First World War

and Army of Occupation

War Diary

France, Belgium and Germany

3 DIVISION
76 Infantry Brigade
Headquarters
1 January 1918 - 31 March 1919

WO95/1434

The Naval & Military Press Ltd
www.nmarchive.com
Published in association with The National Archives

Published by

The Naval & Military Press Ltd

Unit 10 Ridgewood Industrial Park,

Uckfield, East Sussex,

TN22 5QE England

Tel: +44 (0) 1825 749494

www.naval-military-press.com

www.nmarchive.com

This diary has been reprinted in facsimile from the original. Any imperfections are inevitably reproduced and the quality may fall short of modern type and cartographic standards.

Contents

Document type	Place/Title	Date From	Date To
Heading	76 Infantry Bde. H.Q. 1918 Jan To 1919 Mar.		
Heading	3rd Division 76th Inf. Bde. Bde. Headquarters 1918 Jan-1919 Mar		
Heading	76 Infantry Bde. H.Q. 1918 Jan To 1919 Mar.		
Miscellaneous	Box 1434 Loose Fragment could not locate		
Heading	3rd Division B.H.Q. 76th Infantry Brigade January 1918		
Miscellaneous	3rd Division "Q"	01/02/1918	01/02/1918
Miscellaneous	Casualties for month of January 1918		
War Diary	Blaireville	01/01/1918	27/01/1918
War Diary	Wancourt N. 15d. central	27/01/1918	31/01/1918
Operation(al) Order(s)	76 Infantry Brigade Operation Order No. 70	24/01/1918	24/01/1918
Miscellaneous	Table of moves and Reliefs in connection with 76 Infantry Brigade Operation Order No. 70		
Operation(al) Order(s)	76th Infantry Brigade Operation Order No. 71	29/01/1918	29/01/1918
Heading	3rd Division B.H.Q. 76th Infantry Brigade February Z 1918		
Miscellaneous	3rd Division "Q"	01/03/1918	01/03/1918
War Diary	Wancourt N. 15d.	01/02/1918	28/02/1918
Miscellaneous	Casualties for month of February 1918		
Miscellaneous	To officer Commanding 10th Bn. Royal Welsh Fusiliers	02/02/1918	02/02/1918
Miscellaneous	3rd Division "G" work on Defences, week ending Feb. 4th	05/02/1918	05/02/1918
Operation(al) Order(s)	76th Infantry Brigade Operation Order No. 74	02/02/1918	02/02/1918
Operation(al) Order(s)	76th Infantry Brigade Operation Order No. 75	05/02/1918	05/02/1918
Operation(al) Order(s)	76th Infantry Brigade Operation Order No. 76	08/02/1918	08/02/1918
Operation(al) Order(s)	76th Infantry Brigade Operation Order No. 77	11/02/1918	11/02/1918
Operation(al) Order(s)	76th Infantry Brigade Operation Order No. 78	14/02/1918	14/02/1918
Operation(al) Order(s)	76th Infantry Brigade Operation Order No. 79	17/02/1918	17/02/1918
Operation(al) Order(s)	76th Infantry Brigade Operation Order No. 80	20/02/1918	20/02/1918
Operation(al) Order(s)	76th Infantry Brigade Operation Order No. 81	23/02/1918	23/02/1918
Operation(al) Order(s)	76th Infantry Brigade Operation Order No. 82	26/02/1918	26/02/1918
Heading	3rd Division B.H.Q. 76th Infantry Brigade March 1918 Appendices attached Operation Orders		
War Diary	Wancourt N. 15d. central	01/03/1918	09/03/1918
War Diary	Wancourt N. 15d	10/03/1918	23/03/1918
War Diary	Northumberland Lines	23/03/1918	25/03/1918
War Diary	MI 6a 74	26/03/1918	28/03/1918
War Diary	M 8 66.0.	29/03/1918	31/03/1918
Miscellaneous	Casualties for month of March 1918		
Operation(al) Order(s)	76th Infantry Brigade Operation Order No. 83	28/02/1918	28/02/1918
Operation(al) Order(s)	76th Infantry Brigade Operation Order No. 84	05/03/1918	05/03/1918
Operation(al) Order(s)	76th Infantry Brigade Operation Order No. 85	10/03/1918	10/03/1918
Miscellaneous	Amendment to 76th Infantry Brigade Operation Order No. 85	11/03/1918	11/03/1918
Operation(al) Order(s)	76th Infantry Brigade Operation Order No. 86	16/03/1918	16/03/1918
Operation(al) Order(s)	76th Inf. Bde. O.O. No. 88	20/03/1918	20/03/1918
Operation(al) Order(s)	76th Inf. Bde. O.O. No. 89	26/03/1918	26/03/1918
Operation(al) Order(s)	76th Inf. Bde. O.O. No. 90		
Operation(al) Order(s)	76th Inf. Bde. O.O. No. 91	29/03/1918	29/03/1918

Operation(al) Order(s)	76th Inf. Bde. O.O. No. 92	30/03/1918	30/03/1918
Heading	3rd Division War Diary B.H.Q. 76th Infantry Brigade April 1918 Attached Operation Orders		
War Diary	Divion	01/04/1918	03/04/1918
War Diary	Hersin Chateau	04/04/1918	05/04/1918
War Diary	Sains-En-Gohelle Chateau	06/04/1918	07/04/1918
War Diary	Sains-En-Gohelle	08/04/1918	11/04/1918
War Diary	W 14 b 2.4	11/04/1918	12/04/1918
War Diary	V 12 b 8.2	13/04/1918	13/04/1918
War Diary	Annezin	14/04/1918	14/04/1918
War Diary	W 29 a 8.4	15/04/1918	18/04/1918
War Diary	E4 b. 4.1.	19/04/1918	24/04/1918
War Diary	Annezin E9 b 5.6	24/04/1918	26/04/1918
War Diary	Vendin-lez-Bethune W. 27 C 6.8	27/04/1918	30/04/1918
Operation(al) Order(s)	76th Infantry Brigade Operation Order No. 93	31/03/1918	31/03/1918
Miscellaneous	March Table "A" issued with 76th Infantry Brigade O.O. 93		
Operation(al) Order(s)	76th Infantry Brigade Operation Order No. 94	03/04/1918	03/04/1918
Miscellaneous	March Table to Accompany 76th Infantry Brigade O.O. 94		
Operation(al) Order(s)	76th Infantry Brigade Operation Order No. 95	05/04/1918	05/04/1918
Miscellaneous	March Table to Accompany 76th Infantry Brigade O.O. 95		
Miscellaneous	There are no Operation order no. 96, 97 and 98, as these	01/05/1918	01/05/1918
Operation(al) Order(s)	76th Inf. Bde. O.O. No. 99	14/04/1918	14/04/1918
Operation(al) Order(s)	76th Infantry Brigade Operation Order No. 100	20/04/1918	20/04/1918
Operation(al) Order(s)	76th Infantry Brigade Operation Order No. 101	23/04/1918	23/04/1918
Operation(al) Order(s)	76th Infantry Brigade Operation Order No. 102	25/04/1918	25/04/1918
Heading	76th Brigade 3rd Division B.H.Q. 76th Infantry Brigade May 1918		
War Diary	Vendin-les-Bethune W 27 C 6.8.	01/05/1918	02/05/1918
War Diary	L'Abbaye W 25 a 0.8.	03/05/1918	05/05/1918
War Diary	St Sauveur D 5 a 5.1.	05/05/1918	08/05/1918
War Diary	Bethune E4 b 4.1	09/05/1918	16/05/1918
War Diary	St Sauveur D 5 a 5.1.	17/05/1918	20/05/1918
War Diary	L'Abbaye Chocqucs W 25 a. 0.8.	21/05/1918	30/05/1918
War Diary	L'Abbaye W 25 a. 0.8.	31/05/1918	31/05/1918
Operation(al) Order(s)	76th Infantry Brigade Operation Order No. 103	02/05/1918	02/05/1918
Miscellaneous	Artillery Co-Operation Appendix 1		
Miscellaneous	Amendment No. 1 to 76th Inf. Bde. No. 103 dated May 2nd 1918	03/05/1918	03/05/1918
Operation(al) Order(s)	76th Infantry Brigade Operation Order No. 104	04/05/1918	04/05/1918
Operation(al) Order(s)	76th Infantry Brigade Operation Order No. 105	07/05/1918	07/05/1918
Operation(al) Order(s)	76th Infantry Brigade Operation Order No. 106	11/05/1918	11/05/1918
Operation(al) Order(s)	76th Infantry Brigade Operation Order No. 107	15/05/1918	15/05/1918
Operation(al) Order(s)	76th Infantry Brigade Operation Order No. 108	19/05/1918	19/05/1918
Operation(al) Order(s)	76th Infantry Brigade Operation Order No. 109	23/05/1918	23/05/1918
Operation(al) Order(s)	76th Infantry Brigade Operation Order No. 110	27/05/1918	27/05/1918
Miscellaneous	Casualties for month of May 1918		
Heading	3rd Division B.H.Q. 76th Infantry Brigade June 1918 Attached:- Report on Operations 14/15th Brigade Operation & Move Orders.		
War Diary	L'Abbaye W 25 a 0.8	01/06/1918	04/06/1918
War Diary	St Sauveur D 5a 5.1	05/06/1918	13/06/1918
War Diary	L'Abbaye W 25 a 0.8.	14/06/1918	30/06/1918
Miscellaneous	Casualties for month of June		

Miscellaneous	76th Infantry Brigade Report on Operation carried out on June 14/15th 1918	16/06/1918	16/06/1918
Operation(al) Order(s)	76th Infantry Brigade Operation Order No. 111	01/06/1918	01/06/1918
Operation(al) Order(s)	76th Infantry Brigade Operation Order No. 112	03/06/1918	03/06/1918
Operation(al) Order(s)	76th Infantry Brigade Operation Order No. 113	11/06/1918	11/06/1918
Miscellaneous	76th Infantry Brigade Administrative Instructions, Reference 76th Infantry Brigade Operation Order No. 114	12/06/1918	12/06/1918
Operation(al) Order(s)	76th Infantry Brigade Operation Order No. 114	12/06/1918	12/06/1918
Diagram etc			
Miscellaneous	Amendment No. 1 to 76th Infantry Brigade O.O. No. 114	13/06/1918	13/06/1918
Operation(al) Order(s)	76th Infantry Brigade Operation Order No. 115	16/06/1918	16/06/1918
Operation(al) Order(s)	76th Infantry Brigade Operation Order No. 115 (A)	19/06/1918	19/06/1918
Miscellaneous	Instructions for the move of 76th Infantry Brigade Transport in the event of a withdrawal	16/06/1918	16/06/1918
Miscellaneous	March Table		
Operation(al) Order(s)	76th Infantry Brigade Operation Order No. 116	18/06/1918	18/06/1918
Operation(al) Order(s)	76th Infantry Brigade Operation Order No. 117	22/06/1918	22/06/1918
Operation(al) Order(s)	76th Infantry Brigade Operation Order No. 118	28/06/1918	28/06/1918
Miscellaneous	Instructions for the move of 76th Infantry Brigade Transport in the event of A Withdrawal	30/06/1918	30/06/1918
Miscellaneous	March Table		
Diagram etc			
Heading	3rd Division B.H.Q. 76th Infantry Brigade July 1918 Brigade Operation Orders & Defence Scheme attached		
War Diary	L'Abbaye W. 25a. 0.8.	01/07/1918	31/07/1918
Miscellaneous	Casualties Month of July 1918		
Operation(al) Order(s)	76th Infantry Brigade Operation Order No. 119	04/07/1918	04/07/1918
Operation(al) Order(s)	76th Infantry Brigade Operation Order No. 120		
Operation(al) Order(s)	76th Infantry Brigade Operation Order No. 121	18/07/1918	18/07/1918
Operation(al) Order(s)	76th Infantry Brigade Operation Order No. 122	22/07/1918	22/07/1918
Operation(al) Order(s)	76th Infantry Brigade Operation Order No. 123	27/07/1918	27/07/1918
Miscellaneous	76th Infantry Brigade provisional Defence Scheme (Hinges Sector)	29/07/1918	29/07/1918
Miscellaneous	Ammunition to be maintained in the line Appendix "A"		
Heading	3rd Division War Diary & Appendices, B.H.Q. 76th Infantry Brigade August 1918		
Heading	3rd Division B.H.Q. 76th Infantry Brigade August 1918 Appendices under separate cover		
War Diary	L'Abbaye	01/08/1918	05/08/1918
War Diary	Amettes	06/08/1918	13/08/1918
War Diary	Sus-St Leger	14/08/1918	19/08/1918
War Diary	Birles au Bois	19/08/1918	20/08/1918
War Diary	F 8 d 90.85 (Bde. HQ)	21/08/1918	21/08/1918
War Diary	F 8 d 90.85 Ref. 1/40,000 Combined sheets 51C SE 57d NE 51 b SW 57 C NW	21/08/1918	21/08/1918
War Diary	F 18 b 8.0 Busout on Bucquoyyette Road 3 Entrances accomodation Excellent	22/08/1918	22/08/1918
War Diary	A14 C71 Old Serman	22/08/1918	22/08/1918
War Diary	Dus out in Bank	22/08/1918	23/08/1918
War Diary	A 14 C 7.1	23/08/1918	26/08/1918
War Diary	A 11 b 9.7	27/08/1918	28/08/1918
War Diary	A 11 b 9.7. (Large Serman dug out in Hamerville Trench)	28/08/1918	28/08/1918
War Diary	B10 C 6.0.	29/08/1918	30/08/1918

War Diary	Railway Embankment A 4 d 9.2	31/08/1918	31/08/1918
War Diary	B10 C 6.0.	31/08/1918	31/08/1918
Heading	76th Brigade 3rd Division Appendices B.H.Q. 76th Infantry Brigade August 1918		
Operation(al) Order(s)	76th Infantry Brigade Operation Order No. 124	02/08/1918	02/08/1918
Operation(al) Order(s)	76th Infantry Brigade Operation Order No. 125	04/08/1918	04/08/1918
Operation(al) Order(s)	76th Infantry Brigade Operation Order No. 126	04/08/1918	04/08/1918
Miscellaneous	Table of moves to Accompany 76th Infantry Brigade O.O. No. 126		
Miscellaneous	Administrative Instructions for move of 76th Infantry Brigade	05/08/1918	05/08/1918
Miscellaneous	Embussing and March Table		
Operation(al) Order(s)	76th Infantry Brigade Operation Order No. 127	05/08/1918	05/08/1918
Miscellaneous	Preliminary Instructions for the Entrainment of 76th Infantry Brigade	11/08/1918	11/08/1918
Operation(al) Order(s)	76th Infantry Brigade Operation Order No. 128	13/08/1918	13/08/1918
Miscellaneous	Administrative Instructions to Accompany 76th Infantry Brigade Operation Order No. 128	13/08/1918	13/08/1918
Operation(al) Order(s)	76th Infantry Brigade Operation Order No. 129	13/08/1918	13/08/1918
Miscellaneous	March and Entraining Table to Accompany 76th Infantry Brigade Order No. 128		
Operation(al) Order(s)	76th Infantry Brigade Operation Order No. 130	19/08/1918	19/08/1918
Miscellaneous	March Table to Accompany 76th Infantry Brigade Order No. 130		
Operation(al) Order(s)	76th Infantry Brigade Operation Order No. 131	20/08/1918	20/08/1918
Miscellaneous	Addendum No. 1 to 76th Inf. Bde. Order No. 131	20/08/1918	20/08/1918
Operation(al) Order(s)	76th Infantry Brigade Operation Order No. 132	20/08/1918	20/08/1918
Operation(al) Order(s)	76th Inf. Bde. Order No. 133	21/08/1918	21/08/1918
Operation(al) Order(s)	76th Inf. Bde. Order No. 134	21/08/1918	21/08/1918
Operation(al) Order(s)	76th Inf. Bde. Order No. 135		
Miscellaneous	Machine Guns. Instructions Ref. 76th Infantry Brigade Order No. 135	22/08/1918	22/08/1918
Operation(al) Order(s)	76th Inf. Bde. Order No. 136	26/08/1918	26/08/1918
Miscellaneous	A Form Messages And Signals		
Miscellaneous	'D' Coy. M.G.C. 1 Gds. Bde. (information)		
Operation(al) Order(s)	76th Inf. Brigade Order No. 137	28/08/1918	28/08/1918
Operation(al) Order(s)	76th Infantry Brigade Order No. 138	29/08/1918	29/08/1918
Operation(al) Order(s)	76th Infantry Brigade Order No. 139	30/08/1918	30/08/1918
Operation(al) Order(s)	76th Inf. Bde. Order No. 140		
Miscellaneous	Being Report on Operation Aug. 21st-23rd 76th Infantry Brigade		
Miscellaneous	Points Brought by the Operation		
Miscellaneous	C Form Messages And Signals.		
Heading	3rd Division War Diary & Appendices, B.H.Q. 76th Infantry Brigade September 1918		
Heading	3rd Division War Diary, B.H.Q. 76th Infantry Brigade September 1918 Appendices under separate cover		
War Diary	Bde Hee near of Mory Copse B10 C 6.0	01/09/1918	01/09/1918
War Diary	B10 C 6.0	01/09/1918	03/09/1918
War Diary	Boiry St Martin S 20 a 8.6.	03/09/1918	05/09/1918
War Diary	La Bazeque V. 21. Central	06/09/1918	11/09/1918
War Diary	Douchy F. 9.b. 5.0.	12/09/1918	12/09/1918
War Diary	Sapignies	13/09/1918	16/09/1918
War Diary	Sunken Road I 12 b. 7.2.	17/09/1918	26/09/1918
War Diary	Spoil Head K. 20 Central	27/09/1918	28/09/1918
War Diary	Boggart Hole K. 33. b. 2.7.	29/09/1918	30/09/1918

War Diary	Marcoing L. 22. a. 5.6.	30/09/1918	30/09/1918
Heading	Appendices H.Q. 76th Infantry Brigade September 1918		
Miscellaneous	A Form Messages And Signals		
Miscellaneous	Messages And Signals		
Miscellaneous	A Form Messages And Signals		
Miscellaneous			
Miscellaneous	A Form Messages And Signals		
Miscellaneous	Addenda 8th Infantry Brigade Operation Order No. 70	02/09/1918	02/09/1918
Operation(al) Order(s)	8th Infantry Brigade Operation Order No. 70	01/09/1918	01/09/1918
Miscellaneous	C Form Messages And Signals.		
Miscellaneous			
Operation(al) Order(s)	76th Infantry Brigade Operation Order No. 141	06/09/1918	06/09/1918
Miscellaneous	March Table to Accompany 76th Inf. Brigade Order No. 141		
Miscellaneous	Brief Report on Operation Aug. 29th-Sept. 2nd 76th Infantry Brigade	07/09/1918	07/09/1918
Miscellaneous	Point Brought Out In Operation Of August 30th	07/09/1918	07/09/1918
Operation(al) Order(s)	76th Infantry Brigade Operation Order No. 142	10/09/1918	10/09/1918
Miscellaneous	March Table to Accompany 76th Bde. Order No. 142		
Operation(al) Order(s)	76th Infantry Brigade Operation Order No. 143	11/09/1918	11/09/1918
Miscellaneous	March Table Accompany 76th Brigade Order No. 143		
Operation(al) Order(s)	76th Infantry Brigade Order No. 144	15/09/1918	15/09/1918
Operation(al) Order(s)	76th Infantry Brigade Order No. 145	25/09/1918	25/09/1918
Miscellaneous	76th Infantry Brigade Administrative Instructions issued with 76th Infantry Brigade Order No. 145	25/09/1918	25/09/1918
Operation(al) Order(s)	76th Infantry Brigade Order No. 146	25/09/1918	25/09/1918
Miscellaneous	76th Infantry Brigade Administrative Instructions No O.R./17	27/09/1918	27/09/1918
Miscellaneous	A Form Messages And Signals		
Miscellaneous	Report on operations Sept. 26th-28th 1918 76th Infantry Brigade	05/10/1918	05/10/1918
Miscellaneous	Point Brought out by the operations	05/10/1918	05/10/1918
Miscellaneous	Messages And Signals		
Heading	3rd Division War Diary & Appendices B.H.Q. 76th Infantry Brigade October 1918		
Heading	76th Brigade 3rd Division War Diary, B.H.Q. 76th Infantry Brigade October 1918 Appendices under separate cover		
War Diary	Marcoing L. 22. a. 6.6.	01/10/1918	07/10/1918
War Diary	Masniers G 20. a 7.2.	07/10/1918	08/10/1918
War Diary	L. 22. a 6.6.	08/10/1918	09/10/1918
War Diary	Boggart Hole K. 33. b 2.C.	09/10/1918	13/10/1918
War Diary	Marcoing 10 Rue de La Gare L. 23.a. 7.9.	14/10/1918	19/10/1918
War Diary	Catteniers	20/10/1918	20/10/1918
War Diary	Quievy	21/10/1918	22/10/1918
War Diary	Solesmes	22/10/1918	23/10/1918
War Diary	Romeries	23/10/1918	29/10/1918
War Diary	Vertain	30/10/1918	31/10/1918
Heading	3rd Division Appendices 76th Infantry Brigade October 1918		
Miscellaneous	A Form Messages And Signals		
Operation(al) Order(s)	76th Infantry Brigade Order No. 147	07/10/1918	07/10/1918
Miscellaneous	Administrative Instructions Ref. 76th Bde. Order No. 147	07/10/1918	07/10/1918
Miscellaneous	A Form Messages And Signals		

Miscellaneous	C Form Messages And Signals.		
Miscellaneous	Report on operations October 1st 1918 76th Infantry Brigade	10/10/1918	10/10/1918
Miscellaneous	Administrative Instructions Ref. 76th Bde. Order No. 147	07/10/1918	07/10/1918
Operation(al) Order(s)	76th Infantry Brigade Order No. 148		
Miscellaneous	76th Infantry Brigade Administrative Instructions	12/10/1918	12/10/1918
Miscellaneous	Amendment No. 1 to 76th Infantry Brigade Administrative Instructions dated 12th October 1918	12/10/1918	12/10/1918
Operation(al) Order(s)	76th Infantry Brigade Order No. 149	18/10/1918	18/10/1918
Miscellaneous	March Table to Accompany 76th Inf. Brigade Order No. 149		
Miscellaneous	76th Infantry Brigade Administrative Instructions to Accompany 76th Infantry Bde. Order No.	18/10/1918	18/10/1918
Miscellaneous	March Table to Accompany order 12/10/18		
Miscellaneous	76th Infantry Brigade Warning Order	19/10/1918	19/10/1918
Miscellaneous	76th Infantry Brigade March Table For Move 22nd October 1918		
Operation(al) Order(s)	76th Infantry Brigade Order No. 150	22/10/1918	22/10/1918
Miscellaneous	Addenda to 76th Inf. Brigade Order No. 150	22/10/1918	22/10/1918
Miscellaneous	Report on operations October 22nd-24th 1918 76th Infantry Brigade	01/11/1918	01/11/1918
Miscellaneous	Point Brought to Notice	01/11/1918	01/11/1918
Operation(al) Order(s)	76th Infantry Bde. Order No. 151		
Operation(al) Order(s)	76th Infantry Brigade Order No. 152	27/10/1918	27/10/1918
Miscellaneous	Table of reliefs to Accompany 76th Brigade Order No. 152		
Operation(al) Order(s)	76th Infantry Brigade Order No. 153	29/10/1918	29/10/1918
Heading	3rd Division War Diary & Appendices 76th Infantry Brigade November 1918		
Heading	76th Brigade. 3rd Division B.H.Q. 76th Infantry Brigade. November 1918 Appendices Under Separatecover		
War Diary	Carnieres	01/11/1918	02/11/1918
War Diary	Quievy	03/11/1918	03/11/1918
War Diary	Romeries	04/11/1918	08/11/1918
War Diary	Frasnoy	09/11/1918	10/11/1918
War Diary	La Longueville	11/11/1918	15/11/1918
War Diary	Neuemenil	16/11/1918	20/11/1918
War Diary	Cousolre	21/11/1918	24/11/1918
War Diary	Thuin	25/11/1918	25/11/1918
War Diary	Nalinnes	26/11/1918	26/11/1918
War Diary	Mettet	27/11/1918	28/11/1918
War Diary	Rouillon	29/11/1918	29/11/1918
War Diary	Braibant	30/11/1918	30/11/1918
War Diary	Jannee	30/11/1918	30/11/1918
Heading	3rd Division 76th Infantry Brigade Appendices 76th Infantry Brigade November 1918		
Operation(al) Order(s)	76th Infantry Brigade Order No. 155	01/11/1918	01/11/1918
Miscellaneous	76th Infantry Brigade Administrative Instructions (To Accompany 76th Inf. Bde. Order No. 155)	02/11/1918	02/11/1918
Operation(al) Order(s)	76th Infantry Brigade Order No.156	03/11/1918	03/11/1918
Miscellaneous	76th Infantry Brigade Administrative Instructions (To Accompany 76th Inf. Bde. Order No. 156)	03/11/1918	03/11/1918
Operation(al) Order(s)	76th Infantry Brigade Order No. 158	07/11/1918	07/11/1918

Miscellaneous	76th Infantry Brigade Administrative Instructions (To Accompany 76th Inf. Bde. Order No. 158)	07/11/1918	07/11/1918
Operation(al) Order(s)	76th Infantry Brigade Order No. 159	09/11/1918	09/11/1918
Miscellaneous	March Table to Accompany 76th Brigade Order No. 159		
Miscellaneous	76th Infantry Brigade Administrative Instructions (To Accompany 76th Inf. Bde. Order No. 159)	09/11/1918	09/11/1918
Miscellaneous	76th Infantry Brigade Administrative Instructions (To Accompany 76th Inf. Bde. Order No. G. 706)	15/11/1918	15/11/1918
Miscellaneous	A Form Messages And Signals		
Operation(al) Order(s)	76th Infantry Brigade Order No. 162	17/11/1918	17/11/1918
Operation(al) Order(s)	76th Infantry Brigade Order No. 163	19/11/1918	19/11/1918
Operation(al) Order(s)	76th Infantry Brigade Order No. 164	23/11/1918	23/11/1918
Operation(al) Order(s)	76th Infantry Brigade Order No. 165	24/11/1918	24/11/1918
Miscellaneous	76th Infantry Brigade Administrative Instructions (To Accompany 76th Inf. Bde. Order No. 165)	24/11/1918	24/11/1918
Operation(al) Order(s)	76th Infantry Brigade Order No. 166	26/11/1918	26/11/1918
Miscellaneous	March Table		
Miscellaneous	76th Infantry Brigade Administrative Instructions (To Accompany 76th Inf. Bde. Order No. 166)	25/11/1918	25/11/1918
Operation(al) Order(s)	76th Infantry Brigade Order No. 167	27/11/1918	27/11/1918
Miscellaneous	March Table		
Miscellaneous	A Form Messages And Signals		
Miscellaneous	Administrative Instructions to Accompany 76th Inf. Brigade Order No. 167	27/11/1918	27/11/1918
Operation(al) Order(s)	76th Infantry Brigade Order No. 168	28/11/1918	28/11/1918
Miscellaneous	March Table		
Miscellaneous	Addendum to 76th Inf. Brigade Order No. 169	28/11/1918	28/11/1918
Miscellaneous	76th Infantry Brigade Administrative Instructions (To Accompany 76th Inf. Bde. Order No. 168)	28/11/1918	28/11/1918
Operation(al) Order(s)	76th Infantry Brigade Order No. 169	29/11/1918	29/11/1918
Miscellaneous	March Table		
Miscellaneous	Messages And Signals		
Miscellaneous	76th Infantry Brigade Administrative Instructions (To Accompany 76th Inf. Bde. Order No. 169)	29/11/1918	29/11/1918
Heading	3rd Division B.H.Q. 76th Infantry Brigade December 1918 Appendices under separate cover		
Miscellaneous			
War Diary	Jannee	01/12/1918	04/12/1918
War Diary	Baillonville Soy	05/12/1918	05/12/1918
War Diary	Manhay	06/12/1918	06/12/1918
War Diary	Hebronval	07/12/1918	07/12/1918
War Diary	Cierreux (Halte)	08/12/1918	08/12/1918
War Diary	Cierreux Chateaux	09/12/1918	11/12/1918
War Diary	Grufflingen	11/12/1918	11/12/1918
War Diary	Manderfield	12/12/1918	12/12/1918
War Diary	Baasem	13/12/1918	13/12/1918
War Diary	Blankenheim	14/12/1918	14/12/1918
War Diary	Eicherscheid	15/12/1918	15/12/1918
War Diary	Hunstereifel	16/12/1918	16/12/1918
War Diary	Euskirchen	17/12/1918	17/12/1918
War Diary	Ahrem	18/12/1918	18/12/1918
War Diary	Gymnich Chateaux	19/12/1918	22/12/1918
War Diary	Gymnich	23/12/1918	31/12/1918
Heading	3rd Division Appendices 76th Infantry Brigade December 1918		

Miscellaneous	76th Infantry Brigade Football League		
Operation(al) Order(s)	76th Infantry Brigade Order No. 170	03/12/1918	03/12/1918
Miscellaneous	March Table		
Operation(al) Order(s)	76th Infantry Brigade Order No. 171	04/12/1918	04/12/1918
Miscellaneous	March Table		
Miscellaneous	76th Infantry Brigade Administrative Instructions (To Accompany 76th Inf. Bde. Order No. 171)	04/12/1918	04/12/1918
Operation(al) Order(s)	76th Infantry Brigade Order No. 172	05/12/1918	05/12/1918
Miscellaneous	March Table		
Miscellaneous	Accommodation in the new area will be allotted as under		
Miscellaneous	76th Infantry Brigade Administrative Instructions (To Accompany 76th Inf. Bde. Order No. 172)	06/12/1918	06/12/1918
Operation(al) Order(s)	76th Infantry Brigade Order No. 173	06/12/1918	06/12/1918
Miscellaneous	March Table		
Miscellaneous	76th Infantry Brigade Administrative Instructions (To Accompany 76th Inf. Bde. Order No. 173)	06/12/1918	06/12/1918
Operation(al) Order(s)	76th Infantry Brigade Order No. 174	07/12/1918	07/12/1918
Miscellaneous	March Table		
Miscellaneous	76th Infantry Brigade Administrative Instructions (To Accompany 76th Inf. Bde. Order No. 174)	07/12/1918	07/12/1918
Miscellaneous	A Form Messages And Signals		
Operation(al) Order(s)	76th Infantry Brigade Order No. 175	10/12/1918	10/12/1918
Miscellaneous	March Table		
Operation(al) Order(s)	76th Infantry Brigade Order No. 175	10/12/1918	10/12/1918
Miscellaneous	Special order of the Day by Brigadier General F.E. Metcalfe, C.M.G., Commanding 76th Infantry Brigade	09/12/1918	09/12/1918
Miscellaneous	76th Infantry Brigade Administrative Instructions (To Accompany 76th Inf. Bde. Order No. 175)	10/12/1918	10/12/1918
Operation(al) Order(s)	76th Infantry Brigade Order No. 176	11/12/1918	11/12/1918
Miscellaneous	March Table		
Operation(al) Order(s)	76th Infantry Brigade Order No. 177	12/12/1918	12/12/1918
Miscellaneous	March Table		
Miscellaneous	76th Infantry Brigade Administrative Instructions (To Accompany 76th Inf. Bde. Order No. 176)		
Operation(al) Order(s)	76th Infantry Brigade Order No. 178	13/12/1918	13/12/1918
Miscellaneous	March Table		
Miscellaneous	76th Infantry Brigade Administrative Instructions (To Accompany 76th Inf. Bde. Order No. 178)	13/12/1918	13/12/1918
Operation(al) Order(s)	76th Infantry Brigade Order No. 179	14/12/1918	14/12/1918
Miscellaneous	March Table		
Miscellaneous	76th Infantry Brigade Administrative Instructions (To Accompany 76th Inf. Bde. Order No. 179)	14/12/1918	14/12/1918
Operation(al) Order(s)	76th Infantry Brigade Order No. 180	15/12/1918	15/12/1918
Miscellaneous	March Table		
Miscellaneous	76th Infantry Brigade Administrative Instructions (To Accompany 76th Inf. Bde. Order No. 180)	15/12/1918	15/12/1918
Operation(al) Order(s)	76th Infantry Brigade Order No. 181	16/12/1918	16/12/1918
Miscellaneous	March Table		
Miscellaneous	76th Infantry Brigade Administrative Instructions (To Accompany 76th Inf. Bde. Order No. 181)	16/12/1918	16/12/1918
Operation(al) Order(s)	76th Infantry Brigade Order No. 182	17/12/1918	17/12/1918
Miscellaneous	March Table		
Miscellaneous	76th Infantry Brigade Administrative Instructions (To Accompany 76th Inf. Bde. Order No. 182)	17/12/1918	17/12/1918
Operation(al) Order(s)	76th Infantry Brigade Order No. 183	18/12/1918	18/12/1918

Miscellaneous	March Table		
War Diary	Gymnich	01/01/1919	01/03/1919
War Diary	Cologne	02/03/1919	17/03/1919
War Diary	Cologne 59 Hohenstofen Ring	18/03/1919	31/03/1919

76 INFANTRY BDE. H.Q.

1918 JAN TO 1919 MAR.

1434

3RD DIVISION
76TH INFY BDE

BDE HEADQUARTERS

~~JAN – DEC – 1918~~

1918 JAN – 1919 MAR

76 INFANTRY BDE. H.Q.

1918 JAN TO 1919 MAR.

1434

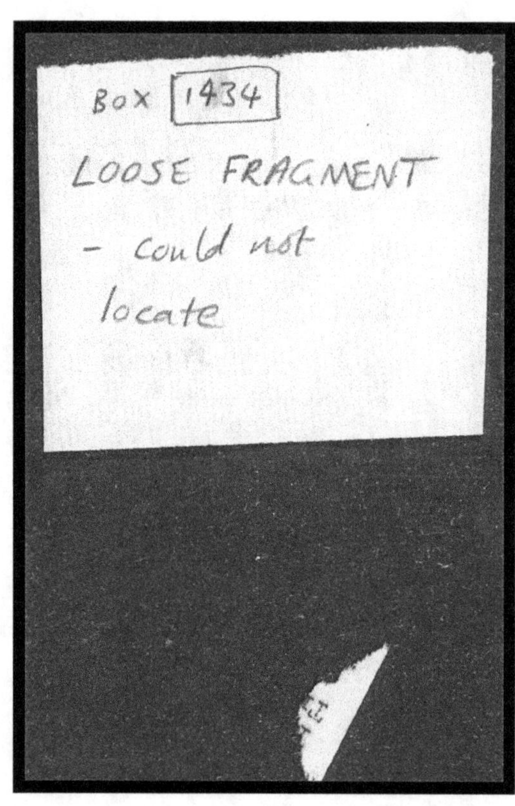
Box 1434
LOOSE FRAGMENT
- could not
locate

3rd Division.

B. H. Q.

76th INFANTRY BRIGADE.

JANUARY 1918

3rd.Division "Q".

Herewith War Diary for Month of January 1918.

Lt.,Col.,
1/2/18. Commanding 76th.Infantry Brigade.

CASUALTIES FOR MONTH OF JANUARY 1918.

****

	Officers.	O.R.
Killed	.	1
Wounded	.	4
Gassed	.	8

Instructions regarding War Diaries and Intelligence Summaries are contained in F. S. Regs., Part II. and the Staff Manual respectively. Title pages will be prepared in manuscript.

WAR DIARY
or
INTELLIGENCE SUMMARY.
(Erase heading not required.)

H.Q.,76th.INFANTRY BRIGADE.
January 1918.

Army Form C. 2118.

Vol 28

Place	Date 1918.	Hour	Summary of Events and Information	Remarks and references to Appendices
BLAIREVILLE	Jan.		Fine.	
	1.	11a.m.	Asst.Staff Captain took over R.E. Dumps at HENDECOURT.	
			G.O.C. and Staff Captain inspected all the camps.	
		3 p.m.	Staff Captain inspected camps and transport lines with a view to ascertaining what material was required for repairs.	
			All units improving their camps.	
	2.	10a.m.	Fine.	
		12 noon	Staff Captain visited all units.	
		2.30p.m.	G.O.C. and B.M. went round the training area.	
	3		Fine.	
			Elementary training begun.	
		9 a.m.	S.C. reconnoitred the line from L'HOMME MORT to 2,500 yds North of ST.LEGER.	
		10.30a.m.	G.O.C. and B.M. went round the training area.	
	4		Fine.	
		9a.m.	B.M. reconnoitred the line.	
		11.30a.m.	G.O.C. went to CAMIERS to attend M.G.Course.	
		12noon	Asst.S.C. inspected the baths in BLAIREVILLE.	
			Units commenced bathing.	
	5		Fine.	
		11 a.m.	S.C.visited units.	
		3 p.m.	Asst.S.C. inspected the Brigade Dump at HENDECOURT.	
	6	11 a.m.	S.C. went to see the 8th.K.O.R.L.	
		2 p.m.	B.M. wemt to DENIERS to see about timber.	
	7		Fine. Thaw during the night.	
		11 a.m.	S.C. wne to BEAUMETZ re firewood.	
			B.M. visited units.	
		3.30p.m.	G.O.C. returned from CAMIERS.	

A5834 Wt. W4973/M687 750,000 8/16 D. D. & L. Ltd. Forms/C.2118/13.

Army Form C. 2118.

Instructions regarding War Diaries and Intelligence Summaries are contained in F. S. Regs., Part II. and the Staff Manual respectively. Title pages will be prepared in manuscript.

WAR DIARY
or
INTELLIGENCE SUMMARY.
(Erase heading not required.)

Place	Date 1918.	Hour	Summary of Events and Information	Remarks and references to Appendices
BLAIRE-VILLE.	Jan. 8		Snowing.	
		8.30 a.m.	G.O.C. inspected 1st.Gordon Hldrs.	
	9		Snowing.	
		10.30a.m.	G.O.C. inspected 2nd.Suffolk Regt.	
	10		Much warmer.	
		10.30a.m.	G.O.C. inspected 10th.R.W.F.	
		3 p.m.	Corps Commander inspected 1st.Gordon Hldrs.,8th.K.O.R.L and T.M.Battery.	
	11		Wet.	
		10.30a.m.	G.O.C. visited 8th.K.O.R.L.	
	12		Fine.	
		10.30a.m.	G.O.C. inspected M.G.C. and T.M.Battery.	
		3 p.m.	Corps Commander inspected 10th.R.W.F. and 2nd.Suffolk Regt.	
	13		Fine.	
		10.30a.m.	G.O.C. went on leave. Lt.,Col.,HUNT,D.S.O.,8th.K.O.R.L.,took over command of the Brigade.	
	14		Fine.	
		9 a.m.	76th.M.G.C. left BLAIREVILLE for BOYELLES.	
		11 a.m.	Lt.Col.,HUNT visited the units.	
	15	10.30a.m.	B.M. went to see 9th.M.G.C.	
		11 a.m.	Lt.Col.HUNT went round the units.	
		3 p.m.	B.M. visited the 1st.Gordon Hldrs.	
	16	10 a.m.	Lt.Col.HUNT reconnoitred the line.	
			B.M. prepared Trench Mortar Scheme.	
	17		Wet.	
		3 p.m.	B.M.& S.C. went to Div.H.Q. and 8th.and 9th.Bdes.	

A5834 Wt. W4973/M687 750,000 8/16 D. D. & L. Ltd. Forms/C.2118/13.

Army Form C. 2118.

Instructions regarding War Diaries and Intelligence Summaries are contained in F. S. Regs., Part II. and the Staff Manual respectively. Title pages will be prepared in manuscript.

WAR DIARY
or
INTELLIGENCE SUMMARY.
(Erase heading not required.)

Place	Date 1918.	Hour	Summary of Events and Information	Remarks and references to Appendices
BLAIREVILLE	Jan.			
	18		Wet.	
			Routine.	
	19		Fine.	
		11 a.m.	Lt.Col.HUNT inspected units. Testing of ground flares by aeroplanes.	
		2.30 p.m.	B.M.& S.C. went to 123rd.Bde.H.Q.	
		3 p.m.	Lt.Col.HUNT inspected transport lines.	
	20		Fine.	
		12 nonn	S.C. visited units.	
			Routine.	
	21		Wet.	
		11 a.m.	Lt.Col.HUNT and S.C. inspected units.	
		2 p.m.	Asst.S.C. inspected 103rd.Inf.Bde area.	
	22		Wet.	
		10.30 a.m.	S.C. went to 103rdzBde.H.Q.,also to CARLISLE LINES & STONE SIDING.	
		11 a.m.	Lt.Col.HUNT visited units.	
		3.30 p.m.	Lt.Col.HUNT went to see 2nd.Suffolk Regt.,and 10th.R.W.Fus.	
	23		Wet.	
		10.30a.m.	Lt.Col.HUNT took the A.A.& Q.M.G. and S.C. of 103rd.Bde. around the area.	
	24	11 a.m.	Demonstration by 1 Company and 1 Platoon of 1st.Gordon Hldrs.,of fire power.	
			O.O.No.70 issued.	
	25		Fine.	
		11 a.m.	Lt.Col.HUNT and S.C. visited the units.	
		1 p.m.	2nd.Suffolk Regt.,and 1st.Gordon Hldrs.,left BLAIREVILLE for MERCATEL AREA.	
		4 p.m.	Lt.Col.HUNT attended Major General's conference at Div.H.Q.	
			Reliefs complete. 5.15 p.m. 1st.Gordon H. 8 p.m. 2nd.Suffolk Regt.	Vide O.O.70 copy attachd.

Instructions regarding War Diaries and Intelligence Summaries are contained in F. S. Regs., Part II. and the Staff Manual respectively. Title pages will be prepared in manuscript.

WAR DIARY
or
INTELLIGENCE SUMMARY.
(Erase heading not required.)

Army Form C. 2118.

Place	Date 1918.	Hour	Summary of Events and Information	Remarks and references to Appendices
BLAIREVILLE	Jan. 26		Fine.	
		11 a.m.	Lt.Col.HUNT went up to 103rd.Bde.H.Q.	
			Asst.S.C. took dumps' personnel to new area and arranged reliefs.	
			2nd.Suffolk Regt.,relieved 25th.N.Fus. in the line,Right Sub-Section.	
		7.20 p.m.	Relief complete.	
			1st.Gordon Hldrs.,relieved 26th.N.Fus. in the Left Sub-Section.	
		8.40 p.m.	Relief complete.	
	27		Fine.	
		9 a.m.	Bde.H.Q. closed.	
			Capt.FURNELL,Q.O.,and personnel moved to new area by light railway.	
WANCOURT,		10 a.m.	Bde.H.Q. opened.	
N.15d.central		2 p.m.	B.M. visited H.Q. of the right Battalion.	
		2.30 p.m.	Capt.FURNELL and I.O. inspected the Brigade Dumps.	
		3 p.m.	Div.Commander called to see Lt.Col.HUNT.	
		4.5 p.m.	10th.R.W.F. arrived at CARLISLE LINES.	
		5.30 p.m.	8th.K.O.R.L. arrived in Support Position. 1 Coy and Battn.H.Q. in N.15d.,2 Coys in MARLIERES CAVES, 1 Coy in EGRET Trench.	
	28		Fine.	
		10 a.m.	Lt.Col.HUNT went round the line with Major General.	
		10.30a.m.	S.C. inspected dumps,water point and c.	
			I.O. went round the line.	
		3 p.m.	Capt.FURNELL inspected dumps.	
			B.M. went to Battn.H.Q. and T.M.B. in the line.	
			Situation quiet.	
	29		Fine. Situation quiet.	
		10 a.m.	O.O.No.71 issued.	
			Lt.Col.HUNT went round the line,Right Battn.Front.	
		2 p.m.	do. Left Battn.Front.	
			B.M. went round the line.	

Army Form C. 2118.

WAR DIARY
or
INTELLIGENCE SUMMARY.
(*Erase heading not required.*)

Instructions regarding War Diaries and Intelligence Summaries are contained in F. S. Regs., Part II. and the Staff Manual respectively. Title pages will be prepared in manuscript.

Place	Date	Hour	Summary of Events and Information	Remarks and references to Appendices
WANCOURT N.15d.central	1918. Jan.			
	29	2 p.m.	S.C. visited Q.M. stores of all units.	
			Capt.FURNELL inspected Brigade Dumps and gum boot stores.	
	30		Fine. Situation quiet.	
		4 a.m.	Lt.Col.HUNT went round the line.	
		9 a.m.	B.M. went round the line with Major HALL,R.E.	
		2 p.m.	Capt.FURNELL went round the trabsport lines and details camps re improvement of same.	
			Inter-Battalion reliefs completed.	Vide O.O.71 attachd.
		8 p.m.	8th.K.O.R.L. relieve 2nd.Suffolk Regt.	
		10 p.m.	10th.R.W.F. relieve 1st.Gordon Hldrs.	
	31		Fine. Misty. Situation quiet.	
		4 a.m.	Lt.Col.HUNT went round the line.	
		9 a.m.	B.M.went round the line.	
		2 p.m.	Lt.Col.HUNT and S.C. inspected Transport lines and details camp.	
		10 p.m.	O.O.72 issued to units.	
	31/1/18.		Lt.,Col., Commanding 76th.Infantry Brigade.	

A5834 Wt. W4973/M687 750,000 8/16 D. D. & L. Ltd. Forms/C.2118/13.

SECRET.
****

Copy No...21.

76th.INFANTRY BRIGADE OPERATION ORDER NO.70.

Reference 1/20,000 Sheets 51c.S.E. & 51b.S.W., and Trench Map GUEMAPPE.

24th.January 1918.

1. The 3rd.Division (less Artillery) will relieve the 34th. Division (less Artillery) in the Left Sector of the VI Corps front.

2. The 76th.Inf.Brigade will relieve the 103rd.Inf.Brigade (34th.Division) in the Left Section of the Divisional front in accordance with the attached table of moves and reliefs.

3. 76th.Coy.,M.G.C. will move into the line under the orders of the G.O.C. 34th.Division.

4. Details of reliefs will be arranged between Commanding Officers concerned; and the completion of all moves and reliefs will be reported to Brigade H.Q.

5. Trench Stores,maps,defence schemes,photos and documents relating to the area will be taken over by relieving units.
Trench Store Cards will be sent to Brigade H.Q. withinh 24 hours of relief.

6. One Officer and one N.C.O. per Company in the front line, and one Officer and one N.C.O. per M.G.Coy.,are being left in the line for 24 hours after relief.

7. Guides will be provided by Front Line and Support Battalions of the 103rd.Inf.Brigade at the rate of one per Platoon,one per Company H.Q. and one per Battalion H.Q.

8. Command of the Section will pass to the O.C. 76th.Inf. Brigade at 11 a.m. on Jan.27th.

9. 76th.Inf.Brigade H.Q. will close at BLAIREVILLE at 9 a.m. on Jan.27th.,and open at N.15d.4.3. on arrival.

10. ACKNOWLEDGE.

R.C.Stevenson
Captain,
Brigade Major,76th.Infantry Brigade.

Issued to Signals at 10 a.m.

Copies to:-

1. Bde.Commdr.	15. Left Group R.F.A.
2. 8th.K.O.R.L.	16. S.S.O.,3rd.Div.
3. 2nd.Suffolk R.	17. No.2 Coy.,Train.
4. 10th.R.W.F.	18. Area Commdt.,HENDECOURT.
5. 1st.Gordon H.	19. Camp Commdt.,CARLISLE LINES.
6. 76th.Coy.M.G.C.	20. A.P.M.,3rd.Div.
7. 76th.T.M.B.	21. B.M.
8. 529th.F.Co.R.E.	22. S.C.
9. 7th.Fd.Amb.	23. Bde.Signal Offr.
10. 3rd.Div."G".	24. War Diary.
11. 3rd.Div."Q".	25. War Diary.
12. 8th.Inf.Bde.	26. File.
13. 9th.Inf.Bde.	
14. 103rd.Inf.Bde.	

TABLE OF MOVES AND RELIEFS IN CONNECTION WITH 76th, INFANTRY BRIGADE
OPERATION ORDER NO.70.

Date. Jany.	Unit.	From	To	In relief of:-	Guides Rendezvous.	Instructions.
25th.	2nd.Suffolk Regt. less Transport.	No.2 Camp, BLAIREVILLE.	Support position.	9th.(N.H.)Bn. N.Fus.	N.21a.8.9. 5 p.m.	By Bus to MERCATEL.VIDE separate detailed orders for embussing. Bus column to start at 3 p.m.
25th.	Transport, 2nd.Suffolk Regt.	-do-	CARLISLE LINES.	Transport of 9th.(N.H.) Bn. N.Fus.		Leave No.2 Camp at 3.30 p.m. Route:- BLAIREVILLE, FICHEUX, MERCATEL.
25th.	1st.Gordon Hldrs.	No.5 Camp HENDECOURT.	CARLISLE LINES.	24/27th.Bn. N.Fus.		March Route - Road junction S.8b.1.5. - Road junction M.15b.6.0. - BEAURAINS. To clear HENDECOURT at 2p.m.
Night 26/27th.	2nd.Suffolk Regt.	Support Position.	Front Line, Right Sub-Section.	26th.Bn. N.Fus.	Support Battn. H.Q.,5 p.m.	
Night 26/27th.	1st.Gordon Hldrs.	CARLISLE LINES.	Front Line, Left Sub-Section.	25th.Bn.N.Fus.	N.21a.8.9. 5 p.m.	Via NEUVILLE VITASSE.
27th.	8th.K.O.R.L.	No. [illegible] Camp.	Support position.	25th.Bn.N.Fus.	N.21a.8.9. 5 p.m.	By Bus to MERCATEL, vide separate detailed orders for embussing. Bus column to start at 3 p.m.
27th.	Transport, 8th.K.O.R.L.	No.4 Camp	CARLISLE LINES.	Transport, 25th.Bn.N.Fus.		Leave No.4 Camp at 3.30 p.m. Route:- BLAIREVILLE - FICHEUX - MERCATEL.
27th.	10th.R.W.F.	No.3 Camp	Reserve Position, CARLISLE LINES.	26th.Bn.N.Fus.		March Route:- BLAIREVILLE - FICHEUX - Rd.junct. (M.27c.2.8.) Road junction M.15b.6.0. To enter BLAIREVILLE at 2 p.m.
27th.	76th.T.M.B.	No.5 Camp	Line	103rd.T.M.B.	To be arranged between C.O's concerned.	By Bus to MERCATEL, in same convoy as 8th. K.O.R.L. Not to be East of N.21a.8.9.before 5 p.m.

Movement in daylight East of MERCATEL will be by Platoons at 200 yards distance.

SECRET.
****

Copy No.20....

76th. INFANTRY BRIGADE OPERATION ORDER NO.71.

Reference Sheets U.T.S.312,312a.,313,1/10,000,
Sheet 51b.S.W.,1/20,000. — 29th.January 1917

1. The following reliefs will take place in the LEFT SECTION on the night January 30th./31st.

(a) 8th.Bn.King's Own (R.L.) Regt. will relieve 2nd.Bn.The Suffolk Regt.,in the Right Sub-Section.
(b) 10th.Bn.Rl.Welch Fus.,will relieve 1st.Bn.The Gordon Hldrs.,in the Left Sub-Section.

2. On relief,the 2nd.Bn.Suffolk Regt.,will move into Reserve at CARLISLE LINES.

1st.Bn.Gordon Hldrs.,will move into Support and be disposed as follows:-

H.Q. and 2 Coys............ N.16c.
1 Company .... MARLIERES CAVES.
1 Company .... EGRET Trench.

3. Details of reliefs will be arranged between O's.C. concerned, and their completion reported to Brigade H.Q.

4. Head of the column of Reserve Battalion will not pass Traffic Control Post at N.20b.7.8. before 5 p.m.
Movement in daylight East of the ARRAS - BAPAUME Road will be by Platoons at 200 yards interval.

5. Trench Store Cards will be sent to Brigade H.Q. within 24 hours of relief.

6. Relieving Battalions will carry on the work begun by the Battalions in the line.
Separate orders will be issued to O.C.,1st.Bn.Gordon Hldrs., re working parties.

7. O.C.,1st.Bn.Gordon Hldrs.,will find the 3.30 p.m. shift on Jan.30th.,for work under 181st.Tunnelling Company R.E.

8. ACKNOWLEDGE.

H.C.H. Lollops.
Captain,
Issued to Signals 10 a.m. A/Brigade Major,76th.Infantry Brigade.

Copies to:-
1. G.O.C.
2. 8th.K.O.R.L.
3. 2nd.Suffolk Regt.
4. 10th.R.W.Fus.
5. 1st.Gordon Hldrs.
6. 76th.Coy.,M.G.C.
7. 76th.T.M.B.
8. 3rd.Div."G".
9. 3rd.Div."Q".
10. 160th.Bde.R.F.A.
11. 529th.Fd.Co.R.E.
12. D.M.G.O.,3rd.Div.
13. D.T.M.O., "
14. 9th.Inf.Bde.
15. 12th.Inf.Bde.
16. Camp Comdt.,CARLISLE (LINES.
17. B.M.
18. S.C.
19. Bde.Sig.Offr.
20. War Diary
21. War Diary.
22. File.

3rd Division.

B.H.Q. 76th INFANTRY BRIGADE ::: FEBRUARY Z 1918.

HEADQUARTERS
Date 2·III·18
I.O.....
76th INFANTRY BDE.

3rd.Division "Q".

Herewith War Diaries for Month of February 1918.

M.C. Ayton 2/Lt.,
for Brigadier-General,
Commanding 76th.Infantry Brigade.

1/3/18.

Instructions regarding War Diaries and Intelligence Summaries are contained in F. S. Regs., Part II. and the Staff Manual respectively. Title pages will be prepared in manuscript.

Army Form C. 2118.

WAR DIARY
or
INTELLIGENCE SUMMARY.

H.Q. 76th. Infantry Brigade.

(Erase heading not required.)

Vol 29

Place	Date 1918.	Hour	Summary of Events and Information	Remarks and references to Appendices
WANCOURT. N.15d.	Feb. 1		Fine.Misty.Situation quiet.	
		9 a.m.	Conference of Battalion Commanders,Brigade H.Q.	
			Capt.FURNELL inspected Dumps and Gum-boot Stores.	
		10 a.m.	Divisional Commander called to see Col.HUNT.	
		11.30 a.m.	O.O.73 issued to units.	
		5 p.m.	Orders for disbanding 10th.R.W.F. received and Administrative Instructions issued to Unit by Staff Captain.	
		4 p.m.	Col.HUNT went to H.Q.,12th.Inf.Bde.	
		8.30 p.m.	Relief Complete,10th.R.W.F. and 1st.Gordon Hldrs.	
	2		Fine.Bright.Situation quiet.	
		9 a.m.	Brigade Major went round line re work of Pioneer Battalion.	
		11 a.m.	Divisional Commander addressed 10th.R.W.F. at CARLISLE LINES. Col.HUNT attended.	
		12 noon	" " inspected Brigade Transport Lines with Col.HUNT.	
		2 p.m.	Col.HUNT went round theline.	
			Staff Captain went to see 10th.R.W.F. re disbandment.	
		8 p.m.	O.O.74 issued.	
			Letter of thanks for past work sent to 10th.R.W.F. by Brigade Commander................	Letter attchd.
	3.		Fine. Bright. Situation quiet.	
		9 a.m.	Capt.FURNELL went round line re water points.	
		10 a.m.	Col.HUNT inspected T.M.Battery's and M.G.Coy's back billets.	
		2 p.m.	" went round Left Battalion front.	
		8.30 p.m.	Relief complete. 2nd.Suffolk Regt.,and 8th.K.O.R.L	Vide O.O. 74.
	4		Fine. Dull. Situation quiet.	
		2 p.m.	Brigade Major went round the line.	
			Staff Captain went to Details.	
		3.30 p.m.	Divisional Commander called to see Col.HUNT.	
	5		Fine. Bright. Situation quiet.	
		10 a.m.	Col.HUNT inspected Transport Lines.	
		12 noon	A.A.& Q.M.G. visited Brigade H.Q. with reference to the disposal of remainder of 10th.R.W.F.	

A5834 Wt. W4973/M687 750,000 8/16 D. D. & L. Ltd. Forms/C.2118/13.

Army Form C. 2118.

Instructions regarding War Diaries and Intelligence Summaries are contained in F. S. Regs., Part II. and the Staff Manual respectively. Title pages will be prepared in manuscript.

WAR DIARY
or
INTELLIGENCE SUMMARY.
(Erase heading not required.)

Place	Date 1918.	Hour	Summary of Events and Information	Remarks and references to Appendices
WANCOURT. N.15d.	Feb. 5	2 p.m.	Officers and 150 O.R.,10th.R.W.F. left for 9th.Bn.in motor lorries.	
			Brigade Major and Capt.FURNELL went round the line.	
		8 p.m.	O.O.75 issued.	
			Work on defences report for Week Ending Feb.4th.,forwarded to Div.	Vide B/2212 attchd.
	6		Fine. Dull.	
		10 a.m.	Col.HUNT and Staff Captain went round the line.	
		2 p.m.	Brigade Major and Capt.FURNELL went round the line.	
		7 p.m.	Relief complete. 1st.Gordon Hldrs.,and 8th.K.O.R.L.	Vide O.O. 75.
	7		Dull. Some rain. Situation quiet.	
		9 a.m.	Col.HUNT went round the line.	
		2 p.m.	Staff Captain took over 10th.R.W.F. transport which is now attached to Brigade.	
		4 p.m.	Divisional Commander called at Bde H.Q.	
	8		Dull. Wet.	
		5 a.m.	Brigade Major and Capt.FURNELL went round the line.	
		9 a.m.	Col.HUNT and Staff Captain went to see departure of 10th.R.W.F.	
		9.30 a.m.	10th.R.W.F. left CARLISLE LINES for BAILLEULVAL,by march route and came under orders of (VI Corps.	
		11 a.m.	Army Commander and Div.Commander went round the BLUE Line.	
		3 p.m.	Col.HUNT went round the line.	
		8 p.m.	O.O.76 issued.	
		6.30 a.m.	Hostile artillery and T.M's opened a barrage S of the COJEUL RIVER. Later the barrage developed on the N side. Our artillery replied at a slow rate of fire on enemy front and support lines. On the S side of the COJEUL the enemy gradually ceased fire at 7.30 a.m. On the N side the barrage continued until 8 a.m. Heaviest firing occured on the CAMBRAI Road, HOE & APE SUPPORTS,SHIKAR AVENUE,NEW BISON,SOUTHERN AVENUE & SHOVEL Trench. The 8th.K.O.R.L. suffered several casualties. The 2nd.Suffolk Regt. Nil. No raid was attempted on our front. All was quiet at 8.30 a.m.	
	9		Fine. Bright. Situation quiet.	
		10 a.m.	Staff Captain inspected detail camp.	
		12.15 p.m.	Divisional Commander called at Bde H.Q.	

A5834 Wt. W4973/M687 750,000 8/16 D. D. & L. Ltd. Forms/C.2118/13.

Instructions regarding War Diaries and Intelligence Summaries are contained in F. S. Regs., Part II. and the Staff Manual respectively. Title pages will be prepared in manuscript.

WAR DIARY
or
INTELLIGENCE SUMMARY.
(*Erase heading not required.*)

Army Form C. 2118.

3.

Place	Date 1918.	Hour	Summary of Events and Information	Remarks and references to Appendices
WANCOURT. N.15d.	Feb. 9	2 p.m.	Visited 9th.Inf.Bde.H.Q.	
		2.30 p.m.	Went round Right Battalion front.	
		3 p.m.	Brigade Major and Capt.FURNELL went round Left Battalion front.	
		7.55 p.m.	Relief of 2nd.Suffolk Regt.,and 1st.Gordon Hldrs.,complete. .... Vide	O.O.76.
	10		Fine. Dull. Situation quiet.	
		5.30 a.m.	Capt.FURNELL reconnoitred the COJEUL VALLEY with C.R.E.	
		9 a.m.	Col.HUNT went round the line.	
		2 p.m.	Brigade Major went round the line with O.C."D" Coy.,20th.K.R.R.C.(Pioneers) re wiring.	
		3 p.m.	Capt.PLAYFAIR returned to duty from Hospital.	
	11		Fine. Dull. Situation quiet.	
		7.15 a.m.	Col.HUNT and Staff Captain went to Tank Demonstration at BRAY SUR SOMME.	
		8 p.m.	O.O.77 issued to units.	
	12		Fine. Bright. Situation quiet.	
		7.15 a.m.	Brigade Major went to Tank Demonstration at BRAY.	
		10 a.m.	Col.HUNT went round M.G.Positions.	
		2 p.m.	Capt/s TROLLOPE & FURNELL went round the line.	
		7.25 p.m.	Inter-Battalion relief complete. .... Vide	O.O.77.
	13		Dull. Wet. Situation quiet.	
		9 a.m.	Staff Captain inspected new work on Details Camp.	
		10 a.m.	Brigade Major went round the line.	
		11.45 a.m.	Capt.TROLLOPE returned to Division.	
	14		Fine. Dull. Situation quiet.	
		10.30 a.m.	Brigade Major and Capt.FURNELL went round the line.	
		12.30 p.m.	Divisional Commander visited Bde H.Q.	
		8 p.m.	O.O.78 issued to units.	
		12 mdt.	G.O.C. returned to Bde.from leave.	
	15		Fine. Dull.Situation quiet.	

A5834 Wt. W4973/M687 750,000 8/16 D. D. & L. Ltd. Forms/C.2118/13.

Army Form C. 2118.

WAR DIARY
or
INTELLIGENCE SUMMARY.
(Erase heading not required.)

Instructions regarding War Diaries and Intelligence Summaries are contained in F. S. Regs., Part II. and the Staff Manual respectively. Title pages will be prepared in manuscript.

Place	Date 1918.	Hour	Summary of Events and Information	Remarks and references to Appendices
WANCOURT. N.15d.	Feb. 15	10.30 a.m.	G.O.C. and Capt.FURNELL went round the line.	
		2 p.m.	Col.HUNT left Brigade to rejoin his Battalion.	
		8.25 p.m.	Relief of 1st.Gordon Hldrs.,by 8th.K.O.R.L. complete.	Vide 0.0.78.
	16		Fine. Bright. Situation quiet.	
		9.45 a.m.	Divl.Commander called at Bde.H.Q. to see G.O.C.	
		10.15 a.m.	G.O.C. and B.M. went round the line.	
		3 p.m.	Capt.FURNELL visited Transport Lines and Details Camp.	
	17		Fine. Bright. Situation quiet.	
		10 a.m.	Staff Captain went to CARLISLE LINES to make arrangements for billetting 10th.R.W.F.	
		1.30 p.m.	G.O.C. went round the line.	
		3 p.m.	0.0.79 issued to units.	
	18		Fine. Bright. Situation quiet.	
		2 p.m.	G.O.C. and Staff Capt.,inspected Transport Lines and Details Camp.	
		9.30 a.m.	Divl.,Cmdr.,called to see Gen.PORTER.	
		7.15 p.m.	Relief of 2nd.Suffolk Regt.,by 1st.Gordon Hldrs.,complete. —	Vide 0.0.79.
	19		Fine. Bright. Situation quiet.	
		6.30 a.m.	G.O.C. and Capt.FURNELL went round the line.	
			8th.K.O.R.L. captured 2 prisoners of the 1st.R.E.I.R.,221st.Divn.	
	20		Fine. Bright. Situation quiet.	
		6.30 a.m.	G.O.C. and Brigade Major went round the line.	
		2 p.m.	Capt.FURNELL went round the line.	
		8 p.m.	0.0.80 issued to units.	
	21		Dull. Wet in morning,fine later. Situation quiet.	
		7 a.m.	Brigade Major went round the line.	
		11 a.m.	G.O.C.and Staff Captain reconnoitred NEUVILLE VITASSE for dug-outs.	
		2 p.m.	Capt.FURNELL went round line with G.S.O.3.	
		7.50 p.m.	Relief of 2nd.Suffolk Regt.,by 8th.K.O.R.L. complete.	Vide 0.0.80.

Instructions regarding War Diaries and Intelligence Summaries are contained in F. S. Regs., Part II. and the Staff Manual respectively. Title pages will be prepared in manuscript.

WAR DIARY
or
INTELLIGENCE SUMMARY.
(*Erase heading not required.*)

Army Form C. 2118.

Place	Date 1918.	Hour	Summary of Events and Information 5.	Remarks and references to Appendices
WANCOURT. N.15d.	Feb. 22		Dull. Wet. Situation quiet.	
		6.30 a.m.	G.O.C. and Capt.FURNELL went round the line.	
		2 p.m.	Brigade Major went round the line.	
	23		Fine. Dull. Situation quiet.	
		10 a.m.	B.M. went round the line.	
		12 noon	Divl.,Commander visited Brigade H.Q.	
		2.30 p.m.	G.O.C. and Capt.FURNELL reconnoitred NEUVILLE VITASSE for dug-outs.	
		3 p.m.	O.O.81 issued to units.	
	24		Fine. Dull. Situation quiet.	
		6.30 a.m.	G.O.C. and Capt.FURNELL went round the line.	
		10 a.m.	B.M.went round the line.	
		7 p.m.	Relief complete.	Vide O.O.81 attachd.
	25		Wet. Situation quiet.	
		10 a.m.	G.O.C. inspected M.G. emplacements.	
		2.30 p.m.	Divl.,Commander conferred with G.O.C. at Bde.,H.QM	
		4 p.m.	Conference of Battalion Commanders at Brigade H.Q.	
	26		Fine. Bright. Situation quiet.	
		6 a.m.	G.O.C.& B.M. went round the line.	
		9 a.m.	O.O.82 issued to units.	
		12 noon	Capt.FURNELL left for attachment to Divl.,H.Q.	
	27		Fine. Dull. Situation quiet.	
		6 a.m.	B.M.& S.C. visited line.	
		8.30 p.m.	Relief complete. 1st.Gordon Hldrs.,relieved 2nd.Suffolk Regt.	Vide O.O.82 attchd.
	28		Fine. Cloudy. Situation quiet.	
		6 a.m.	G.O.C.& Lt.FIRTH went round line (Right sector)	
		2 p.m.	B.M. and 2/Lt.AYTON visited Right Battalion H.Q.	
		8 p.m.	O.O.83 issued to units.	
	28/2/18.		W.C. Ayton 2/Lt.for Brigadier-Gen., Commanding 76th.Infantry Brigade.	

A5834 Wt. W4973/M687 750,000 8/16 D. D. & L. Ltd. Forms/C.2118/13.

CASUALTIES FOR MONTH OF FEBRUARY 1918.

****

	Killed.	Wounded.	Missing.	Gassed.	Remarks.
Officers	-	1	-	-	-
O.R.	10	48	2	6	

To:- Officer Commanding 10th.Bn.Royal Welch Fusiliers.

Brigadier-General PORTER,D.S.O.,is on leave and at present does not know that the 10th.Bn.Royal Welch Fusiliers is to be lost to the Brigade.

Lt.,Col.,HUNT,D.S.O.,however,feels absolutely certain that he is voicing General PORTER's wishes in conveying his thanks to the Battalion for their splendid work in the past,for their loyalty and esprit-de-corps and for their gallantry on all occasions.

For General PORTER he wishes the Officers,Non-Commissioned Officers and Men "God speed" and "Farewell".

Captain,
A/Brigade Major,76th.Infantry Brigade.

2/2/18.

3rd.Division "G".   B/2212.

WORK ON DEFENCES, Week Ending Feb.4th.

WIRE.

100 yards double apron from post E.E. Northwards in front of existing wire.

70 yards double apron in front of Post B.B.
75 " " " across CAMBRAI Road.
50 " " " between Posts M.M. & L.L.

In addition, 1200 gooseberries have been put in the existing wire in front line.

FIRE TRENCHES.

Front line. Has been deepened almost throughout by 1 foot New firebays built and existing ones improved. Revetting and trench-boarding are in progress.

HERON Support. Work on clearing out continued. Five fire - bays built.

TAIL. Deepened two feet from GOAT to KESTREL.

HOE Support. Deepened where necessary. Traverses and firebays built and improved.

NEW BISON. 30 yards deepened 2 feet and revetting commenced.

NEW GANNET. 40 yards of trench cleared. Eight firebays built and revetted.

EGRET. Parapet and parados revetted for 100 yards.

COMMUNICATION TRENCHES.

KESTREL AVENUE. 300 yards cleared down to trench boards from EGRET Eastwards.

SHIKAR AVENUE. Berme of 3 feet cleared for 150 yards.

DURHAM AVENUE. 80 yards deepened one foot.

SOUTHERN AVENUE. From front line to HOE SUPPORT bermed two feet wide.

m GOAT LANE & MONKEY LANE.

Work of clearing and berming continued.

Forward post on CAMBRAI Road dug, firestepped and wired.

Two forward posts in COJEUL VALLEY dug and wired.

The 529th.(E.R.) Fd., Coy., R.E. and attached infantry working party have completed the foolowing work:-

1. New Battalion H.Q. in EGRET.
2. Work on dugout in HOE SUPPORT.
3. 262 yards of SHIKAR AVENUE revetted.
4. 92 yards of SOUTHERN AVENUE revetted.

Captain,

5/2/18.   for Lt., Col., Commanding 76th. Inf. Bde.

SECRET.
****

Copy No.....

76th. INFANTRY BRIGADE OPERATION ORDER NO.74.

Reference Shoots 312, 312a, & 313, 1/10,000.
Sheet 51b.SW., 1/20,000.

2nd. February 1918.

1. On the night Feb.3rd./4th., the 2nd.Bn.The Suffolk Regt., will relieve 8th.Bn.King's Own (R.L.) Regt., in the right sub-section

2. On relief, the 8th.Bn.King's Own (R.L.) Regt., will move into Brigade Support.

3. Trench Store Cards will be forwarded to Brigade H.Q. within 24 hours of relief.

4. Completion of relief will be reported to Brigade H.Q.

5. ACKNOWLEDGE.

H.W. Trollope
Captain,
A/Brigade Major, 76th. Infantry Brigade.

Issued to Signals 8 p.m.

Copies to:-
1. G.O.C.
2. 8th.K.O.R.L.
3. 2nd.Suffolk Regt.
4. 10th.R.W.F.
5. 1st.Gordon Hldrs.
6. 76th.Coy.M.G.C.
7. 76th.T.M.B.
8. 3rd.Div."G".
9. 3rd.Div."Q".
10. 160th.Bde.R.F.A.
11. 529th.(E.R.)Fd.Co.R.E.
12. D.M.G.O.3rd.Div.
13. D.T.M.O. "
14. 9th.Inf.Bde.
15. 12th.Inf.Bde.
16. B.M.
17. S.C.
18. Bde.Sig.Offr.
19. War Diary.
20. War Diary.
21. File.

SECRET.
****
Copy No. 19 ..

76th. INFANTRY BRIGADE OPERATION ORDER NO.75.

Reference Sheets 312, 312a., & 313, 1/10,000
Sheet 51b.SW., 1/20,000.

5th. February 1918.

1. On the night Feb.6/7th., 8th.Bn.King's Own (R.L.) Regt., will relieve 1st.Bn.Gordon Hldrs., in the Left Sub-Section.

2. On relief, the 1st.Gordon Hldrs., will move into Brigade Support.

3. Details of relief will be arranged between Officers Commanding concerned.

4. Trench Store Cards will be forwarded to Brigade H.Q. within 24 hours of relief.

5. Completion of relief will be sent to this office.

6. ACKNOWLEDGE.

H.W.Thollope.
Captain,
A/Brigade Major, 76th. Infantry Brigade.

Issued to Signals 8 p.m.

Copies to:-

1.	G.O.C.	11.	529th.Fd.Co.R.E.
2.	8th.K.O.R.L.	12.	D.M.G.O. 3rd.Div.
3.	2nd.Suffolk R.	13.	D.T.M.O. "
4.	10th.R.W.F.	14.	9th.Inf.Bde.
5.	1st.Gordon H.	15.	12th. "
6.	76th.M.G.C.	16.	B.M.
7.	76th.T.M.B.	17.	S.C.
8.	3rd.Div."G".	18.	Bde.Sig.Offr.
9.	" "Q".	19.	War Diary
10.	160th.Bde.R.F.A.	20.	War Diary.
		21.	File.

SECRET.
****

76th. INFANTRY BRIGADE OPERATION ORDER NO.76. Copy No. 15
****

Reference Sheets 312,312a.,& 313,1/10,000
Sheet 51b.SW.,1/20,000. 8th.February 1918.

1. On the night Feb.9/10th.,the 1st.Bn.Gordon Hldrs.,will relieve the 2nd.Bn.Suffolk Regt.,in the Right Sub-Section.

2. On completion of relief the 2nd.Bn.Suffolk Regt.,will move into Brigade Support.

3. Details of relief will be arranged between C.O's concerned.

4. Trench Store Cards will be forwarded to Brigade H.Q.within 24 hours of relief.

5. The 2nd.Bn.Suffolk Regt.,will take over the spoil carrying parties from 1st.Bn.Gordon Hldrs.,commencing with the 3.30 p.m. shift on Feb.9th..

6. ACKNOWLEDGE.

H.W. Tollope.
Captain,
A/Brigade Major,76th.Infantry Brigade.

Issued to Signals 8 p.m.

Copies to:-

1.	G.O.C.	11.	D.M.G.O.3rd.Div.
2.	8th.K.O.R.L.	12.	D.T.M.O. "
3.	2nd.Suffolk Regt.	13.	9th.Inf.Bde.
4.	1st.Gordon Hldr.	14.	44th.Inf.Bde.
5.	76th.M.G.C.	15.	B.M.
6.	76th.T.M.B.	16.	S.C.
7.	3rd.Div."G".	17.	Bde.Sig.Offr.
8.	3rd.Div."Q".	18.	War Diary.
9.	160th.Bde.R.F.A.	19.	War Diary.
10.	529th.(E.R.)Fd.Co.R.E.	20.	File.

SECRET.
****

76th.INFANTRY BRIGADE OPERATION ORDER NO.77. Copy No.18.

****

Reference Sheets 312,312a.,& 313,1/10,000.
Sheet 51b.SW.,1/20,000. 11th.February 1918.

1. On the night Feb.12/13th.,the 2nd.Suffolk Regt.,will relieve 8th.K.O.R.L. in the left sub-section.

2. On completion of relief 8th.K.O.R.L. will move into Brigade Support.

3. Details of relief will be arranged between C.O.'s concerned.

4. Completion of relief to be reported to Brigade H.Q.

5. Trench Store Cards will be forwarded to Brigade H.Q. within 24 hours of relief.

6. 8th.K.O.R.L. will take over the 3.30 p.m. shift of working party under 181st.Tunnelling Company.

7. ACKNOWLEDGE.

H.W.Lobb[?] for
Captain,
Brigade Major,76th.Infantry Brigade.

Issued to Signals 8 p.m.

Copies to:-

1.	Lt-Col-Cmdg.	11.	D.M.G.C.3rd.Div.
2.	8th.K.O.R.L.	12.	D.T.M.O. "
3.	2nd.Suffolk Regt.	13.	9th.Inf.Bde.
4.	1st.Gordon Hldrs.	14.	44th. "
5.	76th.Coy.M.G.C.	15.	B.M.
6.	76th.T.M.B.	16.	S.C.
7.	3rd.Div."G".	17.	Bde.Sig.Off.
8.	3rd.Div."Q".	18.	War Diary.
9.	Left Group R.F.A.	19.	War Diary.
10.	529th.(E.R.)Fd.Co.R.E.	20.	File.

SECRET.

::*:*:*:*:*

76th.INFANTRY BRIGADE OPERATION ORDER NO.78. Copy No..21

::*:*:**:**:**:**:**:**:**:*:*:*:*:*:*:*:*:*:*

Reference Sheets 312,312a.,& 313,1/10,000.
Sheet 51b.SW.,1/20,000.

14th.February 1918.

1. On the night Feb.15/16th.,8th.Bn.K.O.R.L. will relieve 1st.Bn.Gordon Hldrs.,in the Right Sub-Section.

2. On relief 1st.Bn.Gordon Hldrs.,will move into Brigade Support.

3. Details of relief will be arranged between C.O's concerned,and completion reported to Brigade H.Q.

4. H.Q.,8th.Bn.K.O.R.L. will be established in EGRET Trench,O.19c.6.6.

5. Trench Store Cards will be sent in to Brigade H.Q. within 24 hours of relief.

6. 1st.Bn.Gordon Hldrs.,will find the 3.30 p.m. shift on Feb.15th., for the 181st.Tunnelling Company.

7. ACKNOWLEDGE.

[signature] Captain,
Brigade Major,76th.Infantry Brigade.

Issued to Signals 8 p.m.

Copies to:-

1.	Lt.Col.Cmdg.	11.	D.M.G.C.3rd.Div.
2.	8th.K.O.R.L.	12.	D.T.M.O. "
3.	2nd.Suffolk R.	14.	181st.Tunn.Coy.
4.	1st.Gordon H.	15.	9th.Inf.Bde
5.	76th.M.G.C.	16.	44th. "
6.	76th.T.M.B.	17.	B.M.
7.	3rd.Div."G".	18.	S.C.
8.	3rd.Div."Q".	19.	Bde.Sig.Offr.
9.	Left Group R.F.A.	20.	War Diary.
10.	529th.Fd.Co.R.E.	21.	"
		22.	File.

SECRET.
::*:*:*:*
Copy No.19.

76th. INFANTRY BRIGADE OPERATION ORDER NO.79.
:

Reference Sheets 312, 312a., & 313, 1/10,000.
Sheet 51b., SW., 1/20,000.

17th., February 1918.

1. On the night Feb.18/19th., 1st. Gordon Hldrs., will relieve 2nd. Suffolk Regt., in the Left Sub-Section.

2. On relief 2nd. Suffolk Regt., will move into Brigade Support.

3. Details of relief will be arranged between C.O's concerned, and completion reported to Brigade H.Q.

4. Trench Store Cards will be sent into Brigade H.Q. within 24 hours of relief.

5. 2nd. Suffolk Regt., will find the 3.30 p.m. shift on Feb.18th., for the 181st. Tunnelling Company.

6. ACKNOWLEDGE.

B.Blanton
Captain,
Brigade Major, 76th. INFANTRY BRIGADE.

Issued to Signals 3 p.m.

Copies to:-

1. G.O.C.
2. 8th. K.O.R.L.
3. 2nd. Suffolk Regt.
4. 1st. Gordon Hldrs.
5. 76th. Coy. M.G.C.
6. 76th. T.M.B.
7. 3rd. Div. "G".
8. 3rd. Div. "Q".
9. Left Group R.F.A.
10. 529th. (E.R.) Fd. Co. R.E.
11. D.M.G.C. 3rd. Div.
12. D.T.M.O. "
13. 181st. Tunn. Coy.
14. 9th. Inf. Bde.
15. 44th. "
16. B.M.
17. S.C.
18. Bde. Sig. Offr.
19. War Diary.
20. "
21. File.

SECRET.
****
Copy No 16..

76th. INFANTRY BRIGADE OPERATION ORDER NO.80.

Reference UTS Sheets 1/10,000.
Sheet 51b., SW., 1/20,000.

20th. February 1918.

1. On the night Feb.21st./22nd., 2nd. Suffolk Regt., will relieve 8th.K.O.R.L. in the Right Sub-Section.

2. On relief 8th.K.O.R.L. will move into Brigade Support.

3. Details of relief will be arranged between C.O's concerned, and completion reported to Brigade H.Q.

4. Trench Store Cards will be sent to Brigade H.Q. within 24 hours of relief.

5. 8th.K.O.R.L. will find the 2 p.m. shift on Feb.21st., for the 257th. Tunnelling Company.

6. ACKNOWLEDGE.

[signature] Captain,
Brigade Major, 76th. Infantry Brigade.

Issued to Signals 8 p.m.

Copies to:-

1.	G.O.C.	11.	D.M.G.C. 3rd. Div.
2.	8th.K.O.R.L.	12.	D.T.M.O. "
3.	2nd. Suffolk Regt.	13.	9th. Inf. Bde.
4.	1st. Gordon Hldrs.	14.	8̶4th. "
5.	76th. M.G.C.	15.	B.M.
6.	76th. T.M.B.	16.	S.C.
7.	3rd. Div. "G".	17.	Bde. Sig. Offr.
8.	3rd. Div. "Q".	18.	War Diary.
9.	Left Group R.F.A.	19.	"
10.	529th. (E.R.) Fd. Co. R.E.	20.	File.

SECRET.
****
Copy No. 19

76th. INFANTRY BRIGADE OPERATION ORDER NO.81.
****

Reference UTS Sheets 1/10,000.
Sheet 51b.,SW.,1/20,000. 23rd.February 1918.

1. On the night Feb.24th./25th.,8th.K.O.R.L. will relieve 1st. Gordon Hldrs.,in the Left Sub-Section.

2. On relief,1st.Gordon Hldrs.,will move into Brigade Support.

3. Details of relief will be arranged between C.O's concerned,and completion reported to Brigade H.Q.

4. Trench Store Cards will be sent in to Brigade H.Q. within 24 hours of relief.

5. 1st.Gordon Hldrs.,will find the 2 p.m. shift on Feb.24th.,for the 257th.Tunnelling Company.

6. ACKNOWLEDGE.

Issued to Signals 3 p.m.

S. Playfair
Captain,
Brigade Major,76th.Infantry Brigade.

Copies to:-

1.	G.O.C.	11.	D.M.G.O. 3rd.Div.
2.	8th.K.O.R.L.	12.	D.T.M.O. "
3.	2nd.Suffolk Regt.	13.	9th.Inf.Bde.
4.	1st.Gordon Hldrs.	14.	44th. "
5.	76th.Coy.M.G.C.	15.	B.M.
6.	76th.T.M.B.	16.	S.C.
7.	3rd.Div."G".	17.	Bde.Sig.Offr.
8.	3rd.Div."Q".	18.	War Diary.
9.	Left Group R.F.A.	19.	"
10.	529th.(E.R.)Fd.Co.R.E.	20.	File.

SECRET.
****

76th.INFANTRY BRIGADE OPERATION ORDER NO.82.
****

Copy No. 16.

Reference UTS Sheets 1/10,000.
Sheet 51b.,SW.,1/20,000.

26th.February 1918.

1. On the night Feb.27/28th.,1st.Gordon Hldrs.,will relieve 2nd.Suffolk Regt.,in the Right Sub-Section.

2. On relief,2nd.Suffolk Regt.,will move into Brigade Support.

3. Details of relief will be arranged between C.O's concerned and completion reported to Brigade H.Q.

4. Trench Store Cards will be sent in to Brigade H.Q. within 24 hours of relief.

5. 2nd.Suffolk Regt.,will find the 2 p.m. shift on Feb.27th.,for the 257th.Tunnelling Company.

6. ACKNOWLEDGE.

Issued to Signals 9 a.m.

B. Playfair
Captain,
Brigade Major,76th.Infantry Brigade.

Copies to:-

1.	G.O.C.	11.	D.M.G.O.3rd.Div.
2.	8th.K.O.R.L.	12.	D.T.M.O. "
3.	2nd.Suffolk Regt.	13.	9th.Inf.Bde.
4.	1st.Gordon Hldrs.	14.	44th. "
5.	76th.Coy.M.G.C.	15.	B.M.
6.	76th.T.M.B.	16.	S.C.
7.	3rd.Div."G".	17.	Bde.Sig.Offr.
8.	3rd.Div."Q".	18.	War Diary.
9.	Left Group R.F.A.	19.	"
10.	529th.(E.R.)Fd.Co.R.E.	20.	File.

3rd Division.

B. H. Q.

76th INFANTRY BRIGADE

MARCH 1918

Appendices attached:

Operation Orders.

Instructions regarding War Diaries and Intelligence Summaries are contained in F. S. Regs., Part II. and the Staff Manual respectively. Title pages will be prepared in manuscript.

WAR DIARY
or
INTELLIGENCE SUMMARY.
(Erase heading not required.)

Army Form C. 2118.

Headquarters

76th.Inf.Brigade.

V.R. 30

Place	Date 1918.	Hour	Summary of Events and Information	Remarks and references to Appendices
WANCOURT N.15d. central.	Mch. 1		Fine. Frosty. Situation quiet.	
		6 a.m.	B.M.visited Left Battn front.	
		2 p.m.	G.O.C. and S.C. visitedDivision for conference.	
	2		Fine. Frosty. Clear. Situation quiet.	
		4.30 a.m.	Corps Commander and G.O.C. visitedline.	
		3 p.m.	Divisional Commander conferred with G.O.C. at Brigade H.Q.	
		9 p.m.	Relief complete. (2nd.Suff.Regt and 8th.K.O.R.L.,1st.Gdn Hldrs and 7th.K.S.L.I.) Vide O.O.83	
	3		Dull. Misty situation quiet.	
			G.O.C. and B.M. went round the line.	
	4		Dull. Misty. Situation quiet.	
			B.M.went round the line.	
		2 p.m.	Conference of Battn Cmdrs.,at Brigade H.Q.	
	5		Dull. Misty. Situation ~~XXXXX~~.normal.	
		8 a.m.	B.M. went round the line.	
		8 p.m.	O.O.84 issued to units.	
		9.15 p.m.	Relief complete. "B"Coy.1st.G.H.relieved "W"Coy.2nd.Suff.Regt who came out to practice raid.	
	6		Fine. Clear. Situation normal.	
		6 a.m.	G.O.C. and 2/Lt.AYTON went round Right Sector.	
		12 noon	Divl Cmdr.,called to see G.O.C.	
	7		Fine. Clear. Situation normal.	
		8.30 p.m.	2nd.Suff.Regt.,relieved by 1st.G.H.and 8th.K.O.R.L. in Support Position vide O.O.84.	
	8		Fine. Clear. Situation normal.	
		6 a.m.	G.O.C. and S.C. went round the line.	
	9		Fine. Clear. Situation normal.	
		3 p.m.	Divl Cmdr called to see G.O.C.	
			B.M. and I.O. went round Second System.	

A5834 Wt. W4973/M687 750,000 8/16 D. D. & L. Ltd. Forms/C.2118/13.

Army Form C. 2118.

Instructions regarding War Diaries and Intelligence Summaries are contained in F. S. Regs., Part II. and the Staff Manual respectively. Title pages will be prepared in manuscript.

WAR DIARY
or
INTELLIGENCE SUMMARY.

(Erase heading not required.)

Place	Date	Hour	Summary of Events and Information	Remarks and references to Appendices
	1918			
WANCOURT N15d	MAR.		Fine misty - Situation normal	
	10	8pm	Units issued with O.O. 85	
	11		Fine misty - situation normal	
		8 am	G.O.C. attended conference at 8th Bde. H.Q	
		8pm	O.O.85 (amendment) issued	
	12		Fine situation quiet	
		8 am	G.O.C. & 2/Lt AYTON went round line	
		9pm	Relief complete (8th KORL R relieved 1st G.H. & 2nd Suffolk Regt. moved up to 2nd System) - - - - - - -	VIDE O.O.85
	13 14 15 16		} Fine situation quiet.	
		6am	G.O.C. & S.C went round line	
		1pm	Corps Commander called	
		3pm	O.O.86 issued to units.	
	17		Fine situation quiet	
		9 am	B.M went round line	
		9pm	Relief complete (8th KORLR & 2nd Suffolk) - - - - - - - - - - -	VIDE O.O.86
	18		Fine situation quiet	
		6am	G.O.C went round line	
	19		Wet situation quiet	
		6am	B.M went round line.	
	20		Wet - situation quiet	
		6am	G.O.C went round line	
	21		Fine misty.	
		5.10	Enemy put down heavy bombardment chiefly on our support & reserve lines & WANCOURT. A Gas projector attack was launched against the 44th Inf. Bde. on our left but their casualties were slight. The enemy attempted to enter O post but were driven off by L.G. & rifle fire. Barrage particularly heavy on WANCOURT. H.Q. 8th KORL moved from WANCOURT to STAG TRENCH. Coy. of 8th KORL left MARLIÈRE caves to Sunken Rd. near Bde. H.Q (N15d). 2 platoons to BUZZARD Trench. Scattered shelling - apparently no fixed targets.	

A5834. Wt. W4973/M687. 750,000. 8/16. D. D. & L. Ltd. Forms/C.2118/13.

Instructions regarding War Diaries and Intelligence Summaries are contained in F. S. Regs., Part II. and the Staff Manual respectively. Title pages will be prepared in manuscript.

WAR DIARY
or
INTELLIGENCE SUMMARY.
(Erase heading not required.)

Army Form C. 2118.

Place	Date Mar	Hour	Summary of Events and Information	Remarks and references to Appendices
WANCOURT N15d	22		Situation quieter	
		11.30pm	Orders received to withdraw to YELLOW line (3rd System) 2nd in Command & 1 off per Battn came to Bde HQ. Orders were sent to Battns placing withdrawal N of River COJEUL under O/c 2nd Suffolk & S of River under O/c 8th KORLR	
	23	1am	Front line withdrew	
		2.30am	do do (2nd System) withdrew	0087
		3.30am	Reserve do (do) do. All 3 Battn HQ moved to old Bde HQ (N15d3.4)	
Northumberland Lines.		7am	Bde HQ moved to NORTHUMBERLAND Lines. Dispositions:- 8th KORL (Right Front) 1st G.H. (left front) 2nd Suffolk (whole of Reserve line)	
		9am	Enemy appeared over WANCOURT RIDGE. Day passed fairly quietly. Enemy shelled back areas. Also did a lot of sniping & artillery shelled enemy movement.	
		12noon	Attack on 1 G.H. & 8th KORL repulsed.	
	24.	1pm	do on left of 1st G H. The enemy reached our wire but were completely repulsed	
		2pm	with heavy losses. Units issued with O.O. 88	
	25		Enemy quieter all night. 2nd Suffolk withdrawn to GREEN line 1st G H & 8th KORLR took over front & reserve lines	O.O 88
Mila 74	26.		Situation quiet.	
	27		do. do. (BDE H.Q. [illegible]) units. 1.15pm O.O 89 issued to units	
		5.30pm	Enemy attempt to bomb down SHAFT SWITCH was frustrated by 8th KORLR. At the same time a party advanced down Sunken Road at N22 central. These were also successfully dealt with. 11am O.O. 90 issued. 3rd Div O. O1222 received.	

A5834 Wt. W4973/M687 750,000 8/16 D. D. & L. Ltd. Forms/C.2118/13.

Instructions regarding War Diaries and Intelligence Summaries are contained in F. S. Regs., Part II. and the Staff Manual respectively. Title pages will be prepared in manuscript.

WAR DIARY
or
INTELLIGENCE SUMMARY.

(Erase heading not required.)

Army Form C. 2118.

Place	Date	Hour	Summary of Events and Information	Remarks and references to Appendices
M16a7.4	Mar 27/28		2nd Suffolk relieved 1st G.H. 1st G.H. to NEUVILLE VITASSE Switch & GREEN line — —	0.0.89
		12.10am	do do do 1st G.H. to Army line 4th System — — — — — — —	0.0.90
		3 am	Enemy bombardment started on back area.	
		5.50 am	S.O.S. went up on our front.	
			~~Enemy ... NEUVILLE VITASSE — WANCOURT.~~	
			2nd Suffolk holding line of bivouacs in sunken road (TILLOY — WANCOURT)	
		10 am	8th KORL. holding CT from N15b1.4 to N21b2.4.	
		12.10pm	Enemy reported about FEUCHY CHAPEL.	
		1.20	All 3 Battns holding NEUVILLE Switch & Green Line.	
		3pm	Lt Col. JAMES M.C. (8th KORLR) killed.	
		4pm	1st G.H. ordered to throw back left flank through M14a.	
		9.25pm	Right flank of Bde. fell back in rear of NEUVILLE. Orders issued to re-establish line & gain touch with Right Bde.	
		5pm	3rd Div. GA. 293 received.	
			~~Bde H.Q. moved to M8c6.~~	
		7.pm	B.M. 207 issued. 12 midnight. BM207 complied with. — — — —	BM207
M8c6.0.	29		3rd Div. O.O. 223 received.	
		~~H.Q.~~	5 am Bde H.Q. moved to M8c6.0.	
		11pm	Situation. 1st G.H. in touch with Enemy in M13c7.0. holding GREEN line northwards. 2nd Suffolk withdrawn to M18. 8th KORLR in position M23b & M24a & b.	
	30		Situation quieter	
		9 am	O.O. 92 issued.	
		2 am	76th Inf Bde relieved by 21st Canadian Inf. Battn. — — — — — — —	0.0.91
		4pm	76th Inf Bde. moved to WARLUZEL — SOMBRIN area — — — —	0.0.92
	31		Wet.	
		9pm	O.O. 93 issued.	

M. C. Ayton 2/Lt
for Brig. Genl.
76th Inf. Bde.

A5834 Wt. W4973/M687 750,000 8/16 D. D. & L. Ltd. Forms/C.2118/13.

CASUALTIES FOR MONTH OF MARCH 1918.

	Killed.	Wounded.	Missing.
Officers.	6	23	13.
O.R.	134	556	602.

SECRET.
****

Copy No...

76th.INFANTRY BRIGADE OPERATION ORDER NO.83.

Reference 1/20,000 51b.,SW.
and UTS.Maps 1/10,000 dated 16/2/18. 28th.Feb.1918.

1. The 3rd.Divisional front is being re-adjusted,and will be held with the 9th.Infantry Brigade on the right,the 8th.Infantry Brigade in the centre,and the 76th.Infantry Brigade on the left.

2. The new 76th.Infantry Brigade front will be held with one Battalion in line,one Battalion in support,and one Battaion in Brigade Reserve at CARLISLE LINES.

3. The following reliefs will take place on the night March 2nd./3rd.:-

(a) 7th.K.S.L.I. (8th.Infantry Brigade) will relieve 1st. Gordon Hldrs.,in that portion of the front between the present inter-brigade boundary and the new inter-brigade boundary. (vide map attached *)

(b) 2nd.Suffolk Regt.,will relieve 8th.K.O.R.L. in the present Left Sub-section,and will relieve 1st.Gordon Hldrs.,in that portion of the front between the present inter-battalion boundary and the new inter-brigade boundary.

4. On completion of the above reliefs,-

(a) 8th.K.O.R.L. will move into Brigade Reserve at CARLISLE LINES.

(b) 1st.Gordon Hldrs.,will move into Brigade Support with the advanced company in the line LION - EGRET (N.of KESTREL) instead of in STAG as at present.

5. Trench Stores and maps,photos etc.,relating to the area to be taken over by the 8th.Inf.Brigade will be handed over to 7th.K.S.L.I. by O.C.,1st.Gordon Hldrs.

6. Details of above reliefs will be arranged between C.O's concerned and their completion reported to Brigade H.Q.

7. Separate orders will be issued for reconnaissances etc.,to be made by Battalion in Brigade Reserve at CARLISLE LINES.

8. Trench Store Cards will reach Brigade H.Q. within 24 hours of relief.

9. 1st.Gordon Hldrs.,will find the 2 p.m. shift for 257th. Tunnelling Coy.,on March 2nd.

10. ACKNOWLEDGE.

[signature]
Captain,
Issued to Signals 8 p.m. Brigade Major,76th.Infantry Brigade.

Copies to:-
1. G.O.C.
2. 8th.K.O.R.L. *
3. 2nd.Suffolk Regt. *
4. 1st.Gordon Hldrs. *
5. 76th.T.M.B. *
6. Left Group R.F.A.
7. 529th.Fd.Co.R.E.
8. 76th.Coy.3rd.M.G.Bn.
9. 3rd.Div."G".
10. 3rd.Div."Q".
11. 8th.Inf.Bde.
12. 9th.Inf.Bde.
13. 44th.Inf.Bde.
14. D.M.G.C.
15. D.T.M.O.
16. No.2 Coy.,Train.
17. 7th.Fd.Amb.
18. B.M.
19. S.C.
20. Bde.Sig.Offr.
21. War Diary.
22. War Diary.
23. File.
24. "

SECRET.
****

Copy No,...1

76th.INFANTRY BRIGADE OPERATION ORDER NO.84.
****

Reference 1/20,000 51b.SW.,and
UTS.Maps 1/10,000 d.16/2/18.

5th.March 1918.

1. The following reliefs and moves will be carried out in the Left Section on the night March 7/8th.:-

(a) 1st.Gordon Hldrs.,will relieve 2nd.Suffolk Regt.,in the line

(b) 8th.K.O.R.L. will move up into Brigade Support.

2. After relief,2nd.Suffolk Regt.,will move into Brigade Reserve at CARLISLE LINES.

3. Details of relief will be arranged between C.O's concerned and their completion reported to Brigade H.Q.

4. Trench Store Cards will reach Brigade H.Q. within 24 hours of relief.

5. 8th.K.O.R.L. will move via NEUVILLE VITASSE - Control Post N.21a.5.8. - thence by duck-board track to Support Battalion H.Q., N.18c.4.4.,and will not reach MARLIERE before 6 p.m. March 7th..

6. ACKNOWLEDGE.

S Playfair
Captain,
Brigade Major,76th.Infantry Brigade.

Issued to Signals 8 p.m.

Copies to :-
1. G.O.C.
2. 8th.K.O.R.L.
3. 2nd.Suffolk Regt.
4. 1st.Gordon Hldrs.
5. 76th.T.M.B.
6. Left Gp.3rd.D.A.
7. 529th.Fd.Co.R.E.
8. 76th.Coy.3rd.M.G.Bn.
9. 3rd.Div."G".
10. 3rd.Div."Q".
11. 8th.Inf.Bde.
12. 9th.Inf.Bde.
13. 44th.Inf.Bde.
14. D.M.G.O.
15. D.T.M.O.
16. 7th.Fd.Amb.
17. B.M.
18. S.C.
19. Bde.Sig.Offr.
20. War Diary.
21. "
22. File.
23.

SECRET.
****

Copy No. 21..

76th. INFANTRY BRIGADE OPERATION ORDER NO.85.

Reference 1/20,000 51b.,SW.,and WANCOURT
Special Sheet 1/10,000 Edition 1a.   10th.March 1918.

1. The following reliefs and moves will be carried out in the Left Section on the night March 12/13th.:-

(a) 8th.K.O.R.L. will relieve 1st.Gordon Hldrs.,in the line

(b) 2nd.Suffolk Regt.,will move up into Brigade Support.

2. After relief,1st.Gordon Hldrs.,will move into Brigade Reserve at CARLISLE LINES.

3. Details of reliefs will be arranged between C.O's concerned and their completion reported to Brigade H.Q.

4. There will be no movement,except of advanced parties, forward of MARLIERE before 7 p.m. March 12th.

5. Trench Store Cards will reach Brigade H.Q. within 24 hours of relief.

6. ACKNOWLEDGE.

R Playfair
Captain,
Issued to Signals 8 p.m.   Brigade Major,76th.Infantry Brigade.

Copies to:-
1. G.O.C.
2. 8th.K.O.R.L.
3. 2nd.Suffolk Regt.
4. 1st.Gordon Hldrs.
5. 76th.T.M.B.
6. Left Gp.R.F.A.
7. 529th.Fd.Co.R.E.
8. 233rd.M.G.C.
9. 3rd.Div."G".
10. 3rd.Div."Q".
11. 8th.Inf.Bde.
12. 9th.Inf.Bde.
13. 44th.Inf.Bde.
14. D.M.G.C.
15. D.T.M.O.
16. 7th.Fld.Amb.
17. B.M.
18. S.C.
19. Bde.Sig.Offr.
20. War Diary.
21. "
22. File.

SECRET.
****

AMENDMENT TO 76th. INFANTRY BRIGADE
OPERATION ORDER NO.85.
****

Cancel para.1 (b) and para.2, and substitute:-

2. 2nd. Suffolk Regt., and 1st. Gordon Hldrs., will move into the Second System on the South and North of the COJEUL Valley respectively.

On relief, 2 platoons 8th. K.O.R.L. will move from RAKE into KEY.

Cancel para.4 and substitute:-

4. 2nd. Suffolk Regt., will leave CARLISLE LINES at 6 p.m. March 12th.

W. G. Playfair.
Captain,
Brigade Major, 76th. Infantry Brigade.

11/3/18.

Addressed all recipients of O.O.85.

SECRET.

Copy No....20

76th. INFANTRY BRIGADE OPERATION ORDER NO.86.

Reference 1/20,000 51b.,SW.,and WANCOURT
Special Sheet 1/10,000 Edition 1a. 16th.March 1918.

1. 2nd.Suffolk Regt.,will relieve 8th.K.O.R.L. in the FIRST SYSTEM,Left Section,on the night March 17/18th.

2. On relief,8th.K.O.R.L. will move into the SECOND SYSTEM, (SOUTH),taking over the dispositions of 2nd.Suffolk Regt.

1st.Gordon Hldrs.,will remain in the SECOND SYSTEM (NORTH).

3. Details of relief will be arranged between C.O's concerned and their completion reported to Brigade H.Q.

4. There will be no movement,except of advanced parties, forward of MARLIERE before 7 p.m. March 17th.

5. Trench Store Cards will reach Brigade H.Q. within 24 hours of relief.

6. ACKNOWLEDGE.

R Playfair
Captain,
Brigade Major,76th.Infantry Brigade.

Issued to Signals 3 p.m.

Copies to:-
1. G.O.C.
2. 8th.K.O.R.L.
3. 2nd.Suffolk Regt.
4. 1st.Gordon Hldrs.
5. 76th.T.M.B.
6. Left Gp.R.F.A.
7. 233rd.M.G.C.
8. 529th.(E.R.)Fd.Co.R.E.
9. 3rd.Div."G".
10. 3rd.Div."Q".
11. 8th.Inf.Bde.
12. 9th.Inf.Bde.
13. 44th.Inf.Bde.
14. D.M.G.O.
15. D.T.M.O.
16. 7th.Fld.Amb.
17. B.M.
18. S.C.
19. Bde.Sig.Offr.
20. War Diary.
21. "
22. File.

Secret. Copy No.

76th Inf. Bde. O.O. 88

Ref. attchd. Map
1/20,000 57.B. S.W.

24th March 1918

1. The 3rd Divl. front will be held by 3 Brigades in line.

2. Tonight, Mch 24/25th, 76th Inf Bde will hand over to 9th Inf. Bde the portion of the front and Reserve lines, Third System, South of the new boundary (vide attchd map)

3. Inter-Bde and Battn. boundaries are shown on the attached map.

4. 8 K.O.R.L. will hold the right, 1st Gordon Hldrs the left of 76th Bde front, each with 2 companies in the front line and 2 in the Reserve line.

5. 2nd Suffolk Regt will be withdrawn on relief to the Army line in N.13a. and c. and the vicinity.

6. All Battn H.Q.s will remain as at present.

7. The 4th R. Fus will be the left Battn. 9th Inf. Bde and will be disposed in depth in the front and reserve lines.

8. Officers from 4 R. Fus will report to H.Q. of 8 K.O.R.L. and 2nd Suffolk Regt this afternoon to arrange details.

Completion and dispositions to be reported as usual.

Bde H.Q. will move later to the vicinity of M.17; all concerned will be notified of exact location and time of move.

8. Acknowledge.

(Sd) J.G. Playfair Captain
BM 76th Inf. Bde

Issued 1pm

Copies
1. 8 K.O.R.L.
2. 2 Suff. Regt
3. 1. G. Hldrs
4. 76 T.M.B.
5. 9 Inf Bde
6. 8th "
7. 3 Div G
8. Rf. Coy 3. Div.

Secret Copy

76th Inf. Bde. O.O. No. 89

Ref. 1/20,000 51B.S.W.
Ed. 7c

26th March 1918

1. 2nd Suffolk Regt. will relieve 1st Gordon Hldrs in the front and reserve lines Third System during the night Mch 26/27th

2. On relief 1. Gordon Hldrs will occupy the Army line, Fourth System now held by 2. Suffolk Regt. and will also occupy the new Switch line N.8c.8.0 (Sunken Road) through N.14 a. and c to N.14 c.0.0. (N.E. corner of NEUVILLE VITASSE)

3. Completion of reliefs and dispositions will be reported, as usual.

4. Acknowledge.

(Sd) J.S.O. Playfair Capt.
BM 76th Inf. Bde

Issued 1.15 pm

Copies to:–
1. 8th Bde
2. 2. Suffolk Regt
3. 1. Gordon Hldrs
4. 76 TMB
5. Left Gp. RFA
6. 3 Div G
7. 9 Inf Bde
8. ...
9. File

Secret Copy No.

76th Inf. Bde O.O. 91

Ref. 51b SW 1/20,000 and LENS 11

29th March 1918

1. 4th Canadian Bde will relieve 76th and part of 9th Bde tonight taking over 76th Bde front with one Battn, the 21st Can. Battn.

2. H.Q. 21st Can. Battn will be in present H.Q. 1st N. Fus M24 c.1.9

Lt Col T.L. Lideman DSO, Cmdg., 2nd Bn. Suffolk Regt and one officer per Battn will be at H.Q. 1 N Fus at 11 pm tonight.

3. 21st Bn. is to be disposed as follows:-

Right Coy From BEAURAINS - NEUVILLE VITASSE Road to about the WHITE POST Track

Left Coy From WHITE POST Track to junction with 4th Bde

Support Coys In old trenches M18.

4. When O.C. 21st Can. Bn. is satisfied that his Bn is in position, he will inform O.C. 2 Suffolk Regt who will then order all 3 Bns 76th Bde to withdraw, and will notify Bde H.Q. by code word "LIKEMAN"

5. Battns will reform about M.16 and march by companies at 300 yards interval to RIVIERE.

Route :- Bde Report Centre M16 a. 5.6 — AGNY - WAILLY.

6. No troops 76th Bde will be withdrawn until orders are received from O.C. 2nd Suffolk Regt.

7. Men of M.G.C., T.M.B. etc with Battns will be withdrawn with them

-3-

8. Guides will report to 2/Lt AYTON 2 Suffolk Regt., at the Double NISSEN Hut, CARNIBLE LINES at 9.30pm as follows:-

4 guides 8th KORL for the relieving Bn's Right Coy
4 " 1. G.H. " " " " Left Coy
4 " 2nd Suff R. " " " " Support Coys

Each party of guides will be under an officer or Senior N.C.O.

9. Acknowledge

Issued 4.30pm (Sd) I.S.O. Playfair Captain
Bm. 76th Inf. Bde

Copies 1. 8 KORL
2. 2 Suff R
3. 1. G. H.
4. 76 TMB
5. Left Gp. 3 DA
6. 9th } Bdes
7. 44th }
8. 4th Can }
9. 3. Div G
10. ____________

"Secret" Copy No

76th Inf Bde No 92

Ref LENS 11 1/100,000   30th March 1918

G.O. [illegible]

1. 76th Bde will move to the WARLUZEL — SOMBRIN area today as follows:-

2. Starting Point

Cross Roads just East of E in GROSVILLE

Unit	Time to reach S.P.
Bde HQ	2.30pm
8 KORL	2.35pm
2 Suffolk Regt	2.50pm
1 Gordon Hdrs	3.5 pm
76th TMB	3.20pm
7th Fd Amb.	3.25pm

Route:- COUY EN ARTOIS – FOSSEUX — SOMBRIN

3. Transport (less cookers) will move via SIMENCOURT under the orders of Bde T.O. joining the column in rear of 7th Fd Amb. at COUY EN ARTOIS.

4. Billetting parties will meet the Staff Captain at the TMB office SOMBRIN at 2.30pm

5. Acknowledge.

(Sd) [illegible] Captain

BM. 76th Inf Bde.

Issued 9am

Copies
1. 8 KORL
2. 2 Suff Regt
3. 1 Gordon Hrs
4. 76th TMB
5. Bde T.O.
6. 7 F Amb
7. [illegible]
8. 3rd Div [illegible]
9. TM SOMBRIN

3rd Division

WAR DIARY

B. H. Q.

76th INFANTRY BRIGADE

APRIL 1 9 1 8

Attached - Operation Orders.

Army Form C. 2118.

Instructions regarding War Diaries and Intelligence Summaries are contained in F. S. Regs., Part II. and the Staff Manual respectively. Title pages will be prepared in manuscript.

WAR DIARY
or
INTELLIGENCE SUMMARY.

(Erase heading not required.)

76th Infantry Bde H.Q.

1/3

Place	Date	Hour	Summary of Events and Information	Remarks and references to Appendices
DIVION.	APRIL 1st		Fine - clear.	
		9am.	Brigade moved from SOMBRIN - WARLUZEL area to DIEVAL - DIVION area by bus.	0093
		4 pm.	Lt-Col. G.C. Stubbs resumed command of 2nd Suffolks vice Lt Col G.L. Likeman	
	2nd		Fine - clear	
		12.30pm	GOC & BM reconnoitred MAISTRE LINE with Div. General.	
			Lt-Col G.L. Likeman assumed command of 8th K.O.R.L.	
		2.0 pm	Orders issued to 8th KORL to move from DIEVAL to DIVION	
		10.0 pm	Above order cancelled.	
	3rd		Dull - clear	
		8.30am	Bn & Coy Comdrs reconnoitred MAISTRE LINE with BM & 2Lt. Bowden.	
		1.00am	OO94 issued to units	
	4th		Dull - Showery - Misty	0094.
HERSIN CHATEAU		9.0am	Brigade moved from DIEVAL - DIVION area to HERSIN area.	
			GOC. BM & 2Lt. Bowden with Bn - Comdrs reconnoitred localities at NOEUX-les-MINES and NOYELLES.	
	5th		Dull - rainy	
		10.0am	GSO2 & Staff Captain visited BOYEFFLES & BOUVIGNY - BOYEFFLES to obtain billets.	
		2.0pm	GOC & GSO1 visited Noulette Huts and Marqueffles Camp	
		10.0pm	OO 95 issued to units	
SAINS-EN-GOHELLE CHATEAU.	6th		Dull - clear	0095
		10.0am	Brigade moves from HERSIN area to LES BREBIS - FOSSE 10 - MARQUEFFLES FM area	
	7th		Bright - Clear.	
		10.30am	GOC & BM reconnoitred localities with Div. Comdr. at NOULETTE. AIX-NOULETTE and BULLY-GRENAY.	

VR 31

A5834 Wt. W4973/M687 750,000 8/16 D. D. & L. Ltd. Forms/C.2118/13.

Army Form C. 2118.

Instructions regarding War Diaries and Intelligence Summaries are contained in F. S. Regs., Part II. and the Staff Manual respectively. Title pages will be prepared in manuscript.

WAR DIARY
or
INTELLIGENCE SUMMARY.
(Erase heading not required.)

Place	Date	Hour	Summary of Events and Information	Remarks and references to Appendices
SAINS-EN-GOHELLE	APRIL 8th		Dull - showery.	
		9.0am	GOC & BM visited Bns at work on MAISTRE LINE and reconnoitred CITE CALONNE.	
		3.0pm.	Div. Comdr. held conference with GOC & Bn. Comdrs at Bde. Hqrs. [	
		6.0pm.	Officer of 1st Corps Cyclists reported, to act as Guide for the Brigade for the area.	
	9th		Dull - misty.	
		10.0am	Warning order issued to Brigade to be ready to move at an hour's notice	
		11.0am	GOC set out for MAROC locality but returned owing to thick mist	
		3.0pm	GOC & S.C. visited Major-Genl. Thwaites Comdg. 46th Div. at BRAQUEMONT	
		2.30pm	Major CB Nichols - 2nd Suffolk Regt. reported for duty at Bde Hqrs.	
		8.30pm	Div - Comdr. called to see GOC	
	10th.		Dull - clear	
		4.30am	Bde. Hqrs stood to, owing to heavy drum fire on LA BASSÉE front.	
	11th.	9.0am	Dull clear	
			Brigade ordered to move to BARLIN area.	
		10.0am	Above order cancelled	
		11am	Brigade ordered to move by bus to HINGES area.	
		2.0pm	Brigade moved off	
		6.0pm	Brigade Hqrs opened in Chateau Hinges	
W14 b 2.4.		11.0pm	Brigade Hqrs moved to W14 b. 2.4.	
		7.0pm	Brigade Dispositions. 1st Gordon Hlanders manned line of LA BASSEE CANAL from W11a 6.0 to W 3.6 3.8	6
			2nd Suffolks and 8th K.O.R.L in reserve, bivouaced behind HINGES	
		6.30pm	Div - Comdr. conferred with GOC and GOC 8th Brigade	
	12th.	1.30am	8th K.O.R.L ordered to be attached to 8th Brigade.	

A5834 Wt. W4973/M687 750,000 8/16 D. D. & L. Ltd. Forms/C.2118/13.

Instructions regarding War Diaries and Intelligence Summaries are contained in F. S. Regs., Part II. and the Staff Manual respectively. Title pages will be prepared in manuscript.

WAR DIARY
or
INTELLIGENCE SUMMARY.
(Erase heading not required.)

Army Form C. 2118.

Place	Date	Hour	Summary of Events and Information	Remarks and references to Appendices
W14 b 2.4.	APRIL 12th		Fine - clear.	
			BM reconnoitred line of LA BASSÉE CANAL.	
		7.30 am	BM & 2Lt. Bowden visited Hqrs of 2nd Suffolks and 1st G.H.	
		2.30 pm		
		10.0 am	Owing to German Cavalry reported in ROBECQ. 2nd Suffolks ordered to hold line of LA BASSÉE CANAL from P29 c 7.2 to Q 32 a 7.0.	
		7.0 pm	Div - Genl saw GOC and GOC 11th Brigade.	
		8.0 pm	2nd Suffolk regt relieved by a Battn of 11th Brigade and moved into support behind 1st Gordon Highlanders, ~~who~~ holding from W11 a 60 to Q 32 a 60.	
		10.30 pm	Bde Hqrs moved to V12 b 8.2	
V12 b 8.2.	13th		Fine - misty - clear by 11.0 am.	
		6.0 pm	Div - Genl saw GOC.	
		~~[illegible]~~	~~[illegible] moved to units~~	
		11.0 pm	Bde relieved by 10th Brigade and moved into Div - Reserve in VENDIN - LES - BETHUNE area	
		midnight	Bde - Hqrs opened at ANNEZIN (E9 b 4.5)	
ANNEZIN	14th		Dull - clear.	
		8 am	BM and ~~Lt~~ Firth visited HQ of 8th Bde.	
		3.0 pm	OO 99 issued to units.	
		9.0 pm	Brigade relieved 8th Brigade. 2nd Suffolks - right front from X6 c 3.1 to X13 a 2.8 (inclusive)	OO 99
			1st Gordon Highlanders, left front from X13 a 2.8 to W17 b 2.7.	
			8th K.O.R.L in support in SÉVELINGUE LINE W23 b 2.2 to W24 d 1.5.	
		9. pm	Bde Hqrs opened at W29 a 8.4	
W29 a 8.4	15th	2.30 am	Relief Complete.	

A5834 Wt. W4973/M687 750,000 8/16 D. D. & L. Ltd. Forms/C.2118/13.

Instructions regarding War Diaries and Intelligence Summaries are contained in F. S. Regs., Part II. and the Staff Manual respectively. Title pages will be prepared in manuscript.

WAR DIARY
or
INTELLIGENCE SUMMARY.
(Erase heading not required.)

Army Form C. 2118.

Place	Date	Hour	Summary of Events and Information	Remarks and references to Appendices
W29a8.4.	15th		Dull - clear.	
		11 am	BM. visited Hqrs of Battalions.	
		12.30 pm	Div. Comdr. visited Bde Hqrs.	
		10.0 pm	GOC went round line.	
	16th		Dull - clear.	
		5. pm	GOC went to HQ. of 9th Bde for conference with GOC Division and GOC 8th + 9th Bdes.	
	17th		Dull - hazy.	
		4.40 am	Artillery fired counter preparation fire.	
		6.30 pm	Div - Comdr. Called to see G.O.C	
	18th	1.0 am	Enemy opened heavy back area and counter battery fire.	
			Dull - showery - misty - visibility very poor.	
		7 am	Heavy drum fire on 1st Div. on our right in neighbourhood of LOISNE.	
			Heavy back area shelling all day on our front.	
		1.0 pm	Bde Hqrs. moved from W29a8.4 to W23c 85.40	
		11.0 pm	Bde Hqrs moved from W23c 85.40 to E4b 4.1.	
E4b.4.1.	19th		Dull - clear.	
		3.0 pm	BM visited HQ of Battalions	
		9.0 pm	GOC and Lt. Forth ~~visited~~ went round line of right Battn.	
	20th		Dull - clear - visibility good.	
		3.0 pm	GOC visited GOC 11th Brigade.	
		4.30 pm	OO 100 issued to units.	
		10.0 pm	Bde - front extended. 2nd Suffolk Regt taking from X8c 3.2 to W18b 2.5	
			1st Gordon Highlanders from W18b 2.5 to W11a 6.0 (exclusive).	OO 100
	21st	1.20 am	Relief complete	

A5834 Wt. W4973/M687 750,000 8/16 D. D. & L. Ltd. Forms/C.2118/13.

Instructions regarding War Diaries and Intelligence Summaries are contained in F. S. Regs., Part II. and the Staff Manual respectively. Title pages will be prepared in manuscript.

WAR DIARY
or
INTELLIGENCE SUMMARY.
(Erase heading not required.)

Army Form C. 2118.

Place	Date	Hour	Summary of Events and Information	Remarks and references to Appendices
E 4 b 4.1	APRIL 21st		Bright - clear.	
		2.0 pm	B.M. + 2Lt. Bowden visited Hqrs of Battns	
		9.0 pm	G.O.C + Lt. Firth went round line.	
	22nd		Bright - clear.	
			Situation quiet.	
	23rd		Bright - clear. Visibility good.	
		10.0 am	O.O. 101 issued to units.	
		2.0 pm	Div. Genl called to see G.O.C.	
		10.0 pm	Bde. relieved by 9th Inf. Bde.	O.O. 101.
			Bde moved into Divl Reserve in VENDIN - ANNEZIN area.	
	24th	1.30 am	Relief complete.	
			Bde Hqrs closed at E 4 b 4.1 and opened at ANNEZIN. E 9 b 5.6.	
ANNEZIN E 9 b 5.6.			Bright - clear -	
	25th		Dull - clear.	
		6.30 am	GOC and Lt-Col Stubbs reconnoitred HINGES - VAUDRICOURT Line.	
		11.0 am	BM and Staff Captain reconnoitred OBLINGHEM area to find suitable Hqrs for Brigade	
		3.0 pm	GOC attended Divisional General's conference at Hqrs. of 9th Inf Bde.	
		6.30 pm	GOC visited 8th K.O.R.L.R.	
		11.30 pm	O.O. 102 issued to units	
	26th.		Dull - clear.	
		3.30 pm	GOC visited 8th KORL and 1st Gordon Highlanders	
		10.0 pm	Bde relieved 11th Inf Bde and part of 9th Inf. Bde.	OO 102
		9.15 pm	Bde hqrs closed at ANNEZIN	
		10.0 pm	Bde Hqrs opened at VENDIN-lez-BETHUNE W 27 c 6.8.	

Instructions regarding War Diaries and Intelligence Summaries are contained in F. S. Regs., Part II. and the Staff Manual respectively. Title pages will be prepared in manuscript.

WAR DIARY
or
INTELLIGENCE SUMMARY.
(Erase heading not required.)

Army Form C. 2118.

Place	Date	Hour	Summary of Events and Information	Remarks and references to Appendices
	APRIL 26th		Disposition 8th K.O.R.L. W17b.2.7 to W10b86	
			2nd Suffolk Regt W10b.86 to LA PANNERIE W4a88 (inclusive);	
			1st Gordon Highlanders in support in Hangars nr. Chau. de WERPPE (W19a4.2)	
VENDIN-lez-BETHUNE W27c 6.8	27th	12.50 am	Relief complete	
			Dull - clear - visibility good.	
		6.0 am	BM and Lt Firth went round line	
		11.0 am	Dw. Genl. called to see G.O.C	
		9.0 pm	G.O.C went round line	
	28th		Dull - clear. Hazy.	
		11.30 am	Dw. Genl. called to see G.O.C. and Lt Col Stubbs.	
	29th		Dull: Visibility fair.	
		6.0 am	BM went round line	
		12.0 noon	Dw Genl called to see G.O.C.	
		1.0 pm	Major Congreve - XIII Corps called.	
	30th		Dull - misty. clear by midday.	
		5.0 am	G.O.C + BM reconnoitred defence system.	
		10.0 am	CRE visited Bde HQ.	
		3.0 pm	CRA visited Bde HQ.	

A5834 Wt. W4973/M687 750,000 8/16 D. D. & L. Ltd. Forms/C.2118/13.

SECRET.
****

Copy No. 18.

76th. INFANTRY BRIGADE OPERATION ORDER NO. 93.

Reference LENS 1/100,000, Sheet 11
Edition 2.

31st. March 1918.

1. The dismounted personnel of the 76th. Infantry Brigade, 3rd. Battn. M.G.C., 7th. Fld., Amb., and 3rd. Div. T.M. Batteries will move by Bus to the DIEVAL Area on April 1st.

2. The Bus Column will be drawn up facing West on the AVESNES LE COMTE - LIENCOURT Road with its head just above the O in LIENCOURT.
Moves to the embussing point will be in accordance with the attached March Table "A".

3. The debussing point will be between DIEVAL and OURTON on the ST. POL - BRUAY Road.

4. An officer from each unit will be at the Cross Roads just North of T in LIENCOURT at 9.15 a.m.

5. Signal time will be sent by D.R. to each unit in SOMBRIN and WARLUZEL between 7 a.m. and 8 am. on April 1st.

6. Moves of transport to the ST. POL South Area will be in accordance with March Table "B" attached.

7. Transport will move from the ST. POL South Area to the DIEVAL Area under the orders of C.R.A., 3rd. Division.
8 Locations of units in the DIEVAL Area will be notified later.

9 Acknowledge

Captain,
Brigade Major, 76th. Infantry Brigade.

Issued to Signals 9 a.m.

Copies to:-
1. G.O.C.
2. 8th. K.O.R.L.
3. 2nd. Suff. Regt.
4. 1st. Gordon Hldrs.
5. 76th. T.M.B.
6. 3rd. Div. T.M.B's.
7. 3rd. Bn. M.G.C.
8. 7th. Fld. Amb.
9. 3rd. Div. "G".
10. 3rd. Div. "Q".
11. C.R.A., 3rd. Div.
12. A.P.M. "
13. T.M., SOMBRIN.
14. B.M.
15. S.C.
16. Bde. Sig. Offr.
17. War Diary.
18. "
19. File.

March Table "A" issued with 76th. Infantry Brigade O.O.93.
****

Unit.	Starting Point.	Time to reach S.P.	Route.	Remarks.
2nd. Suffolk Regt.	Junction of SOMBRIN - GRAND RULLECOURT and BARLY - WARLUZEL Roads.	8.35 a.m.	GRAND RULLECOURT - Road junction just S of T in LIENCOURT. - Cross Roads S of M in APPEGREMES.	
76th. Bde. H.Q.) 76th. T.M.B.)		8.39 a.m.		
3rd. Battn. M.G. Corps.		8.42 a.m.		
1st. Gordon Hldrs.	Road junction 300 yards north of WARLUZEL Church.	8.40 a.m.	do.	
7th. Fld. Amb.		8.44 a.m.	do.	
8th. K.O.R.L.		8.47 a.m.	do.	
3rd. Div. T.M. Batteries.	(see remarks column)		BARLY - AVESNES LE COMTE.	To reach S. end of AVESNES LE COMTE at 9.10 a.m.

SECRET.
****

Copy No....

76th.INFANTRY BRIGADE OPERATION ORDER NO.94.

****

Reference LENS 1/100,000,Sheet 11,Edition 2. 3rd.April 1918.

1. 76th.Infantry Brigade Group will march to the HERSIN Area on April 4th.,in accordance with the attached March Table.

2. Billeting parties will report to the Town Major, HERSIN at 11 a.m. April 4th.

3. Brigade H.Q. will close at DIVION at 10 a.m. and open at HERSIN on arrival.

4. ACKNOWLEDGE.

Captain,

Issued at 10.30 p.m. Brigade Major,76th.Infantry Brigade.

Copies to:-
1. G.O.C.
2. 8th.K.O.R.L.
3. 2nd.Suff.Regt.
4. 1st.Gordon Hldrs.
5. 76th.T.M.B.
6. 529th.Fd.Co.R.E.
7. 7th.Fd.Amb.
8. 3rd.Div."G".
9. 3rd.Div."Q"
10. 8th.Inf.Bde.
11. 9th. "
12. A.P.M.,3rd.Div.
13. T.M.,DIVION.
14. CAMBLAIN CHATELAIN.
15. DIEVAL.
16. HERSIN.
17. Bde.Sig.Offr.
18. War Diary.
19. "
20. File..

MARCH TABLE TO ACCOMPANY 76th. INFANTRY BRIGADE O.O.94.

Unit.	Starting Point.	Time to reach S.P.	Route.	Remarks.
Brigade H.Q.	Cross Roads $\frac{1}{2}$ mile due East of N in DIVION.	11.00 a.m.	HOUDAIN - MAISNIL LES RUITZ - BARLIN.	
2nd. Suffolk Regt.		11.5 a.m.		
76th. T.M.B.		11.14 a.m.		
1st. Gordon Hldrs.		11.17 a.m.		
7th. Fd. Amb.		11.25 a.m.		
8th. K.O.R.L.		11.30 a.m.		
529th. Fd. Co. R.E.		11.38 a.m.		

SECRET.
****

Copy No.23...

76th.INFANTRY BRIGADE OPERATION ORDER NO.95.

****

Reference 36b.,1/40,000. 5th.April 1918.

1. 76th.Infantry Brigade will move on April 6th.,in accordance with the attached March Table.

2. 1st.Gordon Hldrs.,will remain at FOSSE 10.

3. The following distances will be maintained:-

In rear of each Company............... 100 yards.
In rear of Battn.transport............ 500 yards.

4. Brigade H.Q. will close at COUPIGNY at 10 a.m. April 6th. and open at SAINS EN GOHELLE on arrival.

5. ACKNOWLEDGE.

[signature]
Captain,
Brigade Major,76th.Infantry Brigade.

Issued to Signals at 10 p.m.

Copies to:-
1. G.O.C.
2. 8th.K.O.R.L.
3. 2nd.Suffolk Regt.
4. 1st.Gordon Hldrs.
5. 76th.T.M.B.
6. 3rd.Div."G".
7. 3rd.Div."Q".
8. 529th.Fd.Co.R.E.
9. 7th.Fld.Amb.
10. A.P.M.,3rd.Div.
11. 8th.Inf.Bde.
12. 9th. "
13. T.M.,HERSIN.
14. LES BREBIS.
15. SAINS EN GOHELLE.
16. BOUVIGNY.
17. BOYEFFLES.
18. 2 Coy.Train.
19. B.M.
20. S.C.
21. Bde.Sig.Offr.
22. War Diary.
23. "
24. File.

MARCH TABLE TO ACCOMPANY 76th.INFANTRY BRIGADE O.O.95.

Unit.	Starting point.	Time to reach S.P.	Route.	Destination.	Billeting parties report.
Brigade H.Q.	Road junction,Q.5d.3.8.	11 a.m.	Cross Roads R.7b.0.7.	SAINS EN GOHELLE.	
76th.T.M.B.	-do-	11.5 a.m.	-do-	-do-	To T.M.,SAINS EN GOHELLE,11 a.m.
2nd.Suffolk Regt.	-do-	11.10 a.m.	-do- Road junction R.2c.2.7.- road junct.,R.5c.4.7.	LES BREBIS.	To T.M.,LES BREBIS by 11 a.m.
8th.K.O.R.L.	To leave camp at 11 a.m.		BORING NO.517 - BOYEFFLES - BOUVIGNY BOYEFFLES.	MARQUEFFLES HUTS, (R.26a.9.9.)	At MARQUEFFLES HUTS by 11 a,m.

There are no operation orders No.96,97 and 98,as these numbers were omitted by mistake.

S.A. Bowden 2/Lt.,
for Brigadier-General,
Commanding 76th.Infantry Brigade.

1/5/18.

Secret.

Copy No.

76th Inf. Bde. O.O. 99

Ref. Sheet 36a S.E. 1/20,000
and BETHUNE 1/40,000

14th April 1918

1. 76th Inf. Bde. will relieve 8th Inf. Bde. tonight.

2. 2nd Suff. Regt. will take over the front from CANAL DE LA LAWE at PONT TOURNANT (exclusive) to the BETHUNE - LOCON Road (inclusive) from 7th K.Shrp. and 2 R. Scots.

3. 1st Gordon Hdrs. will take over from BETHUNE - LOCON Road (exclusive) to PT. LEVIS AVELETTE (inclusive) from 8th K.O.R.L.

Troops of 7th K.Shp. and 8th T.M.B. in this sector will be under the orders of O.C. 8th K.O.R.L. for relief.

4. On relief by 1 Gordon Hdrs. 8th K.O.R.L. will relieve 1st R.S.F. in the SEVELINGUE line and come into 76th Bde. Reserve.

5. Platoon guides will be at the Barge W.23B.1.1. for 2 Suffolk Regt. at 9.0 p.m. and at the Barge W.17D.2.1. for 1st Gordon Hdrs at 9.30 p.m.

Platoons will reach the Canal at 5 minute intervals.

6. Dispositions of 2 Suffolk Regt. and 1 Gordon Hdrs. will be as verbally explained to C.O's. Detailed dispositions to be reported to Bde. H.Q. as soon as possible after relief.

7. The 12 L.G. teams Tank Corps will not be used East of the Canal W.17 and W.23. Disposition of these guns will be notified to Battalions later.

8. Bde. H.Q. will close at ANNEZIN at 9.0 pm and open at W.29A.9.8 on arrival.

9. Acknowledge.

[signature]
Captain
B.M. 76th Inf. Bde.

Issued at 3pm

1. 8 K.O.R.L.
2. 2 Suff. Regt.
3. 1 G. Hdrs.
4. 76 T.M.B.
5. 8 Inf. Bde.
6. 3 Div. G.
7. 42 Bde. R.F.A.
8. Bde. T.O.
9. Det. 11th Bn. Tank Corps
10.
11.
12.

SECRET.
****

Copy No....

76th.INFANTRY BRIGADE OPERATION ORDER NO.100.

Reference LOCON 1/10,000,Edition 7. 20th.April 1918.

1. 76th.Inf.Bde is to extend its left to the Drawbridge at W.11a.5.0.exclusive.

2. The following reliefs will therefore be carried out on the night April 20th/21st.

(a) 2nd.Suffolk Regt will take over from 1st.Gordon Hldrs as far West as the Farm W.18b.2.3. (exclusive to 2nd.Suffolk Regt.)

(b) 1st.Gordon Hldrs will take over from 1st.Rifle Brigade (11th.Inf.Bde) from AVELETTE Drawbridge to the Drawbridge,W.11a.5.0. (exclusive to 1st.Gordon Hldrs.)

Details will be arranged between C.O's concerned.

3. After relief,the boundary between Battalions 76th.Inf.Bde will run as follows:-

Farm W.18b.2.3. and Farm W.18d.15.40.(both inclusive to 1st.Gordon Hldrs) - thence along western edge of orchards to W.24b.05.90. - thence to Canal Bridge W.24c.0.1. (inclusive to 2nd.Suffolk Regt.)

4. After relief,the left boundary 76th.Inf.Bde will run as follows:-

Bridge W.11a.5.0. (exclusive) - W.16d.9.8. - W.16c.0.4.

5. 1 Platoon 8th.K.O.R.L. will remain at AVELETTE Bridge as at present.

6. Completion of reliefs will be reported as usual,and sketch of dispositions forwarded as soon as possible.

7. ACKNOWLEDGE.

[signature]

Captain,
Brigade Major,76th.Infantry Brigade.

Issued at 4.30 p.m.

Copies to:-
1. 8th.K.O.R.L.
2. 2nd.Suffolk Regt.
3. 1st.Gordon Hldrs.
4. 76th.T.M.B.
5. 3rd.Div."G".
6. 8th.Inf.Bde.
7. 9th.Inf.Bde.
8. 11th.Inf.Bde.
9. Left Gp.R.F.A.
10. 529th.Fd.Co.R.E.
11. "A" Coy.,3rd.Bn.M.G.C.
12.

SECRET.
****

Copy No.....

76th.INFANTRY BRIGADE OPERATION ORDER NO.101.
****

Ref.1/20,000 Sheet 36a.SE. & 36b.NE. 23rd.April 1918.

1. 76th.Inf.Bde will be relieved by 9th.Inf.Bde during the night April 23rd./24th.

2.

13th.King's	will relieve	2nd.Suffolk Regt	on the Right.
4th.R.F.	" "	1st.Gordon Hldrs	" " Left.
1st.N.F.	" "	8th.K.O.R.L.	in Reserve.
9th.T.M.B.	" "	76th.T.M.B.	

3. Details of reliefs will be arranged between C.O's concerned and completion reported to Brigade H.Q.

5. Brigade H.Q. will close at E.4b.4.1. on completion of reliefs, and will open at ANNEZIN on arrival

5. Units will take over billets vacated by relieving units.

6. ACKNOWLEDGE.

(Sd) [signature]

Captain,
Brigade Major,76th.Infantry Brigade.

Issued at 10 a.m.

Distribution over.... /

Copies to:-

1. 8th.K.O.R.L.
2. 2nd.Suffolk Regt.
3. 1st.Gordon Hldrs.
4. 76th.T.M.B.
5. Left Gp.R.F.A.
6. " 3rd.Bn.M.G.C.
7. 529th.(E.R.)Fd.Co.R.E.
8. 3rd.Div."G".
9. 8th.Inf.Bde.
10. 9th.Inf.Bde.
11. 11th.Inf.Bde.
12.
13.
14.

SECRET.
****

Copy No......

76th.INFANTRY BRIGADE OPERATION ORDER NO.102.
****

Reference 1/20,000 Sheet 36a.SE.,
and 1/40,000 BETHUNE Combined Sheet. 25th.April 1918.

1. The Boundary between 3rd.and 4th.Divisions is to be adjusted to run as follows:-

LA PANNERIE (inclusive to 3rd.Div.) - N.corner of Orchard in W.8d. - road junction W.13a.9.2. - road junction W.13c.3.8. - road junction W.23b.8.9.

2. On the night April 26th./27th.,76th.Inf.Bde will relieve:-

(a) 9th.Inf.Bde from the junction of the present front line with the CANAL about W.17b.2.8. to PT.LEVIS,W.11a.6.0.,(exclusive).

(b) 11th.Inf.Bde (4th.Div) from PT.LEVIS,W.11a.6.0.,inclusive, to road junction W.4a.9.8. (inclusive).

3. The 76th.Inf.Bde front will be held by 8th.K.O.R.L. on the right,and 2nd.Suffolk Regt on the left.
Boundary between Battalions:- the HINGES - LE VERTBOIS FME Road,inclusive to 8th.K.O.R.L.

4. 8th.K.O.R.L. will relieve:-

(a) Troops of 4th.R.Fus on the Canal Bank between the junction of the front line with the CANAL about W.17b.2.8. and PT.LEVIS,W.11a.6.0., (exclusive).

(b) 1 Coy 1st.R.Brigade between PT.LEVIS,W.11a.6.0.,(inclusive) and the road at W.11a.1.9. (inclusive).

(c) Troops of 1st.Rif.Brig.at HINGETTE and LE PLOUY FME.

5. 2nd.Suffolk Regt will relieve:-

(a) 1 Coy 1st.Rif.Brig.between the road at W.11a.1.9. (exclusive) and PONT L'HINGES (exclusive).

(b) 1 Coy 1st.Som.L.I.between PONT L'HINGES (inclusive) and road junction W.4a.9.8. (inclusive).

(c) Troops of 1st.Rif.Brig.and 1st.Som.L.I.in the area LE CAUROY - LE VERTANNOY.

6. 1st.Gordon Hldrs.,will relieve 1st.Hampshire Regt in Brigade Reserve at LANNOY,and will not leave present billots before 9.30 p.m.

7. Details of all above reliefs, and of relief of 11th.T.M.B. by 76th.T.M.B., will be arranged between C.O's concerned, and completion reported to 11th.Inf.Bde H.Q., W.8d.1.6.

8. 8th.K.O.R.L. and 2nd.Suffolk Regt will march by platoons at 100 yards distance.

Leading platoon 8th.K.O.R.L. will pass the Level Crossing W.27a.4.1. at 8.30 p.m.; leading platoon 2nd.Suffolk Regt at 9 p.m.

9. 76th.Inf.Bde front will be covered by 1½ Bdes R.F.A., and by 1½ Coys 3rd.Bn.M.G.C.

There will be no Vickers' Guns North of the Canal.

10. Brigade H.Q. will close at ANNEZIN at 9 p.m., and open at W.27c.5.9. on arrival.

A representative of 76th. Infantry Brigade H.Q. will be at H.Q., 11th.Inf.Bde., W.8d.1.6., until completion of reliefs.

11. ACKNOWLEDGE.

[signature]

Captain,

Issued at 11.30 p.m. Brigade Major, 76th.Infantry Brigade.

Copies to:-
1. G.O.C.
2. 8th.K.O.R.L.
3. 2nd.Suffolk Regt.
4. 1st.Gordon Hldrs.
5. 76th.T.M.B.
6. 40th.Bde.R.F.A.
7. 529th.Fd.Co.R.E.
8. 3rd.Bn.M.G.C.
9. 3rd.Div."G".
10. 3rd.Div."Q".
11. 8th.Inf.Bde.
12. 9th. "
13. 11th. "
14. 7th.Fld.Amb.
15. S.S.O.
16. B.M.
17. S.C.
18. Bde.Sig.Offr.
19. War Diary.
20. War Diary.
21. File.
22.

76th Brigade.

3rd Division.

<u>B. H. Q.</u>

<u>76th INFANTRY BRIGADE.</u>

<u>M A Y 1918.</u>

Army Form C. 2118.

Instructions regarding War Diaries and Intelligence Summaries are contained in F. S. Regs., Part II. and the Staff Manual respectively. Title pages will be prepared in manuscript.

WAR DIARY
or
INTELLIGENCE SUMMARY.
(Erase heading not required.)

Headquarters 76th Inf. Brigade

Vol 32

Place	Date	Hour	Summary of Events and Information	Remarks and references to Appendices
VENDIN-lez-BETHUNE. W27c 6.8.	MAY 1st		Dull - Clear. Visibility good. Situation quiet.	
		10.0 am	Dv. Genl called.	
	2nd		Bright - hazy. clear by mid-day. Situation normal.	
		4.30 am	G.O.C and BM went round line.	
		9.30 pm	Bde Hqrs closed at VENDIN-lez-BETHUNE and opened at L'ABBAYE near CHOQUES. W25a 0.8.	
		8.0 pm	OO 103 issued to units	
L'ABBAYE W25a 0.8.	3rd		Bright clear. visibility good. Situation normal.	
		5.0 am	BM went round line	
		11.30 am	Lt Col Woolfe Murray DSO MC called.	
		3.0 pm	BM went to Hqrs of 8th KORL.	
		5.0 pm	BM returned with Lt Col J.L. Likeman DSO.	
		5.15 pm	G.O.C conferred with O's Comdg 1st G.H. 8th KORL and 42nd Bde. R.F.A.	
	4th	2.30 am	Under cover of artillery and machine gun barrages, 5 platoons of 1st Gordon Hldrs attacked and captured orchard W11a+b. 2 MG's and 40 prisoners were taken. In conjunction 8th KORL established a post at W11d central and 2nd Suffolk Regt and 8th KORL established a post at W11a 15.90. Casualties 3 OR Killed 2 off. 10 OR wounded.	OO 103.
		5.0 am	Enemy put down heavy barrage on Canal Bank for half an hour No infantry action followed.	
		10.0 am	OO 104 issued to units.	
			Bright - Clear.	
		3.0 pm	Dv. Genl called.	
		3.30 pm	G.O.C visited Hqrs of 1st Gordon Hldrs.	
		10.0 pm	Bde relieved by 9th Inf. Bde.	OO 104

A5834 Wt. W4973/M687 750,000 8/16 D. D. & L. Ltd. Forms/C.2118/13.

Army Form C. 2118.

Instructions regarding War Diaries and Intelligence Summaries are contained in F. S. Regs., Part II. and the Staff Manual respectively. Title pages will be prepared in manuscript.

WAR DIARY
or
INTELLIGENCE SUMMARY.
(Erase heading not required.)

Place	Date	Hour	Summary of Events and Information	Remarks and references to Appendices
	May 5th	3.am	Enemy attacked our new positions in orchard W11a+b. He was successfully repulsed by rifle and L.G. fire and Grenades.	
		5.am	Relief complete	
			Brigade Hqrs closed at L'Abbaye and opened at St Sauveur D5a 5.1.	
St SAUVEUR D5a 5.1.			Dull - Showery.	
		11.0.am	Div. Genl called.	
			Disposition of units while in divisional reserve.	
			8th KORL. In trenches. E1a 5.3 to E1d 6.2.	
			2nd Suffolk Regt. In trenches. E1a 2.2 to E7a 1.7.	
			1st Gordon Hldrs. In Bank of CLARENCE RIVER V24 a and d.	
	6th		Bright - clear.	
		6.am	BM and O.C. 529 3rd Coy. reconnoitred line joining Suffolk and Perth lines.	
		10.30am	Corps Commander and G.O.C visited 2nd Suffolk Regt and 8th KORL.	
		3.0pm	BM went to Division	
		3.10pm	G.O.C. visited Transport lines	
		3.30pm	Div. Comdr. called.	
		4.0pm	G.S.O. 2 from G.H.Q called.	
			During night 6/7th 8th KORL and 1st Gordon Hldrs worked on	
	7th		Wet.	
		9.am	BM reconnoitred line joining Inverness and Lancaster Lines.	
		10.30am	GOC and BM went to Divisional Depot.	
		7.0pm	OO 10.5 issued.	

Instructions regarding War Diaries and Intelligence Summaries are contained in F. S. Regs., Part II. and the Staff Manual respectively. Title pages will be prepared in manuscript.

WAR DIARY
or
INTELLIGENCE SUMMARY.
(Erase heading not required.)

Army Form C. 2118.

Place	Date	Hour	Summary of Events and Information	Remarks and references to Appendices
St SAUVEUR D5a 5.1	May 8th		Fine - Bright	
		11.0 am	BM and S.C. visited 8th Inf. Bde	
		12.30 pm	G.O.C. went to 8th Inf. Bde	
		2.0 pm	GOC attended conference with Divl. Genl at Div. H.Q.	
		9.30 pm	Bde H.Q. closed at St Sauveur and opened at BETHUNE E4b 4.1.	OO 105.
			Bde relieved 8th Inf. Bde in right Sector.	
			8th K.O.R.L on right front — 1st Gordon Hdrs on left front	
			2nd Suffolk Regt in support.	
BETHUNE E4b 4.1	9th	1.10 am	relief complete.	
			Fine - bright. Vis. very good Situation normal and quiet.	
		5.0 am	GOC went round line	
		2.0 pm	BM visited Hqrs. of Battns.	
		10.30 am	Divl. Genl. called	
			Night 9/10 Artillery fired Concentration and creeping barrage	
	10th		Dull - misty. Situation normal and very quiet.	
		3.0 am	8th KORL captured two prisoners of 99th I.R. 220th Div, in PONT TOURNANT.	
		5.0 am	G.O.C. + I.O went round line.	
		11.0 am	Div - Genl called.	
		3.0 pm	BM. and S.C went to see new Hqrs, being constructed in Canal bank	
	11th		Bright - clear Situation normal - very quiet in forenoon -	
		5.0 am	BM went round line	
		3.0 pm	Div - Genl called	
		8.0 pm	OO 106 issued.	

A5834 Wt. W4973/M687 750,000 8/16 D. D. & L. Ltd. Forms/C.2118/13.

Instructions regarding War Diaries and Intelligence Summaries are contained in F. S. Regs., Part II. and the Staff Manual respectively. Title pages will be prepared in manuscript.

WAR DIARY
or
INTELLIGENCE SUMMARY.
(Erase heading not required.)

Army Form C. 2118.

Place	Date	Hour	Summary of Events and Information	Remarks and references to Appendices
BETHUNE E4641.	MAY		Dull - Showery. Situation unchanged.	
	12th	3.0am	Heavy hostile gas shelling of our batteries.	
		5.0am	GOC went round line	
		2.0pm	BM went round Hqrs. of battns.	
		4.0pm	Div - Genl called.	
		8.0pm	2nd Suffolk Regt relieved 8th KORL in right sub sector.	00106
		11.35pm	Relief complete.	
	13th		Fine - vis. good. Situation normal.	
		11.0am	Div. Genl called.	
		9.40pm	Boche put up three green lights - mistaken for S.O.S and artillery opened.	
	14th		Dull - clear. Situation unchanged.	
		5.0am	GOC went round line.	
		1.0pm	Div - Genl called.	
		4.0pm	G.S.O I called.	
	15th		Bright - Clear. Situation normal.	
		6.0am	BM & S.C went round line.	
		6.0pm	Div. Genl called.	
		8.0pm	OO 107 issued.	
	16th		Fine - clear. vis - good. Situation normal.	
		12.30pm	Div. Genl called.	
		9.0pm	9th Inf. Bde relieved 76th Inf Bde.	00107
		11.0pm	Bde Hqrs closed at E46 4.1 and opened at St Sauveur D5a 5.1	

A5834 Wt. W4973/M687 750,000 8/16 D. D. & L. Ltd. Forms/C.2118/13.

Instructions regarding War Diaries and Intelligence Summaries are contained in F. S. Regs., Part II. and the Staff Manual respectively. Title pages will be prepared in manuscript.

WAR DIARY
or
INTELLIGENCE SUMMARY.
(Erase heading not required.)

Army Form C. 2118.

Place	Date	Hour	Summary of Events and Information	Remarks and references to Appendices
St SAUVEUR D5a 5.1.	MAY 17th		Relief Complete	
			Bright - Clear.	
			Bde in Div Reserve in CHOCQUES area.	
			Dispositions	
			8th KORL. in bivouacs in E1c and E7a	
			2nd Suffolk Regt in bivouacs in D6d and E1c	
			1st Gordon Hldrs in billets - bivouacs & huts in D6b.	
		2.30 pm	GOC & BM went to see demonstration of message rockets at D5a 6.6.	
		6.0 pm	Div - Genl. called.	
	18th		Bright - Clear - Vis - very good.	
			Units bathing.	
			During night 18/19 2nd Suffolk Regt were out digging cable trench near Hinges.	
	19th		Fine - clear - vis. very good	
		11.30 am	G.O.C visited units.	
			During nights 19/20 1st Gordon Hldrs were out digging cable trench in Hinges	
		8.0 pm	OO 108 issued	
	20th		Fine - clear. vis. good	
		2.0 pm	GOC visited units.	
		4.0 pm	Div. Genl called.	00108
		10.0 pm	Bde relieved 8th Inf. Bde in Left Sector.	
		10.0 pm	Bde HQrs closed at St SAUVEUR and opened at L'Abbaye. Chocques	

A5834 Wt. W4973/M687 750,000 8/16 D. D. & L. Ltd. Forms/C.2118/13.

Army Form C. 2118.

Instructions regarding War Diaries and Intelligence Summaries are contained in F. S. Regs., Part II. and the Staff Manual respectively. Title pages will be prepared in manuscript.

WAR DIARY
or
INTELLIGENCE SUMMARY.
(Erase heading not required.)

Place	Date	Hour	Summary of Events and Information	Remarks and references to Appendices
L'Abbaye Chocques W25d.0.8.	May		Bright – Clear. Situation normal.	
	21st	2.30 am	Relief complete.	
			Dispositions – 8th KORL. Right Front. 2nd Suffolks. Left front. 1st Gordon Hdrs. in support.	
		5.0 am	GOC went round line.	
		2.30 pm	B.M. went round line.	
	22nd		Bright – vis. good. Situation normal. Artillery fairly active.	
		5.0 am	BM went round line.	
		10.30 am	Div. Comdr. called.	
	23rd		Bright clear. vis. good. Situation normal. Hostile artillery quiet.	
		5.0 am	GOC & S.C went round line.	
		2.30 pm	Div. Comdr. called.	
		8.0 pm	OO 109 issued	
	24th	1.30 am	2 Platoons 2nd Suffolk Regt. raided enemy post at W5c 2.8. Several of enemy were killed but no identification obtained.	
			Dull – showery. vis. very bad. Situation normal. Artillery very quiet.	
		5.30 am	G.O.C. went round line.	
	24th	10.0 pm	1st Gordon Hdrs relieved 2nd Suffolk Regt in left sub-sector.	OO 109.
	25th	1.0 am	Relief complete.	
			Bright. clear. Situation normal. Artillery fairly quiet.	
		1.15 am	150 Yellow Cross Gas shells fell near Rt. Bn. HQ W22a 3.7	
		5.0 am	BM went round line	
		5.0 pm	Div Genl. Called.	

A5834 Wt. W4973/M687 750,000 8/16 D. D. & L. Ltd. Forms/C.2118/13.

Army Form C. 2118.

Instructions regarding War Diaries and Intelligence Summaries are contained in F. S. Regs., Part II. and the Staff Manual respectively. Title pages will be prepared in manuscript.

WAR DIARY
or
INTELLIGENCE SUMMARY.

(Erase heading not required.)

Place	Date	Hour	Summary of Events and Information	Remarks and references to Appendices
L'Abbaye. Chocques W25a 0.8.	MAY 26th		Dull - Showery. Situation normal	
		1.30am to 4.0am	Continuous gas shelling of W19 with Yellow Cross. About 3000 rounds were fired.	
		5.0 am	GOC went round line.	
		6.0 pm	Div. Comdr called.	
	27th		Bright clear. Situation normal. Hostile artillery very active	
			During night 26/27 a new post was established and dug at W5C 45.10	
		5.0 am	B.M. went round line.	
		8.0 pm.	OO 110 issued to units.	
	28th		Bright - Clear. Situation. Hostile aircraft abnormally active. Hostile Artillery very active on back areas	
		2.30 am to 3.30 am	Heavy gas shelling of HINGES area with Yellow Cross, and of W16d 3.3 with Green and Blue Cross	
		1.0 pm	Lt Col Likeman DSO. came for Conference with G.O.C.	
		3.0 pm	Corps Commander called	
		5.0 pm	Brig - Genl Fisher DSO called	
		5.30 pm	Div. Comdr. called.	
		3.0 pm	BM went up line with 2/Lt. Taylor.	
			Inter Battalion Relief. 2nd Suffolk Regt relieved 8th KORL in right Sub sector	OO110
	29th	1.0 am	Relief complete.	
			Bright - clear. Situation normal. Slight increase in artillery and EA activity	
		11.30 am	Contact patrol aeroplane came over Bde H.Q. to practice receiving messages from ground.	
		6.0 pm	Div. Comdr. called.	
	30th		Bright. clear. Situation normal. Artillery and aircraft very active	
		5.30 am	BM went round line.	
		3.0 pm	Message rocket experimental test between Support Bn Hqrs and Bde Hqrs	
			During night 30/31st Blue Cross Gas shells fell nr. Bde Hqrs.	

A5834 Wt. W4973/M687 750,000 8/16 D. D. & L. Ltd. Forms/C.2118/13.

Army Form C. 2118.

Instructions regarding War Diaries and Intelligence Summaries are contained in F. S. Regs., Part II. and the Staff Manual respectively. Title pages will be prepared in manuscript.

WAR DIARY
or
INTELLIGENCE SUMMARY.

(Erase heading not required.)

Place	Date	Hour	Summary of Events and Information	Remarks and references to Appendices
L'Abbaye W25a 0.8.	May 31st.		Bright clear. Situation normal. Artillery active during night, quiet during day.	
		5.0am	G.O.C. went round line.	
		2.0pm	Lt Col. J.L. Likeman D.S.O. came down to see G.O.C.	
		3.0pm	G.O.C. attended Div. Comdr's Conference at Hqrs. of 8th Inf. Bde. BETHUNE	

SECRET.
****

Copy No. 14

76th. INFANTRY BRIGADE OPERATION ORDER NO.103.

Reference LOCON 1/10,000 Ed. 7. 2nd. May 1918.

1. At an hour ZERO (to be notified later) during the night of May 3rd./4th., 1st. Gordon Hldrs., will attack and capture the orchard in W.11a.& b.

2. The attack will be delivered by 5 platoons, and will be supported by artillery and M.G. fire in accordance with the attached programmes.

3. The assaulting troops will be on their assembly positions half an hour before ZERO. All troops of 8th.K.O.R.L. will then be withdrawn from the Breastwork round the bridgehead at W.11a.6.0.

4. One platoon 8th.K.O.R.L. will be assembled at about W.11c.95.50. half an hour before ZERO.
At ZERO hour this platoon will advance and dig in with 2 sections at about W.11d.5.5., and 2 sections in support at about W.11d.05 .65.
The post at W.11a.85.00. will remain as at present.

5. At ZERO hour the posts of 8th.K.O.R.L. and 2nd.Suffolk Regt. now at W.10b.95.70. will advance 150 yards along the road and dig in at about W.11a.15.90.

6. On completion of the operation, the outpost line of 1st. Gordon Hldrs., will be established along the German trench through W.11b.2.5., thence along the N.E. edge of the orchard to its Northern corner.
There will be a L.G. section at about W.11a.75.70.

7. The opening of the Field Artillery Barrage at ZERO is the signal for the co-operating Machine Guns to open fire.

8. O.C., 529th.(E.R.)Fd.Co.R.E. will arrange for a footbridge to be across the Canal at W.11c.7.8. by 10.30 p.m. on May 3rd., and will arrange for this bridge to be swung inshore by day.

9. Prisoners will be sent to Brigade H.Q.

10. O's.C., 2nd.Suffolk Regt., 1st. Gordon Hldrs., and "B" Coy 3rd.Bn. M.G.C. will each send a representative to H.Q. 8th.K.O.R.L. at 11 p.m. on May 3rd., to synchronize watches.

11. After the operation all troops of 1st. Gordon Hldrs East of the Canal will come under the orders of O.C. 8th.K.O.R.L.

12. ACKNOWLEDGE.

B. Playfair
Captain,
Brigade Major, 76th. Infantry Brigade.

Issued at 8 p.m.

Copies to:-
1. G.O.C.
2. 8th.K.O.R.L.
3. 2nd.Suff.Regt.
4. 1st.Gordon Hldrs.
5. 76th.T.M.B.
6. Left Gp.R.F.A.
7. 529th.Fd.Co.R.E.
8. 3rd.Div."G".
9. 8th.Inf.Bde.
10. 9th. "
11. 12th. "
12. "B"Coy 3rd.Bn.M.G.C.
13. 3rd.Bn.M.G.C.
14. War Diary.
15. "
16. File.

APPENDIX 1.
****

ARTILLERY CO-OPERATION.
****

1. ZERO to ZERO plus 5 mins.

18 pdrs....... 5 batteries W.11a.60.72. - W.11a.93.32. - W.11b.51.30.

2 batteries W.5c.85.05. - W.11b.22.71.

1 battery W.5d.08.40. - W.5d.40.10.

2. ZERO plus 5 mins.to ZERO plus 8 mins.

18 pdrs....... 3 batteries W.5d.08.40. - W.11b.55.82.

3 batteries W.5c.85.05. - W.11b.25.70.

3. ZERO plus 8 mins.to ZERO plus 1 hour.

18 pdrs....... 3 batteries W.5d.08.40. - W.11b.55.82.

4. STANDING BARRAGES. (ZERO to ZERO plus 1 hour).

2 batteries 4.5"Hows. Area W.5c.27.18. - W.5c.60.18.- W.5b.0.0. - W.5a.5.0.

1 section 4.5" Hows. House W.12c.15.55.

HEAVY ARTILLERY. Enclosures and hedges in W.6a. W.6c.,W.12a. Q.35d.,and defences in W.5b.

** ** ** ** ** ** **

APPENDIX 2.
****

MACHINE GUN CO-OPERATION.
****

No.of guns.	Location.	From.	Until.	Target.	Rate.
10	HINGES Area.	ZERO.	ZERO plus 20 mins.	Old practice trenches about W.5c.45.70. - W.5c.65.80.	1 b.p.g.per 5 mins.
10	-do-	ZERO plus 20 mins.	ZERO plus 2 hours.	-do-	1 b.p.g.per 15 mins.
4	LONG CORNET.	ZERO plus 15 mins.	ZERO plus 2 hours.	W.12a.0.1. to W.12a.0.9.	1 b.p.g.per 10 mins.
2	W.10c.	ZERO plus 15 mins.	ZERO plus 2 hours.	W. 5d.25.65.to W.5d.4.4.	1 b.p.g.per 10 mins.

*** *** *** *** *** ***

AMENDMENT NO.1
to 76th.Inf.Bde.No.103 dated May 2nd.1918.

****

APPENDIX 1. "ARTILLERY CO-OPERATION", para.2.,

for "8mins." read "9 mins."

Captain,

3/5/18 Brigade Major, 76th. Infantry Brigade.

Copy to each recipient of O.O.103.

SECRET.

Reference 76th.Inf.Bde.O.O.103, para.1.

ZERO hour will be 2.30 a.m. on May 4th.

Captain,

3/5/18. Brigade Major, 76th. Infantry Brigade.

Copy to each recipient of O.O.103.

SECRET.
****

Copy No....

76th.INFANTRY BRIGADE OPERATION ORDER NO.104.

Reference 1/20,000 Sheets 36a.SE. and 36b.N.E.

4th.May 1918.

1. 76th.Inf.Bde will be relieved by 9th.Inf.Bde on the night May 4/5th.

2. (a) 1st.N.F.will relieve 8th.K.O.R.L. plus 3 platoons 1st.Gordon Hldrs.,on the right.
   (b) 4th.R.F.will relieve 2nd.Suffolk Regt.on the left.
   (c) 13th.King's will relieve 1st.Gordon Hldrs.,(less 3 platoons) in Brigade Reserve.
   (d) 9th.T.M.B.will relieve 76th.T.M.B.

3. Details of relief will be arranged between C.O's concerned and completion reported to Brigade H.Q.W.25a.0.8.

4. Aeroplane photographs,trench stores and details of work in hand will be handed over to relieving units.
Receipts for S.A.A.,Bombs,Very Lights and S.O.S.Grenades will be sent to Brigade H.Q.within 24 hours of relief.

5. 170 rounds S.A.A.and 1 shovel per man will be brought out of the line.

6. Destinations of units of 76th.Inf.Bde after relief will be notified as soon as possible.

7. 76th.Inf.Bde.H.Q.will close at W.25a.0.8. on completion of relief and move to ST.SAUVEUR,where reports of arrival in the new area will be sent.

8. ACKNOWLEDGE.

[signature]
Captain,
Brigade Major,76th.Infantry Brigade.

Issued at 10 a.m.

Copies to:-
1. G.O.C.
2. 8th.K.O.R.L.
3. 2nd.Suffolk Regt.
4. 1st.Gordon Hldrs.
5. 76th.T.M.B.
6. Left Gp.R.F.A.
7. 529th.Fd.Co.R.E.
8. "B"Coy.3rd.Bn.M.G.C.
9. 3rd.Div."G".
10. 8th.Inf.Bde.
11. 9th.Inf.Bde.
12. 12th.Inf.Bde.
13. S.S.O.,3rd.Div.
14. B.M.
15. S.C.
16. Bde.Sig.Offr.
17. War Diary.
18. "
19. File.
20.

SECRET.
****

Copy No......18

76th.INFANTRY BRIGADE OPERATION ORDER NO.105.

Reference 1/20,000 Sheets 36a.S.E.
and 36b.N.E.

7th May 1918

1. The 76th.Inf.Bde. will relieve 8th.Inf.Bde.in the Right Section of the 3rd.Divisional Front on the night May 8/9th.

2. (a) 8th.K.O.R.L.will relieve 7th.K.S.L.I.on the right.
   (b) 1st.Gordon Hldrs will relieve 1st.R.S.F.on the left.
   (c) 2nd.Suffolk Regt will relieve 2nd.R.Scots in Support.
   (d) 76th.T.M.B.will relieve 8th.T.M.B.

3. Battalions will start to leave their present areas as follows:-
8th.K.O.R.L. - 8.30 p.m.,1st.Gordon Hldrs - 9 p.m., 2nd.Suffolk Regt 9.30 p.m.

4. Details of relief will be arranged between C.O's concerned and their completion reported to Brigade H.Q.

5. Maps showing dispositions will be forwarded as soon as possible after relief.

6. Lists of Trench Stores taken over should reach Brigade H.Q. within 24 hours of relief.

7. Brigade H.Q.will close at ST.SAUVEUR at 9 p.m. on May 8th.,and open at E.4b.4.1. on arrival.

8. ACKNOWLEDGE.

[signature]
Captain,
Brigade Major,76th.Infantry Brigade.

Issued at 9 p.m.

Copies to:-
1. G.O.C.
2. 8th.K.O.R.L.
3. 2nd.Suffolk Regt.
4. 1st.Gordon Hldrs.
5. 76th.T.M.B.
6. Right Gp.R.F.A.
7. 529th.Fd.Co.R.E.
8. "C"Coy.3rd.Bn.M.G.C.
9. 3rd.Div."G".
10. 8th.Inf.Bde.
11. 9th. "
12. 7th.Fld.Amb.
13. D.T.M.O.,3rd.Div.
14. B.M.
15. S.C.
16. Bde.Sig.Offr.
17. War Diary.
18. "
19. File.

SECRET.
****

Copy No..16..

76th.INFANTRY BRIGADE OPERATION ORDER NO.106.

Ref.1/20,000 Sheets 36a.S.E., and 36b.N.E.

11th.May 1918.

1. 2nd.Suffolk Regt.,will relieve 8th.K.O.R.L. in the Right Sub-section of the 76th.Inf.Brigade front on the night May 12th./13th.

2. On relief,8th.K.O.R.L.will move into Support positions in the INVERNESS and DUMBARTON LINES.

3. 8th.K.O.R.L. will not relieve the posts of 2nd.Suffolk Regt.,at about W.24a.9.7. These will continue to be held by 2 platoons 2nd.Suffolk Regt.

4. Details of relief will be arranged between C.O's concerned and completion reported to Brigade H.Q.

5. ACKNOWLEDGE.

[signature], Captain,
Brigade Major,76th.Infantry Brigade.

Issued at 8 p.m.

Copies to:-

1. G.O.C.
2. 8th.K.O.R.L.
3. 2nd.Suffolk Rgt.
4. 1st.Gordon Hldrs.
5. 76th.T.M.B.
6. Rt.Gp.R.F.A.
7. " 3rd.Bn.M.G.C.
8. 529th.Fd.Co.R.E.
9. 3rd.Div."G".
10. 8th.Inf.Bde.
11. 9th. "
12. 137th. "
13. B.M.
14. S.C.
15. Bde.Sig.Offr.
16. War Diary.
17. "
18. File.

SECRET.
****

Copy No. 20

76th. INFANTRY BRIGADE OPERATION ORDER NO.107.

Reference 1/20,000 Sheets 36a.S.E. and 36b.N.E. — 15th. May 1918.

1. 76th. Inf. Bde. will be relieved by 9th. Inf. Bde. on the night May 16/17th.

2. (a) 13th. King's will relieve 2nd. Suffolk Regt. on the right.
   (b) 4th. R.F. " " 1st. Gordon Hldrs. on the left.
   (c) 1st. N.F. " " 8th. K.O.R.L. in support.
   (d) 9th. T.M.B. " " 76th. T.M.B.

3. Details of above reliefs will be arranged between C.O's concerned, and completion reported to Brigade H.Q., E.4b.4.1.

4. Aeroplane photographs, trench stores, and details of work in hand will be handed over to relieving units.
   Receipts for Trench Stores will be sent to Brigade H.Q. within 24 hours of relief.

5. On relief, 76th. Inf. Bde. will move into Divisional Reserve in the CHOCQUES Area. Exact locations of units will be notified later.

6. 76th. Inf. Bde. H.Q. will close at E.4b.4.1. on completion of relief, and move to ST. SAUVEUR, where reports of arrival in the CHOCQUES Area will be sent.

7. ACKNOWLEDGE.

[signature]
Captain,
Brigade Major, 76th. Infantry Brigade.

Issued at 8 p.m.

Copies to:-
1. G.O.C.
2. 8th. K.O.R.L.
3. 2nd. Suffolk Rgt.
4. 1st. Gordon Hldrs.
5. 76th. T.M.B.
6. Right Gp. R.F.A.
7. 529th. Fd. Co.
8. Right Gp. 3rd. Bn. M.G.C.
9. 3rd. Div. "G".
10. " "Q".
11. 8th. Inf. Bde.
12. 9th. Inf. Bde.
13. 139th. Inf. Bde.
14. S.S.O., 3rd. Div.
15. 7th. Fld. Amb.
16. B.M.
17. S.C.
18. Bde. Sig. Offr.
19. War Diary.
20. "
21. File.

SECRET.
****

Copy No. 19.

76th. INFANTRY BRIGADE OPERATION ORDER NO.108.

Ref.1/20,000 Sheet 36a.S.E.
and 36b.N.E.

19th., May 1918.

1. 76th. Infantry Brigade will relieve 8th. Inf. Bde. in the Left Section of the Divisional front on the night May 20th./21st.

2. (a) 8th.K.O.R.L. will relieve 7th.K.S.L.I. on the right.
(b) 2nd.Suffolk Regt. will relieve 1st.R.S.F. on the left.
(c) 1st.Gordon Hldrs. will relieve 2nd.Royal Scots in Support.
(d) 76th.T.M.B. will relieve 8th.T.M.B.

Details of the above reliefs will be arranged between C.O's concerned, and completion reported to Brigade H.Q., W.25a.0.8.

3. Battalions will start to leave their present areas as follows:-

8th.K.O.R.L. .... 9 p.m.
2nd.Suffolk Regt. ...... 9.30 p.m.
1st.Gordon Hldrs .... 10 p.m.

4. Aeroplane photographs, trench stores, and details of work in hand will be taken over.
Receipts for trench stores will be sent to Brigade H.Q. within 24 hours of relief.

5. Sketch maps showing dispositions will be forwarded as soon as possible after relief.

6. Brigade H.Q. will close at ST.SAUVEUR at 10 p.m. on May 20th., and open at L'ABBAYE on arrival.

7. ACKNOWLEDGE.

[signature]
Captain,
Brigade Major, 76th. Infantry Brigade.

Issued at 8 p.m.

Distribution over...... /

Copies to:- 1. G.O.C.
2. 8th.K.O.R.L.
3. 2nd.Suffolk Regt.
4. 1st.Gordon Hldrs.
5. 76th.T.M.B.
6. Left Gp.R.F.A.
7. 529th.Fd.Co.R.E.
8. 3rd.Div."G".
9. 8th.Inf.Bde.
10. 9th "
11. S.S.O.,3rd.Div.
12. 7th.Fld.Amb.
13. 3rd.Bn.M.G.C.
14. D.T.M.O.,3rd.Div.
15. B.M.
16. S.C.
17. Bde.Sig.Offr.
18. War Diary.
19. "
20. File.

SECRET.
****

Copy No....

76th.INFANTRY BRIGADE OPERATION ORDER NO.109.

Ref.1/20,000 Sheets 36a.S.E. and 36b.N.E.

23rd.May 1918.

1. 1st.Gordon Hldrs.will relieve 2nd.Suffolk Regt.in the Left Sub-section on the night of May 24th./25th.

2. Details will be arranged between C.O's concerned and completion reported to Brigade H.Q.

3. Aeroplane photographs and trench stores will be handed over.

4. On relief,2nd.Suffolk Regt.will move into the Support positions occupied by 1st.Gordon Hldrs.

5. ACKNOWLEDGE.

Captain,
Brigade Major,76th.Infantry Brigade.

Issued at 8 p.m.

Copies to:-
1. G.O.C.
2. 8th.K.O.R.L.
3. 2nd.Suffolk Regt.
4. 1st.Gordon Hldrs.
5. 76th.T.M.B.
6. Left Gp.R.F.A.
7. " 3rd.Bn.M.G.C.
8. 529th.(E.R.)Fd.Co.R.E.
9. 3rd.Div."G".
10. 3rd.Div."Q".
11. 8th.Inf.Bde.
12. 9th. "
13. 11th. "
14. 7th.Fld.Amb.
15. B.M.
16. S.C.
17. War Diary.
18. War Diary.
19. File.

SECRET.
****
Copy No. 18...

76th. INFANTRY BRIGADE OPERATION ORDER NO.110.

Ref.1/20,000 Sheets 36a.S.E. and 36b.N.E.

27th. May 1918.

1. 2nd.Suffolk Regt.will relieve 8th.K.O.R.L. in the Right Sub-section on the night of May 28/29th.

2. Details will be arranged between C.O's concerned and completion reported to Brigade H.Q.

3. Aeroplane photographs and trench stores will be handed over.

4. On relief, 8th.K.O.R.L. will move into the Support positions occupied by 2nd.Suffolk Regt.

5. ACKNOWLEDGE.

[signature]
Captain
Brigade Major, 76th. Infantry Bde.

Issued at 8 p.m.

Copies to:-
1. G.O.C.
2. 8th.K.O.R.L.
3. 2nd.Suffolk Regt.
4. 1st.Bn.Gordon Hldrs.
5. 76th.T.M.B.
6. Left Gp.R.F.A.
7. " 3rd.Bn.M.G.C.
8. 529th.(E.R.)Fd.Co.R.E.
9. 3rd.Div."G".
10. 3rd.Div."Q".
11. 8th.Inf".Bde.
12. 9th. "
13. 12th. "
14. 7th.Fld.Amb.
15. B.M.
16. S.C.
17. War Diary.
18. War Diary.
19. File.

Casualties for Month of May, 1918.

	Officers.
Killed.	1
Wounded.	13
Wounded. (at duty)	2
Missing.	1
Gassed.	5

	Other Ranks.
Killed.	42
Wounded.	229
Missing.	11
Gassed.	159

3rd Division.

B. H. Q.

76th INFANTRY BRIGADE.

JUNE 1918.

Attached :-

Report on Operations 14/15th.

Brigade Operation & Move Orders.

Instructions regarding War Diaries and Intelligence Summaries are contained in F. S. Regs., Part II. and the Staff Manual respectively. Title pages will be prepared in manuscript.

WAR DIARY
or
INTELLIGENCE SUMMARY.
(Erase heading not required.)

Army Form C. 2118.

Headquarters 76th Brigade (Inf)

Vol 33

Place	Date	Hour	Summary of Events and Information	Remarks and references to Appendices
L'Abbaye W25a 0.8	June 1st		Bright. Clear. Situation normal.	
		5.0 am	G.O.C. went round line	
		3.0 pm	O.O. 111 issued.	
	2nd	12.30 am	Under cover of Artillery barrage party of 8th KORL under 2/Lieut Rumsey raided enemy posts at W11b 45.25. 1 off + 10 R captured and a number of enemy killed. Prisoners belonged to 3rd Coy 31st RIR 18th Res Div.	
			Situation normal — Visibility good.	
		3.0 pm	BM went up line.	
			Inter Battalion relief. 8th KORL relieved 1st Gordon Hldrs in left sub-sector.	OO 111
	3rd		Bright — Visibility good. Situation normal. Artillery not quite so active.	
		5.0 am	G.O.C. went round line	
		9.0 am	Capt. Meares, 1st Essex Regt. (G50 3. XIII Corps) attached to Brigade for one month.	
		11.0 pm	Div. Comdr. Called.	
		11.0 am	Corps Comdrs called.	
		8.0 pm	O.O. 112 issued.	
	4th		Fine clear. Situation normal. Hostile Aircraft less active than usual. G.O.C. awarded C.M.G.	
		10.0 pm	Inter Brigade Relief. 76th Inf. Bde relieved by 9th Inf. Bde. in HINGES Section.	
St Sauveur. D5a 5.1	5th	am	Relief Complete. Bde H.Q. closed at L'Abbaye and opened at St Sauveur.	OO 112.
			Troops resting and bathing.	
	6th		Bright – clear.	
		10.30 am	G.O.C. visited 8th KORL and Congratulated raiding party.	

A5834 Wt. W4973/M687 750,000 8/16 D. D. & L. Ltd. Forms/C.2118/13.

Army Form C. 2118.

WAR DIARY
or
INTELLIGENCE SUMMARY.
(Erase heading not required.)

Instructions regarding War Diaries and Intelligence Summaries are contained in F. S. Regs., Part II. and the Staff Manual respectively. Title pages will be prepared in manuscript.

Place	Date	Hour	Summary of Events and Information	Remarks and references to Appendices
St Sauveur. D5a5.1	June 7th		Bright. Fine. Battalions Training.	
		10.0am	Div. Comdr. and G.O.C visited 2nd Suffolks, 8th KORL and 76th T.M.B. at work.	
	June 8th		Fine - Clear. Battalion. Training	
		10.30am	GOC and S.C. visited 61st Div.	
		9.0am	BM and Capt Meares. taped out practice trenches.	
	June 9th.		Fine. Clear. Battalions Training	
			During night of 9/10th 8/KORL relieved 4th Royal Fus who came under the orders of GOC 76th Inf Bde, 8/KORL being under orders of 9th Inf. Bde	
	June 10th		Fine Clear.	
		9.0am	BM & S.C. went up line to arrange dumps etc.	
		6.0pm	Div. Comdr called to see G.O.C.	
		9.0pm	GOC. went to Division to see CRA.	
	June. 11th		Fine. Clear. Battalion Training	
		10.30am	Corps Commander called to see Battalion at work.	
		4.30pm	GOC went to 11th Bde. 4th Division.	
		8.0pm	OO 113 issued	
	June 12th.		Fine - Clear. Battalions Training.	
		10.30am	Div. Comdr. & G.O.C. watched units practising the attack	
			G.O.C. stayed at Division until 2.0 pm.	
		10.30pm	GOC. watched units practising the attack by night.	
		10.0am	OO 114 issued.	

A5834 Wt. W4973/M687 750,000 8/16 D. D. & L. Ltd. Forms/C.2118/13.

Instructions regarding War Diaries and Intelligence Summaries are contained in F. S. Regs., Part II. and the Staff Manual respectively. Title pages will be prepared in manuscript.

WAR DIARY
or
INTELLIGENCE SUMMARY.
(Erase heading not required.)

Army Form C. 2118.

Place	Date	Hour	Summary of Events and Information	Remarks and references to Appendices
St Sauveur. D5a5.1	JUNE 13th		Bright - clear. Units training.	
		5.0pm	Bde Hqrs closed at St SAUVEUR and opened at L'Abbaye. W25a 0.8.	OO 113.
			76th Inf. Bde relieved 9th Inf Bde.	
			2nd Suffolk Regt on right front. 1st Gordon Hldrs. on left front.	
			8th K.O.R.L remained in support and came under orders of GOC 76th Inf Bde	
			4th Royal Fus. came under orders of GOC 9th Inf. Bde.	
L'Abbaye. W25a 0.8.	June 14th	3.0am	~~Bde~~ Relief complete.	
			Bright. Clear. Situation normal.	
		5.0am	GOC went round line.	
		11.45pm	Under cover of artillery and M.G. barrages an attack was carried out, in conjunction with 9th Inf Bde, with 2nd Suffolk Regt on right, and 1st Gordon Hldrs on left, against enemy positions in W4b and W5c & d. The operation was entirely successful and the objective (bend in Ford Lane at W5d 55.15, along road, to Q34d 4.2) was gained. Enemy barrage was slight. A machine gun in the Assault Course at W5d 3.5 held out for some time, but was eventually cleared up. A machine gun in the ruined house at Q34d 7.1 held up the centre of the Gordon Hldrs until daylight, but it then withdrew and our line was established on the objective. Touch was gained with 11th Inf. Bde on left and 9th Inf. Bde. on right.	
			Total of prisoners captured in whole operation amounted to 4 officers, 2 aspirant officers and 177 OR. of 18th Res. Div.	
	15th		Bright - clear. Hostile Artillery fairly active. During the day enemy barraged the Canal Bank at intervals, and harassed roads in and round HINGES	
		2.0pm	BM went round Battns	
		3.30pm	Capt Meares & 2/Lt Bowden went to Battle Hqrs of 1st Gordons.	

Army Form C. 2118.

Instructions regarding War Diaries and Intelligence Summaries are contained in F. S. Regs., Part II. and the Staff Manual respectively. Title pages will be prepared in manuscript.

WAR DIARY
or
INTELLIGENCE SUMMARY.
(*Erase heading not required.*)

Place	Date	Hour	Summary of Events and Information	Remarks and references to Appendices
L'Abbaye W25a 0.8.	June 16th		Dull – Showery in morning. Situation Quiet.	
		1.0 pm	OO 115 issued.	
			2nd Suffolk Regt took over whole front.	
			1st Gordon Hldrs moved into Bde. Reserve in CHOCQUES area.	OO 115.
	17th	1.0 am	Relief complete.	
			Bright – Clear. Vis. very good. Situation quiet except from 6.0 am to 9.0 am when area round Canal Bank was heavily shelled.	
		9.0 am	Capt Playfair went on leave. Capt GK Meares took over as Brigade Major.	
		10.30 am	Corps Commander visited Bde, and saw 1st Gordon Hldrs.	
		12 noon	Mr Philip Gibbs, War Correspondent, interviewed G.O.C. about the attack.	
		5.0 pm	Div! Comdr. called to see G.O.C.	
	18th		Bright – Vis. good. Situation Quiet. Hostile Artillery much quieter.	
		5.0 am	GOC went round line.	
		3.0 pm	Div. Comdr. called.	
		11.0 pm	OO 116 issued.	
	19th		Dull – Showery. Situation very quiet.	
		11.0 am	GOC and Staff Captain visited transport lines	
		11.30 am	B.G.G.S. XIII Corps called.	
			Inter Battalion Relief. 8/KORL relieved 2/Suffolk Regt in front line	
			1st Gordon Hldrs relieved 8/KORL in Support.	OO 116
			2/Suffolk Regt moved into Brigade Reserve in CHOCQUES area.	
	20th	1.45 am	Relief complete.	
			Dull Showery. Bright by 11.0 am. Situation very quiet.	

A5834 Wt. W4973/M687 750,000 8/16 D. D. & L. Ltd. Forms/C.2118/13.

Instructions regarding War Diaries and Intelligence Summaries are contained in F. S. Regs., Part II. and the Staff Manual respectively. Title pages will be prepared in manuscript.

WAR DIARY
or
INTELLIGENCE SUMMARY.
(Erase heading not required.)

Army Form C. 2118.

Place	Date	Hour	Summary of Events and Information	Remarks and references to Appendices
L'Abbaye W25a 0.8.	June 20th	4.30am	G.O.C. and Staff Captain went round GORDON LINE.	
	21st		Bright. Clear. Some showers. Situation quiet. Bursts on canal bank during the night 21/22.	
		10.0am	Div. Comdr called.	
		4.0pm	G.O.C. visited 2nd Suffolk Regt. and watched "Z" Coy Sports.	
			During the night 21/22 patrol of 8/K.O.R.L captured prisoner of ... W5d 7.5.,	
			Prisoner belonged to 7th Coy II Bn 23rd R.I.R. 12th R.D.	
	22nd		Dull - Showery. Brighter during the afternoon. Situation quiet.	
		4.30am	G.O.C. went round line.	
		2.0pm	Capt Meares and 2/Lt Borden went round Bn. Hqrs.	
		3.0pm	OO 117 issued to units.	
		5.0pm	G.O.C. went to 2/Suffolk Regt to see sports of Hqrs Coy.	
	23rd		Showery. Bright and dull alternately. Situation quiet. Some artillery activity during the night.	
		10.0am	Intelligence Officer 8th Div. American Army attached to Bde. for instruction	
			Inter Battalion relief	
			1st Gordon Highrs relieved 8/KORL in forward section.	
			2/Suffolk Regt relieved 1/Gordon Hdrs in Support.	OO 117
			8/KORL returned to Chocques area in Brigade Reserve.	
	24th	1.0am	Relief complete.	
			Dull - Showery. Situation quiet.	
		5.0am	G.O.C. went round line.	

A5834 Wt. W4973/M687 750,000 8/16 D. D. & L. Ltd. Forms/C.2118/13.

Instructions regarding War Diaries and Intelligence Summaries are contained in F. S. Regs., Part II. and the Staff Manual respectively. Title pages will be prepared in manuscript.

WAR DIARY
or
INTELLIGENCE SUMMARY.
(Erase heading not required.)

Army Form C. 2118.

Place	Date	Hour	Summary of Events and Information	Remarks and references to Appendices
L'Abbaye W25a0.8.	June 25th		Dull - Showery. Situation quiet.	
	26th		Bright at intervals. Vis. not good. Situation quiet.	
		10.0 am	G.O.C went up line.	
		1.0 pm	Capt G.K. Meares proceeded to 5th Div.	
			Capt T. Pickard-Cambridge, 2nd Suffolk Regt. assumed duties as Brigade Major.	
	27th		Bright. Fairly Clear. Situation quiet.	
		10.0 am	G.O.C visited 8/KORL at rest.	
	28th	6.0 am	Creeping barrage for three minutes on our front, in conjunction with minor operation carried out by Corps on our left. Hostile retaliation fairly heavy, particularly on the Aberdeen line, the orchard and canal bank round Pont d'Hinges. Hostile fire slackened at 6.30 am and ceased at 7.0 am.	
			Dull. Showery day.	
		10.30 am	Div. Comdr. called.	
			Div. Comdr & G.O.C visited 8/KORL at training, and also the transport lines of 8/KORL and 2/Suffolk Regt.	
		3.0 pm	OO 118 issued	
	29th		Bright at intervals. Situation normal. Artillery very active during the night.	
		5.0 am	GOC went round line.	
		1.0 pm	Lt Col Stubbs DSO came to Bde. Hqrs to see GOC.	
		9.0 pm	Lt Col Perry ? M.C. came into Bde. Hqrs to see GOC re relief.	

A5834 Wt. W4973/M687 750,000 8/16 D. D. & L. Ltd. Forms/C.2118/13.

Army Form C. 2118.

Instructions regarding War Diaries and Intelligence Summaries are contained in F. S. Regs., Part II. and the Staff Manual respectively. Title pages will be prepared in manuscript.

WAR DIARY
or
INTELLIGENCE SUMMARY.

(Erase heading not required.)

Place	Date	Hour	Summary of Events and Information	Remarks and references to Appendices
L'Abbaye W25a0.8	29th		Inter Battalion relief. 2nd Suffolk Regt relieved 1/Gordon Hldrs in front system. 1/Gordon Hldrs returned to rest in CHOCQUES area. 8/KORL relieved 2/Suffolk Regt in support.	OO118.
	30th	1.10 am	Relief complete. Artillery very active during the night.	
			Bright clear – Situation unchanged.	
		11.0 am	GOC reconnoitred lines of defence	
		12 noon	Div. Comdr. called –	

[signature]
Brig Genl.
Commanding 76th Inf. Bde.

A5834 Wt. W4973/M687 750,000 8/16 D. D. & L. Ltd. Forms/C.2118/13.

CASUALTIES FOR MONTH OF JUNE.

==*=*=*=*=*=*=*=*=*=*=*=*=*

OFFICERS.

Killed.	Wounded.	Gassed.
6	10	1

Other Ranks.

Killed.	Wounded.	Missing.	Gassed.
62	299	21	5

War Diary 

B/2723.

76th. INFANTRY BRIGADE

Report on operation carried out on June 14/15th.1918.

2nd.Suffolk Regt and 1st.Gordon Hldrs were assembled by 11.30p.m. without incident.

The night was quiet, and the enemy apparently unsuspecting. At 11.45 p.m. the artillery barrage opened, the synchronization being good. All ranks speak highly of the barrage.

2nd.Suffolk Regt.

Opposition was encountered by the Centre Company from the Assault Course, W.5d.2.4. where 2/Lt.FRANKS was killed. In some cases the sections, advancing in columns of file, missed some enemy posts which opened fire from the rear, before being dealt with by the supporting platoons.

On arrival on the objective the Centre and Left Companies found that a gap existed between them in which some of the enemy were still holding out. A platoon under 2/Lt.BENNETT was sent forward from the Reserve Company, cleared the opposition and filled the gap.

The left of the Right Company was held up by a M.G.post at about W.5d.3.4., the Platoon Commander and Platoon Sergeant being wounded. While trying to ascertain the situation, the Company Commander was also wounded. 2/Lt.COOK, M.C., D.C.M., commanding the right front platoon, had reached his objective having himself shot a German Machine Gunner and put the remainder of the post out of action. His platoon was digging in when he received news of the situation on his left. He at once assumed command of the Company, organized a bombing attack, and cleared up the resistance. His prompt action was most commendable.

2nd.Suffolk Regt was in touch throughout with 4th.R.F. on the right and 1st.Gordon Hldrs on the left.

1st.Gordon Hldrs.

The outer flanks of the assaulting companies gained their objectives up to time, maintaining touch with 2nd.Suffolk Regt on the right and 1st.Rif.Brigade on the left.

In the centre, however, opposition was encountered at once, principally from the front line posts about W.4b.9.5. and the ruined buildings Q.34d.7.1. It is possible that these were missed by the barrage, though it is difficult to ascertain this for certain. These posts were eventually rushed by the two left platoons of the Right Support Company, under covering fire from Lewis Guns and rifles from the left, several of the enemy being killed and the remainder captured.

In the assaulting companies both Company Commanders and 2 platoon Commanders were killed, and both C.S.M's seriously wounded.

CONSOLIDATION.

Both Battalions succeeded in digging in on their objectives, although most of the digging had to be done after daylight, owing to the time spent in overcoming opposition.

MEDICAL.

The medical arrangements were admirable, and the wounded quickly cleared by No.7 Field Ambulance. The advanced Car Post was a decided advantage.

contd..... / CAPTURES

CAPTURES.

About 100 prisoners were captured by the Brigade. Order of Battle and identifications were normal.

Several important maps were captured, and about 12 light machine guns are now in action against the enemy.

ENEMY ATTITUDE.

The enemy artillery reply was weak, probably owing to our C.B.work.

The attack was a surprise, though one officer prisoner said that the shelling of Q.34d. had given rise to some suspicion.

Since the attack enemy activity has taken the form of violent bursts of artillery fire on, and on either side of the Canal Bank, lasting from 10 to 20 minutes each. Numerous enemy balloons have been up during the hours of daylight.

SIGNALLING COMMUNICATION.

(a) Buried line remained through all the time.

(b) Message rockets fired from the forward posts could be heard by the look-out man, but could not be recovered.

(c) Telephones and Lucas Lamps worked satisfactorily.

(d) Two P.B.& A.sets were taken across the Canal to communicate with Battn.H.Q., W.10c.1.9. They did not work satisfactorily, owing, it is thought, to the Canal itself.

CASUALTIES.

2nd.Suffolk Regt............ 1 Officer killed.
5 Officers wounded.
85 O.R. K.W.or M.

1st.Gordon Hldrs............ 4 Officers killed.
3 Officers wounded.
15 O.R.killed.
127 O.R.wounded.

8th.K.O.R.L................. 2 O.R.wounded.

TOTAL........................5 Officers killed.
8 Officers wounded.
229 O.R. K.W.or M.

16/6/18.

Brigadier-General,
Commanding 76th.Infantry Brigade.

SECRET.
****
Copy No.18.

76th. INFANTRY BRIGADE OPERATION ORDER NO.111.

Ref.1/20,000 Sheets 36a.S.E.
and 36b.N.E.

1st. June 1918.

1. 8th.K.O.R.L.Rgt. will relieve 1st.Gordon Hldrs. in the Left Subsection of the 'HINGES section' on the night of June 2nd./3rd.

2. Details will be arranged between C.O.'s concerned and completion reported to Brigade H.Q.

3. Aeroplane photographs and trench stores will be handed over.

4. On relief, 1st.Gordon Hldrs. will move into the Support positions occupied by 8th. K.O.R.L.Rgt.

5. ACKNOWLEDGE.

[signature]
Captain,
Brigade Major, 76th. Infantry Brigade.

Issued at 3 p.m.

Copies to:-
1. G.O.C.
2. 8th.K.O.R.L.
3. 2nd.Suffolk Rgt.
4. 1st.Gordon Hldrs.
5. 76th.T.M.B.
6. Left Gp.R.F.W.
7. " 3rd.Bn.M.G.C.
8. 529th.(E.R.) Fd.Coy.,R.E.
9. 3rd.Div."G".
10. 3rd.Div."Q".
11. 8th.Inf.Bde.
12. 9th.Inf.Bde.
13. 12th.Inf.Bde.
14. 7th.Fld.Amb.
15. B.M.
16. S.C.
17. War Diary.
18. War Diary.
19. File.

SECRET.
****

Copy No..19.....

76th. INFANTRY BRIGADE OPERATION ORDER NO. 112.

Reference 1/20,000 Sheets 36a.S.E.
and 36b.N.E. 3rd.June 1918.

1. The 76th.Inf.Bde. will be relieved by 9th. Inf.Bde. in the HINGES SECTION on the night of June 4th./5th.

2. 13th.King's will relieve 2nd.Suffolk Rgt. on the Right.
1st. N.Fus. will relieve 8th.K.O.R.L.Rgt. on the left.
4th. R.Fus. will relieve 1st.Gordon Hldrs. in Support.
9th.T.M.Battery will relieve 76th. T.M.Battery.

3. Details of reliefs will be arranged between C.O.'s concerned and completion reported to Brigade H.Q. at L'ABBAYE.

4. Aeroplane photographs and trench stores will be handed over to relieving Units.

Receipts will reach Brigade H.Q. within 24 hours of relief.

5. Units will take over accommodation in the CHOCQUES Area as follows:-

8th.K.O.R.L.R.	from	1st.N.Fus.
2nd.Suffolk R.	"	4th.R.Fus.
1st.Gordon H.	"	13th.King's.
76th.T.M.Bty.	"	9th.T.M.Bty.

6. 76th.Inf.Bde.H.Q. will close at L'ABBAYE on completion of relief, and move to ST. SAUVEUR, where reports of arrival in the new area will be sent.

7. ACKNOWLEDGE.

[signature]
Captain,
Issued at 8 p.m. Brigade Major, 76th. Infantry Brigade.

Copies to :-
1. G.O.C.
2. 8th.K.O.R.L.
3. 2nd.Suffolk Rgt.
4. 1st.Gordon H.
5. 76th.T.M.B.
6. Left Group R.F.A.
7. " " 3rd.Bn.M.G.C.
8. 529th.(E.R.)Fld.Coy.R.E.
9. 3rd.Div."G".
10. 3rd.Div."Q".
11. 8th.Inf.Bde.
12. 9th.Inf.Bde.
13. 10th.Inf.Bde.
14. 7th.Fld.Amb.
15. B.M.
16. S.C.
17. Bde.Signal Off.
18. T.M.CHOCQUES.
19. War Diary.
20. Do.
21. File.

SECRET.
****

Copy No..19.

76th.INFANTRY BRIGADE OPERATION ORDER NO.113.

****

Reference 1/10,000 Sheet LOCON Ed.8. 11th.June 1918.

1. The 3rd.Division front is to be held by 3 Brigades in line,8th.Bde on the Right,9th.Bde in the Centre,76th.Bde on the Left.

2. The boundary between 9th.and 76th.Bdes is as shown on the tracing already issued to units 76th.Bde.

3. The new inter-battalion boundary will be as follows:-
W.5a.70.35. - ditch from W.5a.65.25. to Canal Bank at W.10b.55.80. (all inclusive to Right Battn.) - thence to road junction W.10c.4.9. (inclusive to Left Battn.).

4. 76th.Inf.Bde will take over its new front from 9th.Inf. Bde on the night June 13th./14th.with 2nd.Suffolk Regt on the Right and 1st.Gordon Hldrs on the Left. Reliefs will be carried out as follows:-

(i) 2nd.Suffolk Regt. will march off from its present area at 10.15 p.m. June 13th.relieving:-

(a) troops of 13th.KING'S north of the new Brigade Southern Boundary.
(b) troops of 1st.N.F. south of the new inter-battalion Boundary.

(ii) 1st.Gordon Hldrs. will march from its present area at 9.30 p.m. June 13th.,relieving 1st.N.F.less troops mentioned in para.4 (i) b above.

(iii) 9th.T.M.B. will withdraw from present positions at 11 p.m.

76th.T.M.B.will move into positions as follows:-

2 guns in the hedge about W.5c.45.10.
2 guns in the trench about W.4a.9.8.

5. Aeroplane photographs and trench stores will be taken over.

6. Details of the above reliefs will be arranged between C.O's concerned and completion reported to Brigade H.Q.

7. 76th.Inf.Bde H.Q. will close at ST.SAUVEUR at 5 p.m. June 13th.,and open at L'ABBAYE at the same time.

8. ACKNOWLEDGE.

W.Playfair
Captain,
Brigade Major,76th.Infantry Brigade.

Issued at 8 p.m.

Copies to:-
1. G.O.C.
2. 8th.K.O.R.L.
3. 2nd.Suffolk Regt.
4. 1st.Gordon Hldrs.
5. 76th.T.M.B.
6. Left Gp.R.F.A.
7. " 3rd.Bn.M.G.C.
8. 529th.Fd.Co.R.E.
9. 3rd.Div."G".
10. " "Q".
11. 8th.Inf.Bde.
12. 9th.Inf.Bde.
13. 20th.K.R.R.C.
14. 3rd.Bn.M.G.C.
15. 7th.Fld.Amb.
16. B.M.
17. S.C.
18. Bde.Sig.Offr.
19. War Diary.
20. "
21. File.

SECRET.

76th. INFANTRY BRIGADE ADMINISTRATIVE INSTRUCTIONS.

Reference 76th. INFANTRY BRIGADE OPERATION ORDER NO.114.

Ref. Sheet 36A.S.E.4. — 12th. June 1918.

1. DUMPS.

(A). Battalion Dumps are being formed at the following points and will be completed night 12th/13th.:-

2nd.Suffolk Regt.	W.11a.8.4. (approx).
1st.Gordon Hldrs.	W.4c.6.6. (approx).

Each Dump will contain :-

S.A.A.	50 Boxes
Very Lights, white.	3 Boxes.
S.O.S.	36 Grenades.
Tins of water.	125
Rations (Preserved).	700
Chloride of Lime.	200 lbs.

Spare Lewis Gun Magazines will be dumped across the Canal under Battalion arrangements.

(B). 400 rounds Stokes 3" Ammunition, with components, has been dumped at W.10a.1.1.

This will be carried forward to Gun positions under arrangements of O.C. 76th.L.T.M.Battery.

(C). Dumps of wiring material for use of 529th.Fld.Coy.R.E. and 1 Coy.20th.K.R.R.C. on night 15th/16th have been formed North of Canal at sites selected by these units.

2. SPECIAL STORES.

Following special stores have been issued to 2nd.Suffolk Rgt., 1st.Gordon Hldrs.:-

Each Battalion:-	Shovels	700	(1 per man to be carried)
	Sandbags.	2000	(2 per man to be carried)
	No.35 Rifle Grenades.	480	) up to these numbers to be
	No.23 " " (25% rodded)	480	carried on the men as required.
	Wire Cutters, Mk.V. or Wire Breakers	75	) To be carried on the
	S.O.S.	36	) man as required.
	Very Lights, white	2 Boxes)	
	Red Flares.	250	(2 men in each section to carry 2 Flares each).
	Tracing Tapes	20	
	Spare Box Respirators.	50	

3. RATIONS.

Rations per diem for consumption 15th/&16th. June for troops taking part in the attack :-

Unit.	Preserved Rations P.M. & Biscuits.	Rum.	Solidified Alcohol.	Chloride of Lime.
2nd.Suff.Rgt.	700	700	150 tins.	200 lbs.
1st.Gordon H.	700	700	150 "	200 "
76th.T.M.Bty.	30	30	15 "	Nil.

The above Rations and Stores will be issued to Units on 12th. inst. at Refilling Point.

Rations for consumption by Battalions on 16th. inst. will be placed on Dumps North of Canal (vide para.1 A.) under Brigade arrangements. Rations for consumption 15th inst. will be carried on the man.

76th.L.T.M.Bty. will carry on the man Rations for 15th and 16th. inst.

Full instructions re Rations have been issued to those concerned under this office No. A/41/6 dated 11/6/18.

4. MEDICAL ARRANGEMENTS.

Regimental Aid Posts.

2nd.Suffolk Rgt.	W.11a.0.4. (approx.):
1st.Gordon Hldrs.	W.4c.8.4.

Canal will be bridged at these two points.

O.C.No.7th.Field Ambce. will arrange for wounded brought to these R.A.P's to be cleared to the Car Post at VERTANNOY via Relay Post to be established by him at W.10a.1.1.

A third bridge will be available for wounded at W.11a.2.2. and O.C.No.7th.Field Ambce. will arrange to take over any wounded brought across this bridge. Walking wounded will be directed to the Advanced Dressing Station at L'ABBAYE.

5. BRIDGES.

Additional floating bridges are being put over the Canal at approximately the following points by 529th.Field Coy.R.E. on night June 14th/15th.:-

W.11a.2.2.
W.10b.5.8.
W.4c.6.5.

[signature]

Captain,
Staff Captain, 76th. Infantry Brigade.

Copies to :-

1. 8th.K.O.R.L.
2. 2nd.Suff.Rgt.
3. 1st.Gordon H.
4. 76th.T.M.Bty.
5. 529th.F.Coy.,R.E.
6. 7th.Field Ambce.
7. 20th.K.R.R.C.
8. Left Gp.3rd.Bn.M.G.C.
9. 3rd.Div."Q". (for information)
10. War Diary.
11. Do.
12. File.

SECRET.
****

Copy No....

76th.INFANTRY BRIGADE OPERATION ORDER NO.114.

Reference 1/10,000 Sheet 36a.S.E.4 (LOCON) Ed.8.

12th.June 1918.

1. (a) With a view to securing a greater depth in defence on the East bank of the LA BASSEE Canal, the 3rd.Division will advance its front on the night 14th./15th.June to the line - Q.34d.4.2. - FORD LANE - TURBEAUTE CT at W.12a.0.8. - thence along the West bank of this stream to W.12c.1.6. - thence to W.18b.5.8. where it will connect up with our present front line.

(b) The 4th.Division is advancing its extreme right flank to gain touch with the left flank of the 3rd.Division about Q.34d.40.25.

(c) The operation will be carried out as a surprise without a preliminary bombardment.

2. The advance on the front of the 3rd.Division will be carried out by the 9th.Inf.Brigade on the Right and the 76th.Inf.Bde on the Left.

3. The attack on the 76th.Inf.Brigade front will be carried out by 2nd.Suffolk Regt on the Right and 1st.Gordon Hldrs.on the Left. Boundary between Battalions:-

Canal Bank at W.10b.55.80. - thence along ditch to W.5a.65.25. - FORD LANE about W.5a.70.35. - all inclusive to 2nd. Suffolk Regt.

4. 4th.R.Fus.(9th.Inf.Bde) is attacking on the Right of 2nd.Suffolk Regt; 1st.Rifle Brigade (11th.Inf.Bde) on the Left of 1st.Gordon Hldrs.

5. 2nd.Suffolk Regt and 1st.Gordon Hldrs will be in their assembly positions by 11 p.m. June 14th. There will be no movement before 10.15 p.m., and no troops will be forward of our present front line before ZERO.

6. 8th.K.O.R.L. At 10.15 p.m. 2 Coys 8th.K.O.R.L. will move from the SHROPSHIRE LINE to garrison the GORDON LINE between the Brigade Boundaries. 2 Coys will remain in the SHROPSHIRE LINE. 4 Lewis Gun Sections will move to the Canal Bank in the Right Battalion Area and 2 L.G. Sections to the Canal Bank in the Left Battalion Area.

7. TASKS. Tasks are allotted as follows:-

(a) 2nd.Suffolk Regt. To capture and consolidate the line of FORD LANE from the bend at W.5d.55.15. (inclusive) to a point 100 yards N.W. of the cross roads W.5a.85.25.

(b) 1st.Gordon Hldrs. To capture and consolidate the line of FORD LANE from a point 100 yards N.W. of the cross roads W.5a.85.25.to the cross roads W.5a.1.9. (inclusive) - building Q.34d.7.1. (inclusive) - gaining touch with 1st.Rif.Brigade at the ditch about Q.34d.4.2.

8. At ZERO hour (to be notified later) :-

(a) The Field Artillery H.E. and Shrapnel barrages will open, the former on the front line of enemy posts, the latter on a line 150 yards beyond.

contd...... / (b)

(b) The Machine Gun Barrage will open on the line of the final objective.

The opening of the Field Artillery Barrage will be the signal for the Heavy Artillery and Machine Guns to open fire.

(c) The attacking Infantry will advance close up under the Artillery Barrage and await its lifting.

9. At ZERO plus 8 minutes:-

(a) The Field Artillery barrages will begin to creep forward at the maximum rate of 100 yards in 4 minutes.

(b) The M.G.Barrage will lift to a line 300 yards beyond the final objective.

(c) The Infantry will advance behind the H.E.Barrage to the final objective.

10. As soon as the objective is gained, the Artillery and Machine Guns will form protective barrages; covering parties will be pushed forward, and the digging of posts commenced.

11. The line of the objective will be held as an outpost line.

Each attacking Battalion will hold the captured ground with 2 Coys forward of the present front line, and 2 Coys in the present front line and supporting posts.

12. 250 Red Ground Flares will be issued to each attacking Battalion.

Should the situation be obscure, a Contact Aeroplane will go up on the morning of June 15th.

The most advanced Infantry will light Red Ground Flares to indicate their position if called for by an aeroplane sounding its Klaxton Horn or firing white lights.

Flares will not be lit unless called for by an aeroplane.

13. Prisoners will be sent to Brigade H.Q.

14. A watch, synchronised with the artillery, will be sent round to Battalion H.Q. between 6 p.m. and 7 p.m. on June 14th.

15. ACKNOWLEDGE.

R Marfair
Captain,

Issued at 10 a.m. Brigade Major, 76th. Infantry Brigade.

Copies to:-
1. G.O.C.
2. 8th.K.O.R.L.
3. 2nd.Suffolk Regt.
4. 1st.Gordon Hldrs.
5. 76th.T.M.B.
6. Left Gp.R.F.A.
7. " 3rd.Bn.M.G.C.
8. 529th.Fd.Co.R.E.
9. 20th.K.R.R.C.
10. 3rd.Div."G".
11. " "Q".
12. 8th.Inf.Bde.
13. 9th. "
14. 11th. "
15. C.R.A., 3rd.Div.
16. C.R.E. "
17. 7th.Fld.Amb.
18. 3rd.Bn.M.G.C.
19. B.M.
20. S.C.
21. Bde.Sig.Offr.
22. War Diary.
23. "
24. File.

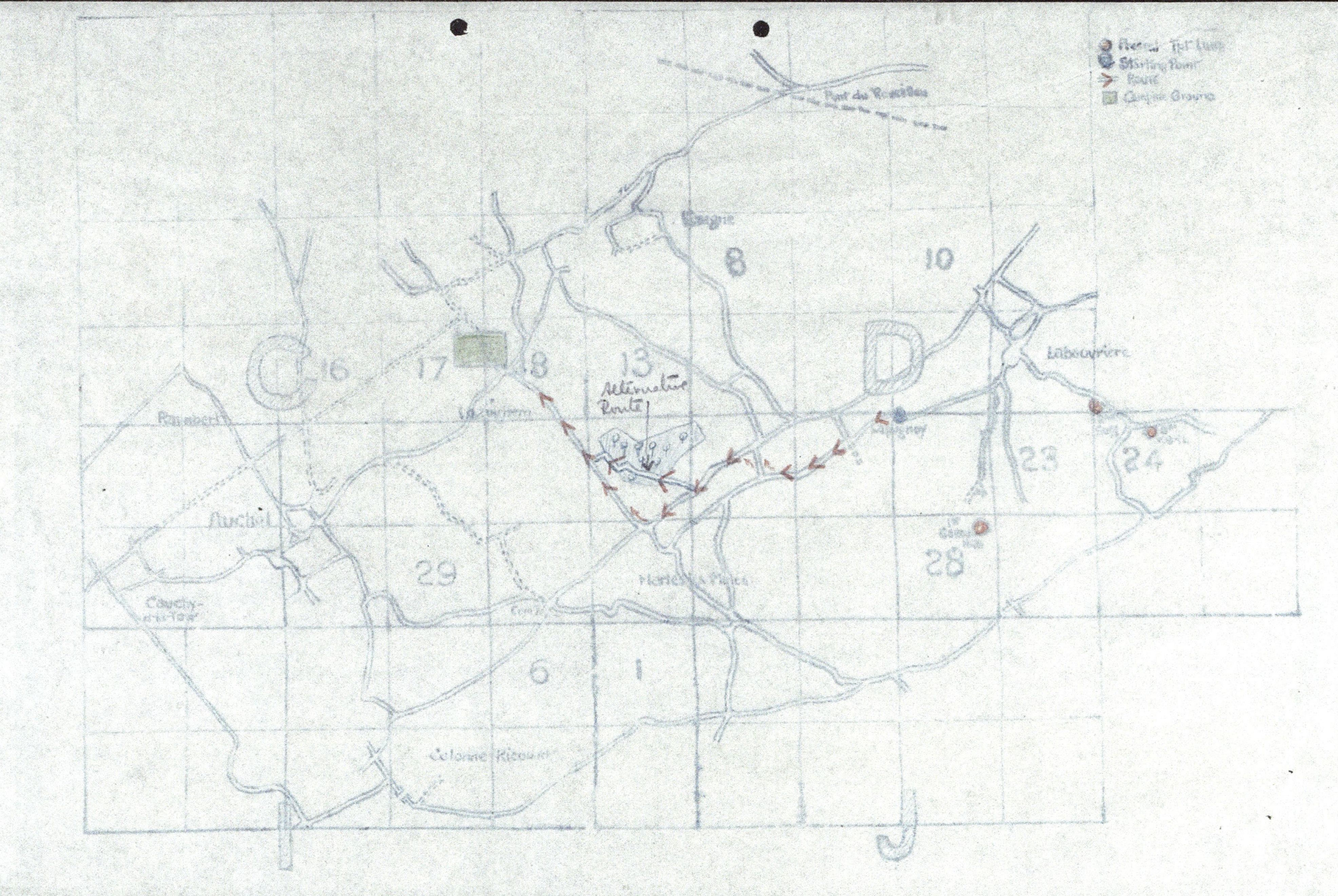

Starting Point
Route
Alternative Route
Labourière
Auchel
8
10
13
16
17
18
23
24
28
29
6
1
C
D
J

AMENDMENT No.1 TO 76th.INFANTRY BRIGADE O.O.NO.114.

****

<u>Para.6.</u> After "At 10.15 p.m." insert "on June 15th./16th.".

After "4 Lewis Gun Sections will move" insert "at 10.15 p.m. on June 14th./15th."

<u>Add new para.16.</u>

"Troops taking part in the advance will wear the following distinguishing marks:- All Officers, Platoon and Section Commanders will wear a White Band, at least 4 inches broad, on each arm above the elbow. The remainder will wear a similar band on the right arm above the elbow".

[signature]
Captain,
Brigade Major, 76th. Infantry Brigade.

13th. June 1918.

Copies to all recipients of O.O.114.

** ** ** ** **

SECRET.
****

Copy No....

76th. INFANTRY BRIGADE OPERATION ORDER NO.115.

Ref.1/20,000 Sheets 36a.S.E. and 36b.N.E.

16th. June 1918.

1. 2nd. Suffolk Regt will take over tonight, June 16th./17th., the whole front at present held by 2nd. Suffolk Regt and 1st. Gordon Hldrs.

2. Details of necessary reliefs will be arranged between C.O's concerned, and completion reported to Brigade H.Q.

3. On relief, 1st. Gordon Hldrs will move into Brigade Reserve in the CHOCQUES Area. Battn.H.Q. - D.5c.7.9.

4. 2 Coys 8th.K.O.R.L. will move at 10.30 p.m. from the SHROPSHIRE LINE to garrison the SUFFOLK LINE within the Brigade Boundaries.
H.Q. 8th.K.O.R.L. will remain at W.15d.4.7.

5. ACKNOWLEDGE.

C.C. Playfair

Captain,
Brigade Major, 76th. Infantry Brigade.

Issued at 1 p.m.

Copies to:-
1. G.O.C.
2. 8th.K.O.R.L.
3. 2nd.Suffolk Regt.
4. 1st.Gordon Hldrs.
5. 76th.T.M.B.
6. Left Gp.R.F.A.
7. " 3rd.Bn.M.G.C.
8. 529th.Fd.Co.R.E.
9. 20th.K.R.R.C.
10. 3rd.Div."G".
11. " "Q".
12. 8th.Inf.Bde.
13. 9th. "
14. 11th. "
15. 7th.Fld.Amb.
16. B.M.
17. S.C.
18. Bde Sig.Offr.
19. War Diary.
20. "
21. File.

SECRET
****

Copy No......

76th.INFANTRY BRIGADE OPERATION ORDER NO.115 (A).
****

Ref.Map LOCON 1/10,000 Ed.8 36a.S.E.4. 19th.June 1918.

1. On the night 17th./18th.June the 9th.Inf.Brigade extended its front so as to include the road running N.E.from W.11b.0.5.

2. The dispositions of the 2nd.Suffolk.Regt holding the 76th.Inf.Bde front remained unchanged as there were no posts to be handed over.

3. ACKNOWLEDGE.

J.K. Meares
Captain,
Issued at 3 p.m. for Brigade Major,76th.Infantry Brigade.

Copies to:-
1. G.O.C.
2. 8th.K.O.R.L.
3. 2nd.Suffolk Regt.
4. 1st.Gordon Hldrs.
5. 76th.T.M.B.
6. Left Gp.R.F.A.
7. " 3rd.Bn.M.G.C.
8. 529th.Fd.Co.R.E.
9. 20th.K.R.R.C.
10. 3rd.Div."G".
11. " "Q".
12. 8th.Inf.Bde.
13. 9th. "
14. 11th. "
15. 7th.Fld.Amb.
16. B.M.
17. S.C.
18. Bde.Sig.Offr.
19. War Diary.
20. "
21. File.

SECRET.

INSTRUCTIONS FOR THE MOVE OF 76TH. INFANTRY BRIGADE TRANSPORT IN THE EVENT OF A WITHDRAWAL.

1. In the event of it becoming necessary to withdraw in a Westerly direction, the Transport of the Brigade will retire from their present positions in accordance with attached March Table.

2. The Brigade Transport (less Pack Convoy - vide para. 6) will move under the orders of Capt.D.R.G.RENFREW, 1st.Bn.Gordon Hldrs, Brigade Transport Officer, who will receive orders direct from 3rd.Division "Q".

On receipt, by telegram, of the code word "PACK", he will warn the Brigade Group Transport to be ready to move off within one hour : this will include the warning of the 529th.(E.R.) Field Coy.,R.E. and No.7 Field Ambulance, but these two Units will not actually move except under the order of the C.R.E. and A.D.M.S.
(A copy of this telegram will be repeated by 3rd. Division "Q" to Brigade H.Q. who will repeat to Units for information only).

3. Orders for the move of the Divisional Train will be arranged for separately by 3rd.Division "Q" direct.

4. On receipt by the Brigade Transport Officer of the code word "MOVE", he will send orders for Units to move in accordance with attached March Table. The order to move will give the ZERO Hour.

5. When it becomes evident, from the situation either on the Divisional front or on the flanks, that a move Westwards is to be expected, each Unit of the Brigade Group, including the 529th.Field Coy.,R.E. and No.7 Field Ambulance will send a mounted or cyclist orderly to report to the Brigade Transport Officer. The orderlies of the 529th.Field Coy.,R.E. and No.7 Field Ambulance will rejoin their Units after delivering the instructions to "PACK", but the remaining orderlies will stay with the Brigade Transport Officer throughout the subsequent move.

6. On receipt of the word "PACK", each Battalion will send 2 limbers and 6 pack animals loaded with S.A.A. from Mobile Reserve (24 Boxes per limber and 2 per pack animal) to the Sandpits, D.24b., with a N.C.O. in charge. The senior of the three N.C.O.'s will take command of the whole convoy and will report at once to Brigade Rear H.Q. (now at No.7 Billet, LABEUVRIERE) to the Officer who will be there.

This transport will remain behind under orders of the above Officer and will not move with the rest of the Transport.

7. A reserve of rations for 27 men and 30 horses for 48 hours is being formed at the Sandpits under the Transport Officer of 8th.Bn.K.O.R.L.Rgt. These rations will be handed over to the Pack Convoy before the Brigade Transport moves.

8. The Brigade and Regimental Transport Officers will, if time permits, reconnoitre the route allotted to them (vide attached sketch), also the area they will occupy in the new locality.

R.W.Stevenson.
Captain,
Staff Captain, 76th. Infantry Brigade.

16th.June 1918.

Copies to :-
1. 8th.K.O.R.L.Rgt.
2. 2nd.Suffolk Rgt.
3. 1st.Gordon Hldrs.
4. 529th.(E.R.) Fld.Coy.,R.E.
5. 7th.Field Ambce.
6. Brigade Transport Officer.
7. T.O.8th.K.O.R.L.Rgt.
8. T.O.2nd.Suffolk Rgt.
9. 3rd.Division "Q" (for information).
10. War Diary.
11. Do.
12. File.

MARCH TABLE.

Unit Transport. Order of March.	Present Location.	Starting Point.	Hour of Start.	ROUTE.	Destination.	Remarks.
1st.Gordon H.	D.28b.8.7.	LABEUVRIERE - LAPUGNOY Road. Head of Column at D.22a.1.9.	ZERO	LAPUGNOY Station - Level Crossing D.20d.6.8. - Road Junction D.20b.4.4. * - Cross Roads D.25b.2.9. - LOZINGHEM - Camping Ground at C.17b. and C.18a. (Sheet 36 B.) Note:- * Alternative route shown on attached sketch may be used, as Cross Roads D.25b.2.9. is liable to be congested.	Camping Ground at C.17b. and C.18a. (Sheet 36 B.)	
8th.K.O.R.L.	D.24b.5.8.		ZERO plus 4 mins.			
76th.Bde. H.Q.	D.24b.5.8.		Do.			76th.Brigade H.Q.Transport will march under orders of T.O.8th.K.O.R.L. Whole Transport will march under orders of Brigade Transport Officer.
2nd.Suffolk Rgt.	D.18c.1.3.		ZERO plus 8 mins.			

SECRET.
****

Copy No....

76th. INFANTRY BRIGADE OPERATION ORDER NO.116.

Ref.1/20,000 Sheets 36a.S.E. and 36b.N.E.

18th. June 1918.

1. The 8th.K.O.R.L.will relieve the 2nd.Suffolk Regt on the 76th.Brigade front on the night 19th./20th.June.

2. Details of necessary reliefs will be arranged between C.O's concerned, and completion reported to Brigade H.Q.

3. On relief, the 2nd.Suffolk Regt will move into Brigade Reserve in the CHOCQUES Area in the trenches vacated by the 1st.Gordon Hldrs. Battn. H.Q.will be at D.5c.7.9.

4. The 1st.Gordon Hldrs will relieve the 8th.K.O.R.L.in the BATTLE ZONE, and will be disposed as follows:-

1 Coy on Canal Bank
2 Coys in GORDON LINE.
1 Coy in SUFFOLK LINE.
Battn.H.Q. - W.15d.4.7.

5. ACKNOWLEDGE.

J K Meares
Captain,
Issued at 11 p.m. for Brigade Major, 76th. Infantry Brigade.

Copies to:-
1. G.O.C.
2. 8th.K.O.R.L.
3. 2nd.Suff.Regt.
4. 1st.Gordon Hldrs.
5. 76th.T.M.B.
6. Left Gp.R.F.A.
7. " 3rd.Bn.M.G.C.
8. 529th.Fd.Co.R.E.
9. 20th.K.R.R.C.
10. 3rd.Div."G".
11. " "Q".
12. 8th.Inf.Bde.
13. 9th. "
14. 11th. "
15. 7th.Fld.Amb.
16. B.M.
17. S.C.
18. Bde.Sig.Offr.
19. War Diary.
20. "
21. File.

SECRET.
****

Copy No....

76th.INFANTRY BRIGADE OPERATION ORDER No.117.

Ref.1/20,000 Sheets 36a.S.E. and 36b.N.E. — 22nd.June 1918.

1. The 1st.Gordon Hldrs will relieve the 8th.K.O.R.L. on the 76th.Inf.Bde.front on the night 23rd./24th.June.

2. Details of necessary reliefs will be arranged between C.O's concerned and completion reported to Brigade H.Q.

3. On relief, the 8th.K.O.R.L.will move into Brigade Reserve in the CHOCQUES Area in the trenches vacated by the 2nd.Suffolk Regt. Battn.H.Q.will be at D.5c.7.9.

4. The 2nd.Suffolk Regt will relieve the 1st.Gordon Hldrs in the BATTLE ZONE and will be disposed as follows:-

Canal Bank .... 1 Coy plus 1 Platoon.
GORDON LINE .... 2 Coys less 1 Platoon.
SUFFOLK LINE .... 1 Coy

Battn.H.Q. - W.15d.4.7.

5. ACKNOWLEDGE.

Issued at 3 p.m.

[signature]
Captain,
for Brigade Major, 76th. Infantry Brigade.

Copies to:-
1. G.O.C.
2. 8th.K.O.R.L.
3. 2nd.Suffolk Regt.
4. 1st.Gordon Hldrs.
5. 76th.T.M.B.
6. Left Gp.R.F.A.
7. " 3rd.Bn.M.G.C.
8. 529th.Fd.Co.R.E.
9. 20th.K.R.R.C.
10. 3rd.Div."G".
11. " "Q".
12. 8th.Inf.Bde.
13. 9th. "
14. 11th. "
15. 7th.Fld.Amb.
16. B.M.
17. S.C.
18. Bde.Sig.Offr.
19. War Diary.
20. "
21. File.

SECRET.

Copy No. ..

76th. INFANTRY BRIGADE OPERATION ORDER NO.118.

Ref.1/20,000 Sheets 36a.S.E. and 36b.N.E. — 28th.June 1918.

1. The following reliefs will be carried out in the HINGES Sector on the night 29th./30th.June:-

(a) 2nd.Suffolk Regt will relieve 1st.Gordon Hldrs in the FORWARD ZONE.

(b) 8th.K.O.R.L. will relieve 2nd.Suffolk Regt in the BATTLE ZONE, and will be disposed as follows:-

Canal Bank............ 1 Coy (plus 1 Platoon)
GORDON LINE........... 2 Coys (less 1 Platoon).
SUFFOLK LINE.......... 1 Coy.

Battn.H.Q............. W.15b.05.95.

2. On relief, 1st.Gordon Hldrs will move into Brigade Reserve in the CHOCQUES Area, taking over the trenches vacated by 8th.K.O.R.L. Battn.H.Q. will be at D.5c.7.9.

3. Details of reliefs will be arranged between C.O's concerned, and completion reported to Brigade H.Q.

4. Trench Store Cards will be forwarded to Brigade H.Q. with 24 hours of relief.

5. ACKNOWLEDGE.

T.D. Pickard-Cambridge Captain,
for Brigade Major, 76th. Infantry Brigade.

Issued at 3 p.m.

Copies to:-
1. G.O.C.
2. 8th.K.O.R.L.
3. 2nd.Suffolk Regt.
4. 1st.Gordon Hldrs.
5. 76th.T.M.B.
6. Left Gp.R.F.A.
7. " 3rd.Bn.M.G.C.
8. 529th.Fd.Co.R.E.
9. 20th.K.R.R.C.
10. 3rd.Div."G".
11. " "Q".
12. 8th.Inf.Bde.
13. 9th. "
14. 12th. "
15. 7th.Fd.Amb.
16. B.M.
17. S.C.
18. Bde.Sig.Offr.
19. War Diary.
20. "
21. File.

SECRET.
****

INSTRUCTIONS FOR THE MOVE OF 76TH. INFANTRY TRANSPORT IN THE EVENT OF A WITHDRAWAL.

(The Instructions issued on 16th. June 1918 are hereby cancelled and (the following substituted).

MOVE "A".

1. In the event of it becoming necessary to withdraw in a Westerly direction, The Transport of the Brigade will retire from their present positions in accordance with the attached March Table.

2. The Brigade Transport (less Pack Convoy - vide para.6) will move under the orders of Capt.D.R.G.RENFREW, 1st.Bn.Gordon Hldrs., Brigade Transport Officer, who will receive orders direct from 3rd.Division "Q".
On receipt, by telegram, of the code word "PACK", he will warn the Brigade Group Transport to be ready to move off within one hour : this will include the warning of the 529th.(E.R.)Field Coy.,R.E. and No.7 Field Ambulance, but these two units will not actually move except under the order of the C.R.E. and A.D.M.S.
(A copy of this telegram will be repeated by 3rd.Division "Q" to Brigade H.Q. who will repeat to units for information only).

3. Orders for the move of the Divisional Train will be arranged for separately by 3rd.Division "Q" direct.

4. On receipt by the Brigade Transport Officer of the code word "MOVE", he will send orders for units to move to destination "A" in accordance with attached March Table and sketch (Route shewn in RED). The order to move will give the ZERO Hour.

5. When it becomes evident, from the situation either on the Divisional front or on the flanks, that a move Westwards is to be expected, each unit Transport of the Brigade Group, including the 529th.Field Coy.R.E. and No.7 Field Ambulance, will send a mounted or cyclist orderly to report to the Brigade Transport Officer. The orderlies of the 529th.Field Coy.,R.E. and No.7 Field Ambulance will rejoin their units after delivering the instructions to "PACK", but the remaining orderlies will stay with the Brigade Transport Officer throughout the subsequent move.

6. On receipt of the word "PACK", each Battalion will send two limbers and 6 pack animals loaded with S.A.A. from Mobile Reserve (24 boxes per limber and 2 per pack animal) to the Transport Lines of 1st.Bn.Gordon Hrs., D.28b.8.7., with a N.C.O. in charge. The senior of the three N.C.O.'s will take command of the whole convoy and will report at once to Brigade Rear H.Q.(now at No.7 Billet, LABEUVRIERE) to the officer who will be there.
This transport will remain behind under orders of the above officer and will not move with the rest of the Transport.

7. A reserve of rations for 27 men and 30 horses for 48 hours is being formed at the Transport Lines of 1st.Bn.Gordon Hrs. under the Brigade Transport Officer. These rations will be handed over to the Pack Convoy before the Brigade Transport moves.

8. The Brigade and Regimental Transport Officers will, if time permits, reconnoitre the route allotted to them, also the area they will occupy in the new locality.

MOVE "B".

1. If the situation demands a further withdrawal than that laid down in MOVE "A" above, the code word "DOUBLE MOVE" will be sent by 3rd.Division "Q" to the Brigade Transport Officer.

2. On receipt of this code word, all instructions hold as for MOVE "A", except that the march will be continued through to FERFAY (destination "B") as shewn on March Table and attached sketch (in BLUE).

3. On arrival at destination "B", camps and sites may be selected in the neighbourhood of the village, but all billets in the village must be reserved for accommodation of reinforcing troops. In allotting accommodation, Infantry will invariably be given priority over all Transport.

[illegible] Captain,

30th.June 1918. Staff Captain, 76th. Infantry Brigade.

MARCH TABLE.
****

Unit Transport. Order of March.	Present Location.	Starting Point.	Hour of Start.	R O U T E.	Continuation of Route for MOVE "B".	Destination "A".	Destination "B".	Remarks
1st.Gordon Hrs.	D.28b.5.8.	LABEUVRIERE - LAPUGNOY Road.	ZERO	LAPUGNOY Station - Lovel Crossing D.20d.6.8. - Road junction D.20b.4.4.x - Cross Roads D.25b.2.9. - LOZINGHEM.	C.11d.7.0. - thence through C.17a. - C.16d.- C.22a. - C.21b.& c - CAUCHY - A - LA TOUR - FERFAY.	Camping Ground at C.17b. and C.18a. (Shoot 36B.)	FERFAY.	76th.Bde.H.Q. Transport will march under orders of T.O. 1st.Gordon H. Whole Transport will march under Brigade Transport Officer.
76th.Bde. H.Q.	D.29a.1.9.	Head of Column at D.22a.1.9.	ZERO					
2nd.Suffolk Rgt.	D.28c.1.3.		ZERO plus 4 mins.					
* 8th.K.O.R.L. Rgt.	D.29c.4.3.		ZERO plus 8 mins.	x Note:- Alternative route shewn on attached sketch may be used, as Cross Roads D.25b.2.9. are liable to be congested.				* 8th.K.O.R.L. may proceed via PLACE-A-BRUAY-MARLES LES MINES Road and join Bde. Group in rear of 2nd.Suff.Rgt. at D.25b.2.9. at ZERO plus 20 mins.
* see Remarks for alternative route for 8th.K.O.R.L.Rgt.								

Copies to :-

1. 8th.K.O.R.L.Rgt.
2. 2nd.Suffolk Rgt.
3. 1st.Gordon Hldrs.
4. 529th.(E.A.) Field Coy.,R.E.
5. 7th.Field Ambulance
6. Brigade Transport Officer.
7. T.O.8th.K.O.R.L.Rgt.
8. T.O.2nd.Suffolk Rgt.
9. 3rd.Division "Q".
10. War Diary.
11. Do.
12. File.

Ferlay

Allouagne

Labeuvrière

Alternative Route

Cauchy à la Tour

Calonne Ricouart

1st S.H

8th K.O.R

2nd Suff.

Present Transport Lines

Starting Point

Destination "A"

Route "A"

Destination "B"

Route "B"

3rd Division.

B. H. Q.

76th INFANTRY BRIGADE.

JULY 1918.

Brigade Operation Orders & Defence Scheme attached.

Instructions regarding War Diaries and Intelligence Summaries are contained in F. S. Regs., Part II. and the Staff Manual respectively. Title Pages will be prepared in manuscript.

WAR DIARY
or
INTELLIGENCE SUMMARY
(Erase heading not required.)

Headquarters,
76th.Infantry Brigade.

JULY 1918.

Army Form C. 2118.

34

Place	Date 1918.	Hour	Summary of Events and Information	Remarks and references to Appendices
L'ABBAYE, W.25a.0.8.	July 1	10 a.m.	G.O.C.visited 1st.Gordon Hldrs in Reserve.	
		3 p.m.	2/Lt.BOWDEN departed for 6 months tour of duty in England.Duties taken over by Capt. A.H.POLLOCK,M.C.	
			Weather bright and clear.	
	2	5 a.m.	G.O.C.went round front line.	
		1 a.m.	Enemy raided 2nd.Suffolk Regt. They were repulsed leaving 2 dead.	
		1 p.m.	Major PERRY lunched at Bde H.Q.	
	3	10 a.m.	Capt.PLAYFAIR,D.S.O.,M.C.(Bar),returned from leave. Capt.STEVENSON departed to England on staff course at CAMBRIDGE.	
			Capt.FURNELL took over duties of Staff Captain.	
		12 noon	G.O.C.Division visited Bde H.Q.	
			G.O.C.Bde and Capt.PLAYFAIR visited 1st.Gordon Hldrs in Reserve.	
			Gen.MORLAND,XIII Corps visited Bde H.Q.	
	4	4 a.m.	G.O.C.went round the line.	
		11 a.m.	B.M. do.	
		2 p.m.	S.C.attended War Savings Meeting at Division.	
			Weather bright and clear.	
	5	2 p.m.	S.C.and Capt.A.H.POLLOCK,M.C.,visited Battn.H.Q.in the line.	
		3 p.m.	Major ROOS,8th.K.O.R.L.reported to Bde H.Q.for duty,stayed to dinner and went to 8th.K.O.R.L. Details.	
			Maj.PEARSON and Capt.GAMMELL called at Bde on way to line.	
			8th.K.O.R.L.relieved 2nd.Suffolk Regt in forward zone.	
			1st.Gordon Hldrs relieved 8th.K.O.R.L.in Battle Zone.	
			Weather still fine.	
	6	4 a.m.	8th.K.O.R.L.captured 1 O.R.of the 23rd.R.I.R.,12th.Res.Div. (Normal).	
		12 noon	Gen.BIRDWOOD,G.O.C.,Fifth Army,visited Bde Staff with G.O.C.Division.	
	7		S.C.and G.O.C.visited 2nd.Suffolk Regt in training.	
			S.C.and B.M.visited Battn.in the line.	

2449 Wt. W14957/M90 750,000 1/16 J.B.C. & A. Forms/C.2118/12.

Army Form C. 2118.

Instructions regarding War Diaries and Intelligence Summaries are contained in F. S. Regs., Part II. and the Staff Manual respectively. Title Pages will be prepared in manuscript.

WAR DIARY
or
INTELLIGENCE SUMMARY
(Erase heading not required.)

Place	Date 1918.	Hour	Summary of Events and Information	Remarks and references to Appendices
L'ABBAYE, W.25a.0.8.	July 8	9 a.m.	G.O.C.and S.C.inspected transport of units in BOIS DES DAMES.	
		4 p.m.	G.S.O.1 and G.S.O.3 visited Bde H.Q.	
	9		Gen.MORLAND inspected Battn.in Reserve,2nd.Suffolk Regt.during training,attended by G.O.C. Divn.,G.O.C.Bde.,and B.M.	
			Gen.MORLAND inspected the transport of units in the afternoon. S.C.and G.O.C.Bde attended.	
			Capt.A.H.POLLOCK,M.C.,and Lt.TAYLOR went round the line and visited Battn.H.Qrs.	
	10	4 a.m..	B.M.went round the line.	
			8th.K.O.R.L.raided and captured 2 O.R.,23rd.R.I.R.(Normal).	
		10.30 a.m.	G.O.C.Divn.,called at Bde.	
	11	4 a.m.	G.O.C.went round line.	
		8 p.m.	Lt.Col.,STUBBS and Adjutant came to dinner on way to line.	
		11 p.m.	1st.Gordon Hldrs relieved 8th.K.O.R.L.in front line,night 11/12th. 2nd.Suffolk Regt relieved 1st.Gordon Hldrs in support. 8th.K.O.R.L.went back to ST.SAUVEUR.	
	12	4 a.m.	B.M.went round line.	
		11 a.m.	Gen.ELLIOT called at Bde.	
		2.30 p.m.	B.M.and Capt.POLLOCK visited Battn.H.Q.in line.	
	13	11 a.m.	Gen.STEWART,XIII Corps,and Maj.CARTHEN,Wing Cmdr.,R.A.F.,visited Bde.	
		8 p.m.	Lt.,Col.,PERRY,M.C.,and Maj.MORGAN,M.C.,8th.K.O.R.L.dined at Bde H.Q.	
	14	4 a.m.	S.C.and G.O.C.went round the line.	
		8 p.m.	Gen.KENTISH and Col.MUNROE,Gordon Hldrs.,visited Bde and stayed to dinner.	
	15	12.30 noon	G.O.C.and S.C.visited left Brigade.	
	16		Fine. Nothing to report.	

2449 Wt. W14957/M90 750,000 1/16 J.B.C. & A. Forms/C.2118/12.

Army Form C. 2118.

WAR DIARY
or
INTELLIGENCE SUMMARY
(Erase heading not required.)

Instructions regarding War Diaries and Intelligence Summaries are contained in F. S. Regs., Part II. and the Staff Manual respectively. Title Pages will be prepared in manuscript.

Place	Date 1918.	Hour	Summary of Events and Information	Remarks and references to Appendices
L'ABBAYE, W.25a.0.8.	July 17	5 a.m.	B.M.went round the line.	
		3 p.m.	Capt.POLLOCK went round line.	
		2 a.m.	2nd.Suffolk Regt relieved 1st.Gordon Hldrs.,8th.K.O.R.L.relieved 2nd.Suffolk Regt in Battle Zone.	
	18	5 a.m.	G.O.C.and S.C.went round the line.	
			Capt.PICKNARD-CAMBRIDGE went on leave.	
			G.O.C.Divn.,and Capt.GOULDING dined at Bde.	
	19	5 a.m.	B.M.went round the line.	
		10 a.m.	Gen.CHARLES attached to Bde in order to take over whilst Gen.PORTER goes on leave.	
		5 p.m.	Col.HERBERT A/G.O.C.8th.Bde called and stayed to tea.	
			Showery during day.	
	20	5 a.m.	Gen.PORTER and S.C.went round line.	
			Lt.Col.PERRY and Major ROOS,8th.K.O.R.L.came to lunch at Bde.	
			Q.M.8th.K.O.R.L.called on way to line.	
			M.G.Battn.relieved,and Capt.BLOWER M.G.C.took over.	
			Thunderstorm during afternoon.	
	21	10 a.m.	Gen.PORTER handed over to Gen.CHARLES and proceeded on leave.	
		12 noon	G.O.C.Div.visited Bde and conferred with G.O.C.	
		3 p.m.	Col.PRAGNELL called.	
			Gen.CHARLES went round line.	
		2 p.m.	S.C.attended conference re Corps Horse Show.	
			Weather good,visibility fair.	
	22	5 a.m.	B.M.went round line.	
		10 a.m.	Bde I.O.and Div.I.O.visited line.	
		3 p.m.	G.O.C.went round line with Capt.BLOWER,O.C.,M.G.C.	
		4 p.m.	G.S.O.3 visited Bde.	

2449 Wt. W14957/M90 750,000 1/16 J.B.C. & A. Forms/C.2118/12.

Army Form C. 2118.

Instructions regarding War Diaries and Intelligence Summaries are contained in F. S. Regs., Part II. and the Staff Manual respectively. Title Pages will be prepared in manuscript.

WAR DIARY
or
INTELLIGENCE SUMMARY
(Erase heading not required.)

4.

Place	Date 1918.	Hour	Summary of Events and Information	Remarks and references to Appendices
L'ABBAYE, W.25a.0.8.	July 23	10 a.m.	G.O.C.and B.M.visited Battns in the line.	
		11 a.m.	Col.PRAGNELL called to say goodbye before going tonthe 3rd.Cav.Divn.	
		11.30 a.m.	Col.KELLY,Fifth Army and Maj.HENDERSON,XIII Corps visited Bde H.Q.	
		5 p.m.	G.O.C.and Capt.POLLOCK visited Left Bde H.Q.	
		12.30 a.m.	8th.K.O.R.L.relieved the 2nd.Suffolk Regt in Forward Zone.	
		12.15 a.m.	1st.Gordon Hldrs relieved 8th.K.O.R.L in the Battle Zone.	
			Weather showery,cleared up later in the day.	
	24	12.30 noon	Gen.BIRDWOOD and G.O.C.Divn.called at Bde H.Q.	
		2 p.m.	G.O.C.and B.M.went round the line.	
			Capt.FURNELL attended Bde Conference re Corps Horse Show.	
		4 p.m.	O.C.,M.G.C.called re M.G's on the Canal Bank.	
		8.30 p.m.	G.O.C.went round the line with Lt.Col.PERRY.	
			Weather dull in morning,bright and sunny in afternoon.	
	25	10 a.m.	G.O.C.visited 2nd.Suffolk Regt on Range.	
		2 p.m.	Capt.CHIPPER came to take over B.M. from Capt.PLAYFAIR.	
			S.C.visited Bde details.	
		5 p.m.	B.M.and Capt.CHIPPER visited 2nd.Suffolk Regt in Reserve.	
			Weather showery.	
	26	10 a.m.	G.O.C.visited Battns in the line.	
		11 a.m.	XXXXXXXXXXXXXXX.A.A.& Q.M.G.visited H.Q.	
		8 p.m.	G.O.C.and B.M.went to 2nd.Suffolk Regt to dinner.	
			Weather wet.	
	27	8 a.m.	2nd.Suffolk Regt went to AUCHEL Training Area and returned owing to bad weather.	
			Sig.Offr.visited Battns in the line.	
			Capt.RUSSELL,D.S.O.,M.C.,attached to Bde for commencement of Staff Course.	
			Weather wet and showery all day.	

Army Form C. 2118.

WAR DIARY
or
INTELLIGENCE SUMMARY
(Erase heading not required.)

Instructions regarding War Diaries and Intelligence Summaries are contained in F. S. Regs., Part II. and the Staff Manual respectively. Title Pages will be prepared in manuscript.

Place	Date 1918	Hour	Summary of Events and Information	Remarks and references to Appendices
			5.	
L'ABBAYE, W.25a.0.8.	July 28	8 a.m.	S.C.and G.O.C.attended Divl.,Competition preparatory to Corps Horse Show and competition.	
		12 noon	Lt.Col.VIGERS,Corps Signal Officer,called at Bde re laying of cables.	
		2 p.m.	2nd.in command M.G.C.,and O.C.,3rd.Div.Sig.Coy.,called at Bde.	
		9.30 p.m.	G.O.C.went round outpost line with Lt.Col.PERRY M.C.,8th.K.O.R.L.	
	29	9 a.m.	Capt.PLAYFAIR,D.S.O.,M.C.,(Bar) departed for England reported Senior Officers' School, ALDERSHOT as Instructor.	
		9.30 a.m.	G.O.C.Divn.,and G.O.C.Bde went round the line.	
		12 mid.	8th.K.O.R.L.relieved 2nd.Suffolk Regt in the Forward Zone,1st.Gordon Hldrs relieved 8th.K.O.R.L.in the Battle Zone.	
	30	7 a.m.	S.C.went round the line.	
		5 p.m.	XIII Corps Cmdr visited Bde.	
	31	2 p.m.	B.M.reconnoitred SHROPSHIRE LINE.	
		3.30 p.m.	S.C.spoke to 8th.K.O.R.L.re War Saving Certificates.	
			G.O.C.visited Battns in the line.	

** ** ** ** ** **

C. C. Stubbs Lt. Colonel,
Commanding 76th.Infantry Brigade.

2449 Wt. W14957/M90 750,000 1/16 J.B.C. & A. Forms/C.2118/12.

CASUALTIES MONTH OF JULY 1918.

** ** ** ** ** ** **

	Killed.	Wounded.	Missing.	Gassed.
Officers	3			
O.R.	14	72		

** ** ** **

SECRET.
****

Copy No....

76th.INFANTRY BRIGADE OPERATION ORDER NO.119.

Reference 1/20,000 Sheets 36a.S.E.
and 36b.N.E.

4th.July 1918.

1. The following reliefs will be carried out in the HINGES Section on the night July 5th./6th.:-

(a) 8th.K.O.R.L.will relieve 2nd.Suffolk Regt in the FORWARD ZONE.
(b) 1st.Gordon Hldrs will relieve 8th.K.O.R.L.in the BATTLE ZONE.

2. On relief,2nd.Suffolk Regt will move into Brigade Reserve in the Area vacated by 1st.Gordon Hldrs. Battn.H.Q.,ST.SAUVEUR,D.5c.7.9.

3. Details of relief will be arranged between C.O's concerned,and completion reported to Brigade H.Q.

4. Trench Store Cards will reach Brigade H.Q.within 24 hours of relief.

5. ACKNOWLEDGE.

[signature]
Captain,
Brigade Major,76th.Infantry Brigade.

Issued at 10 a.m.

Copies to:-
1. G.O.C.
2. 8th.K.O.R.L.
3. 2nd.Suffolk Regt.
4. 1st.Gordon Hldrs.
5. 76th.T.M.B.
6. Left Gp.R.F.A.
7. " 3rd.Bn.M.G.C.
8. 529th.Fd.Co.R.E.
9. 20th.K.R.R.C.
10. 3rd.Div."G".
11. " "Q".
12. 8th.Inf.Bde.
13. 9th. "
14. 12th. "
15. 7th.Field Amb.
16. B.M.
17. S.C.
18. Bde.Sig.Offr.
19. War Diary.
20. "

SECRET.

Copy No. 19..

76th. INFANTRY BRIGADE OPERATION ORDER No.120.

Reference 1/20,000 Sheets 36a.S.E.
and 36b.N.E.

1. The following reliefs will be carried out in the HINGES Section on the night July 11th./12th.:-

(a) 1st.Gordon H'ders will relieve 8th.K.O.R.L. in the FORWARD ZONE.
(b) 2nd.Suffolk Regt will relieve 1st.Gordon H'drs in the BATTLE ZONE.

2. On relief, 8th.K.O.R.L.will move into Brigade Reserve in the area vacated by 2nd.Suffolk Regt.

3. Details of relief will be arranged between C.O's concerned, and completion reported to Brigade H.Q.

4. Trench Store Cards will reach Brigade H.Q.within 24 hours of relief.

5. ACKNOWLEDGE.

[signature]
Captain,
Brigade Major, 76th. Infantry Brigade.

Issued at 3 p.m.

Copies to:-
1. G.O.C.
2. 8th.K.O.R.L.
3. 2nd.Suffolk Regt
4. 1st.Gordon H'ldrs
5. 76th.T.M.B.
6. Left Gp.R.F.A.
7. " M.G.C.
8. 529th.Fd.Co.R.E.
9. 20th.K.R.R.C.
10. 3rd.Div."G",
11. " "Q".
12. 8th.Inf.Bde.
13. 9th. "
14. 10th. "
15. 7th.Field Amb.
16. D.M.
17. S.C.
18. Bde.Sig.Offr.
19. War Diary.
20. "
21. File.

SECRET.
****

Copy No..19....

76TH. INFANTRY BRIGADE OPERATION ORDER NO. 121.

Reference 1/20,000 Sheets 36a. S.E.
and 36b. N.E.

16th. July 1918.

1. The following reliefs will be carried out in the HINGES Section on the night July 17th/18th :-

(a). 2nd.Suffolk Rgt. will relieve 1st.Gordon Hldrs. in the FORWARD ZONE.

(b). 8th.K.O.R.L.Rgt. will relieve 2nd.Suffolk Rgt. in the BATTLE ZONE.

2. On relief, 1st.Gordon Hldrs. will move into Brigade Reserve in the area vacated by 8th. K.O.R.L.Rgt.

3. Details of relief will be arranged between C.O.'s concerned, and completion reported to Brigade H.Q.

4. Trench Store Cards will reach Brigade H.Q. within 24 hours of relief.

5. All aeroplane photographs will be handed over to relieving Units.

6. ACKNOWLEDGE.

R. Playfair
Captain,
Brigade Major, 76th. Infantry Brigade.

Issued at 3 p.m.

Copies to :-
1. G.O.C.
2. 8th.K.O.R.L.
3. 2nd.Suffolk Rgt.
4. 1st.Gordon Hrs.
5. 76th.T.M.Bty.
6. Left Gp.R.F.A.
7. " " M.G.C.
8. 529th.Fld.Coy.R.E.
9. 20th.K.R.R.C.
10. 3rd.Div. "G".
11. 3rd.Div. "Q".
12. 8th.Inf.Bde.
13. 9th.Inf.Bde.
14. 10th.Inf.Bde.
15. 7th.Fld.Ambce.
16. B.M.
17. S.C.
18. Bde.Sig.Off.
19. War Diary.
20. Do.
21. File.

SECRET.

Copy No. 18

76th. INFANTRY BRIGADE OPERATION ORDER NO. 122.

Reference 1/20,000 Sheets 36a. S.E. and 36b. N.E.

22nd. July 1918.

1. The following reliefs will be carried out in the HINGES Section on the night July 23rd./24th.:-

(a). 8th.K.O.R.L.Rgt. will relieve 2nd.Suffolk Rgt. in the FORWARD ZONE.

(b). 1st.Gordon Hldrs. will relieve 8th.K.O.R.L.Rgt. in the Battle ZONE.

2. On relief, 2nd.Suffolk Rgt. will move into Brigade Reserve in the area vacated by 1st.Gordon Hldrs.

3. Details of relief will be arranged between C.O.'s concerned, and completion reported to Brigade H.Q.

4. Trench Store Cards will reach Brigade H.Q. within 24 hours of relief.

5. ACKNOWLEDGE.

[signature]
Captain,
Brigade Major, 76th. Infantry Brigade.

Issued at 10 a.m.

Copies to :-

1. G.O.C.
2. 8th.K.O.R.L.
3. 2nd.Suffolk Rgt.
4. 1st.Gordon Hrs.
5. 76th.T.M.Bty.
6. Left Gp.,R.F.A.
7. ~~7~~
8. 529th.Fld.Coy.,R.E.
9. 20th.K.R.R.C.
10. 3rd.Div. "Q".
11. 3rd.Div. "G".
12. 8th. Inf.Bde.
13. 11th. " "
14. 7th.Fld.Ambce.
15. B.M.
16. S.C.
17. Bde.Sig.Off.
18. War Diary.
19. Do.
20. File.
21. Left Gp.3rd.Bn.M.G.C.

SECRET.

Copy No. 18......

76th. INFANTRY BRIGADE OPERATION ORDER NO. 123.

Refernnce 1/20,000 Sheets 36a.S.E.
and 36b.N.E.

27th. July 1918.

1. The following reliefs will be carried out in the HINGES Section on the night July 29th./30th.:-

(a). 1st.Gordon Hldrs will relieve 8th.K.O.R.L.Rgt. in the FORWARD ZONE.

(b). 2nd.Suffolk Rgt. will relieve 1st.Gordon Hldrs. in the BATTLE ZONE.

2. On relief, 8th.K.O.R.L.Rgt. will move into Brigade Reserve in the area vacated by 2nd.Suffolk Rgt.

3. Details of relief will be arranged between C.O.'s concerned, and completion reported to Brigade H.Q.

4. Trench Store Cards will reach Brigade H.Q. within 24 hours of relief.

5. ACKNOWLEDGE.

C. Chipp[illegible]
Captain,
Brigade Major, 76th. Infantry Brigade.

Issued at 3 p.m.

Copies to :-

1. G.O.C.
2. 8th.K.O.R.L.Rgt.
3. 2nd.Suffolk Rgt.
4. 1st.Gordon Hldrs.
5. 76th.T.M.Bty.
6. Left.Gp.R.F.A.
7. " " 3rd.Bn.M.G.C.
8. 529th. Fld.Coy.,R.E.
9. 20th.K.R.R.C.
10. 3rd.Div."Q".
11. 3rd.Div."G".
12. 9th.Inf.Bde.
13. 11th. " "
14. 7th.Fld.Ambce.
15. B.M.
16. S.C.
17. Bde.Sig.Off.
18. War Diary.
19. Do.
20. File.

SECRET.
****

Copy No....

76th.INFANTRY BRIGADE
PROVISIONAL DEFENCE SCHEME (HINGES Sector).

** ** ** ** ** ** **

Reference Sheets 36a.S.E.) 1/20,000.
36b.N.E.)

1. Provisional Defence Scheme issued under B/2754 of June 19th. 1918 is cancelled.

2. BOUNDARIES.

The Boundary between 76th.Inf.Bde.and the Brigade on the right is:- Bend of road at W.5d.55.10. to W.11a.55.00. (road exclusive to 76th.Inf.Bde.) - W.16a.92.35. - round S.E.edge of HINGES WOOD - W.16c.9.8. - W.25.central.

The boundary between the 76th.Inf.Bde.and the right Brigade of the 4th.Division on the left is:- Q.34d.45.25. - W.8d.6.7. - W.13a.90.25. - W.13c.4.8. - V.27a.1.0.

3. DEFENCES.

The Defences are organised into two Zones:-

(a) A Battle Zone.
(b) A Rear Zone.

(a) The Battle Zone. Consists of the front system,2nd.and 3rd. Systems.

(i) The Front System. Comprises all defences in front of and including the ABERDEEN & CANAL LINES.

(ii) The 2nd.System. Comprises all those defences in rear of the front system up to and including the DUMBARTON & SHROPSHIRE LINES.

(iii) The 3rd.System. Comprises all defences in the REVEILLON - CHOCQUES LINE.

The BETHUNE SWITCH,BETHUNE RETRENCHMENT and CLARENCE SWITCH, form switches between the 2nd.and 3rd.Systems.
BETHUNE RETRENCHMENT includes SHELL TRENCH,VENDIN TRENCH and detached posts in front,also CEMETERY TRENCH and CEMETERY SUPPORT.

(b) The Rear Zone includes all defences in rear of the "BATTLE ZONE".

(c) The "Line of Retention" in the "Battle Zone" will be the PERTH LINE & CANAL LINE.
For the maintenance of this line,every means at the disposal of the Division will be employed.

(d) The following is a brief description of the REVEILLON - CHOCQUES LINE,CLARENCE SWITCH & LILLERS - HOUCHIN LINE.

(i) The REVEILLON - CHOCQUES LINE consists of a front and support line of breastwork and trench and a system of trenches on the forward and reverse slopes of CHOCQUES HILL,which is an important tactical feature as it dominates the whole of the surrounding country.
The CLARENCE SWITCH runs along the Western Bank of the CLARENCE River,the Northern portion only has been constructed, but the river bank itself is defensible.

contd.... (d).

(ii) The LILLERS - HOUCHIN LINE consists of front,support and reserve lines of trench and breastwork.
The main tactical features in this line are the Spur in D.18 and E.13.,the village and chateau of LABEUVRIERE,and the Spur in D.10.

(e) LOCALITIES.
In addition to the various systems of defence in the "Battle" and "Rear" Zones,it is the intention to organise a series of localities and keeps capable of all-round defence. The provision of shell proof accomodation for the garrison is an essential factor in defences of this nature. Many Concrete Machine Gun Nests and Shelters have been completed and others are under construction,and when this work is further advanced, the question of grouping them to form localities will be considered.

4. DISPOSITIONS.

(a) One Battn.in advance of the "Line of Retention"......... 2 Coys in front line, (EDINBURGH LINE).
2 Coys in support in trenches from W.11b.15.70.to W.4a.4.3. (ABERDEEN LINE).

Battalion H.Q......... W.10a.1.1.

(b) One Battn.in "Line of Retention" and 2nd.System....... 1½ Coys in Canal Bank.
1½ Coys in GORDON LINE.
½ Coy in SUFFOLK LINE.

Battalion H.Q......... W.15b.10.95.

(c) One Battn.in rear of 2nd.System...................... Coys in CHOCQUES Area.

Battalion H.Q......... D.5c.7.9.

(d) 76th.L.T.M.Bty.......... 4 guns inposition.

No.of guns.	Location.
2	W.4b.3.2.
2	W.10c.65.65.

5. PRINCIPLES OF DEFENCE.

(a) The rôle of the troops holding the EDINBURGH & ABERDEEN LINES is to break up and disorganise a hostile attack before it reaches the "Line of Retention".
Immediate local counter-attacks by the troops holding these two lines will be delivered on the responsibility of the local commander on the spot to recapture any portion of these lines which may be lost.
The enemy must not be pernitted to approach the Canal.
No ground will be given up and every foot of ground must be stubbornly contested.

(b) The "Line of Retention" will be held at all costs and all the efforts of the Division will be concentrated to this end.

contd...... Para.5.

(c) Troops in and in rear of the "Line of Retention" will not be used for the purpose of regaining ground in advance of this line without orders from higher authority.

(d) Commanders of Battalions holding the EDINBURGH & ABERDEEN LINES will prepare schemes for immediate counter-attacks to regain any portion of these lines which may be lost.

(e) Troops holding the GORDON & SUFFOLK LINES must reconnoitre all wire entanglements between them and the CANAL LINE,and must know the positions of gaps so as to be able to counter-attack through the obstacle.

(f) All Commanders will ensure that the troops under their command are fully acquainted with their rôle in the event of attack, and that the troops in reserve are able to take up their allotted positions in the shortest time possible.

6- ACTION IN CASE OF ATTACK.

In the event of information being received to justify the assumption that an attack is imminent,the following action will be taken:-

(a) All troops will maintain enhanced state of readiness and vigilance,and Brigade Reserve will be prepared to move at short notice.

(b) The Battalion in the 2nd.System will detail guards to ensure that no transport is permitted to move on the roads East of the SHROPSHIRE LINE.

All roads in the front and 2nd.Systems will be blocked and knife rests placed in position across them.

(c) Battalion Commanders will allocate to specified companies the responsibility for blocking each road should occasion arise.

(d) A contact aeroplane provided with smoke bombs will be sent out by the Corps to fly over enemy's lines.

In the event of attack:-

(a) Should parties of the enemy gain a footing on the S.W.bank of the Canal,they must be immediately counter-attacked and driven back by the two companies in the GORDON & SUFFOLK LINES. It will not, however,be the rôle of the Battalion in the 2nd.System to carry out a counter-attack on a large scale; this will be the duty of the Reserve Battalion if necessary.

(b) On receipt of the order "MAN BATTLE STATIONS",the Reserve Battalion in the CHOCQUES Area will occupy the SUFFOLK LINE with 2 Coys,and the SHROPSHIRE LINE with 2 Coys.

This Battalion will be ready to make a counter-attack should the enemy succeed in reaching the Northern slopes of HINGES HILL. This will probably be best accomplished by the 2 Coys in SHROPSHIRE LINE advancing round the Western side of HINGES and taking the enemy in flank,the 2 Coys in SUFFOLK LINE co-operating in this manoeuvre.

The direction of the counter-attack must,however,be governed by the situation. It is possible the enemy may force a crossing through HINGETTE,in which case the counter-attack will be made over the ridge in W.16b.

contd..... para.6.

(c) All working parties in the forward area will report for orders to the Commander of the nearest troops, who will notify their location to Brigade H.Q.

7. S.O.S.

(a) The "S.O.S." is only to be used when an infantry attack developes. The signal will only be sent by the direct order of an officer or platoon commander.

(b) Should the enemy commence an intense bombardment, our artillery and machine guns will reply with their counter-preparation programme.

(c) All available means of communication will be employed in sending an "S.O.S." message. The "S.O.S." takes priority over all other messages.

(d) The "S.O.S." Signal will be repeated at Battn.H.Q. and at the Artillery O.P. Battn.Commanders will arrange for the necessary relay posts in advance of Battn.H.Q. in case of foggy weather.

(e) The artillery must be informed immediately its fire is no longer required.

8. SHORTEN RANGE SIGNAL.

In the event of the enemy reaching the Canal, a "SHORTEN RANGE" Signal consisting of a rocket fired from a mortar, and bursting into 3 lights suspended vertically - GREEN, RED, GREEN - will be sent up at Forward Battn.H.Q. and at the Artillery O.P.

On this Signal, our artillery and machine guns will bring in their barrages to 100 yards N.E. of the Canal.

9. RED SMOKE BOMB FROM AEROPLANE.

A RED smoke bomb dropped by one of our aeroplanes during active operations, indicates that the enemy is forming up for attack on the front opposite which the bomb is dropped.

10. FLANK CO-OPERATION.

(a) In the event of an attack, and it becoming evident that the attack is confined to one flank of the Division only, on to the front of a neighbouring Division, it may be necessary to send one or more of the Battalions in Brigade Reserve to the threatened area.

(b) If such a case involves the use of two or more Battalions, the Commander and Staff will be nominated from Divisional H.Q.

(c) To assist the right flank Division, the reserve Battalions of this Division might be required to move to concentration areas in the QUARRY LOCALITY, E.23d., South of BETHUNE, or CANAL DOCK LOCALITY, E.6, N.E. of BETHUNE. These localities and approaches to them will be reconnoitred by a proportion of Officers and N.C.O's of each Battn. whenever out of the line.

contd..... Para.10.

(d) To assist the left flank Division,the Battalion in reserve of the left and centre Brigades could move from the SHROPSHIRE LINE via LANCASTER & SUFFOLK LINES towards LES HARISOIRS. The remaining reserve Battn.would then,if available,be moved to the SHROPSHIRE LINE in reserve.

11. ANTI-GAS DEFENCE.

(a) The orders contained in Appendix IV of S.S.534 will be strictly adhered to.

Attention is directed to S.S.212 "Yellow Cross Gas Shell and the measures to be taken to counteract their effects".

The most careful training in anti-gas measures and gas discipline will be carried out by all units.

All troops in the Division will wear their gas masks for 1 hour at least twice in each week,and will be worked in them in the use of the weapons with which they are armed.

All Headquarters,or at least a portion of all Headquarters, will be made as gas proof as possible under the supervision of the Divisional Gas Officer,who will carry out frequent inspection. Battalions in Brigade Reserve will be practised in marching in their gas masks.

(b) When an area is shelled with "Yellow Cross" Gas,the gas officer of the unit or units concerned will at once carry out an investigation and advise his Commanding Officer as to whether the concentration of gas is sufficient,or is likely to become sufficient, to warrant the evacuation of the area.

(c) When an area is shelled with gas,Commanders of units in the area affected will at once order respirators to be adjusted and will,when possible,and the tactical situation permits,move their troops to a flank to windward of the shelled area.

The affected area will,NOT be re-occupied until declared free of gas by the gas officer of the unit concerned.

If,for tactical reasons,it is considered essential that posts should be left in the area affected,these posts must be constantly relieved.

It must be borne in mind that when the enemy bombards an area with gas previous to attack,he will rarely advance over the gas affected area but will attempt to gain ground on the flanks. The flanks of the bombarded area must,therefore,be carefully watched.

(d) (i) Reports of gas shelling will be at once forwarded by units to the next higher formation and to the Divisional Gas Officer and will give the following particulars in so far as they can be ascertained:-

(a) Nature of gas.
(b) Degree of intensity in terms of the approximate number of rounds falling per minute.
(c) Area affected.
(d) Suspected location of active hostile batteries.

Reports of gas bombardments with the above information will be at once forwarded to the counter-battery office by Divisional H.Q.

(ii) Reports of any gas shelling of 500 rounds and over will, invariably be passed to all units within 2,000 yards radius of the area affected.

contd.... Para.11.

(iii) Sentries will be posted round an area contaminated by "Yellow Cross" Gas, whose duties will be to warn anyone entering the area to adjust their box respirators.
Sentries will not be withdrawn until the gas officers of the units concerned have declared the area free from gas.

12. ANTI-AIRCRAFT DEFENCE.

(a) The Brigade is responsible for the First and Second Lines of A.A. Defence by Vickers and Lewis Guns.

1st. Line .... In the CANAL LINE.
2nd. Line .... In the SUFFOLK LINE.

(b) In each line guns will be placed in pairs at intervals of 1,000 yards. If single guns are employed these should not be plaaed at greater intervals than 500 yards.

(c) At each position a copy of the orders for A.A. Lewis Guns will be kept.

(d) In addition to the above, all units will be responsible for the A.A. protection of their billets, camps, horse lines and dumps.

C. Chipp[illegible] Captain,
29/7/18. Brigade Major, 76th. Infantry Brigade.

Copies to:-
1. 8th. K.O.R.L.
2. 2nd. Suffolk Regt.
3. 1st. Gordon Hldrs.
4. 76th. T.M.B.
5. Left Gp. R.F.A.
6. " 3rd. Bn. M.G.C.
7. 529th. (E.R.) Fd. Co. R.E.
8. 3rd. Div. "G".
9. 9th. Inf. Bde.
10. 11th. "
11.)
12.)
13.) - Retained.
14.)

Copy of Appendix "A" (Ammunition to be maintained in the line) to all recipients of 76th. Inf. Bde. Provisional Defence Schbme.

** ** ** ** ** ** **

APPENDIX "A".

****

AMMUNITION TO BE MAINTAINED IN THE LINE.

** ** ** ** **

The following amounts of S.A.A.and Grenades will be maintained in the line:-

1. IN THE TRENCHES.

180 rounds S.A.A.per rifle.
20 drums S.A.A.per Lewis-Gun-actually with guns.
1060 rounds S.A.A.per Lewis Gun and spare drums at,or near, Company Headquarters.
4 Grenades per man.

2. ON THE MAN.

120 rounds S.A.A.

3. IN BATTALION DUMPS.

80 rounds S.A.A.per rifle.
1000 rounds S.A.A.per Lewis Gun.
2 Grenades per man.

This must be suitably protected from damage by shell fire.

** ** ** ** ** **

3rd Division

WAR DIARY & APPENDICES

B. H. Q.

76th INFANTRY BRIGADE

AUGUST 1918.

3rd Division.

B. H. Q.

76th INFANTRY BRIGADE.

AUGUST 1 9 1 8

Appendices under separate cover

1.

WAR DIARY

H.Q., 76th Inf. Brigade — August 1918

Place	Date 1918	Hour	Summary of Events & Information	Remarks etc
L'ABBAYE	August			
	1	9.30pm.	G.O.C. attended demonstration of platoon & company in attack at WINGHEM	
		8.30pm.	Signalling Officer visited communications of forward Coy.	
	2	9am.	G.O.C. visited Bn. in reserve to see training	
			B.M. went round line. 8. K.O.R.L. relieved 1st. Gdn. Hdrs., 2. Suff. Regt remained in Canal Bank. O.O. for relief issued at 3pm	Ref. O.O. No 134 App. No C1
		2p.m	I.O. went round line.	
			20th K.R.R.C. started work on trenches in Brigade sector.	
	3	6am.	General Charles departed to England to take over command of 25th Div.	
			Lt. Col. Stubbs, D.S.O., took over temporary command of Brigade.	
			Staff Capt. attended Divisional Horse Show.	
			Capt. Rokhard-Cambridge returned from leave.	
	4		Reserve Battn of Bde relieved by 3. Worcester Regt and 8. K.O.R.L. went to HOZINGHEM and took over the billets vacated by the 8. Glos. Orders for relief of 3. Div by 19th Div published also by Bde	O.O. No 135 app. No. C2
	5		G.O.C. 58th Inf. Bde, Battn Cmdrs and Company Officers visited various Headquarters before taking over the line.	O.O. No 136 app. No C3 Administve Instns C4
			General Porter returned from leave. Col. Stubbs, D.S.O., resumed command of 2nd. Suffolk Regt.	March Table appx No. C5
			The Germans were reported to have retired to their rear lines in front of our sector. Patrols of Gordon Hldrs were sent out to ascertain this. He had gone back on the front of the Division on our left but remained still on our front.	
			Capt. Cambridge went ahead to billet for Bde. Detailed orders for relief of Bde published (by 58th Bde)	O.O. No 137 app. No C6
AMETTES	6		On the night Aug. 6/7th, 1st. Gdn. Hldrs were relieved by the 2. Wiltshire Regt in the front line. 2 Suff. Regt were relieved by 9th R. Welch Regt. 76th L.T.M.B. by the 58th L.T.M.B. Relief went off well. On relief the Battns. were given hot tea before entraining.	Entraining Instructions appx No C7

2.

Place.	Date	Time	Summary of events and information.	Remarks etc
AMETTES			Battns were in busses and clear of reserve areas by 5am: arrived in new billetting areas at 6.15am.	
			2nd Suffolk Regt took over billets at FANCQUENHEM	
			1. Gordon Hdrs " " " " LIERES.	
			76. T.M. Bty " " " " AMETTES.	
			76. Bde H.Q " " " " "	
			E. Yorks. " " " " AMES.	
			The billets of the Battns were fair: those of Brigade bad.	
	7.		Units settled in billets and cleaned up.	
			G.O.C. & C.O.s of Battns held conference at Brigade re training	
	8.		Units bathed and received clean clothing.	
			Commenced Training.	
			G.O.C. visited units in training.	
	9	2.30pm.	Army Commander visited units. G.O.C. visited units in training.	
	10		Units trained until 11am and at 3pm were lined up on the RELY-FERFAY road about ½ mile SE of cross roads at BELLERY for inspection by the King. The G.O.C was presented to the King who arrived at 3.30pm. G.O.C. dined with XIII Corps.	
	11		Usual church parade. G.O.C. visited units in recreation during the afternoon and dined with 1st Gordon Hdrs. Orders were received to move at 12 midnight 11/12th but were cancelled later in day.	
	12	9.am	Corps Horse Show. Training by units was continued, but C.O.s were allowed to send men whom they could spare from training. 1. Gordon Hdrs were runners up in Tug of War.	
		10am.	G.O.C. and B.M. visited units in training.	
			Orders were received for moving on the 14th: units & first line transport by rail, rest of transport by road. Destination at present not published.	

3

Instructions regarding War Diaries and Intelligence Summaries are contained in F. S. Regs., Part II. and the Staff Manual respectively. Title pages will be prepared in manuscript.

WAR DIARY
or
INTELLIGENCE SUMMARY.
(Erase heading not required.)

Army Form C. 2118.

Place	Date	Hour	Summary of Events and Information	Remarks and references to Appendices
Amettes	13th	7am	S.C. left to go on ahead. Bde transport less cookers and 1 limber per Bn paraded at NEDON cross roads at 11.45 pm. Marched to a large field near ANVIN where the day was spent.	O.O. 128 APPX. C 9 O.O. 129. 11 C 10 ENTRAINING & MARCH TABLE
SUS-ST LEGER	14th	9am	Entraining of Bde commenced at FERNES. During day Bde H.Q. and Bns arrived in the new area. The 3rd Division is now back in the 6th Corps. Bde H.Q. billeted in SUS-ST LEGER also 1st Gordon Hldrs and 2nd Suffolk Regt, 8th Kings Own at BEAUDRICOURT. Bde in Army reserve	APPX. No C 9 & C 11
"	15th	1am	G.O.C. reached new area. Training to be carried out — Bn in attack.	
		5pm	G.O.C. attended conference at Div. H.Q.. Bde now in G.H.Q. Reserve. During afternoon 2nd Suffolk Regt was bathed. Area reconnoitred by B.M. during day.	
	16th		Training continued in very hot weather	
	17th		Training continued. G.O.C. attended conference at Div H.Q	
	18th		Church parades. G.O.C. presented M.M. ribbons to 2nd Suffolk Regt. & Major Gen. to 1st Gordon Highlanders. Afternoon various recreational and inter Bn games. Verbal orders received about moving up to Berles au Bois area	
	19th	3pm	G.O.C. and Bn Comdrs motored up to near QUESNOY FARM east of MONCHY au Bois to reconnoitre area for the attack on COURCELLES le COMTE. Bde H.Qrs arrived during evening and G.O.C. who had returned to SUS after the reconnaissance reached Bde H.Qrs at 9.30 pm. Operation Order for move to BERLES au BOIS issued 8 am.	O.O. 130 APPX No C 13 March Table C 12
BERLES au BOIS	20th	2.30am	From this hour units marched into new area. During afternoon Coy Comdrs and other regtl officers reconnoitred the ground for the attack. Operation Orders for the attack issued. G.O.C. arrived at new Bde H.Qrs. F.8.d. 90.85 at 11 pm, went to Div. H.Q. & returned about 1 am 21st. A mist after the previous rain was coming down and promised a very hot day for the 21st	O.O. 131 APPX No C 14 Addl. O.O. 131 APPX No C 15 O.O. 132 APPX No 16

A5834 Wt. W4973/M687 750,000 8/16 D. D. & L. Ltd. Forms/C.2118/13.

Instructions regarding War Diaries and Intelligence Summaries are contained in F. S. Regs., Part II. and the Staff Manual respectively. Title pages will be prepared in manuscript.

4

WAR DIARY
or
INTELLIGENCE SUMMARY.

(Erase heading not required.)

Army Form C. 2118.

Place	Date	Hour	Summary of Events and Information	Remarks and references to Appendices
F8d 90.85 (Bde HQ)	21.8	1am	G.O.C. returned from Div HQ	APP^x No. 32
		2am	Thick mist descending 3 am Bns were resting in their assembly positions (see accompanying map)	
		4.55am	Zero Hour for VI Corps Assault (& 3rd Army). A mist so thick that even when it got light later it was impossible to see more than 100 yds, and when our smoke barrage had fallen, one could not see more than 20 yds. It does not seem quite clear why any smoke was used, probably the long duration of the mist was unexpected	
		about 5.45am	The first of the Bde were seen coming through the mist. It was "Y" Coy of the 2nd Suffolk regt "X" Coy passed on the right about the same time.	
		7a.m.	The 2nd Div who were attacking BLUE LINE (see map APP^x No) reported at 6.55am that all objectives had been taken and that at 5.40am the 8th & 9th Bdes had passed through	
		7.35am	Heard from 1st G.H. that their Bn HQ was moving forward from CALVERLEY COPSE to F24a 5.5 in BLUE LINE. Also from 8th KORL that their Bn was advancing in support of the 1st RSF, Bn HQ moving to "aerodrome trench".	
		7am.	Heard from wounded that 8th Bde were in COURCELLES-LE-COMTE	
		9.42am	Heard from INT. officer 99th Bde that at 8.8am the railway line had been reached	
		9am	Verbal message from Div. that 8th Bde were through COURCELLES and advancing on railway in touch with left Bn of the 9th Bde. G.O.C. 8th Bde had ordered up the 8th KORL in support of the 1st RSF "news" after this was a rather long time in coming to us.	
		about 11am	Received a message from 1st G.H. sent off at 9.5a.m., Bn was assembling in BLUE LINE (A19) Two platoons were missing in the dense fog (they afterwards turned up in plenty of time to fight.) Their present HQ. F24a central moving to HQ. A21d 3.0., but were not in touch with any unit.	
		11.35am	Message from KORL recd 1.30pm saying that after much mopping up in COURCELLES they had taken the railway embankment objective and in touch on the left with the RSL1, who were in touch with the Guards. Div.	

A5834 Wt. W4973/M687 750,000 8/16 D. D. & L. Ltd. Forms/C.2118/13.

5

Army Form C. 2118.

WAR DIARY
or
INTELLIGENCE SUMMARY.
(Erase heading not required.)

Instructions regarding War Diaries and Intelligence Summaries are contained in F. S. Regs., Part II. and the Staff Manual respectively. Title pages will be prepared in manuscript.

Place	Date	Hour	Summary of Events and Information	Remarks and references to Appendices
F8d 90.85 Ref 40,000 Combined Sheets (51C SE (57d NE (51b SW (57c NW	21st	12.35 am	Message from CO. 2nd Suffolk (Lt Col Stubbs DSO) saying that there was some confusion owing to mist also as regards situation on left approx as already received, and that 3 Coys of the Suffolk were holding road from A28 A29 to A28 A32 in support. That one Tank was still in action endeavouring to work along the railway south. The railway was strongly held in vicinity of A28 d 5.5 and in G4A.	
		2.35 pm	Message from 3rd Div. that 63rd Div. are making arrangements to continue advance to railway having had heavy fighting in LOGEAST WOOD and that the 8th & 9th Bde were to cooperate and complete the capture of the railway.	
		5.20 pm	Received wire from Div in continuation of their last message give orders re this operation. Bns of 76th Bde to be drawn into reserve West of COURCELLES where they reverted to command of GOC 70th INF Bde. GOC immediately proceeded to 99th Bde HQ for information about the country etc. and returned at 6 pm	
			At 6.35 pm operation orders were being drafted by the B.M. which were issued at 7.5 pm	O.O. 133 APx No. C18
		9. pm	Orders received from 3rd Div cancelling their order re reorganisation on wire was immediately sent cancelling O.O. 133. although Bns had commenced carrying out OO 133 and consequently to carry out the next order was a difficult process.	
		10.00 pm 11 pm	GOC arrived. This was OO 134 published at 11 p.m. IO and SO went off to new Bde HQ in dug out on BUCQUOY - AYETTE road (F16 b 8.0) at 8 p.m. GOC arrived at Bde H Qrs 11 pm.	O.O. 134 APx No. C19
[illegible]	[illegible]		The 19 G.H carried out an attack when Lt Col Wolff-Murray DSO. MC was wounded see ---	APx C30
			B.M. personally took orders regarding OO 134 to Bns	
[illegible]	22		We were relieving the 1st Berks and a Bn of the KRRC	
		8.40 pm	Message of congratulations from GOC. 3rd Div.	Copy of wire C31

6

WAR DIARY
or
INTELLIGENCE SUMMARY.
(Erase heading not required.)

Army Form C. 2118.

Instructions regarding War Diaries and Intelligence Summaries are contained in F. S. Regs., Part II. and the Staff Manual respectively. Title pages will be prepared in manuscript.

Place	Date	Hour	Summary of Events and Information	Remarks and references to Appendices
F18 b 8.0 Dugout on BUCQUOY–AYETTE road. Bentham's accomodation excellent.	22nd	3 a.m.	1st Berks reported relief complete and shortly after the KRRC reported their relief complete. There had been great difficulty owing to the change of orders as dawn came before Bns had reached their posit ions, and the situation of Bns at dawn was as follows.	
		5.30 am	2nd Suffolk in AERODROME TRENCH South of AYETTE - COURCELLES road. Kings Own north of the road in the same trench. 1st G.H were approximately in the "Blue Line". Owing to the enemy shelling all movement heavily no attempt was made in daylight to conform to O.O. 134. The front was tactically well held although Bns were not in the correct place.	
		7.50 am	Wire from Div. ordering G.O.C. to attend a conference at Div. at 12 noon. The day was intensely hot. This conference was eventually postponed till 2 p.m. S.O.S was seen on our flanks at about 10.50 am	
		11 am	Aeroplane message reported enemy concentration east of COURCELLES opposite railway embankment.	
		4 p.m.	Conference at Bde H Qrs at which all COs attended. Scheme for capture of GOMIECOURT was discussed, resulting in O.O. 135 see Appx No.	O.O. 135 Appx No C 20
			Div on right reported that they could not advance until this village had been captured. Bde HQ were to be advanced to A14 c 7.1 I.O went on to reconnoitre it and guide orderlies from Bns there at 6.30 pm.	
A14 c 7.1 old German dugout in bank.		11.30 pm	G.O.C. arrived and Lt. Col West group comdr R.F.A took up his H.Q. there as well.	
		10.20 pm	Zero hour postponed till 4 am. Operation orders of 8th + 9th Inf Bdes received. 8th Bde were advancing their line to protect our left flank, and our right for a short time would be unprotected as the Germans were still in G.H.Q (250 prisoners were taken from there & about 20 M.Gs when the Div on our right advanced at 11 am, 22nd (about))	
	23rd		The assembly for the attack was accomplished in spite of unexpected resistance from enemy in the Railway Embankment.	

A5834 Wt. W4973/M687 750,000 8/16 D. D. & L. Ltd. Forms/C.2118/13.

67

WAR DIARY
or
INTELLIGENCE SUMMARY.
(Erase heading not required.)

Army Form C. 2118.

Instructions regarding War Diaries and Intelligence Summaries are contained in F. S. Regs., Part II. and the Staff Manual respectively. Title pages will be prepared in manuscript.

Place	Date	Hour	Summary of Events and Information	Remarks and references to Appendices
A14 c 7.1	23rd	4.52 am	2nd Suffolk despatched verbal message to say they were digging in on far side of GOMIECOURT	
		5 am	News came from the 8th KORL that they had advanced through GOMIECOURT and had taken 250 prisoners chiefly from the cellar in the chateau, and a quarter of an hour later the 2nd Suffolk reported about 300 prisoners and capture of objective.	
		6.15 am	Reports from Bns indicated that large numbers of German dead were lying about, and prisoners estimated at over 300. It transpired later that our attack was launched only a few minutes before the Germans themselves intended counter-attacking. 2 field guns were captured by the KORL, and one by the 2nd Suffolk	
		5.50 am	The 2nd Suffolk reported a field gun near ACHIET-LE-GRAND firing direct on their right flank — Artillery counter-battery was requested and obtained. Casualties during the attack were very light.	
		8.5 am	Enemy put smoke barrage across Southern flank of the salient formed by the attack and small parties of enemy were seen moving up railway from South to about grid line between A28 & G4	
		8.22 am.	2nd Suffolk reported they had posts at A29 d 5.2 also in A30 c 2.8 and as these were almost in the opening barrage for the next operation, there was some question of withdrawing them, but eventually the barrage line was altered	
		11 am.	The next operation took place and the 2nd Div passed through the Bde. For the rest of the day Bns were ordered to get the best rest they could. Estimated captures 400 prisoners including 8 officers. 3 field guns and 50 M.Gs. Copy of Bdes summary of operations 21st to 23rd	APPx No C30

A5834 Wt. W4973/M687 750,000 8/16 D. D. & L. Ltd. Forms/C.2118/13.

8

Army Form C

Instructions regarding War Diaries and Intelligence Summaries are contained in F. S. Regs., Part II. and the Staff Manual respectively. Title pages will be prepared in manuscript.

WAR DIARY
or
INTELLIGENCE SUMMARY.
(Erase heading not required.)

Place	Date	Hour	Summary of Events and Information	Remarks and references to Appendices
A14 C 7.1	24th	10am	The G.O.C. visited the Bn H.Qrs of the 2nd Suffolk & 1st Gordons near GOMIECOURT. Verbal orders were received during the morning (about 11 am.) for Bde to move back to areas around DOUCHY. O.O. 136 issued at 3.35 pm. Bns arrived back at about 11 pm and G.O.C. came back to Bde H.Qrs in the place occupied on Aug 21st at 11.30 pm. Bde H.Qrs at A14 C 7.1 closed at 9 pm.	O.O. 136 App No C21
		11pm	Div. O.O. received regarding move to DOUCHY area. Bde in VI Corps reserve.	
	25th		The 1st G.H. were in PURPLE FRONT LINE east of ledge running North from QUESNOY FARM. 8th K.O.R.L. in F10a central. 2nd Suffolk in F10d central. Weather still fine and hot. G.O.C. visited 1st G.H. at 11 am. Messages of congratulation received from Corps Comdr on the success of the operations carried out.	
		4pm.	The Major General met the G.O.C. and O.C. Bns of the Bde at Bde H.Qrs. and conveyed a message of congratulation from the C-in-C. who had personally visited the Major General.	
		5.30pm	G.O.C. visited the 2nd Suffolk and 8th K.O.R.L. returning to Bde H.Qrs at 8.30 pm. Weather looked like changing.	
	26th		Verbal Orders received at 11.30 am to relieve the 1st Guards Bde Support Bn near HAMELINCOURT. Weather had changed and was very showery and wet during morning, making the roads very difficult for transport in places. Weather cleared in the afternoon. Orders for move in Appendix Nos in margin. G.O.C. was promised a car by the Guards Div. at noon, but it never arrived, and finally he got a 3rd Div. car at 4.30 pm to reconnoitre area. Bde H.Qrs opened at A11 b 9.7 at 9.50 pm.	G225 App No C22 G226 " C23 G228 " C24

A5834 Wt. W4973/M687 750,000 8/16 D. D. & L. Ltd. Forms/C.2118/13.

9

Army Form C. 2118.

Instructions regarding War Diaries and Intelligence Summaries are contained in F. S. Regs., Part II. and the Staff Manual respectively. Title pages will be prepared in manuscript.

WAR DIARY
or
INTELLIGENCE SUMMARY.
(Erase heading not required.)

Place	Date	Hour	Summary of Events and Information	Remarks and references to Appendices
A 11 b 9.7	27th		Morning rain falling, remained showery all day	
		2.15pm	Verbal message received ordering 1 Bn of Bde to get ready to move up in support of 1st Guards Bde. The location of units at this time was (REF APPx No) 1st G.H in trench in B 1 c 0 3 to about B 7 a 6 5. 2nd Suffolk in trench A 5 c 7.9 to A 12 a 0.7 8th KORL in HAMMEL SWITCH in B 1 a & b. 8th KORL were ordered to support the Guards and OC 8th KORL at 3pm moved off to report to 1st Guards Bde HQ in B 1 b 3.5	
		5.15pm	8th KORL were moving up as required by Guards Bde, their HQ moving to B 2 c 7 2. and were under command of GOC 1st Guards Bde.	
		9 p.m.	GOC visited 1st Guards Bde at 9 p.m where he was given verbal instructions regarding the coming operation. Situation on the Guards front was roughly:— Owing to the advance up North at MONCHY & WANCOURT that during the night the Germans might withdraw. At dawn, therefore if this was found to be the case the 1st Guards Bde would advance with the 8th KORL about a mile behind and the remainder of the 76th Inf Bde in reserve ready to push right through. If only slight opposition was met with tanks were detailed to deal with it. The 2nd Suffolk & 1st G.H. were ordered to hold themselves in readiness to move off at an hour's notice after 6 am on the 28th. The weather was still showery	
		10.30pm	Verbal orders issued regarding this operation on return of G.O.C	
	28th	7am	It was found that the Germans had not withdrawn and the operation did not take place as the 1st Guards Bde had orders not to indulge in a general action	
		1.45am	Instructions sent to HQ D Coy M.G. Coy to be ready to move at ½ hours notice	G 254
		4am	Operation order regarding move issued (see appendix) meanwhile wire sent to Bns to be ready to move at 6 am.	Appx No. C25
		7am	Operation cancelled.	
		1.45pm	1st Guards Bde informed GOC 76th Inf Bde that he had ordered 8th KORL to move forward to support centre at B 9 b 0.5 at 12.40 pm.	

10

Instructions regarding War Diaries and Intelligence Summaries are contained in F. S. Regs., Part II. and the Staff Manual respectively. Title pages will be prepared in manuscript.

WAR DIARY
or
INTELLIGENCE SUMMARY.
(Erase heading not required.)

Army Form C. 2118.

Place	Date	Hour	Summary of Events and Information	Remarks and references to Appendices
A11b9.7. (large German dugout in HAMERVILLE TRENCH)		6.55 pm	Received instructions to relieve 1st Guards Bde in front line to-night 28/29th	
		7 pm	Instructions sent to O.C. B Coy M.G. Corps to move his Coy to 1st Guards Bde H Qrs and to report to 76th Inf Bde HQrs for instructions, meanwhile to send an officer to 1st Guards Bde to arrange relief.	
		8 pm	O.O. No 137 issued regarding relief of 1st Guards Bde by 76th Inf. Bde. See appendix	appendix No C26
		8.15 pm	I.O. went on ahead to reconnoitre new Bde HQrs at B10c 6.0 which was a mined dugout with one shaft at the moment being the rear Bn H Qrs of the 2nd Grenadier Guards	
B10c 6.0.		10.30 pm	Bde H Qrs personnel arrived at about 10.30 pm and the G.O.C. at 1.30 pm. Relief was complete at about midnight. The situation and accurate position of the front line was rather obscure, also as regards touch on right and left flanks	
	29th		The K.O. were roughly on a line C1a 6.2 to C7a central (see appendix) and U25d 2.3 to C1 central	appx No C33
			The G.H. were roughly on a line from C7a central to B18b 3.6. 2nd Suffolk in support at BANKS RESERVE. The 8th Middlesex of the 167th Bde 56th Div. were on our left in LEG LANE, BUNHILL RESERVE and PELICAN AVENUE. Germans were posted strongly in ECOUST with MGs and the 1st G.H. had touch with them at C13b 6.5. The G.H. captured a prisoner on patrol during the day. Our patrols were very active and managed to work through to a point South of LONGATTE (an 8th KORL patrol), and established the fact that the enemy were holding ECOUST - LONGATTE and ridge south east. as well as a MG nest at B18b 6.5	
		4 pm	Major General visited Bde HQrs and verbal orders were received at 7.45 pm for the 76th Bde to attack ECOUST + LONGATTE. See operation order No 138 issued at 11.30 pm	
		8 pm	Conference at Bde H.Q. OCs 2nd Suffolk, 1st G.H. and arty group Comdr were present	Appendix No C27

A5834 Wt. W4973/M687 750,000 8/16 D. D. & L. Ltd. Forms/C.2118/13.

WAR DIARY II

PLACE	DATE	HOUR	SUMMARY OF EVENTS	Ref to APPxs
B10c 6.0.	30th	4 am	2nd Suffolk Regt and 1st Gordons attacked ECOUST and LONGATTE. The 2nd Suffolk had the villages in their boundary and the 1st GH were to make a defensive right flank, the left flank was protected by our alleged possession of BULLECOURT. Reports came in at about 6 am that ECOUST was taken but that the 2nd Suffolk had famed up in the intense darkness, (nights at present are exceptionally dark), too far forward and had suffered somewhat from our opening barrage. They withdrew reformed and were advancing on LONGATTE.	
		6.30am	Received news that objectives had been taken and 1 Coy was in BULLECOURT AV.	Ref APPx No C33.
		8.30am	Reports from FOOs indicated that 2nd Suffolk was withdrawing from ECOUST. Later news showed that they had been attacked on the left flank and rear by a strong counter-attack from "STATION REDOUBT" of BULLECOURT, "RAILWAY RESERVE" and "BULLECOURT AV" all of which it was understood before the attack took place was in the hands of the 56th Div. 2 platoons of the Suffolk were cut off and all who returned had to fight their way back. A line was taken up C13c 2.8 along VRAUCOURT RESERVE to C13b 6.0 thence due North along thin line of wire (ref APPx No) to C7b 8.0 thence to ECOUST support C1d 9.1 and along that Div. boundary U26c 1.3.	
		11am	Endeavours were to be made, according to verbal instructions from G.O.C. 3rd Div, to advance line to grid dividing C7 and C8 — at any rate at dusk	
		12 noon	G.O.C. 9th Bde visited Bde H.Qrs. with a view to finding out what was known of the situation as the 9th Bde were to take over front from the SUFFOLK and K.O.R.L. and at dawn attack ECOUST & LONGATTE again. 1st GH were to attack with them under 9th Bde command. O.O. issued at 9 p.m. The relief took place during the night and the G.O.C. arrived back at the new Bde HQrs in the railway embankment at A5c 0.3 at 5 am on 31st.	Ref O.O. 139 APPx No C29
		8 p.m.	I.O. went on ahead with instructions to take over as Bde H.Qrs. the old 1st Guards Bde HQrs in T25d 0.1. On arriving there he received instructions from the S.C. to go to the railway embankment instead meeting the ration limber and advanced party en route and direct them to A5c 0.3	

12

WAR DIARY.

PLACE	DATE	HOUR	SUMMARY OF EVENTS	Reference.
B10c 6.0	30th		2nd Suffolk on being relieved withdrew to MORY SWITCH between B9d 6.4 and JUDAS SWITCH (B9a 3.9). HQrs. at B9b 1.4. The 8th KORL less 1 Coy (who were to attack with 9th Bde (1st O.O. No139) withdrew to MORY SWITCH from B9a 3.9 to B1d 6.8.	APPX No C 33 (Map)
RAILWAY EMBANKMENT A4d 9.2	31st	10am	Heard that 1st G.H. had got their objective and that ECOUST and LONGATTE were once more in British hands (9th Bde).	
		2pm	Heard that Germans had retaken LONGATTE and that situation between ECOUST and VRAUCOURT RESERVE (where the 1st S.H. were) was obscure	(Map) APPX No C 33
		5.20pm	Received verbal orders for 76th Bde to take over Southern half of Div boundary O.O 140 published about midnight confirming verbal orders issued earlier in evening. I.O moved off at 6.15 pm to take over new Bde HQrs in B10c 6.0 where "B" Coy M.G. Corps were situated. At 7pm verbal instructions recd. regarding renewal of the attack	O.O. No 140 APPX No C29
B10c 6.0.		10pm	G.O.C. returned to take over command of the Bde once more from this location. Main features of the plans for the attack were that the 1st G.H. were to push eastwards during the night along NORBUIL SWITCH, (This was merely a spitlocked trench 18" deep, in places where it was occupied it had been deepened and was therefore more of a series of holes) at 3 am 2 Coys of the KORL were to push over the open ground in C14a & b & C15a, these orders were issued verbally at a conference at Bde HQrs. at which G.O.C. 9th Bde. Lt Col Vickery DSO, RFA (Group commander) and the O.Cs 1st G.H and 8th KORL were present. The 3 Coy Comdrs of the KORL were there and then shewn their task, while their Coys were lying outside Bde HQ and from the conference went straight to their assembly positions. 9th Bde (4 R.F) on the left were to co-operate and push forward with the KORL across the open ground while the 1st N.F. worked up northern leg of NORBUIL SWITCH to meet the 76th Bde at Bde boundary C9d 3.7, the MGs were still holding [illegible]	

13

WAR DIARY

PLACE	DATE	HOUR	SUMMARY OF EVENTS.	REFERENCES.
B10c 6.0	31st	10.30pm to 11.45pm	(Conference at Bde HQ) — between us and the objective or our objective was not reached by 6am on 1.9.18 a smoke barrage and heavy artillery co-operation was to be put down on the sunken roads in C9a b&d (running NW & SE) and C15 b&c (running NE & SW) Under cover of which 8 whippet tanks were detailed to help decide the battle and get our objectives. There was some question of a creeping barrage if our objective had not been reached by 6am. Owing to the difficulty of communication, however, and the consequent danger of an alternative plan which might have brought our barrage down on those who had pushed on farthest both GOC's refused to have it, merely asking the artillery to cooperate as already stated	
		11.30pm	Owing to some slight shelling round the entrance and approach to the Bde HQ the Coys awaiting their Coy Comdrs (who were at the conference) moved off to one side but very soon were reorganized and moved off under guides from the 1st Gds who knew the country	

C. [signature]
Brigadier General
Commanding 76th Inf. Bde

Sept 6/18

76th Brigade.

3rd Division.

A P P E N D I C E S

B. H. Q.

76th INFANTRY BRIGADE :::: AUGUST 1918.

C1

SECRET.
****

Copy No. 16....

76th. INFANTRY BRIGADE OPERATION ORDER NO. 124.

Ref. 1/20,000 Sheets 36a.S.E.
and 36b.N.E.

August 2nd.1918.

1. The following reliefs will be carried out in the HINGES Section on the night August 4th./5th.

(a) 8th.K.O.R.L. will relieve 1st.Gordon Hldrs in the System forward of Canal.

2. On relief, 1st.Gordon Hldrs will move into Brigade Reserve in the area vacated by 8th.K.O.R.L.

3. 2nd.Suffolk Regt will remain in CANAL LINE and 2nd.System.

4. Details of relief will be arranged between C.O's concerned and completion reported to Brigade H.Q.

5. Trench Store Cards will reach Brigade H.Q. within 24 hours of relief.

6. ACKNOWLEDGE.

C. Chipp Captain,
Brigade Major, 76th. Infantry Brigade.

Issued 8 p.m.

Copies to:-
1. G.O.C.
2. 8th.K.O.R.L.
3. 2nd.Suffolk Regt.
4. 1st.Gordon Hldrs.
5. 76th.T.M.B.
6. Left Gp.R.F.A.
7. " 3rd.Bn.M.G.C.
8. 529th.(E.R.)Fd.Co.R.E.
9. 3rd.Div."G".
10. " "Q".
11. 9th.Inf.Bde.
12. 11th. "
13. 7th.Field Amb.
14. B.M.
15. S.C.
16. Bde.Sig.Offr.
17. War Diary.
18. "
19. 20th.K.R.R.C.
20. File.

C2

SECRET.

****

Copy No.22..

76th. INFANTRY BRIGADE OPERATION ORDER NO.125.

Reference Sheets 36a.) 1/40,000.
44b.)

August 4th.1918.

1. The 3rd.Division will be relieved in the line by the 19th.Division.
The Infantry reliefs will take place on the nights August 5/6th., and August 6/7th.
After relief, the 3rd.Division will move into the BOMY Area.

2. The following move will take place on August 4th.:-
8th.K.O.R.L. from present position in Brigade Reserve to LOZINGHEM.
Route:- ALLOUAGNE.
Not to enter LOZINGHEM before 5 p.m.

3. 8th.K.O.R.L. will take over the billets now occupied in LOZINGHEM by the 8th.Gloucester Regt.
Billeting parties will report at Town Major's Office, LOZINGHEM.

4. A Battalion of 57th.Inf.Brigade will move into camps and billets now occupied by 8th.K.O.R.L. during the afternoon of August 4th.

5. All documents relating to the area including detail for working parties will be handed over to incoming Battalion of 57th.Inf.Brigade. Receipts will be obtained and forwarded to these Headquarters by 6 p.m. August 5th.

6. Completion of move will be reported to 76th.Bde H.Q.

7. Orders for further moves will be issued later.

8. 76th.Inf.Bde.O.O.124 is hereby cancelled.

9. ACKNOWLEDGE.

C. Chipper Captain,
Brigade Major, 76th. Infantry Brigade.

Issued at 2 p.m.

Copies to:-
1. G.O.C.
2. 8th.K.O.R.L.
3. 2nd.Suffolk Regt.
4. 1st.Gordon Hldrs.
5. 76th.T.M.B.
6. Left Gp.R.F.A.
7. " 3rd.Bn.M.G.C.
8. 529th.(E.R.)Fd.Co.R.E.
9. 9th.Inf.Bde.
10. 12th.Inf.Bde.
11. 7th.Fld.Amb.
12. B.M.
13. S.C.
14. Bde.Sig.Offr.
15. 3rd.Div."G"
16. " "Q".
17. Bde.T.O.
18. Bde.Supply Offr.
19. No.2 Coy.,Train.
20. 57th.Inf.Bde.
21. 20th.K.R.R.C.
22. War Diary.
23. "
24. File.
25.} Retained.
26.}

C 3

SECRET.
****

Copy No.....22

76th.INFANTRY BRIGADE OPERATION ORDER NO.126.

Ref.HAZEBROUCK Sheet 1/100,000. August 4th.1918.

1. The 76th.Infantry Brigade will be relieved in the HINGES Section by the 58th.Infantry Brigade on the night 6/7th.August.

2. On relief,units will move in accordance with the attached table.

3. The following distances will be maintained by units on the march:-

Between Companies........................ 100 yards.
Between transport of units when Brigaded 100 yards.
Between Battalions....................... 500 yards.
Between units and their transport....... 100 yards.

Particular attention will be paid to march discipline.

4. Units of the 19th.Division located in the 3rd.Divisional Area will come under the tactical control of G.O.C.,3rd.Division.
Similarly,units of the 3rd.Division in 19th.Divisional Area, will come under the tactical control of G.O.C.,19th.Division.

5. Detailed orders for the relief and move will be issued later.

6. ACKNOWLEDGE.

C. Chipper Captain,
Issued at 8 p.m. Brigade Major,76th.Infantry Brigade.

Copies to :-
1. G.O.C.
2. 8th.K.O.R.L.
3. 2nd.Suffolk Regt.
4. 1st.Gordon Hldrs.
5. 76th.T.M.B.
6. Left Gp.R.F.A.
7. " 3rd.Bn.M.G.C.
8. 529th.(E.R.)Fd.Co.R.E.
9. 9th.Inf.Bde.
10. 12th.Inf.Bde.
11. 7th.Field Amb.
12. B.M.
13. S.C.
14. Bde.Sig.Offr.
15. 3rd.Div."G"
16. " "Q".
17. Bde.T.O.
18. Bde.Supply Offr.
19. No.2 Co.Train.
20. 58th.Inf.Bde.
21. 20th.K.R.R.C.
22. War Diary.
23. "
24. File.
25.) Retained.
26.)

TABLE OF MOVES to accompany 76th. INFANTRY BRIGADE 0.0.No.126.

Serial No.	Date.	Unit.	From.	To.	Remarks.
1.	Aug.6th.	8th.K.O.R.L.	LOZINGHEM.	AMES Area.	By route march.
2.	6/7th.	2nd.Suffolk Regt.	Support on relief.	AMES Area.	By Bus from CHOCQUES. Embus on REVEILLON - CHOCQUES Road.
3.	6/7th.	1st.Gordon Hldrs	Front line on relief.		
4.	6/7th.	76th.L.T.M.B.	On relief.		

C4

SECRET.
****

ADMINISTRATIVE INSTRUCTIONS FOR MOVE OF 76TH. INFANTRY BRIGADE.

1. Reference 76th. Infantry Brigade O.O.126 of August 4th. 1918 :

Units will move to AMES Area in accordance with the attached table.

2. Billeting parties will be detailed as follows:-

8th.K.O.R.L.Rgt.	1 Off.	6 N.C.O.'s.
76th. T.M.Battery.	1 Off.	1 N.C.O.
529th.Field Coy.,R.E.	1 Off.	2 N.C.O.'s.
Brigade H.Q.	-	3 N.C.O.'s.

They will report at Area Commandants' Office, NEDONCHELLE, at 12 noon to-morrow, 6th. instant.

They will be met by Lieut. PICKARD-CAMBRIDGE who is now in the Area.

2nd.Suffolk Regt.	1 Off.	6 N.C.O.'s.
1st.Gordon Hrs.	1 Off.	6 N.C.O.'s.

These will report to Billet Warden for LIERES and FANCQUENHEM at No.33 Billet, LIERES, at 12 noon, 6th. instant.

Billeting parties will travel on lorries detailed to carry stores, etc.

3. Lorries will report to units as under for conveyance of Packs and Stores :-

Unit.	Date & Time.	Report at	No. of Lorries.
2nd.Suffolk Rgt.	9 a.m., Aug. 6th.	Details Camp (D.18c.1.3.)	2
1st.Gordon Hrs.	Do.	Div.Fuel Dump,D.22d.7.4.	2
Brigade H.Q.	Do.	No.7 Billot,LABEUVRIERE.	1
76th.T.M.Battery.	Do.	Bde. H.Q.,L'ABBAYE.	1
8th.K.O.R.L.Rgt.	Do.	Chateau, LOZINGHEM.	2

4. Transport of 2nd.Suffolk Rgt. and 1st.Gordon Hldrs., with the exception of 2 Cookers, and Limbers required to convey Lewis Guns, etc., from line, will proceed to new areas under orders of Battalion Transport Officers.

They will not enter their respective billeting areas before 6 p.m.

Transport of Brigade H.Q., with exception of Mess Cart and Signal Section Transport, will be attached to 1st.Gordon Hldrs for this move.

5. O.C. Battalions will arrange for 2 Cookers each from 2nd. Suffolk Regt. and 1st.Gordon Hldrs. to supply hot tea to their men on arrival at embussing point - LE BOUDOU.

An Officer from each Battalion will be in charge of these arrangements. He will report at Brigade H.Q. at 2 p.m., 6th. inst., for instructions.

6. The Agricultural party from 2nd. Suffolk Rgt. have been ordered to report at their Details Camp at 6 p.m. to-morrow, 6th. instant. This party will be conveyed to new area on second journey of one of the stores lorries.

7. Rations for consumption 7th. inst. will be delivered to Battalions in new area to-morrow evening, 6th. inst., at about 7 p.m.

T. J. Furnell
Captain,
A/Staff Captain, 76th. Infantry Brigade.

5th.August 1918.

C5

EMBUSSING AND MARCH TABLE.

Unit.	Embussing Point,	Date.	Time of Departure.	Destination.	Route.
2nd.Suffolk Rgt.	LE BOUDOU on REVEILLON CHOCQUES Road. Head of column facing East.	Aug. 7th.	5 a.m.	FANCQUENHEM.	Station D.5central,- LAPUGNOY Northern Rd. D.16b. - Cross Roads I.10c. - FERFAY - AMES.
1st.Gordon H.	Do.	Do.	Do.	LIERES.	Do.
529th.Fld.Coy.R.E.	Do.	Do.	Do.	AMETTES.	Station D.5 central - LAPUGNOY Northern Rd.D.16b. - Cross Roads I.10c.- FERFAY
76th.T.M.Bty.	Do.	Do.	Do.	AMETTES.	Do.
Brigade H.Q.	Do.	Do.	Do.	AMETTES.	Do.

Unit.	Starting Point.	Date.	Time.	Destination.	Route.
8th.K.O.R.L.Rgt.	LOZINGHEM.	Aug.6th.	Not to enter AMES before 5 p.m.	AMES.	LOZINGHEM - AUCHEL - CAUCHY A LA TOUR - FERFAY - AMES.
No.2 Coy., 3rd.Div. Train.		Do.	Under orders of O.C. No.2 Coy.,3rd. Div. Train.	BELLERY.	

C6.

SECRET.
****

Copy No...23...

76th.INFANTRY BRIGADE OPERATION ORDER No.127.

Ref.Sheets 36a. } 1/40,000.
44b. }

and HAZEBROUCK 5a.,1/100,000. August 5th.1918.

1. Further to 76th.Inf.Brigade Operation Order No.126.

2. On night August 6/7th.,following reliefs will take place:-

1st.Gordon Hldrs will be relieved by 2nd.Wiltshire Regt in front line.
2nd.Suffolk Regt " " " " 9th.Bn.The Welch Regt.
Reserve Battn.area will be occupied by 9th.R.W.Fus.
76th.L.T.M.Bty will be relieved by 58th.L.T.M.Bty.

3. Guides on a basis of 1 per platoon,1 per Company H.Q.,and 2 per Battn.H.Q.,also 1 per gun and 1 for H.Q.,L.T.M.B.,will report to relieving units at D.5d.3.1.on ECQUE-CHOCQUES Road at 7.30 p.m.

Guides for front line posts will be picked up at Front Battn. Headquarters.

4. Work programmes,parties,air photographs,maps,defence schemes and trench store lists will be handed over and receipts forwarded to 76th.Bde.H.Q.by 6 p.m. August 7th.

5. Further details will be arranged direct between C.O's concerned.

6. (a) Completion of relief will be reported by wiring "Not known".

(b) Arrival in AMES Area,and location of Headquarters will be reported to 76th.Bde.H.Q.in AMETTES.

7. Bde.H.Q.will close at L'ABBAYE on completion of relief and open at AMETTES at 7 p.m.,August 6th.

8. Administrative orders issued herewith.

9. ACKNOWLEDGE.

C. Chipper Captain,
Brigade Major,76th.Infantry Brigade.

Issued at 8 p.m.

Copies to:-
1. G.O.C.
2. 8th.K.O.R.L.
3. 2nd.Suffolk Regt.
4. 1st.Gordon Hldrs.
5. 76th.T.M.B.
6. Left Gp.R.F.A.
7. " 3rd.Bn.M.G.C.
8. 529th.(E.R.)Fd.Co.R.E.
9. 9th.Inf.Bde.
10. 12th. "
11. 58th. "
12. 7th.Field Amb.
13. B.M.
15. S.C.
16. Bde.Sig.Offr.
17. 3rd.Div."G"
18. " "Q".
19. Bde.T.O.
20. Bde.Supply Offr.
21. No.2 Coy.,Train.
22. 20th.K.R.R.C.
23. War Diary.
24. "
25. File.
26. Retained.

C7

SECRET.
****

PRELIMINARY INSTRUCTIONS FOR THE ENTRAINMENT OF 76TH. INFANTRY BRIGADE.

1. The following notes are issued for guidance in the event of the Brigade being called on to entrain at PERNES at short notice.

2. The Entraining Officer, Major H.N.MORGAN, M.C., 8th.Bn.K.O.R.L.Rgt., and the Detraining Officer, Major W.G.CHANDLER, 2nd.Bn.Suffolk Rgt., will report to the R.T.O. at entraining station half an hour before the arrival of the first unit of the Brigade Group. Major MORGAN will remain until the last train of the Group is ready to leave.
Major Chandler will travel by the first train, and will be on duty at the detraining station until all the Units in the Brigade Group have detrained.

3. One Company of 1st.Bn.Gordon Hrs (with Cookers and teams), entraining on the last train from PERNES, will report to the R.T.O. $3\frac{1}{2}$ hours before the departure of the first train. This Coy. will be responsible for loading all trains of the Brigade Group and will itself entrain upon the last train.
One Company of 8th.Bn.K.O.R.L.Rgt., (Cooker and team complete) will travel on the 1st. train and will be responsible for the unloading of all trains of the Brigade Group at the detraining station.

4. Battalions' Transport should arrive at entraining station 3 hours before the time of the departure of the train and the personnel $1\frac{1}{2}$ hours.

5. A complete Marching-out State, showing the number of Officers, men, horses, G.S.Wagons, 2-wheeled wagons and cycles, should be sent with the transport of each Unit to the Entraining Officer, who will hand them to the R.T.O. for checking purposes.
Limbered G.S.Wagons will be counted as 2-wheeled vehicles on this State.

6. Supply and baggage wagons will accompany Units in every case. Supply wagons will rejoin their Train Companies as soon as they have been unloaded in the new area.
Water Carts should be full on entrainment.

7. The entrainment of all units must be completed half an hour before the time of departure of the train, when it will be moved from the loading siding.

8. Breast Ropes for horse trucks must be provided by the units themselves: Ropes for lashing vehicles on flat trucks will be provided by the Railway.

9. Piquets should be provided at all stops from each end of the train to prevent troops leaving.

10. All doors of covered trucks and carriages on the right hand side of the train will be kept closed. No personnel or Stores should be allowed in the Brake Vans at each end of the train, or on the roofs of the trucks. No covered truck should be used for baggage as it restricts the space available for personnel.

11. It is hoped to get an allotment of lorries for surplus kit and stores. If this is not possible, all surplus kit and stores will be dumped at a central spot, the location of which will be notified later, under a guard.
Units will arrange to collect and dump all kit and stores which cannot be carried on their transport at a billet in their area at once, so as to facilitate collection when necessity arises.
O.C. Units will arrange to hand over to the Area Commandant any surplus articles for which they have no further use, as the accommodation in the lorries or at the Dump will be limited.

(continued)

12. Units will draw rations for consumption on the day following the day of arrival in the new area before entraining.

13. Small advance parties will be held in readiness to proceed to the new area at short notice. They will be sent to arrive in the new area 24 hours in advance of their unit to arrange billets.

14. The following Routes will be taken to PERNES Station by Infantry Battalions of the Brigade Group:-

TRANSPORT.

LIERES - AMES - FERFAY. Road through B.5b., B.6c.,B.12a. and c.
FERFAY - FLORINGHEM - PERNES via Road through H.6 and 11 to PERNES Station, I.13a.1.5.

INFANTRY, MARCHING.

Same route as Transport to FLORINGHEM, thence to PERNES Station by road through H.6d. and H.12b. and d.

15. Billeting Certificates will be rendered to the Mayor of the Commune by Units for all billets now occupied before departure.

T. F. Funnell Captain,
A/Staff Captain, 76th. Infantry Brigade.

11th.August 1918.

Copies to :- 1. G.O.C.
2. 8th.K.O.R.L.Rgt.
3. 2nd.Suffolk Rgt.
4. 1st.Gordon Hldrs.
5. 76th.T.M.Bty.
6. 3rd.Bn.M.G.C.
7. 7th.Fld.Ambce.
8. 529th.Fld.Coy.,R.E.
9. No.2 Coy. Train.
10. B.M.
11. S.C.
12. Bde.Signal Off.
13. Bde.Supply Off.
14. Major H.N.MORGAN,M.C.
15. Major W.G.CHANDLER.
16. 3rd. Div. "Q".
17. Bde. Q.M.Sgt.
18. War Diary.
19. Do.
20. File.
21. Bde. Transport Off.

C8

SECRET.
****

Copy No...

76th.INFANTRY BRIGADE ORDER NO.128.

Ref.Maps 1/100,000 LENS 11 & HAZEBROUCK 5a. — August 13th.1918.

1. The 3rd.Division personnel with certain transport is commencing entraining about 3 p.m.,August 13th.
76th.Inf.Brigade Group with transport to be laid down will entrain on August 14th.

2. For purposes of the move to entraining station and entrainment one company Pioneer Battalion will be included in the Brigade Group.

3. Instructions for entrainment and March Table will be issued later.

4. Detraining station for personnel of Brigade Group will be WARLINCOURT,and for transport.MONDICOURT. Destination.SAULTY-LARBRET Area.

5. Major H.N.MORGAN,M.C.,8th.K.O.R.L.,will be entraining officer.
Major W.G.CHANDLER,2nd.Suffolk Regt.,will be detraining officer and will travel by the first train.

6. Billet ing parties will travel by the first train of the 76th.Inf.Brigade Group.

7. All transport of 76th.Inf.Bde.Group not proceeding by rail will march under the command of O.C. No.2 Coy. 3rd.Div.Train,who will send on billeting parties furnished with the numbers of officers,O.R. and animals,to the Area Commandant.ANVIN.

Route:- NEDONCHELLE - FONTAINE-LEZ-BOULANS - HEUCHIN.

Destination:- ANVIN - WAVRANS Area.

INSTRUCTIONS:- To pass NEDONCHELLE Church at 12 midnight August 13th./14th. Orders for march night 14th./15th.will be received from Area Commandant.ANVIN.

8. Distances to maintained on the march by troops and transport will be as laid down in 76th.Inf.Brigade Order No.126.
Particular attention will be paid to march discipline.

9. ACKNOWLEDGE.

C. Chipp[illegible] Captain,
Brigade Major,76th.Infantry Brigade.

Issued at 7 a.m.

Copies to:-
1.G.O.C.
2.8th.K.O.R.L.
3.2nd.Suffolk Regt.
4.1st.Gordon Hldrs.
5.76th.T.M.B.
6.20th.K.R.R.C.(Pioneers)
7.8th.Inf.Bde.
8.9th. "
9.7th.Lield Amb.
10.529th.Field Co.R.E.
11.No.2 Coy Train.
12.B.M.
13.S.C.
14. Bde.Sig.Offr.
15. Bde.Transport Offr.
16. Bde.Supply Offr.
17. Major MORGAN.
18. Major CHANDLER.
19. 3rd.Div."G".
20. " "Q".
21. War Diary.
22. "
23. File.
24. }
25. } Retained.
26. }

C9

SECRET.
****

ADMINISTRATIVE INSTRUCTIONS TO ACCOMPANY 76TH. INFANTRY BRIGADE OPERATION ORDER NO. 128.

1. The Brigade Group, plus 1 Coy. Pioneer Battalion, will entrain in tactical trains at PERNES on 14th. instant. Detraining stations will be WARLINCOURT (personnel) and MONDICOURT (transport).

2. The Entraining Officer, Major H.N.MORGAN, M.C., 8th.K.O.R.L.Rgt. and the Detraining Officer, Major W.G.CHANDLER, 2nd.Suffolk Regt., will report to the R.T.O. at PERNES as laid down in para. 2 of Preliminary Instructions dated 11th. instant.

3. All units will forward a complete Marching-Out State to Brigade H.Q. by 6 p.m. to-night, 13th. inst., shewing the numbers of Officers, O.R., Horses, G.S.Wagons, G.S.Limbers, 2-wheeled Vehicles and Cycles proceeding by train. G.S.Wagons will be counted as two 2-wheeled vehicles. These States will be consolidated and 2 copies sent to the Entraining Officer, who will hand one copy to the R.T.O.,PERNES on arrival at station.

4. One Coy. 1st.Bn.Gordon Hldrs. will be responsible for loading & unloading transport. They will report to R.T.O.PERNES Station 3½ hours before time of departure of train to convey transport. They will be responsible for unloading this train at MONDICOURT.

5. Probable length of journey 2½ hours.

[illegible] will arrive at the entraining station 1 hour

AMENDMENT TO ADMINISTRATIVE INSTRUCTIONS.

Reference Administrative Instructions issued with O.O.No.128, para. 7, Rations for 15th. inst. will be drawn by units from MONDICOURT Station on arrival and not as stated.

C9

Captain,
13/8/18. A/Staff Captain, 76th. Infantry Brigade.

9. Railhead will change [illegible]
instant.

10. Billeting parties will be sent by the first train allotted to the Brigade Group.

Field Ambulance Advanced Parties will proceed by Motor Ambulance.

11. Entraining Programme for Brigade Group will be issued later.

12. Lorries will be detailed as under to convey stores and surplus ki[illegible]

One lorry to each Battalion reporting at Battn.H.Q. at 5.30 a.m.,14th.i[illegible]
One lorry to Brigade H.Q. " " " 5. 0 a.m. "
One lorry to 76th.T.M.Battery " " " 5. 0 a.m.

These lorries will be loaded as quickly as possible and will proceed to MONDICOURT, where loads will be dumped immediately. No second journey is possible. A small unloading party (not more than 5) will be detailed to proceed with lorries. They will unload the lorries on arrival at MONDICOURT and will remain in charge of them until they can be removed.

T. J. [illegible]
Captain,
13th August 1918. [illegible] Captain, 76th. Infantry Brigade.

Same Distribution as for O.O. No. 128.

C9

SECRET.
****

ADMINISTRATIVE INSTRUCTIONS TO ACCOMPANY 76TH. INFANTRY BRIGADE OPERATION ORDER NO. 128.

1. The Brigade Group, plus 1 Coy. Pioneer Battalion, will entrain in tactical trains at PERNES on 14th. instant. Detraining stations will be WARLINCOURT (personnel) and MONDICOURT (transport).

2. The Entraining Officer, Major H.N.MORGAN, M.C., 8th.K.O.R.L.Rgt. and the Detraining Officer, Major W.G.CHANDLER, 2nd.Suffolk Regt., will report to the R.T.O. at PERNES as laid down in para. 2 of Preliminary Instructions dated 11th. instant.

3. All units will forward a complete Marching-Out State to Brigade H.Q. by 6 p.m. to-night, 13th. inst., shewing the numbers of Officers, O.R., Horses, G.S.Wagons, G.S.Limbers, 2-wheeled Vehicles and Cycles proceeding by train. G.S.Wagons will be counted as two 2-wheeled vehicles. These States will be consolidated and 2 copies sent to the Entraining Officer, who will hand one copy to the R.T.O.,PERNES on arrival at station.

4. One Coy. 1st.Bn.Gordon Hldrs. will be responsible for loading & unloading transport. They will report to R.T.O.PERNES Station 3½ hours before time of departure of train to convey transport. They will be responsible for umloading this train at MONDICOURT.

5. Probable length of journey 2½ hours.

Dismounted Personnel will arrive at the entraining station 1 hour nd transport 3 hours before the time of departure.

In addition to the Iron Rations, the unconsumed portion of the y's rations will be carried on the man. Rations for consumption the day llowing will be delivered by the Supply wagons at the entraining station. l units will send a representative to the station at a time to be notiod later to take over these rations, and will be responsible for loading em on the train conveying their transport.

Motor Ambulances will proceed by road.

9. Railhead will change from CALONNE RICOUART to FREVENT on 14th. instant.

10. Billeting parties will be sent by the first train allotted to the Brigade Group.

Field Ambulance Advanced Parties will proceed by Motor Ambulance.

11. Entraining Programme for Brigade Group will be issued later.

12. Lorries will be detailed as under to convey stores and surplus ki

One lorry to each Battalion reporting at Battn.H.Q. at 5.30 a.m.,14th.i
One lorry to Brigade H.Q. " " " 5. 0 a.m. "
One lorry to 76th.T.M.Battery " " " 5. 0 a.m.

These lorries will be loaded as quickly as possible and will proceed to MONDICOURT, where loads will be dumped immediately. No second journey is possible. A small unloading party (not more than 5) will be detailed to proceed with lorries. They will unload the lorries on arrival at MONDICOURT and will remain in charge of them until they can be removed.

T. J. [signature]
Captain,

13th.August 1918. Staff Captain, 76th. Infantry Brigade.

Same Distribution as for O.O. No. 128.

C10

SECRET.
****

Copy No.19..

76th.INFANTRY BRIGADE ORDER No.129.

Ref.1/100,000 LENS 11. August 13th.1918.

1. The 3rd.Division is being transferred from the Fifth to the Third Army and will move to the VI Corps Area. On arrival in VI Corps Area the 3rd.Division will be held in Third Army Reserve.

2. 76th.Infantry Brigade will be disposed in the area SUS ST. LEGER - BEAUDRICOURT. Brigade Headquarters SUS ST.LEGER.
Para.4 of 76th.Inf.Brigade Order No.128 is amended accordingly.

3. All transport moving by road on arrival in the ANVIN - WAVRANS Area will come under the orders of O.C.3rd.Divl.Train, who will issue the necessary orders for the march for the night 14th./15th.August.

4. Location of Headquarters and arrival in billets will be reported to Brigade H.Q.as soon as possible after completion of move.

5. Brigade Headquarters will close at AMETTES at 11.30 a.m. August 14th.and will open at SUS ST.LEGER on arrival.

6. ACKNOWLEDGE.

C. Chipper Captain,
Brigade Major, 76th.Infantry Brigade.

Issued at 8 p.m.

Copies to:-
1. G.O.C.
2. 8th.K.O.R.L.
3. 2nd.Suffolk Regt.
4. 1st.Gordon Hldrs.
5. 76th.T.M.B.
6. "C"Coy.20th.K.R.R.C.(Pioneers).
7. 7th.Field Amb.
8. 529th.(E.R.)Fd.Co.R.E.
9. No.2 Coy Train.
10. B.M.
11. S.C.
12. Bde.Signal Offr.
13. Bde.Transport Offr.
14. Bde.Supply Offr.
15. Major MORGAN.
16. Major CHANDLER.
17. 3rd.Div."G".
18. " "Q".
19. War Diary.
20. "
21. File.
22.)
23.)
24.) Retained.
25.)
26.)

Reference Sheet 36b.

C11

SECRET.
****

MARCH AND ENTRAINING TABLE
TO ACCOMPANY 76th. INFANTRY BRIGADE ORDER No.128.

** ** ** ** ** **

Date.	Unit.	Starting point	Time	Route	Train No.	Train leaves.	Remarks.
Aug.14th.	Personnel only:- 8th.K.O.R.L. 529th.Field Co.R.E. 7th.Field Amb. Divl.Employment Co.) Traffic.) "C"Coy.Pioneer Bn.)	Cross Roads in FERFAY, B.18a.8.5. arrive PERNES Station 9.45 a.m.	8.35 a.m. 8.45 a.m. 8.48 a.m.	FERFAY, Cross Roads C.19d.4.4., FLORINGHEM.	1	10.45 a.m.	Under command of Lt.Col.B.H.H.PERRY,M.C.
Aug.14th.	Personnel only:- Brigade H.Q. 2nd.Suffolk Regt 1st.Gordon Hldrs less 1 Coy.	Cross Roads in FERFAY B.18a.8.5.	11.30 a.m. 11.32 a.m. 11.42 a.m.	-do-	2	1.34 p.m.	Under command of Lt.Col.G.C.STUBBS,D.S.O.
Aug.14th.	1st.Line Transport. Water. Cookers. Limbers. Carts. Bde H.Q. - - 1) 8th.K.O. 2 4 2) 2nd.Suffs. 2 4 2) 1st.G.Hdrs 2 4 2) 529th.Fd.Coy. - 1) 7th.Fd.Amb. - 1) "C"Co. Pioneer Bn. 1 1 1 7 13 10	Cross Roads in FERFAY B.18a.8.5. arrive PERNES Station 1.45 p.m.	12.20 p.m.	FERFAY, cross roads C.19d.4.4., FLORINGHEM, PERNES.	3	4.45 p.m.	Under command of an officer to be detailed by O.C. 1st.Gordon Hldrs.
Aug.14th.	1 Coy 1st.Gordon Hldrs.	Cross Roads in FERFAY B.18a.8.5.	12 noon	FERFAY, cross roads C.19d.4.4., FLORINGHEM.			Party for loading and unloading transport. Travel by Train No.3.

P.T.O.

Date.	Unit.	Starting point.	Time.	Route.	Destination.	Remarks.
Aug.13th.	Transport not moving by rail of:-					
	Bde H.Q.	Cross Roads in NEDON, B.8c.6.8.	11.30 p.m.	NEDONCHELLE - FONTAINE-LEZ-BOULANS - HEUCHIN.	ANVIN - WAVRANS Area.	Under command of O.C. No.2 Coy 3rd.Div.Train.
	529th.Fd.Co.R.E.		11.32 p.m.			
	7th.Field Amb.		11.36 p.m.			
	No.2 Coy Train.		11.40 p.m.			
	8th.K.O.R.L.		11.45 p.m.			
	2nd.Suff.Regt.		11.49 p.m.			
	1st.Gordon Hdrs,		11.53 p.m.			

C. Clifford Capt
Bde Major
76th Inf Bd

SECRET
******

C13

Copy No.

76th INFANTRY BRIGADE OREDR NO. 250.
****

Ref. Map LENS 11, 1/100000

August 19th, 1918.

1. The 3rd Division, less artillery, will concentrate in the area MONCHY-AU-BOIS - BERLES-AU-BOIS - HUMBERCAMP - POMMIER - BEINVILLERS-AU-BOIS - HANNESCAMPS on night 19th/ 20th August.

2. Units of 76th Inf. Bde. Group, less 7th Field Ambce. and No. 2 Coy. Train, will march in accordance with attached march table.
7th Field Ambce. and No. 2 Coy. Train will move under orders to be issued by 3rd Division "Q".

3. Distances between units on the march will be reduced to a minimum.

4. No. unit will march off from billets before 8.30 p.m.

5. First line transport will accompany units on the march and will park under arrangements which will be issued later.

6. One officer and ten men per Battalion will report to Lt. K.M. WALKER, 2nd suffolk Regt., at 76th Bde. H.Q. at 4 p.m. to reconnoitre and picket route.

7. Administrative instructions will be issued later.

8. Brigade H.Q. will close at SUS ST. LEGER at 8.30 p.m. and open at BERLES AU BOIS on arrival.

9. ACKNOWLEDGE.

Issued at 8 a.m.

sd/ C. Chipper, Captain,
Brigade Major, 76th Infantry Brigade.

Copies to:-
1. G.O.C.
2. 8th K.O.R.L. Regt.
3. 2nd Suffolk Regt.
4. 1st Gordon Hldrs.
5. 76th T.M.Bty.
6. Bde. Transport Officer.
7. Bde. Supply Offr.
8. No. 2 Coy. Train.
9. 529 Fd. Coy. R.E.
10. 7th Field Amb.
11. 3rd Div. "G".
12. " "Q".
13. 8th Inf. Bde.
14. 9th Inf. Bde.
15. B.M.
16. S.C.
17. Bde. Sig. Offr.
18. War Diary.
19. " "
20. File.
21.)
22.)
23.) Retained.
24.)
25.)

PTO

MARCH TABLE TO ACCOMPANY 76th INFANTRY BRIGADE ORDER NO. 130.

Ref. LENS 11.

Unit.	Starting point.	Time.	Route.	Destination.	Remarks.
2nd Suffolk Regt. followed by Bde. H.Q.& T.M.B.	Cross Road 2,000 yds. East of church in SUS ST. LEGER.	9 p.m.	SOMBRIN SAULTY LA HERLIERE LA CAUCHIE.	BERLES AU BOIS.	To follow 8th Bde. Group. To keep to Northern road through SUS ST. LEGER.
1st Gordon Hldrs.	-do-	9.10 p.m.	-do-	-do-	To keep to Northern road through SUS St. LEGER.
8th K.O.R.L.	-do-	9.20 p.m.	-do-	-do-	-do-
529 Field Co. R.E.	Cross roads B 11a 3.5 (Sheet 57d)	10.15 p.m.	POMMERA-Cross roads 500 yds.S.E. of GOMBREMETZ-HUMBERCAMP-POMMIER.	-do-	Not to pass Cross roads 500 yds. S.E. of GOMBREMETZ until M.G. Battn. is clear. Route to be reconnoitred beforehand.

C12

C14

SECRET.
****

Copy No......

76th. INFANTRY BRIGADE ORDER NO. 181.

Ref. Map ERVILLERS 1/20,000 Ed.1.A.
(specially marked)

August 20th. 1918.

1. The Third Army is to press back the enemy towards BAPAUME and prevent them destroying road and railway communication.

2. "Z" day has been notified verbally to all concerned.

3. At ZERO hour the BLUE Line will be attacked by VI and IV Corps by a surprise attack with Tanks.
In the VI Corps Area this will be carried out by 99th. Inf. Bde., 2nd. Divn., on the right and 2nd. Guards Brigade, Guards Divn on the left.

4. At ZERO plus 90 minutes 3rd. Division and Mark V. Tanks will pass through the 99th. Inf. Bde and gain the ARRAS - ALBERT Railway and crossings over it.
This attack will be carried out with 9th. Inf. Bde on the Right, 8th. Inf. Bde on the Left and 76th. Inf. Bde in Support disposed as below:-

8th. Inf. Bde. {	1 Battalion	1 Battn. 1 Battn.	1 Battalion	} 9th. Inf. Bde.
	1 Battalion		1 Battalion	

76th. Inf. Bde {
8th. K.O.R.L. 2nd. Suffolk Regt.
"C" Coy 3rd. Bn. M.G.C.
1st. Gordon Hldrs.

Time of Brigade moving forward from assembly positions will be notified later.

Troops attacking on either flank will be 2nd. Guards Brigade, (Guards Divn.) on left and 188th. Inf. Bde (63rd. Divn.) on right.

5. When the 8th. and 9th. Inf. Bdes reach the ARRAS - ALBERT Railway the 8th. K.O.R.L. will come under the orders of the G.O.C. 8th. Inf. Bde and 2nd. Suffolk Regt under those of G.O.C. 9th. Inf. Brigade. Their task and that of 1st. Gordon Hldrs will then normally be as explained in 3rd. Div. G.S. 1874 (SECRET) already issued.

When the line of the RAILWAY is carried and crossings secured and rendered passable the 2nd. Cavalry Brigade preceded by Whippet Tanks will pass through and gain the GREEN dotted line.

6. During the advance from their assembly positions forward in support of the 8th. and 9th. Brigades the tasks of the 76th. Inf. Brigade will be:-

(a) To support the attack whenever held up.
(b) To protect the rear and flank of these Brigades if the troops on the flanks are held up.
(c) To close any gap between the Brigades should one occur.
(d) To move forward and support the 8th. and 9th. Brigades if heavily counter-attacked.

7. The O.C., "C" Coy 3rd. Bn. M.G.C. will instruct his section commanders and keep in close touch with O's.C. Battalions 76th. Inf. Bde. He will detail one section to be ready to co-operate with each Battn. at the request of the O.C. Battalion in carrying out any of the tasks detailed in para. 6.

8. Any units which are obliged to diverge from their original formation to carry out the above tasks will report their action forthwith to Brigade H.Q. It must be impressed on all commanders that except in case of absolute necessity they are not to be drawn off from the main objective.

9. All units will detail special patrols to keep connection with units on their flanks, front and rear.

10. After ZERO hour a situation report, negative or otherwise, will be rendered every hour.

11. 76th.L.T.M.B. will form a carrying party.

12. 1 Section 529th.(E.R.) Field Co.R.E. attached to 76th.Inf.Bde. will remain at assembly position until ordered otherwise.

13. Artillery orders and time table will be issued separately to all concerned.

14. Headquarters 76th.Inf.Bde will be notified later.

15. Headquarters 188th.Inf.Bde (63rd.Div.) F.21d.2.5.
2nd.Guards Bde (Guards Div.) HENDECOURT.

16. The following signals between Tanks and Infantry will be employed:-

(a) Tanks to Infantry.

Red and Yellow Flag - Broken down - go on.
Green and White Flag - Come on.
Red, White and Blue Flag - British Tank coming back to rally.

(b) Infantry to Tanks.

Helmet on rifle pointed in direction required - Tank wanted.

17. (a) The S.O.S. Signal on the VI Corps front during the operations will be GREEN-GREEN-GREEN.

(b) On the front of the IV Corps on our right the S.O.S. Signal will be RED-GREEN-RED.

18. The leading troops will light flares when called for by a contact aeroplane sounding its Klaxon Horn or dropping smoke parachutes.

19. The 12th.Squadron R.A.F. will arrange to drop S.A.A. for the troops holding forward positions.

20. Prisoner of war cages will be established as follows:-
Near MONCHY-BIENVILLERS Road (E.3d.d.8.5.)
On HUMBERCAMP-LA COUCHIE Road (V.29b.1.9.).

Prisoners will be sent via 76th.Inf.Bde Headquarters.

21. Enemy dugouts will not be occupied unless previously reconnoitred by the special party detailed to examine them for concealed explosive.

22. ZERO hour on "Z" day will be notified later.

23. Watches will be synchronized at 76th.Inf.Bde H.Q. at 7 p.m. on "Y" day.

24. ACKNOWLEDGE.

C. Clifford Captain,
Brigade Major, 76th. Infantry Brigade.

Issued at 3 a.m.

Distribution over.

** ** **

Copies to:- 1. G.O.C.
2. 8th.K.O.R.L.
3. 2nd.Suffolk Regt.
4. 1st.Gordon Hldrs.
5. 76th.T.M.B.
6. "C" Coy 3rd.Bn.M.G.C.
7. 529th.(E.R.)Fd.Co.R.E.
8. 3rd.Div."G".
9. 8th.Inf.Bde.
10. 9th. "
11. 2nd.Guards Brigade.
12. 188th.Inf.Bde.
13. B.M.
14. S.C.
15. Sig.Offr.
16. Int.Offr.
17. War Diary.
18. "
19. File.
20.)
21.)
22.) Retained.
23.)
24.)

SECRET.
****

ADDENDUM NO.1 to 76th.INF.BDE.ORDER No.131.

Ref.1/20,000 AYETTE or ERVILLERS Sheets. Aug.20th.1918.

1. 76th.Inf.Bde.H.Q.will close at BERLES AU BOIS at 9 p.m. August 20th.,and open at F.8d.90.85.on arrival.

2. Headquarters 9th.Inf.Bde from 10 p.m. August 20th will be at F.15d.central.
Headquarters 8th.Inf.Bde will be at F.5b.7.3.

3. Battalionn of 76th.Inf.Bde.and "C" Coy 3rd.Bn.M.G.C. will advance from assembly positions at ZERO.

4. Reference paras.5 and 6 of 3rd.Division G.S.1574 (General Instructions) already forwarded.
In order that the information that the crossings over the Railway are possible for Cavalry and Tanks may be quickly transmitted 8th.and 9th.Inf.Bdes will arrange for the following signals to be made and repeated to the rear:-

on the 9th.Bde.front - GOLDEN RAIN ROCKETS.
on the 8th.Bde.front - ROCKETS BURSTING INTO RED & WHITE LIGHTS.

On these signals being sent up the two leading Battalions of 76th.Inf.Bde i.e.- 2nd.Suffolk Regt and 8th.K.O.R.L. will move up to the Railway ready to move forward in support of the Cavalry.

5. Ref.para.18 of 76th.Bde Order No.131 :-

(a) Aeroplanes will call for flares at:-

ZERO plus 1 hour
" " 3 hours
" " 5 "
" " 7 "

(b) There will be a counter-attack machine in the air from ZERO onwards. The signal to denote the assembly of the enemy to counter-attack is the droppong of a RED smoke bomb over the place where the enemy are seen.

6. The boundary between the 3rd.and Guards Divisions will be continued in an Easterly direction along the grid line dividing squares A.12 and A.18,B.7 and B.13.

7. Amendment to 3rd.Division G.S.1574:-

The Tanks will cross the BLUE Line at ZERO plus 75 minutes.
The Infantry will cross the BLUE Line at ZERO plus 79 minutes.

8. ACKNOWLEDGE.

C. Clifton
Captain,
Issued at 5.30 p.m. Brigade Major,76th.Infantry Brigade.

Copies to all recipients of 76th.Bde Order No.131.

** ** ** ** ** ** ** **

C16

SECRET.
****

Copy No. 16.

76th. INFANTRY BRIGADE ORDER NO. 132.

Ref. Maps LENS 11 & 1/20,000 AYETTE Sheet.

August 20th. 1918.

1. Units of 76th. Inf. Bde Group will move to assembly positions tonight 20th./21st by track already reconnoitred leaving Southern extremity of BERLES AU BOIS as follows:-

76th. L.T.M.B. .... 8.30 p.m.
2nd. Suffolk Regt .... 9 p.m.
followed by 1 Section "C" Coy 3rd. Bn. M.G.C.
8th. K.O.R.L. .... 9.40 p.m.
followed by 1 Section 3rd. Bn. M.G.C.
1st. Gordon Hldrs .... 10.20 p.m.
followed by "C" Coy 3rd. Bn. M.G.C. less two sections, followed by 1 Section 529th. Field Co. R.E.

Companies will march at 5 minutes intervals.

2. Assembly positions will be as follows:-

2nd. Suffolk Regt .... & 1 Section M.G.C.	PURPLE RESERVE between F.1c & E.12d.9.5. approx.
8th. K.O.R.L. .... & 1 Section M.G.C.	PURPLE RESERVE between E.12d.9.5. & E.24a.3.8. approx
1st. Gordon Hldrs .... & "C" Coy 3rd. Bn. M.G.C. less 2 sections.	Area E.11b, d., E.12a, c.
1 Section 529th. Field Coy R.E. ...	Area E.11a.
76th. L.T.M.B.	Area F.8d.
Pack mules	E.12b.0.3.

3. Horse transport of Battalions will be sent back to transport lines HUMBERCAMP on leaving this area.

4. ACKNOWLEDGE.

C. Chippe[?]
Captain,
Brigade Major, 76th. Infantry Brigade.

Issued at 5.30 p.m.

Copies to:-

1. G.O.C.
2. 8th. K.O.R.L.
3. 2nd. Suffolk Regt.
4. 1st. Gordon Hldrs.
5. 76th. T.M.B.
6. "C" Coy. 3rd. Bn. M.G.C.
7. 529th. Field Co. R.E.
8. 3rd. Div. "G".
9. 8th. Inf. Bde.
10. 9th. "
11. 2nd. Guards Bde.
12. 188th. Inf. Bde.
13. B.M.
14. S.C.
15. Sig. Offr.
16. Int. Offr.
17. War Diary.
18. "
19. File.
20.)
21.)
22.) Retained.
23.)
24.)

Ref Map 1/20,000

76th Inf Bde Order No 133 SECRET

C18

1. In accordance with 3rd Div GA196 76th Inf Bde will be withdrawn into Divl Reserve after dark tonight 21/22

8th KORL and 2nd Suffolk Rgt will rejoin 76th Inf Bde under orders of GOC 8th & 9th Inf Bdes respectively

2. On completion of withdrawal units will be located as below:—

8th KORL on hill A9c and A9 central Not to go north of latter on account of Yellow Cross Gas.

1st Gordon Highlanders in A20c & b just west of ridge.

2nd Suffolk Rgt south of AYETTE-COURCELLES road in F18c and A13b west of ridge AERODROME TR to be avoided.

C Coy 3rd MG Bn in F18 just west of 2nd Suffolk Rgt. The 2 sections in 8th & 9th Bdes areas will be withdrawn under orders of GOCs 8th & 9th Bdes and rejoin Coy as above

3. 76th Inf Bde HQ will move to a point in COURCELLES ALLEY to be notified later Hour of closing at present location will be notified later. Reports after 10pm to be sent to junction of COURCELLES ALLEY and AERODROME TR.

[illegible] will notify completion of move [illegible]tions.

5. Units will have to dig themselves in and take special precautions against Yellow Cross Gas.

6. Yellow Cross Gas is present in Squares F12, A7 south of AYETTE - COURCELLES road and in A20 a & b east of ridge.

7. 8th Bde H.Q are at junction of FOCH and MOYBRAIN Trenches A8a. 8.7.

9th Bde H.Q are ~~in sunk road east of RIDGE~~ at A13d. 95.80.

8. acknowledge.

Copies to:-

Capt

1/2 } 8 KORL

Bn. 76. Inf Brigade

3/4 } 2 Suff Rgt

Aug 21/18

5/6 } 1. Gordon Hldrs

7 "C" Coy. ~~X~~ 3. Bn. M.G.C.

8 8 Inf Bde

9 9 " "

10 3 Div. G

11 File

12 99 Inf. Bde

Issued at 7.15 p.m.

by [illegible]

76th Inf Bde Order No. 14 SECRET

Map: Sheet 1/20,000

C19.

Copy No.

[illegible] 21st 1918

1. 76 Bde No. 133 is hereby cancelled.

2. 76 Bde will withdraw tonight 21/22 into [illegible] and take over defence of BLUE LINE from 99th Inf. Bde (2 Div) as follows —

8 K.O. will take over defence of BLUE LINE within Divl. boundary. This line is occupied at present north of the AYETTE – COURCELLES road by 1st Royal Berks.

1st Gordon Hrs will take over [illegible] west of AERODROME from Southern Divl. boundary to AYETTE – COURCELLES road exclusive now occupied by [illegible].

2 Suffolk Regt will take over same [illegible] from AYETTE – COURCELLES road to northern Divl boundary inclusive.

C Coy 3rd M.G. Bn will concentrate west of [illegible] and take over from [illegible] 1 Gordon [illegible] and [illegible]

3. Guides from 1st Royal Berks will meet O.C.'s of 76 Bde Battns at junction of COURCELLES [illegible] and AERODROME [illegible] at 12 midnight.

4. 76 Inf Bde HQ will move to [illegible] on BUCQUOY – AYETTE road near [illegible] and open at 12 midnight 21/22.

5. Ack.

Issued 11 pm.

(Sd) [illegible] Capt.
BM 76th Inf Bde.

Copies – 1 [illegible] 5 [illegible]
2 Suffolk 6 [illegible]
3 G.H.
4 [illegible] Inf Bde

C 20

SECRET

Preliminary 7th Inf. Bde. Order No. 135
Operations

1. The 7th Inf. Bde. will attack and capture GOMIECOURT tonight 22/23 August.
Wilts will be on left
S. Lancs Regt. on right
1 Gordon Hdrs in support.

2. Royal Scots of 8th Bde will attack at same time on left and capture woods in A23a and road junction A16d. 8.7.
Grenadier Guards on right attack at same time.
9th Inf. Bde will take wood about A28c. 7.7

3. Boundaries: left – Grid line through A29 and 23 central.
Right – Grid line through A28 and 29 central.
Dividing line between Battns – Grid line between squares 23 and 29.
Water point in GOMIECOURT 100x south of cross roads including R.E. tank ~~road~~

4. 1 Gordon Hdrs will have two companies in reserve and two companies echeloned on right to protect flank and block sunken road in A28b and d.

5. 8 Tanks (Mk. IV) will take part: 4 to go through village, 2 on each flank. They will cross the railway line at A22 central and A28 central.

6. A creeping barrage of shrapnel and H.E. will start at ZERO 300 yards east of railway and advance at a rate of 100 yards in 4 minutes in front of the tanks.
There will be a standing barrage on GOMIECOURT till caught up by creeper and a protective barrage during consolidation.

7. Line of consolidation about GOMIECOURT Circle Trench.

8. Machine Guns will join creeping and protective barrages and fire on known hostile machine gun ~~posts~~ nests.
8 Guns specially guarding Southern flank of attack.

Contd.

9. Assembly position just west of railway will be taken up by 2.15 a.m.

1. Gordon Highrs will follow 2. Suffolk Regt to assembly position, the latter starting from present position at 9.30 p.m. and former at 10 p.m.

8. K.O.R.L. by another route.

Routes as settled at conference.

10. Battn. H.Q will be:-

2 Suffolk Regt and 1. Gordon Highrs } Blue spot A.21.a.5.1

8. K.O.R.L. to be notified later.

11. 76. Bde H.Q will close at F.16.a.5.3 at 8 p.m. on 22nd and open at A.14.c.?.3 in COURCELLES ABBEY on arrival.

12. White bands will be worn on right arm by all taking part in the attack.

13. ZERO will be 3 a.m. on the 23rd.

ZERO hour will be the firing of the artillery barrage.

14. An officer from Brigade H.Q. will call at Battn. H.Q's about 6 p.m. to synchronise watches.

15. Acknowledge.

Issued at 6 p.m.

C. Cliffer Capt.
Bde Maj 76. Inf. Bde.

Copies

1 8 K.O.R.L.
2 2 Suff Regt.
3 1 G.H.
4 76. Machine Gun Detachment
5 76. Trench Mortar Detachment
6 3 Div G
7 3. Div. R.A.
8 [illegible]
9 File
10 8 Inf Bde
11 9 "
12 —

SECRET

MACHINE GUNS. Instructions

Ref. 76th Infantry Brigade Order No. 135

32 Machine Guns will co-operate in the attack.

12 Guns of B. Coy. attached 9th Brigade will fire on area G.4a. from ZERO to ZERO + 90.

24 Guns will fire on Barrage as under:-

(1). From ZERO + 10 to ZERO + 20 on a line from A.29a.55.00. to A.23c.80.75.

(2). From ZERO + 24 to ZERO + 56 enfilade flanks of village

12 guns from A.23d.40.65 to A.24c.40.75.

12 " " A.29b.00.25 to A.30a.00.20.

These guns will lift in accordance with Artillery Barrage time table.

(3). From ZERO + 60 to ZERO + 90 on a line from

A.30c.00.40 to A.24c.60.75.

This Barrage Line will be S.O.S. Line.

At ZERO + 90 all guns will cease fire and be prepared to fire on S.O.S. Lines when required.

Rates of Fire.

Barrage. One belt per gun per 10 minutes

S.O.S. 300 rounds per gun per minute.

C. Clipper Captain

22/8/18 Brigade Major, 76th Infantry Brigade.

Ref. 1/40000 ERVILLERS

76th Inf. Bde Order No. 136

SECRET

C21

1. The 76th Inf. Bde will move today Aug. 26th into the area between the ACHIET-LE-GRAND – ARRAS Railway and the BAPAUME – ARRAS Road, within the Guards Divisional Boundaries where it will become the support Brigade of the Guards Division, relieving the 3rd Guards Brigade.

2. Battalions will move as follows:–

Unit	Starting Point	Time
8 K.O.R.L.	Road junction	5.15 p.m.
1. Gordon Hdrs	F5d.3.2 in	5.55 p.m.
2. Suffolk Regt	AYETTE.	6.35 p.m.

Battalions will move by platoons at 200 yards distance. They will be met by guides from advance party at Cross Roads in MOYENNEVILLE A3d.9.9.

3. Areas are allotted provisionally as follows:–

8 K.O.R.L. S.29, S.30
2 Suffolk Regt. A.5, A.11 b d, A.12 a c.
1 Gordon Hdrs A.6, b & d, A.12 b d, B.1 a c. (B.7 a c.
"D" Coy M.G. Bn & 156th Fd. Coy R.E. } A.11 a c

4. Transport and M.G. Coy and R.E. section will move later under arrangements to be notified separately.

5. Each Battalion will leave out of action 10% of present strength including a nucleus of specialists.

6. Completion of move, location of H.Q. and disposition to be notified.

7. Brigade H.Q. will close at present location at 7 p.m. and open on arrival at place to be notified later.

8. Acknowledge.

C. Chipper Capt.
B.M., 76th Inf. Bde

Issued 3.35 p.m.

Copies 1 8 K.O.R.L.
2 2 Suff. Regt.
3 1 Gordon Hdrs
4
5
6

"A" Form
MESSAGES AND SIGNALS.

Army Form C. 2121
(In pads of 100)

No. of Message..............

Prefix.............. Code..............m | Words. Charge. | This message is on a/c of: C22 .... Service. | Recd. at..........m.
Office of Origin and Service Instructions | Sent At..........m. To.......... By.......... | SECRET (Signature of "Franking Officer.") | Date.......... From.......... By..........

TO 8 K.O.R.L.
2 Suffolk Regt
1 Gordon Hldrs

Sender's Number.	Day of Month.	In reply to Number.	AAA
* G235	26	Preliminary	Instruction

1. 76 Bde will relieve support Brigade of Guards Divn this evening.
2. Batts will be located in trenches south and west of HAMELINCOURT east of railway.
3. 76 Bde will be under orders of Guards Divn.
4. Route via MOYENNEVILLE. further details as regards time.
5. advance parties etc will be communicated as soon as known.

From 76 Inf Bde
Place
Time

The above may be forwarded as now corrected. (Z) (Sd) C. Chipps Capt.
Censor. Signature of Addressor or person authorised to telegraph in his name.

* This line should be erased if not required.

(4715) Wt. W3253/P511 1,113,336 Shts. 2/18 C. & Co. (C.4)

"A" Form
MESSAGES AND SIGNALS.

Army Form C. 2121
(In pads of 100)
No. of Message..............

Prefix............ Code..............m	Words. Charge.	This message is on a/c of:	Recd. at..........m.
Office of Origin and Service Instructions	Sent	CR3 Service.	Date..............
	At..............m.		From ....
	To..............		
	By..............	(Signature of "Franking Officer.")	By ....

TO
JONE = KORL
LOBI = 2nd SK
QOGO = 1st QH

Sender's Number.	Day of Month.	In reply to Number.	AAA
* G236	26		

Ref. G235 send advance party 1 officer 6 OR. to report to Lt CAMBRIDGE at cross roads AYETTE F11 b.7.5 with bicycles at 3pm. These will reconnoitre new areas and meet Battalion at cross roads MOYENNEVILLE. JONE will start from here about 5 pm then QOGO then LOBI. Orders follow.

From BUTA
Place
Time 2.30pm.

The above may be forwarded as now corrected. (Z) (Sd) O. Chippe Capt.

Censor. Signature of Addressor or person authorised to telegraph in his name.

* This line should be erased if not required.

(4715) Wt. W3253/P511 1,113,336 Shts. 2/18 C. & Co. (E.4)

Army Form C. 2121
(in pads of 100).

"A" Form
MESSAGES AND SIGNALS.

No. of Message....................

Prefix.............Code..............m.	Words	Charge.	This message is on a/c of	Recd. at..........m.
Office of Origin and Service Instructions.	COPY			
	Sent		..........................Service.	Date..................
	At..................m.		C24	From ....
	To..................			
	By..................		(Signature of "Franking Officer.")	By..................

TO		
Transport Officers	8. K.O.R.L.	
	2 Suffolk Regt	
	1. Gordon Hdrs	

Sender's Number.	Day of Month.	In reply to Number.	AAA
* G. 228	26		

Ref. ERVILLERS 1/20,000

Transport will march night 26th to join their Battalions as follows:-

Unit.	Starting Point	Time	Route
8 K.O.R.L.	Rd. junct	8 pm	MOYENNEVILLE
1. Gordon H.	F5d.3.2	8.10pm	
2. Suffolk Rgt.	in AYETTE	8.20pm	

Battalion Areas

8 K.O.R.L.	S29. S30
1 Gordon H.	A6 b,d. A12 b,d, B1a,c B7a,c
2 Suff. Regt.	A9. A11 b,d, A12 a,c.

Location of transport lines will be notified en route.

Transport officers will please either report at Bde H.Q. F8d.9.1 at 7 pm or send a mounted orderly.

From			
Place			
Time			

The above may be forwarded as now corrected. (Z) (Sd) C. Chippen Capt

Censor. Signature of Addressor or person authorised to telegraph in his name

* This line should be erased if not required. Bgr. 76 Inf Bde.

Wt. W492/M1647 100,000 pads. 4/17. W. & Co., Ltd. (E. 1187.)

C25

SECRET

8 KORL
2 Suffolk Regt
1 Gordon Hldrs

"D" Coy. M.G.C.
1 Gds Bde for (information)

G25a. 28/8

1. Troops on our left have Captured FONTAINE LEZ CROSILLES and are advancing. Enemy on our front may withdraw in Consequence.

2. If this takes place 1st. Guards Bde will push on followed by 76. Inf Bde

3. (a) 8 KORL will march under orders of G.O.C. 1. Gds Bde who will inform G.O.C. 76. Inf Bde when they have started.

4. (b) 1. Gordon Hldrs and 2 Suffolk Regt will be ready to move off at 6 am, the former on the right, latter on left.

(c.) 1 Sectn "D" Co. 3Bn. M.G.C. will march between 8 KORL and remainder of 76. Bde. "D" Coy. 3Bn. M.G.C. less 1 section will follow in rear of 76. Bde.

Units as in (b) & (c) will move on receipt of orders from G.O.C. 76. Inf. Bde

4. If this move takes place a report Centre will be established at present 1. Gds Bde H.Q. B17.3.S.

5. Transport lines will remain as at present. Pack mules will be sent to Battns.

6. Acknowledge.

Issued at 4am

(Sd) C. Chippe Capt
BM 76. Bde

Ref. 1/20,000 **76th Inf. Brigade Order No 137** SECRET
51 B. S.W.
57c. N.W. Copy No

C26

Aug. 28/18

1. As far as can be ascertained the situation at 6pm. was as follows:-
167th Bde, 56th Div. on line LEG LANE running through U.30 [illegible]
185th Bde, 62nd Div. joining 1st Guards Bde in S.E. corner of B.1[illegible]
76th Inf. Bde will relieve 1st Guards Bde tonight 28/29th between above boundaries.

2. As ordered verbally by Brigadier General.
1st Gordon Hdrs will take over the line from S.E corner B.12 b as far as junction of BANKS RESERVE and sunken road B.11 b 4.9, exclusive, from 2nd Bn. Grenadier Guards.
[illegible] from junction BANKS RESERVE and sunken road at B.11 b 4.9 along line of road through B.5 d [illegible] and [illegible] to [illegible] and join up with 56th Divn. Patrols will be sent out at dawn to gain touch and kept [illegible] with 167th Bde.
2nd Suffolk Regt will take over from BANKS TRENCH at right Divisional Boundary along trench and road to B.4 central.
"D" Coy 3. M.G. Bn. will take over dispositions from Guards M.G. officer.

3. 1st Gordon Hdrs will start at 7.30 pm. and 2nd Suffolk Regt follow. Guides for 1st Gordon Hdrs will be at B.9 [illegible] at 9 pm.
Relief by [illegible] arranged by 1st Guards Brigade.

4. 76th Bde H.Q. will be with 1st Guards Bde H.Q. till midnight 28/29th and open at B.10 c. 6.0. south of HAMLY COPSE on arrival.

5. The present scheme of operations is to gain ground by means of strong patrols and where found clear to push forward our line. Enemy is to be harassed in his retirement to the greatest extent. O.C. Battalions will not attack villages or other strong points without orders from Brigade H.Q. Such attacks will be carried out in an organized manner with artillery and tank co-operation. It is most important to keep touch with Battns and Brigades on flanks for purpose of co-operation.

6. Acknowledge.

C. Chipper Capt.
B.M. 76th Inf. Brigade

Issued at 8 pm.

Copies to:-
1 [illegible]
2 2nd Suffolk Regt.
3 1. Gdn. Hdrs
4 "D" Co. M.G. Bn.
5 3. Div. "G"
6 1. Gds. Bde
7 8. Inf. Bde
8 9 "
9 [illegible]
10 } Retained
11 }
12 }
13. 185 Inf. Bde
14. 167 "

[illegible]

C 27

1. On the morning of August 30th [illegible] Inf Bde will gain the line C 3 a 3.9 (BULLECOURT AVENUE) in touch with 56th Div. on high ground east and south of LONGATTE — road junction C 8 d 1.6 — thence line of road to southern divisional boundary in trench with 62nd Div. at C 13 d 5.7.

2. Objectives. (a) 2nd Suffolk Regt from [illegible] to track junction C 8 d 1.6 inclusive.

(b) 1st Gordon Highlanders track junction C 8 d 1.6 exclusive to track junction C 13 d 5.9

(c) 8th K.O.R.L. Regt will be in Brigade Reserve.

3. 2nd Suffolk Regt will assemble south of railway U 25 d - C 1 c and attack ECOUST - LONGATTE from the West with the co-operation of Tanks and pass on to objective as in para 2.

56th Division will attack BULLECOURT AVENUE northwards from 16th Bde. Boundary simultaneously.

1st Gordon Highlanders will pivot on their present right up to their objective in touch with 2nd Suffolk Regt.

4. Field Artillery Barrage will open at ZERO on the line U 26 c [illegible] in straight line to C 7 b 70.55 - down the road to C 7 b 3.0 - thence straight line to C 13 a 6.3 - thence due south to track junction [illegible] inclusive.

This barrage will move as follows:-

Open on above line at ZERO and dwell for 10 minutes. Creep at 100 yards per 3 minutes then to final protective line: C 3 b 9.0 in straight line to C 9 c 0.0 - straight [illegible] C 13 d 9.0

Heavy Artillery will bombard ECOUST - LONGATTE and outskirts and also neutralise [illegible] NOREUIL [illegible]

C 27

5. ZERO will be 5 a.m. August 10th
The opening of the artillery barrage will give ZERO hour.

6. Headquarters of 2nd Suffolk Regt and 8th K.O.R.L. will be at cross roads B.5.d.a.8
Headquarters of 1st Gordon Highlanders B.17.a
L'HOMME MORT as at present.

7. Acknowledge

C. Clifford Capt
Bde. Major
76th Inf. Bde.

Issued at 11.30 pm.

Copy No.

1.	8th KORL	9	8th Inf. Bde
2.	2nd Suffolk Regt	10	9th Inf. Bde
3	1st Gordon Hdrs.	11	File
4	D Coy 3rd MG Bn.	12.	War Diary
5	C Tank Detachment	13	"
6	3rd Division G	14	Retained
7.	167th Infantry Brigade	15	
8	185th Infantry Brigade	16	

C28

Inf. [illegible] Aug 30th [illegible]

1. 76th Inf. Bde, less 1st Gordon Hdrs [illegible] and [illegible] will be relieved [illegible] 30/31 by 9th Inf. Bde.

2. 9th Inf. Bde will take over the front as follows.

4th Royal Fusiliers from [illegible] C 7 and C18 to grid line between [illegible]

13th Kings from grid line between [illegible] to [illegible] boundary [illegible]

1st North'd Fusrs, 2 coys [illegible] 1 coy [illegible] 1 coy BANKS TR. [illegible]

3. For purposes of relief the [illegible] 4th Royal Fus. will [illegible] who will [illegible] the taken over by 13th Kings will [illegible] over by [illegible] STUBBS [illegible]

4th Royal Fus. and 13th Kings will be formed [illegible] in battle formation.

4. All [illegible] of 1st Gordon Hdrs [illegible] over by 4th Royal Fus. will [illegible] orders [illegible] of O.C. 1st Gordon Hdrs [illegible] accommodated in [illegible]

[illegible] 3rd [illegible] will [illegible] command of O.C. 1st Gordon Hdrs.

On completion of the relief O.C. 1st Gordon Hdrs will [illegible] 9th Inf. Bde together with [illegible]

5. [illegible] of 1 [illegible] and [illegible] will [illegible] of [illegible] CORSE [illegible] at 8.30 pm.

4th Royal Fusrs [illegible] followed by [illegible] 13th Kings and 1st North'd Fusiliers

C 28

6. As soon as 4th Royal Fusrs and 13th Kings are in position 8th KORL and 2nd Suffolk Regt will be withdrawn.

7. Completion of relief will be notified by sending the word ECOUST

8. 76th Bde H.Q. will close at present location on completion of relief and open at a place to be notified later on arrival.

9. Battalions on relief will be accommodated as follows:-

8th KORL less 1 Coy — MORY SWITCH } exact locations follow
2nd Suffolk Regt — MORY SWITCH

10. Acknowledge

C. [illegible] Capt
Bde Major
76th Inf. Bde.

Issued at 8.0 pm.

Copy No

1	8th KORL	10	3rd Div Q
2	2nd Suff Rgt	11	3rd Div Train No 2 Coy
3	1st Gordon Hdrs	12	Bde. Supply Officer
4	D Coy MG Bn	13	O.C. Details
5	9th Inf Bde	14	File
6	105 Inf Bde	15	War Diary
7	107 Inf Bde	16	" "
8	8th Inf Bde	17	} Retained
9	3rd Div G	18	}

76th Inf. Bde [illegible]

1st

C 29

[illegible] orders [illegible] issued [illegible]

[illegible] the line [illegible]COURT [illegible] and [illegible] SUPT. to C 8 [illegible]

[illegible] 3 a 3.4. [illegible] south [illegible] C 7 [illegible]

1st [illegible] don Hdrs. 76th Inf. Bde [illegible] in [illegible]COURT [illegible]

[illegible]

[illegible] NOREUIL SWITCH and [illegible] TRENCH in [illegible]

[illegible] 9th Inf. Bde. will advance to [illegible]

this objective north of a line [illegible]

76th Inf. Bde [illegible] south of this line.

1st Gordon Hdrs with 1 Coy 8th KORL are attacking [illegible] NOREUIL SWITCH [illegible] towards C 4 [illegible]

[illegible] are doing the same along [illegible] TRENCH.

[illegible] 2 Coys 8th KORL in touch with 4th Royal [illegible] on their left will advance with their right on NOREUIL SWITCH and clear up the ground between NOREUIL SWITCH and northern brigade boundary.

[illegible] of objective is [illegible]

[illegible] with [illegible] north of [illegible]

the two Coys 8th KORL [illegible] to clear [illegible] of ground. A smoke barrage will come down on [illegible] of objective to screen movement of [illegible] and infantry.

5. 2nd Suffolk Regt. will be in Brigade Reserve in

DAWNS TRENCH in B 10, 11.

[illegible] 3rd M.G. Batn. will protect the consolidation.

6. 76th Inf. Bde. H.Q. are at B 10 c 6.0.

H.Q. 8th KORL & 1st Gordon Hdrs. – B 17 a [illegible]

H.Q. 2nd Suffolk Regt. – B 10 [illegible]

Acknowledge.

Issued at 1.45 a.m.

C. [illegible] Capt.

[illegible]

[illegible]

C 30

Brief report of Operations Aug. 21st–23rd

76th Infantry Brigade

Aug. 20. The Brigade with [illegible] Coy 3rd Bn. M.G.C. left BERLES-AU-BOIS after dark on the evening of Aug. 20th and assembled in position about PURPLE RESERVE LINE [illegible] south of MONCHY-AU-BOIS without incident. Quiet night with heavy mist. Bde HQ – F.2.c.9.8

Aug 21st. At ZERO 4.55 a.m. the Brigade acting as Divisional Reserve advanced from assembly position in small columns and followed 8th & 9th Inf. Bdes at about 1,000 yards distance. 8th K.O. were on the left, 2nd Suffolk Regt on the right and 1st Gordon Hdrs followed 1000 yards in rear. 1 Sect. of M.G. Coy was with each of the leading Battns, remainder of Coy with 1st Gordon Hdrs.

A very thick mist covered the battlefield and rendered keeping up direction and touch very difficult. This mist did not lift till about 11 a.m. when neighbourhood of COURCELLES was reached. The open country added to the difficulty and it was necessary to keep to the village in order to maintain direction. The two leading Battalions coming under the orders of 8th and 9th Inf. Bdes on their Brigades reaching the railway line objective, were sent forward to assist in the consolidation. 8th K.O. had a good deal of mopping up to do in COURCELLES and there was still considerable M.G. opposition in squares A.21 and 27 south of the village. The railway line however was made good soon after the fog cleared though the right flank of the 2nd Suffolk Regt was continually troubled by German M.G. fire from west of the railway in G.[illegible] on the 63rd Division front.

In the late afternoon 2 Coys of the Reserve Battalion, 1st Gordon Hdrs were ordered by H.Q. 9th Inf. Bde to co-operate in an attack on the railway embankment just north of ACHIET-LE-GRAND railway station with the 63rd Div. on the right. About 7 p.m. it was found that the attack of 63rd Div had already taken place but had only been partially successful. At the request however of [illegible] ANSON Bn. (63rd Div) the next Battn. on the right, the attack was [illegible] and launched at 7.30 p.m. During [illegible] intense hostile artillery and machine gun fire and lack of artillery support this attack was held up and dug in on the forward slope west of the railway, having gained their advance forward about 500 yards beyond the forward slope.

Night 21st/22nd. During the night Battalions of 76th Bde were withdrawn again into Brigade reserve and relieved 99th Inf. Bde (2nd Div) on the BLUE LINE west of COURCELLES. 76th Bde H.Q. moved to A.16.a.3.3 on the AYETTE–BUCQUOY road.

Aug 22nd. Orders were received in the afternoon for Brigade to capture GOMIECOURT at 4 a.m. Aug. 23rd. C.O.s were assembled at 3.30 p.m. and instructions and orders issued. Bde H.Q. moved next night to A.14.c.7.1

Night 22nd/23rd. Battalions moved off from BLUE LINE about 11 pm to assembly positions west of railway. 8th K.O.R.L. were to capture northern half of village, 2nd Suffolk Regt the southern half and consolidate about the line of GOMIECOURT CIRCLE Trench. 1st Gordon Hdrs were to guard the right flank of the attack with 2 Coys and hold 2 Coys in reserve. One Battn of 6th Inf. Bde was to co-operate and protect northern flank of the attack.

The approach march to assembly positions was quiet, but trouble was experienced by 2nd Suffolk Regt and 1st Gordon Hdrs in taking up position, with their right flank Coys owing to advanced position of the enemy west of the railway. A German M.G. had to be dislodged from assembly position of the flanking Coys of 1st Gordon Hdrs.

ZERO was altered to 4 a.m.

Eight Mark IV Tanks had been ordered to co-operate and assembled in the ridge of DOROTHY Trench at 3.30 a.m. They could not approach closer to the railway owing to observation by enemy in A.22.

Aug. 23rd. Artillery barrage opened well at 4 a.m. and infantry following closely attained all their objectives with few casualties. The tanks had difficulty in crossing the railway and arrived too late to be of assistance. The enemy were taken unawares by the attack and,

During the [illegible] which the troops [illegible] their [illegible] of the [illegible] and [illegible] by [illegible] in ammunition, the enemy and keeping them down in their dugouts and [illegible] to bring up their M.G.

M.G. fire from the railway to the south was the most troublesome feature in the operation.

Capt. Hugo, the liaison officer of the 3rd and 37th Divisions [illegible] and later passed beyond our lines.

"C" & "D" Coys. 3rd Bn. M.G.C. co-operated in the barrage at 4 a.m. 23rd directing special attention to the flank of the attack. 1 Section crossed the railway and covered the right flank by direct fire.

28/8/18

Brigadier-General
Commanding 76th Infantry Brigade

Points brought out

by the operation.

1. Importance of the use of the compass to keep direction and check position on [illegible] landmarks. [illegible] and steel helmets [illegible] be [illegible] in their [illegible].

2. Wounded should be dressed but not removed by stretcher bearers until the fighting is finished.

3. Shovels are indispensable.

4. Owing to initial difficulties tanks were not able to co-operate fully. One tank however rendered very useful service mopping up [illegible]. A supply tank to a Brigade would be invaluable.

An instance occurred of a sergeant going to direct a tank to a M.G. nest being shot at by the tank's 6 pdr gun. Some signal by which tanks recognise our own men approaching would be valuable.

5. Visual signalling worked well. Runners were very hard worked, casualties being heavy [illegible] in Bn. [illegible] 3 [illegible] is the minimum for mobile warfare. Telephone communication was well maintained on Aug. 23rd.

6. It is suggested that only part of the L.G.s should be sent forward at first to avoid loss, the remainder coming up later when consolidation begins, the L.G. section meanwhile fighting with their rifles. This is dependent on the special circumstances under which the attack is undertaken.

A hostile [illegible] was put out of action by a L.G. section firing at 800 yards range.

7. Practice in [illegible] at long distances across country is very desirable. [illegible] invaluable.

[illegible]

8. A definite area of not more than [illegible] down, [illegible] section commanders is considered necessary under [illegible] [illegible] conditions.

9. In dusty weather a chamois or similar brush for keeping breech of rifle in working order should be carried by every man.

"C" Form

Army Form C. 2123.
(In books of 100.)

MESSAGES AND SIGNALS. No. of Message..........

Prefix SM Code [illegible] Words 41	Received	Sent, or sent out	Office Stamp.
£ s. d. Charges to collect	From YC By [illegible]	At C 31 m. To By	
Service Instructions.			

Handed in at VEKA Office [illegible] m. Received [illegible] m.

TO Bdes. = 76th Inf Bde

*Sender's Number	Day of Month	In reply to Number	AAA
BM 209	7		

GOC Congratulates all Ranks on Excellent Work Carried out under Trying and Difficult conditions.

FROM PLACE & TIME VEKA = 3rd Div 8.40 pm

* This line should be erased if not required.

(B 8070) Wt. w. 7496—M857 250,000 Pads. 10/16 H & S (E436.) Forms/C.2123/3.

3rd Division.

WAR DIARY & APPENDICES

B. H. Q.

76th INFANTRY BRIGADE

SEPTEMBER 1918.

3rd Division.

WAR DIARY

B. H. Q.

76th INFANTRY BRIGADE.

SEPTEMBER ~~AUGUST~~ 1918.

Appendices under separate cover

Instructions regarding War Diaries and Intelligence Summaries are contained in F. S. Regs., Part II. and the Staff Manual respectively. Title pages will be prepared in manuscript.

SEPTEMBER, 1918 **WAR DIARY** *or* ~~INTELLIGENCE SUMMARY.~~ (*Erase heading not required.*)

76th Infantry Brigade

Page I

Army Form C. 2118.

VR 36

Place.	Date	Hour	Summary of Events and Information	Remarks and references to Appendices
Bde HQ north of MORY COPSE B10c 6.0.	Sept	6.15am	Ten prisoners brought in by 8th KORL taken on the way to objective by companies which started at 3 am.	
		7.0am	8th KORL reported in position on objective in touch with 4th Royal Fus.rs on left and 1st Gordon Hdrs on right. Patrols pushing on.	
		7.50am	Battalions told to send scouts forward. Wire G 324.	App I G 324
		12.40pm	Reported that scouts had managed to get across valley, but movement in support impossible as any attempt at once heavily shelled. Scouts not yet ~~reported~~ in VRAUCOURT SWITCH. Division informed, G 326	App II G 326
		1.0pm	3rd Div OO 267 received ~~[illegible]~~ stating, if not possible to advance by day, 9th Bde in conjunction with troops on left would come up into line on our left along the NOREUIL SWITCH under cover of a barrage at 6 pm.	App III 3rd D O.O. 267
		3.30pm	G333 embodying 3rd Div OO 267 sent to battalions	App IV G 333
		4.30pm. 5.20pm	G 336 } G 338 } Further reports shewing enemy in VRAUCOURT SW. and NOREUIL	App V G 336, 338
		5.10pm.	G 337 8th KORL and 1st Gordon Hdrs ordered to make no further advance but to hold NOREUIL SW. as a definite line for assembly of 8th Bde	App VI G 337
		2.45pm.	3rd Div OO 268 received re attack of 8th Inf. Bde on morning of Sept 2nd 5.30 am. 8th Bde were asked if they wanted guides but replied in the negative	App VII Div OO 268
		7.10pm.	G 340 to 3 batt.ns stating 8th Bde would pass through. 8th KORL and 1st Gordon Hdrs who would remain in present positions and that 2nd Suffolk Rgt would be under orders of GOC 8th Bde	App VIII G 340

A5834 Wt. W4973/M687 750,000 8/16 D. D. & L. Ltd. Forms/C.2118/13.

Instructions regarding War Diaries and Intelligence Summaries are contained in F. S. Regs., Part II. and the Staff Manual respectively. Title pages will be prepared in manuscript.

September

WAR DIARY
or
INTELLIGENCE SUMMARY.
(Erase heading not required.)

Page 2

Army Form C. 2118.

Place	Date	Hour	Summary of Events and Information	Remarks and references to Appendices
B10c 6.0	1	7.35 pm	8th Bde ~~[illegible]~~ O.O. 70 received.	App IX 8th Bde OO70
	2	9.30 am.	1st Gordon Hdrs reported ~~that about 8 am.~~ parties of 8th Bde and 62nd Div. had come back over the VRAUCOURT SWITCH ridge in disorder but been collected and sent forward again.	
		10.0 am	Learnt that Canadian Corps had broken through DROCOURT – QUEANT line	
		1.50 pm	Learnt that 1 company of 2nd Suffolk had gone up and cleared MACAULAY AVENUE taking 200 prisoners. 3rd Div GB 573	App X GB 573
		1.55 pm	Learnt that Guards Div. had been ordered to move up their two leading brigades into MAIDA VALE.	
		8 pm.	Div OO 269 received re Guards Div. relieving 3rd Div. details to be arranged direct.	
		9 pm.	Bde. Major went to 8th Bde to arrange relief as no Guards representatives had arrived	
		10 pm.	8th KORL and 1st Gordon Hdrs. warned that they would not be relieved by any unit of Guards Div. but would withdraw at 1 am, Sept 3 (GOC 8th Bde had ~~given~~ authority for this withdrawal verbally to Bde, Major) G 344 2nd Suffolk withdrawal under orders of GOC 8th Bde.	App XI G 344
		11.30 pm.	B Coy 3rd MG Bn warned verbally to withdraw at 1 am,	
	3	1 am.	Wire received from 2nd Suffolk asking for cookers at 6 am, Replied 1.15 am by wire confirming. This was not received (by 2nd Suff) till 8 am, together with 8th Bde orders	
		1.45 am.	Bde HQ closed at B10 c 6.0 and moved to BOIRY ST MARTIN.	

September/18 Page 3

Army Form C. 2118.

Instructions regarding War Diaries and Intelligence Summaries are contained in F. S. Regs., Part II. and the Staff Manual respectively. Title pages will be prepared in manuscript.

WAR DIARY
or
~~INTELLIGENCE SUMMARY.~~
(Erase heading not required.)

Place	Date	Hour	Summary of Events and Information	Remarks and references to Appendices
BOIRY ST MARTIN S20a8.6	3	5.30	Bde HQ opened S20a8.6. 8th Bde 0071 for relief ~~issued~~ 12.30 am received.	
		4.30pm	All battalions reported in new area by 2.30pm. No wires accepted for transmission to 3rd Div through Guards Div.	
	4		Reorganising and refitting. Weather for last fortnight had been fine with few showers. Very cold at night latterly.	
	5		~~Refitting and training in fire and movement.~~ Colonel Fraser takes command of the 1st Gordons.	
La Bazéque V.21 Central	6.	9.30am	Left BOIRY ST MARTIN 9.30am arrived at La Bazéque 5.30p.m., having 2hrs. halt at BIENVILLERS. Very hot day but no one fell out on the march.	App XII BO141
— " —	7.		Training areas reconnoitred in the morning. Heavy thunderstorm in the afternoon. Visit from General Burnett.	App XIII Report on [illegible] sent to Div
— " —	8.		Sunday today very wet no training.	
— " —	9.		Training very much hindered owing to occasional heavy showers.	
— " —	10.		Usual training programme carried out occasional showers.	
	11.		Staff Captain went on leave & was replaced by Major Morgan KORL.	
		1.15pm	Left at 1.15p.m. arrived DOUCHY 5.30p.m. H.Q. established in old pill box at F.9.d.5.9.	App XIV BO142

A5834/ Wt. W4973/M687 750,000 8/16 D. D. & L. Ltd. Forms/C.2118/13.

Instructions regarding War Diaries and Intelligence Summaries are contained in F. S. Regs., Part II. and the Staff Manual respectively. Title pages will be prepared in manuscript.

SEPTEMBER 1918. **WAR DIARY** *or* ~~INTELLIGENCE SUMMARY.~~ (*Erase heading not required.*)

Page. IV. 76th Infantry Brigade

Army Form C. 2118.

Place	Date	Hour	Summary of Events and Information	Remarks and references to Appendices
DOUCHY. F.9b.5.0.	12.		Left DOUCHY. 10am arrived SAPIGNIES. H.8.b.2.2.	App. XV. B0103
SAPIGNIES	13.		Platoon training in the morning. Demonstration to all Battns in the afternoon, Tanks cooperating with infantry in the attack	
— " —	14.		Training. Battns in the attack.	
— " —	15.		Move at 2pm arrive FREMICOURT 4pm. Very hot day but troops marched very well. Headquarters bombed at 9.30pm. ~~Enemy~~ plane brought down near BEUGNY	
— " —	16.		Left at 8.30am. H.Q. opened 10am in SUNKEN Rd I12b.4.2. (Div. Reserve). Forward areas reconnoitred, & defence scheme drawn up	App. XVI. B0144
SUNKEN ROAD. I12b.4.2.	17.		Still in Div. Reserve, usual training programe carried out.	
— " —	18.		Usual training in the morning.	
		3.35pm	~~Enemy~~ attack on a three Brigade front, we are ordered to "Stand By" at a minutes notice.	
		8.30pm	Situation in the front slightly improved, reduced to half an hours notice.	
— " —	19.		Front line completely restored, leaving 100 prisoners in our hands. Battns practice the attack in artillery formations.	
— " —	20.	)	Usual training programme. Officers reconnoitre the forward areas.	
— " —	21.	)	Battns. practising the attack	

A5834 Wt. W4973/M687 750,000 8/16 D. D. & L. Ltd. Forms/C.2118/13.

SEPTEMBER 1918 **WAR DIARY** *or* ~~INTELLIGENCE SUMMARY.~~ Page V. Army Form C. 2118.

Instructions regarding War Diaries and Intelligence Summaries are contained in F. S. Regs., Part II. and the Staff Manual respectively. Title pages will be prepared in manuscript.

(*Erase heading not required.*)

76th Infantry Brigade.

Place	Date	Hour	Summary of Events and Information	Remarks and references to Appendices
	Sept			
SUNKEN RD. J.12 b.4.2	22nd		Sunday today no training. Company commanders reconnoitring forward areas	
"	23rd		Battns practising the attack. All units inspected the model of the forward areas.	
"	24th } 25th }		Baths allotted to units in BEAUMETZ. ~~Operation~~ Operation orders for the attack issued	App. XVII. B0145
"	26th	9 p.m	Left the Sunken Road & moved by taped track via BEAUMETZ to assembly positions E. of the CANAL DU NORD	App. XVIII. B0146 attg. adm. march orders
		11 p.m	Bgde H.Q. opened at the SPOIL HEAP K 20 central.	

Army Form C. 2118.

SEPTEMBER **WAR DIARY** or ~~INTELLIGENCE SUMMARY~~ Page VI

(Erase heading not required.)

76th Infantry Brigade

Instructions regarding War Diaries and Intelligence Summaries are contained in F. S. Regs., Part II. and the Staff Manual respectively. Title Pages will be prepared in manuscript.

Map 57c NE.

Place	Date	Hour	Summary of Events and Information	Remarks and references to Appendices
SPOIL HEAP. K 20 Central	27th	12.30am	All Battns reported in their assembly positions East of the Canal Du Nord.	
		5am	Slight rain during the early hours of the morning. Scattered shelling of LONDON SUPPORT & Canal.	
		5.20am	8th Brigade attack the RED LINE, followed closely by the K.O.R.L's. 1st Gordons & 2nd Suffolk Regt. in support.	
		6.30am	8th K.O.R.L's & 1st Gordons assist the 8th Bgde. to capture the RED LINE and a considerable number of prisoners.	
		7.15am	Reported by wounded that the GORDONS had passed through the village of FLESQUIERES, afterwards confirmed by the Bge. observers	
		11am	Success signal (white lights) seen in the BROWN LINE also confirmed by a visual message from 8th K.O.R.L's & 1st Gordons that they had reached & were consolidating on the BROWN LINE.	
		11.20am	Bgde. decided to move forward to the HINDENBURG SUPPORT. LINE. Advance party sent on to reconnoitre new H.Q's.	
		11.30am	Brigade observers report 62nd Div. seen passing through the BROWN LINE. afterwards confirmed by message from O.C 1st GORDONS.	
		3pm	Detailed dispositions received from all Battns.	

2449 Wt. W14957/M90 750,000 1/16 J.B.C. & A. Forms/C.2118/12.

SEPTEMBER WAR DIARY or ~~INTELLIGENCE SUMMARY~~ (Erase heading not required.)

Page VII.

76th Infantry Brigade.

Army Form C. 2118.

Instructions regarding War Diaries and Intelligence Summaries are contained in F. S. Regs., Part II. and the Staff Manual respectively. Title Pages will be prepared in manuscript.

Place	Date	Hour	Summary of Events and Information	Remarks and references to Appendices
SPOILHEAP K 20 Central	27th	3.15pm	Advance party report forward H.Q. taken over by 186th Bgde. Div. advised, and say we will probably withdraw to the Canal ~~area~~, Bgde. decide to remain at the SPOILHEAP. Over 2,000 prisoners reported to have passed through ~~the~~ Div. cage.	
		4pm	~~Battns.~~ reorganise, 62nd Div. ~~reported~~ to be in PREMY AVENUE. Very quiet night spent in the BROWN LINE.	
	28th		Considerable number of prisoners coming in from front & flank Divs. attack ~~reported~~ to be ~~progressing favourably~~	
		2pm	8th K.O.R.L's. & 1st GORDONS withdraw ~~to the~~ HAVRINCOURT ~~area~~, 2nd Suffolk Regt. remain in the HINDENBURG SUPPORT LINE.	
			Bgde ~~H.Q.~~ move to BOGGARTS HOLE, K 33 b 2 7 & open there at 4pm.	
BOGGART HOLE. K.33.b.2.7.	29th		Day spent in resting & cleaning up. Standing By.	App. XIX (? orders & admin. ?)
— " —	30th	5pm	Bgde ordered to move forward to the RIBECOURT ~~area~~ & assemble in squares L 26. & 27. H.Q. given by Division as in L27a in error for L22a.	App. XX.

2449 Wt. W14957/M90 750,000 1/16 J.B.C. & A. Forms/C.2118/12.

Instructions regarding War Diaries and Intelligence Summaries are contained in F. S. Regs., Part II. and the Staff Manual respectively. Title pages will be prepared in manuscript.

SEPTEMBER 1918. WAR DIARY or ~~INTELLIGENCE SUMMARY.~~

(*Erase heading not required.*)

Page VIII.

Army Form C. 2118.

186th Infantry Brigade.

Place	Date	Hour	Summary of Events and Information	Remarks and references to Appendices
MARCOING L.22.a.5.6.	Sept 30th	8pm.	G.O.C. attends conference at the 62nd Div. H.Q. & issues verbal orders to all Battn. C.O's. about 9pm	
		12 midnight.	Battns. move off to there assembly positions, in very heavy rain & guides doubtful of there way.	App. 2L. Report on Battle of Flesquières

J. Clark 2/Lt
for Brigadier General
Commanding 186th Infy Bde.

A5834 Wt. W4973/M687 750,000 8/16 D. D. & L. Ltd. Forms/C.2118/13.

APPENDICES

H. Q. 76th INFANTRY BRIGADE

SEPTEMBER 1918.

(In pads of 100.)

MESSAGES AND SIGNALS.

No. of Message.........

Prefix.......... Code.......... m.	Words.	Charge.	This message is on a/c of:	Recd. at ....m.
Office of Origin and Service Instructions.	Sent		I	Date..........
	At.........m.		..................Service.	From ....
	To..........			
	By..........		(Signature of "Franking Officer.")	By..........

TO				
		LOBI		
	JOLE	BUVI		
	Q090	185 Bde		

Sender's Number.	Day of Month.	In reply to Number.	AAA
* G 724	1		

Scouts will be sent forward ~~[illegible]~~ ~~NOREUIL~~ by JOLE to work along NOREUIL SWITCH in C10 in conjunction with BUVI and also round NOREUIL to the south ~~[illegible]~~ aaa Q090 will push out scouts across NOREUIL valley aaa Dividing line between JOLE and Q090 C15a00 C17c 0.0 aaa If scouts get on ~~[illegible]~~ line will be advanced to next good position by bounds aaa Troops south are going to continue their advance

From BUTA

Place

Time 7.50 am

The above may be forwarded as now corrected. (Z) [illegible signature]

Censor. Signature of Addressor or person authorised to telegraph in his name.

* This line should be erased if not required.

W. W492/M1647 650,000 Pads 5/17 H.W.&V. Ld. (E. 1187.)

"A" Form

MESSAGES AND SIGNALS.

Army Form C. (In pads of 100.)

No. of Message ....

Prefix .... Code .... m. Office of Origin and Service Instructions	Words	Charge.	This message is on a/c of: .... Service. (Signature of "Franking Officer")	Recd. at ...... m. Date .... From .... By ....
	Sent At .... m. To .... By			

TO VEKA

Sender's Number.	Day of Month.	In reply to Number.	AAA
G 326	1		

JOLE just reported patrols out across valley but not yet apparently in VRAUCOURT SWITCH aaa any advance in support at present impossible as all movement is at once heavily shelled from east and south east as any opportunity will be at once seized aaa In any case prepared to advance at dusk aaa ~~[illegible]~~ Is this early enough

From B4+A

Place

Time 12.40pm

The above may be forwarded as now corrected. (Z) [signature]

Censor. Signature of Addressor or person authorised to telegraph in his name

* This line should be erased if not required.

Order No. 1625. Wt. W3253/ P 511 27/2. H. & K., Ltd. (E. 2634).

"A" Form.

Army Form C. 2121
(In pads of 100).

MESSAGES AND SIGNALS.

No of Message

Prefix ... Code ... m. | Words | Charge | This message is on a/c of: | Recd. at ... m.

Office of Origin and Service Instructions. | Sent At ... m. To ... By ... | ... Service. (Signature of "Franking Officer.") | Date ... From ... By ...

TO: 9th Bde, 76th Bde, 8th Bde, CRA, DMGC, 52nd Div, 62 Div, VI Corps, 12th Sqd RAF, Phipps Group RG, CRE. ADMS, Q. Pioneer, Signal

Sender's Number.	Day of Month.	In reply to Number.	AAA
*	1st Sept		

3rd Div Operation Order No 267

1. 9th & 76th Bdes will continue to push forward patrols and gain ground during the day.
As ground is gained the present line will be pushed forward and a new line will be built up by dribbling men forwards.

2. Should it not be possible to advance our line during the day by the above method, a line will be established this evening throughout the whole length of the NOREUIL SWITCH

From

Place

Time

The above may be forwarded as now corrected. (Z)

Censor. Signature of Addressor or person authorised to telegraph in his name.

* This line should be erased if not required.

100,000 Pads. W. 12093. M1217. McC. & Co., Ltd. 1/17. (E. 764). Forms C/2121/11.

"A" Form.
MESSAGES AND SIGNALS.

Army Form C. 2121 (in pads of 100).
No. of Message

Prefix ... Code ... m.	Words	Charge	This message is on a/c of:	Recd. at ... m.
Office of Origin and Service Instructions.	Sent		... Service.	Date
	At ... m.			From
	To			
	By		(Signature of "Franking Officer.")	By

TO

Sender's Number.	Day of Month.	In reply to Number.	AAA
*	1st Sept		

3. With this object in view the 9th Inf Bde will advance at 6.0 pm in conjunction with the 52nd Division on our left and ~~cols~~ will establish themselves on the NOREUIL SWITCH between its junction with LONGATTE TRENCH and the divisional boundary at C.5.C.4.0 where touch will be gained with the 52nd Division.

4. The advance will be made under a creeping barrage.
Zero hour 6.0 pm

5. Acknowledged

4328
1.0pm SM

From 3 Div
Place
Time 11.45 am

The above may be forwarded as now corrected. (Z)

W H Traill Lt Col GS

Censor. Signature of Addressor or person authorised to telegraph in his name.

* This line should be erased if not required.

100,000 Pads. W.12093. M1217. McC. & Co., Ltd. 1/17. (E. 764). Forms C/2121/11.

"A"

MESSAGES AND SIGNALS.

No. of Message.........

Prefix..........Code..........m. Office of Origin and Service Instructions	Words	Charge.	This message is on a/c of: ....Service. (Signature of "Franking Officer")	Recd. at......m.
	Sent		IV	Date..........
	At ....m.			From ....
	To			
	By			By..........

TO { 8 K.O.R.L. / 1st Gordon Hdrs

Sender's Number.	Day of Month.	In reply to Number.	AAA
C 333	1		

1) Should it not be possible to advance our line during the day it will be established this evening throughout the whole length of NOREUIL SWITCH

2) With this object in view 9th Inf Bde will advance at 6.0 pm in conjunction with 53rd Div. on their left and will establish themselves on the NOREUIL SWITCH between its junction with LONGATTE TRENCH and the Div boundary at C 5 a 9.0

3) This advance will be made under creeping barrage. Zero 6 pm.

4) [illegible] ~~[illegible]~~

From 76 Inf Bde

Place

Time 3.30 pm

The above may be forwarded as now corrected. (Z) C. Clarke Capt

..........Censor. Signature of Addressor or person authorised to telegraph

* This line should be erased if not required.

Order No. 1625. Wt. W3253/ P 511 27/2. H. & K., Ltd. (E. 2634).

"A" Form.
MESSAGES AND SIGNALS.

Army Form C. 2121 (in pads of 100).
No. of Message........

Prefix........ Code........ m. | Words | Charge | This message is on a/c of: | Recd. at........ m.

Office of Origin and Service Instructions.

Sent
At........ m.
To........
By........

.... Service.

(Signature of "Franking Officer.")

Date........
From........
By........

TO

Sender's Number. | Day of Month. | In reply to Number. | AAA

8. The Heavy artillery will bombard the LAGNICOURT – NOREUIL road in C.17.d & C 23.b and sunken roads running through C 29.b & C 30.a and will form a creeping barrage in advance of the field artillery barrage.

9. A liaison officer from the 6th and 12th Battn Tanks will be at the HQ 8th Inf Bde.

10. HQrs of Flank Bdes are as follows.
187th Bde (62 Div) – right – HQ. B 27 cent
156th Bde (52 Div) – left – HQ U.7.c 9 8.

From
Place
Time

The above may be forwarded as now corrected. (Z)

.... Censor. Signature of Addressor or person authorised to telegraph in his name.

* This line should be erased if not required.

100,000 Pads. W. 12093. M1217. McC. & Co., Ltd. 1/17. (E. 764). Forms C/2121/11.

“A” Form. Army Form C. 2121
(in pads of 100).
MESSAGES AND SIGNALS. No. of Message............

Prefix............Code............m.	Words	Charge	This message is on a/c of:	Recd. at............m.
Office of Origin and Service Instructions.	Sent		............Service.	Date............
	At............m.			From............
	To............			
	By............		(Signature of “Franking Officer.”)	By............

TO

Sender’s Number.	Day of Month.	In reply to Number.	AAA
*			

11. HQrs 8th Inf Bde will be established at L'HOMME MORT B.17 a. 8 3.
12. Zero hour will be notified.
13. Acknowledge

G332 [illegible]
24th [illegible]

From 3rd Div
Place
Time 1.0 pm

The above may be forwarded as now corrected. (Z) [illegible signature]

............Censor. Signature of Addressor or person authorised to telegraph in his name.

* This line should be erased if not required.

100,000 Pads. W. 12093. M1217. McC. & Co., Ltd. 1/17. (E. 764). Forms C/2121/11.

...Code..........m. | Words | Charge.

Office of Origin and Service Instructions

Sent
At ....m.
To ....
By ....

This message is on a/c of:
VIII ....Service.
SECRET
(Signature of "Franking Officer")

Recd. at......m.
Date..........
From ....
By..........

TO { KORL
2nd Suffolk Rgt
1st Gordon Hdrs }

Sender's Number.	Day of Month.	In reply to Number.	AAA
G 340	1		

(1) 8th Brigade will pass through 9th and 76th Bdes at zero hour tomorrow 2nd Inst from battle positions in rear of present front line.

(2) 8th KORL & 1st Gordon Hdrs will remain in their present positions till further orders.

2nd Suffolk Rgt and one battalion from 9th Inf Bde will come under orders of GOC 8th Inf Bde and will move forward in support of 8th Inf B.

(3) The attack by the 8th Inf Bde will be made under a creeping barrage and in cooperation with Tanks.

(4) Zero hour will be notified later.

From 76 Inf Bde
Place
Time 7.10 pm.

The above may be forwarded as now corrected. (Z)
[illegible]

Censor. Signature of Addressor or person authorised to telegraph in his name

* This line should be erased if not required.

Order No. 1625. Wt. W3253/ P 511 27/2. H. & K., Ltd. (E. 2634).

"A" Form
MESSAGES AND SIGNALS.

No. of Message........

Prefix.........Code.........m. Office of Origin and Service Instructions	Words / Charge. Sent At ....m. To .... By	This message is on a/c of: ....Service. (Signature of "Franking Officer")	Recd. at......m. Date......... From .... By.........

TO		BUVI	195 Inf Bde
	VEKA	BUHI	

Sender's Number.	Day of Month.	In reply to Number.	AAA
G 336	1		

Reports of ~~Patrol~~ patrols and ground observers ~~[illegible]~~ timed early this afternoon state enemy holding VRAUCOURT SWITCH and ~~[illegible]~~ VAULX TRENCH aaa Patrols got as far as railway in valley and were then fired on from posts on ridge aaa Addsd VEKA rptd BUVI BUHI

From BUTA
Place
Time 4.30pm

The above may be forwarded as now corrected (Z) [illegible signature]

Censor. Signature of Addressor or person authorised to telegraph in his name

* This line should be erased if not required.

Order No. 1625. Wt. W3253/ P 511 27/2. H. & K., Ltd. (E, 2634).
8350 ... 9/14. Forms C2121/10.

	Sent		
	At ....m.	............Service.	Date............
	To		From ....
	By	(Signature of "Franking Officer")	By............

TO	VEKA	BUVI BUHI	185 Inf. Bde	

Sender's Number.	Day of Month.	In reply to Number.	AAA
*G 338	1		

Further patrol reports show enemy in NOREUIL with M.G.s which enfilade our line aaa Enemy posts on railway in C15 aaa VRAUCOURT SWITCH held by us in strength aaa our line being heavily shelled and machine gunned 3.40 pm aaa Heavies asked to fire on NOREUIL and counter battery aaa Added VEKA rpt flank below & BUHI

From	BUTA		
Place			
Time	5.20 pm		

The above may be forwarded as now corrected (Z) ....

.... Censor. Signature of Addressor or person authorised to telegraph in his name

* This line should be erased if not required.

Order No. 1625. Wt. W3253/ P 511 27/2. H. & K., Ltd. (E. 2634).

Censor. Signature of Addressor or person authorised to telegraph in his name

* This line should be erased if not required.

8350. S. B. Ltd. Wt. W4843/541—50,000. 9/14. Forms C2121/10.

At ....m. | To .... | By ....

VI

(Signature of "Franking Officer") | From .... | By.........

TO — 8th RORL
1st Gordon Hdrs

Sender's Number.	Day of Month.	In reply to Number.	AAA
G 337	1		

Patrol and observation reports received from 8th RORL & 1st Gordon Hdrs. Information is very valuable and patrol work excellent. Any further information it is possible to obtain will be most useful to us and 8th Bde.

In view of location of enemy and my G 333 No further advance will be made but the line of NOREUIL SWITCH held as a definite line for assembly of 8th Bde.

Retaliation has been asked for on enemy in VRAUCOURT SWITCH and the Heavies will get on to NOREUIL and proceed with counter battery work

From 76 Inf Bde
Place
Time 5.10 pm

The above may be forwarded as now corrected (Z) C. Clayton [illegible]

Censor. Signature of Addressor or person authorised to telegraph in his name

* This line should be erased if not required.

Order No. 1625. Wt. W3253/ P 511 27/2. H. & K., Ltd. (E. 2634).

From
Place
Time

The

Censor. Signature of Addressor or person authorised to telegraph in his name

* This line should be erased if not required.

8350 S. B. Ltd. Wt. W4843/541—50,000. 9/14. Forms C2121/10.

Sent
At
To
By

Advanced Copy

Service.

(Signature of "Franking Officer.")

Date
From
By

TO	8th Bde - BRA - Q 9th Bde - DMGC - ADMS 76th Bde - CRE - Signals	Pioneers 62nd Div VI Corps Phipps group RGA 52nd Div 12 Sqdn RAF Guards Div 6th & 12th Bn Tanks

Sender's Number	Day of Month	In reply to Number	AAA
	1st Sept		

3rd Div Operation Order 268.

1 The VI Corps is to advance tomorrow in conjunction with the XVII Corps on the left. The objectives of the VI Corps and right Div, (52nd Div) of the XVII Corps are shown on attached map. ⊕

2. The attack on the 3rd Div front will be carried out by the 8th Inf Bde which will pass through the 9th and 76th Inf Bdes at zero hour.

3. The 8th Inf Bde will move forward tonight and will be formed up in its battle positions in rear of the

From
Place
Time

⊕ Map to follow

The above may be forwarded as now corrected. (Z)

Censor. Signature of Addressor or person authorised to telegraph in his name

* This line should be erased if not required.

8350 S. B. Ltd. Wt. W4843/541—50,000. 9/14. Forms C2121/10.

"A" Form.
Army Form C. 2121
(In pads of 100).

MESSAGES AND SIGNALS.

No of Message..........

Prefix..........Code..........m.	Words	Charge	This message is on a/c of:	Recd. at..........m.
Office of Origin and Service Instructions.	Sent		..........Service.	Date..........
	At..........m.			From..........
	To..........			
	By..........		(Signature of "Franking Officer.")	By..........

TO

Sender's Number.	Day of Month.	In reply to Number.	AAA
*			

front line of the 9th + 76th Inf Bdes
prior to zero hour.

4. One battalion each of the 76th Inf Bde and 9th Inf Bde will come under the orders of the G.O.C. 8th Inf Bde and will move forward in support to the 8th Inf Bde

5. The attack by the 8th Inf Bde will be made under a creeping barrage and in cooperation with Tanks.

6. 10 Mark IV Tanks and 8 Whippet Tanks are placed at the disposal of the G.O.C. 8th Inf Bde.
the Mark IV Tanks will operate against all trenches between the line of

From

Place

Time

The above may be forwarded as now corrected. (Z)

....
Censor. Signature of Addressor or person authorised to telegraph in his name.

* This line should be erased if not required.

100,000 Pads. W. 12093. M1217. McC. & Co., Ltd. 1/17. (E. 764). Forms C/2121/11.

"A" Form.
MESSAGES AND SIGNALS.

Army Form C. 2121
(In [illegible]s of 100).
No. of Message..........

Prefix.......... Code.......... m.	Words	Charge	This message is on a/c of:	Recd. at .... m.
Office of Origin and Service Instructions.	Sent		..................Service.	Date........
	At .... m.			From........
	To........			
	By........		(Signature of "Franking Officer.")	By........

TO

Sender's Number.	Day of Month.	In reply to Number.	AAA
*			

departure and the Objective.
The Whippet Tanks will operate in
the NOREUIL VALLEY and round
the South and east of LAGNICOURT
7.(a) The two M G Cos in the line will
form a creeping barrage to cover
the advance of the infantry under
arrangements to be made by the
DMGC
(b) The M G Co in Divisional reserve will
move forward tonight in rear of
the 8th Inf Bde to the Sunken road
in C 8 a & c.
G O C 8th Inf Bde will have a call
on this Company if required.

From
Place
Time

The above may be forwarded as now corrected. (Z)

Censor. Signature of Addressor or person authorised to telegraph in his name.

* This line should be erased if not required.

100,000 Pads. W. 12093. M1217. McC. & Co., Ltd. 1/17. (E. 764). Forms C/2121/11.

SECRET.

ADDENDA TO 8th INFANTRY BRIGADE OPERATION ORDER No.70.
2nd September 1918.

Reference para.4.

(a) The 2nd SUFFOLKS will move in support of the 7th K.S.L.I. and will assemble in the Sunken Road in B.18.a. and 17.b. at ZERO minus ½ hour.

(b) The 1st NORTHUMBERLAND FUSILIERS will be prepared to support the 1st ROYAL SCOTS FUSILIERS but will remain in their present position.

(c) Liaison Officers of 1st NORTHUMBERLAND FUSILIERS and 2nd SUFFOLKS will report to H.Q. 8th Infantry Brigade at ZERO hour for further instructions.

(d) 1st NORTHUMBERLAND FUSILIERS and 2nd SUFFOLKS will keep in touch with the situation by means of patrols.

13. COMMUNICATION:

(i) A Forward Report Centre will be established at C.8.a.3.3. tonight: this will be moved forward as the attack progresses.

(ii) Situation Reports even if negative will be sent every hour to Brigade H.Q.

(iii) The mounted troop under Lieut.FAITHORNE will rendezvous at Cross-roads at B.17.b.2.3. at ZERO plus 15 minutes.

14. Battle Order will be worn and will be the same as for the previous operations on the 21st and 23rd August except supporting Coys. only will carry 50% tools and no sandbags will be carried.

15. A.D.S. of 8th Field Ambulance will be established at B.24.a.3.9. which will afterwards move to dugout in C.8.a.2.3.

16. ARTILLERY PROGRAMME:

(a) 18-pdrs. and 4.5 How. Creeping barrages and smoke barrages.
(b) Heavy Artillery will engage selected targets and form a Creeping barra[ge] opening on the line detailed for 4.5 Hows. in para.17 (b) and creeping 300 yds. in advance of the Field Artillery barrage by lifts of 300 yds. in 12 minutes.

17. DETAILS OF CREEPING BARRAGES AND OPENING BARRAGE LINES.

(a) 18-pdrs. (less 1 gun per Bty.)
C.20.b.3.6. - C.14.d.4.0. - C.15.c.0.4. - C.15.central - C.16.a.0.9. - C.11.a.6.0. - C.11.b.0.4. - C.11.b.3.9.

(b) One 18-pdr.per Battery firing smoke and 4.5 Hows. - VRAUCOURT SWITCH, MACAULAY AVENUE, BOLTON ALLEY.
Barrages come down on opening barrage line at ZERO.

At ZERO plus 10 mins. the 18-pdr.barrage advances 100 yds. per 4 mins to the Protective Barrage Line: the 18-pdrs. detailed in para.17 (b) above resume their normal pace in the 18-pdr. Creeping Barrage,when the latter catches them up, the 4.5 Hows. creeping 100 yds. in advanc[e]

Line of Protective Barrage -
18-pdrs. - 400 yds. in advance of the objective.
4.5 Hows. 500 yds. in advance of the objective.
Batteries will remain on this line for 10 mins. and then stop to allo[w] patrols to be pushed out.
During the Creeping Barrage, no fire will be directed on the area enclosed by C.22.b.4.6. - C.23.a.0.9. - C.29.b.9.9. - C.29.a.4.6. This is to ensure a free passage for the Whippets, who will work alon[g] the NE. of the NOREUIL -MORCHIES Rd.

Captain, Bde.Major.

Brigade Major

S E C R E T .

Copy No. 9.

8th INFANTRY BRIGADE OPERATION ORDER No.70.

1st September 1918.

Ref:Map 57c.N.W. 1/20,000.

1. The VI Corps is to advance tomorrow in conjunction with the XVII Corps on the left.

2. The attack on the 3rd Divisional front will be carried out by the 8th Infantry Brigade which will pass through the 9th and 76th Infantry Brigades at ZERO hour.

3. (a) The 8th Infantry Brigade will move forward to-night and will form up on its assembly positions in rear of the front line of the 9th and 76th Infantry Brigades.

(b) Assembly positions will be the Road from C.13.c.1.1. to C.3.b.2.2.

(c) Battalions will move to their assembly positions at the following times :-

1st ROYAL SCOTS FUSILIERS at ZERO minus 5½ hours.
2nd THE ROYAL SCOTS at ZERO minus 4½ hours.
7th K.S.L.I. at ZERO minus 3 hours.

4. The 1st NORTHUMBERLAND FUSILIERS (9th Infantry Bde.) and the 2nd SUFFOLKS (76th Infantry Brigade) will come under the orders of the 8th Infantry Brigade and move in support to the attack.

5. The attack will be carried out under a Creeping Barrage and in co-operation with Tanks.
Battalions will attack in the following order :-

7th K.S.L.I. on the Right.
2nd THE ROYAL SCOTS in the Centre.
1st ROYAL SCOTS FUS.on the Left.

6. Map showing the Objectives and dividing lines between Battalions are issued to Battalion Commanders only.

7. (a) The attack will be supported in its initial stages by a Creeping Barrage from the M.G.Coys. attached to the 9th and 76th Infantry Bdes. as far as the Spur in C.21.central.

(b) One Section 'A' Coy. 3rd M.G.Bn. is attached to each Battalion to assist in the attack and subsequent consolidation.

(c) One Section 'A' Coy. 3rd M.G.Bn. will remain in reserve at L'HOMME MORT.

8. (a) One Section of 4 Tanks attached to 7th K.S.L.I.
Their role will be to work up DUNELM AVENUE and the Sunken Road from C.22.c.1.6. to C.28.b.8.5.
Jumping off point VRAUCOURT RESERVE and NOREUIL SWITCH.

(b) One Section of 3 Tanks attached to 2nd THE ROYAL SCOTS will work up LAGNICOURT TRENCH.
Jumping off point - Junction of LONGATTE TRENCH - NOREUIL SWITCH.

(c) One Section of 3 Tanks attached to 1st ROYAL SCOTS FUSILIERS will work up MACAULEM AVENUE and LEEDS RESERVE.
Jumping off point - IGAREE CORNER (if situation admits).

/(d)

(d) 8 Whippet Tanks will co-operate round the South and East of LAGNICOURT. Instructions have been given by the B.G.C. 8th Infantry Brigade to the Tank Commander.

9. The heavy Artillery will bombard the LAGNICOURT-NOREUIL Road in C.17.d. and C.23.b. and Sunken Roads running through C.29.b. and C.30.a. and will form a Creeping Barrage in advance of the Field Artillery Barrage.

10. Brigade Headquarters will be established at L'HOMME MORT from 9-00 p.m. tonight.

11. All prisoners will be passed back to L'HOMME MORT where they will be collected under Captain KENNEDY, 8th T.M.BATTERY and utilized for carrying parties.

12. ZERO hour will be notified later.

Captain,
Brigade Major, 8th Infantry Brigade.

Issued at 5-30 p.m.

Copies to :- No.1. B.G.C.
2. 2nd The Royal Scots.
3. 1st R.S.Fusiliers.
4. 7th K.S.L.I.
5. 8th T.M.Battery.
6. 3rd Division 'G'.
7. 3rd Division 'Q'.
8. 9th Infantry Bde. (2)
9. 76th Infantry Bde. (2)
10. 187th Infantry Brigade.
11. 156th Infantry Bde.
12. 3rd M.G.Battalion.
13. 'A' Coy.3rd M.G.Bn.
14. 6th Battalion Tanks.
15. 12th Battalion Tanks.
16. No.2 Section 438th (CHES)Fld.Coy.RE.
17. 438th (CHES.)Fld.Coy.R.E.
18. 8th Field Ambulance.
19. 3rd Divisional Arty.
20. Bde.Major.
21. Staff Captain.
22/24. War diary.
25. File.

****

Prefix.....

"C" FORM.
MESSAGES AND SIGNALS.

Army Form C. 2123.
(In books of 100.)
No. of Message ....

Prefix SM Code AK Words 58 | Received. From YCR By | Sent, or sent out. At ....m. To .... By .... | Office Stamp.

Charges to Collect

Service Instructions

Handed in at YCR Office 1 50 p.m. Received 2 2 p.m.

TO BUTA

*Sender's Number.	Day of Month.	In reply to Number.	AAA
GB573	2		

General line runs as follows aaa VRAUCOURT SWITCH MACAULAY AVENUE BOLTON RESERVE aaa One company 2nd Suffolks took 200 prisoners in clearing MACAULAY AVENUE in E 17 a and advanced groups are reported in C 22 b and C 23 a but exact location of these uncertain addsd corps repld flanking divs guards div CRA BUVI BUTA

FROM VEKA
PLACE & TIME 1 50pm

*This line should be erased if not required.

(5866.) Wt. W528/M1970. 100,000 Pads. 5/17. H. W. & V., Ld. (E. 1213.)

SECRET.

Copy No. ...

Ref.: ... .1918.

1. ... the
VI ... visional
Tra...

2. ... will move
to ... nce with
the...

3. ... and will
hal... r dinners.
Pl... resentative
of...

4. ... OMIER and
gui...

5. ... march;-

... ls.
... ls.

6.

7. ... a.m. and
op...

8. ... s will be
fo...

9.

C. Clapper Captain,

Issued at 5.30 a.m. Brigade Major, 76th. Infantry Brigade.

Copies to:-
1. G.O.C.
2. 8th. K.O.R.L.
3. 2nd. Suffolk Regt.
4. 1st. Gordon Hldrs.
5. 76th. T.M.B.
6. 7th. Field Amb.
7. No.2 Co. Train.
8. Bde. Supply Offr.
9. Bde. Transport Offr.
10. Bde. Signal Offr.
11. Staff Capt.
12. 3rd. Div. "G".
13. " "Q".
14. 8th. Inf. Bde.
15. 9th. "
16. War Diary.
17. "
18. File.
19.) Retained.
20.)

SECRET.
****

Copy No....

To .... By .... (Signature of "Franking Officer") By........

TO { 8th K.O.R.L.
1st Gordon Hdrs

Sender's Number.	Day of Month.	In reply to Number.	AAA
G 394	2		

You will not be relieved by any unit of the Guards but will withdraw without further orders at 1 A.M. Sept 3

From 76th Inf Bde
Place
Time 10.pm

The above may be forwarded as now corrected (Z) C. Clifford Capt
Bde Major

.... Censor. Signature of Addressor or person authorised to telegraph in his name

* This line should be erased if not required.

Order No. 1625. Wt. W3253/ P 511 27/2. H. & K., Ltd. (E. 2634).

Ref.Ma ... .1918.

1\. ... the
VI C ... visional
Train ...

2\. ... e will move
to th ... nce with
the a ...

3\. ... and will
halt f ... or dinners.
Places ... presentative
of Bri ...

4\. ... POMIER and
guide ...

5\. ... march;-

... c.
... s.

6\.

7\. ... a.m. and
Open at ...
reports during march to head of column.

8\. Completion of move and location of Headquarters will be reported at once to Brigade H.Q.

9\. ACKNOWLEDGE.

Issued at 5.30 am.

C. Clifford Captain,
Brigade Major, 76th. Infantry Brigade.

Copies to:-
1\. G.O.C.
2\. 8th.K.O.R.L.
3\. 2nd.Suffolk Regt.
4\. 1st.Gordon Hldrs.
5\. 76th.T.M.B.
6\. 7th.Field Amb.
7\. No.2 Co.Train.
8\. Bde.Supply Offr.
9\. Bde.Transport Offr.
10\. Bde.Signal Offr.
11\. Staff Capt.
12\. 3rd.Div."G".
13\. " "Q".
14\. 8th.Inf.Bde.
15\. 9th. "
16\. War Diary.
17\. "
18\. File.
19\.)
20\.) Retained.

SECRET.

Copy No....

76th.INFANTRY BRIGADE ORDER NO.141.

Ref.Map LENS 11. September 6th.1918.

1. The 3rd.Division (less artillery) will move into the VI Corps Reserve Area today,Sept.6th.
3rd.Division "Q" will arrange for the move of Divisional Train and allot them accomodation.

2. 76th.Inf.Brigade together with 7th.Field Ambulance will move to the ST.AMAND - GAUDIEMPRE - LAHERLIERE area in accordance with the attached march table.

3. Battalions will be accompanied by their transport and will halt for 2 hours between MONCHY AU BOIS and BIENVILLERS for dinners. Places allotted for this halt will be pointed out by a representative of Brigade H.Q.

4. Billetting parties will meet units at the church POMMIER and guide them to their allotted areas.

5. The following distances will be maintained on the march;-

Between Companies.................. 100 yards.
Between Battalion and its transport....... 100 yards.
Between Battalions at least.............. 500 yards.

6. Packs will be carried by the men.

7. 76th.Bde H.Q.will close at BOIRY ST.MARTIN at 9.30 a.m. and open at ST.AMAND on arrival.
Reports during march to head of column.

8. Completion of move and location of Headquarters will be reported at once to Brigade H.Q.

9. ACKNOWLEDGE.

C. Chipper Captain,
Brigade Major,76th.Infantry Brigade.

Issued at 3.30 a.m.

Copies to:-
1. G.O.C.
2. 8th.K.O.R.L.
3. 2nd.Suffolk Regt.
4. 1st.Gordon Hldrs.
5. 76th.T.M.B.
6. 7th.Field Amb.
7. No.2 Co.Train.
8. Bde.Supply Offr.
9. Bde.Transport Offr.
10. Bde.Signal Offr.
11. Staff Capt.
12. 3rd.Div."G".
13. " "Q".
14. 8th.Inf.Bde.
15. 9th. "
16. War Diary.
17. "
18. File.
19.) Retained.
20.)

Ref. Map LENS 11.

SECRET.

MARCH TABLE TO ACCOMPANY 76th. INF. BRIGADE ORDER NO.141.

Unit.	Starting Point.	Time.	Route.	Remarks.
76th. Bde. H.Q. & L.T.M.B.	Road junction on MOYENNEVILLE - AYETTE Road 1 mile west of MOYENNEVILLE.	10.45 a.m.	AYETTE, DOUCHY, south of ADINFER Wood, MONCHY, BIENVILLERS, POMMIER.	Halt for 2 hours for dinners between MONCHY & BIENVILLERS. A representative of Brigade H.Q. will meet units and point out place allotted to each. Billeting parties will meet units at church in POMMIER and guide them to their destination. The usual halts at 10 minutes to the clock hour will be observed. Brigade Time will be given by Signals at 9 a.m.
1st. Gordon Hldrs.	-do-	11 a.m.	-do-	
2nd. Suffolk Regt	-do-	11.30 a.m.	-do-	
8th. K.O.R.L.	-do-	12 noon	-do-	
7th. Field Amb.	HAMLINCOURT.	Not before 2.30 p.m.	-do-	To be clear of AYETTE by 4 p.m.

BRIEF REPORT ON OPERATIONS AUG.29th. - SEPT.2nd.

76th.INFANTRY BRIGADE.

XIII

Ref.Maps 1/20,000
51b.S.W.
57c.N.W.and N.E.

B/3025

NIGHT AUG.28th./29th.

76th.Inf.Bde relieved 1st.Guards Bde in the line.

Dispositions - 1st.Gordon Hldrs B.18b.8.0. to B.11b.4.9.
8th.K.O.R.L. B.11b.4.9.northwards to Divisional boundary.
2nd.Suffolk Regt in reserve in BANKS Trench.
Brigade H.Q. - B.10c.6.0.

AUG.29th.

Patrols pushed out and made good to about line through C.1 and C.7 central. Orders received about 8 p.m.for 76th.Bde to capture ECOUST in conjunction with an attack by 56th.Division on our left on BULLECOURT AVENUE.

NIGHT 29/30th.

2nd.Suffolk Regt assembled for the attack in U.25d. and C.1c: objective - C.8d.1.6.to C.3a.8.4. east of LONGATTE. 1st.Gordon Hldrs were to gain the line C.13d.5.9.to 8d.1.6. and refuse their right flank to junction with 62nd.Division. 8th.K.O.R.L in Brigade Reserve in B.6.

The night was extremely dark but assembly was accomplished satisfactorily.

AUG.30th.

Attack started with the opening of the artillery barrage at 5 a.m. Tanks did not get up in time and were ordered back by the Tank Battalion Commander. All objectives were gained and some 150 prisoners were taken. No touch could be obtained however,with 56th.Division although parties worked up BULLECOURT AVENUE. About 7 a.m. the enemy counter-attacked from STATION REDOUBT in left rear of 2nd.Suffolk Regt,at the same time opening T.M.fire from sunken road in C.9a.,and the battalion,suffering heavy casualties,fell back on ECOUST SUPPORT. 1st.Gordon Hldrs similarly had to fall back on their left to line of wire running from C.13b.6.0.to C.7b.2.0. 1 Coy of 8th.K.O.R.L.was sent to prevent any further advance of the enemy down the railway in U.26 and 1 Coy down MAIDA VALE to link up the 2nd.Suffolk Regt and 1st.Gordon Hldrs. These positions were maintained throughout the day.

1st.Gordon Hldrs at dusk pushed forward to about grid line between squares C.7 and C.8 to straighten the front.

At night 76th.Inf.Bde was relieved by 9th.Inf.Bde, 8th.K.O.R.L. less 1 Coy and 2nd.Suffolk Regt being withdrawn on relief,1st.Gordon Hldrs together with 1 Coy 8th.K.O.R.L. remained in line under orders of G.O.C.9th.Inf.Bde and held the front line from Southern Divisional Boundary to grid line between C.7 and C.13.

AUG.31st.

9th.Bde took ECOUST but was held up south of the village. 76th.Bde took over the front at nightfall from southern Divisional Boundary to C.7d.9.2.

NIGHT AUG.31st./Sept.1st.

8th.K.O.R.L.and 1st.Gordon Hldrs advanced without a barrage and took NOREUIL SWITCH; 9th.Inf.Bde taking LONGATTE Trench. There was little opposition,and Whippet tanks which co-operated at 6 a.m. Sept.1st found our troops already on their objective.

SEPT.1st.

Patrols were pushed forward and found NOREUIL and VRAUCOURT SWITCH held by the enemy. Any further movement was stopped by heavy enemy shelling. At 6 p.m. 9th.Bde came up along NOREUIL SWITCH on our left.

SEPT.2nd.

At 5.30 a.m. 8th.Inf.Bde attacked through our line, 2nd.Suffolk Regt being under orders of 8th.Inf.Bde as a reserve. At 10 a.m.the situation in front being obscure,1 Coy of the 2nd. Suffolk Regt was sent forward by 8th.Inf.Bde to clear up VRAUCOURT SWITCH and MACAULAY AVENUE. This was done with few casualties,over 200 prisoners and many machine guns being captured.

Sgd.

Brigadier-General,
7/9/18. Commanding 76th.Infantry Brigade.

POINTS BROUGHT OUT IN OPERATION OF AUGUST 30th.

****

1. Battalion scouts under the Battalion Intelligence Officer were invaluable in reconnoitring assembly positions and also in obtaining information during the battle.

2. Owing to the wide front to be attacked, it was difficult for battalions to keep many men in hand as local reserves: the reserve company of the left battalion had to be employed in mopping up ECOUST.

3. If the tanks had come on although unavoidably late they might have prevented the left flank being turned.

4. A more liberal supply of maps is necessary to make good losses. The printing should be stronger and clearer. The marking of trench lines, which are mostly obliterated, is of less importance than that of natural landmarks. The signs for cuttings and embankments are often indisguishable one from the other.

Signed

Brigadier-General,

7/9/18. Commanding 76th. Infantry Brigade.

C.S.

XIV

SECRET.
****

Copy No.....

76th. INFANTRY BRIGADE ORDER NO.142.

Ref.Map BUCQUOY 1/40,000. Sept.10th.1918.

1. The 76th.Inf.Brigade will move tomorrow into the DOUCHY-AYETTE Area in accordance with the attached march table.

2. Each Battalion will march closed up and followed by its own transport. Packs will be carried by the men.

3. Areas are allotted as follows:-

8th.K.O.R.L....... Square F.9 and including sunken road just east of grid line dividing F.9 and 10. Sunken road in F.9d exclusive.

2nd.Suffolk Regt.. Squares F.10,F.11 a & c.

1st.Gordon Hldrs.. Square F.3 between ROTTEN RAVINE and ADINFER WOOD.

142nd.Field Amb... Square F.4 a & b.

76th.L.T.M.B...... Sunken road near AYETTE SWITCH in F.9d.

76th.Bde H.Q........F.9b.5.0.

4. Billeting parties of 1 officer and 8 O.R.per Battalion will leave at 9 a.m.to reconnoitre their areas. They will meet their units at cross roads in MONCHY E.5a.6.8.and guide them by the best roads into their respective areas.

5. 76th.Bde H.Q.will close at LA BAZEQUE at 1 p.m. and open at F.9b.5.0.on arrival.
Reports during march to head of column.

6. Completion of move and location of headquarters will be reported at once to Brigade H.Q.

7. ACKNOWLEDGE.

C. Chipper
Captain,
Issued at 10 p.m. Brigade Major,76th.Infantry Brigade.

Copies to:-
1. G.O.C.
2. 8th.K.O.R.L.
3. 2nd.Suffolk Regt.
4. 1st.Gordon Hldrs.
5. 76th.T.M.B.
6. 142nd.Field Amb.
7. No.2 Coy Train.
8. Bde Supply Offr.
9. Bde Transport Offr.
10. S.C.
11. 3rd.Div."G".
12. " "Q".
13. 8th.Inf.Bde.
14. 9th. "
15. War Diary
16. "
17. File.
18.)
19.)Retained.
20.)

OVER

Ref.BUCQUOY 1/40,000.

MARCH TABLE TO ACCOMPANY 76th.BDE.ORDER NO.142.

Unit.	Starting point.	Time.	Route.	Remarks.
Bde H.Q. 76th.T.M.B.	Road junction in POMMIER W.25c.2.4.	2.22 p.m.	BIENVILLERS - MONCHY.	Billeting parties will meet units at cross roads in MONCHY F.5a.6.6. and guide them by the best roads into their areas. The usual halts at 10 minutes to the clock hour will be observed. Brigade time will be given by Signals at 12 noon.
2nd.Suffolk Regt	-do-	2.25 p.m.	-do-	
8th.K.O.R.L.	-do-	2.45 p.m.	-do-	
1st.Gordon Hldrs	-do-	3.5 p.m.	-do-	
142nd.Field Amb.	-do-	3.25 p.m.	-do-	

XV

SECRET.

76th. INFANTRY BRIGADE ORDER NO.143.

Copy No.....

Ref. Map 57c.N.W.1/20,000
and LENS 11.

Sept.11th.1918.

1. 76th.Inf Brigade will move tomorrow, Sept.12th., into SAPIGNIES Area in accordance with march table overleaf.

2. The following distances will be maintained on the march:-

Between Coys...................... 100 yards.
" Bn and its transport..... 100 yards.
" Battns at least.......... 500 yards.

3. Areas are allotted as follows:-

8th.K.O.R.L......... Squares H.4d,5c,d,6c. Battn.H.Q.H.2a.1.3.

1st.Gordon Hldrs.... Squares H.2b,3 a,b,4 a.Bn.H.Q.H.1b.8.9.

2nd.Suffolk Regt.... Squares G.12a,b,H.7a,b.Bn.H.Q.G.12a.2.6.

76th.L.T.M.B........ Square H.9a.

142nd.Field Amb..... Squares H.9b,10a.

76th.Bde H.Q........ H.8b.2.2.

4. Advance parties of 1 officer and 6 O.R.per Battalion will leave at 7 a.m. to reconnoitre their areas. They will meet their units on road running S.E.from GOMIECOURT and guide them to their respective areas.

5. 76th.Bde H.Q.will close at F.9b.5.0.at 9 a.m. and open at H.8b.2.2. in SAPIGNIES on arrival.
Reports during march to head of column.

6. Completion of move and location of headquarters to be reported at once to Brigade H.Q.

7. ACKNOWLEDGE.

C. Chipper Captain,
Brigade-Major, 76th. Infantry Brigade.

Issued at 11.30 a.m.

Copies to:-
1. G.O.C.
2. 8th.K.O.R.L.
3. 2nd.Suffolk Regt.
4. 1st.Gordon Hldrs.
5. 76th.T.M.B.
6. 142nd.Field Amb.
7. No.2 Co Train.
8. Bde Supply Offr.
9. Bde Transport Offr.
10. S.C.
11. 3rd.Div."G".
12. " "Q".
13. 8th.Inf.Bde.
14. 9th. "
15. War Diary.
16. "
17. File.
18.)
19.) Retained.
20.)

OVER

Ref.LENS 11.

MARCH TABLE TO ACCOMPANY 76th.BRIGADE ORDER NO.145.

Unit.	Starting point.	Time.	Route.	Remarks.
Bdo H.Q. 76th.L.T.M.B.	Junction of AYETTE - COURCELLES and AYETTE-ARRAS roads.	10.5 a.m.	COURCELLES - GOMIECOURT.	Advanse parties will meet urits on road running S.F.from GOMIECOURT and guido thom to their areas. Brigade time will be given by signals at 8.30 a.m.
8th.K.C.R.L.	-do-	10.10 a.m.	-do-	
1st.Gordon Hldrs	-do-	10.40 a.m.	-do-	
2nd.Suffolk Rogt.	-do-	11.10 a.m.	-do-	
142nd.Field Amb.	-do-	11.40 a.m.	-do-	

wD.

XVI

SECRET.
****

Copy No....

76th.INFANTRY BRIGADE ORDER NO.144.

Ref.Sheet 57c.N.W.
and LENS 11.

September 15th.1918.

1. 76th.Inf Brigade will move into the MORCHIES - BEAUMETZ Area tomorrow Sept.16th in relief of 99th.Inf Brigade.

2. Battalion H.Q.will be:-

8th.K.O.R.L................ J.19b.9.9.
2nd.Suffolk Regt........... J.8c.2.3.
1st.Gordon Hldrs........... J.8c.0.5.

Battalion areas about Battalion H.Q.

3. 3rd.M.G.Bn.H.Q.and 1 Coy 3rd.M.G.Bn about J.13 central.

4. Units will move into this area:-

8th.K.O.R.L.....start 8.30 a.m. - via LABUCQUIERE.
1st.Gordon Hldrs" 8.30 a.m. - via BEUGNY.
2nd.Suffolk Regt" 9.0 a.m. - via BEUGNY.
3rd.Bn.M.G.C.H.Q.and 1 Coy start 9 a.m. - via LABUCQUIERE.

Each Battn will be followed by its transport.

5. 76th.Brigade H.Q.will close at FREMICOURT at 9 a.m. and open at I.12b.7.2.on arrival.

6. Location of transport lines and details will be given later.

7. ACKNOWLEDGE.

8. East of BEUGNY movement will be by platoons at 100 yards distance.

Issued at 9 p.m.

C. Chipp
Captain,
Brigade Major,76th.Infantry Brigade.

Copies to:-
1. G.O.C.
2. 8th.K.O.R.L.
3. 2nd.Suffolk Regt.
4. 1st.Gordon Hldrs.
5. Bde Signal Offr.
6. Bde Transport Offr.
7. No.2 Coy Train.
8. 3rd.Div."G".
9. " "Q".
10. 3rd.Bn.M.G.C.
11. 8th.Inf Bde.
12. 9th. "
13. B.M.
14. S.C.
15. War Diary.
16. "
17. File.

XVII

SECRET.
****
Copy No.20...

76th.INFANTRY BRIGADE ORDER NO.145.
****

Ref.Map 57c.N.E. September 25th.1918.

1. In conjunction with operations elsewhere,VI Corps will attack on Z day at an hour ZERO to be notified later.

2. The 42nd.Division is attacking on the right and the Guards Division on the left of the 3rd.Division.

3. The 3rd.Division is taking the 1st.Objective (RED Line) with 9th.Inf.Brigade on the right and 8th.Inf.Brigade on the left.

4. The 76th.Inf.Brigade will pass through 8th.Inf.Brigade on 1st.Objective at ZERO plus 110 mins.,and capture 2nd.Objective, (BROWN Line) in conjunction with 9th.Inf.Brigade on right. At ZERO plus 270 mins.,185th.Inf.Brigade,62nd.Division,will pass through and take 3rd.Objective (BLUE Line),187th.Inf.Brigade advancing at the same time north and south of RIBECOURT and 9th.Inf.Brigade attacking RIBECOURT. (Vide map attached).

5. The 76th.Inf.Brigade will attack with 8th.K.O.R.L.on right and the 1st.Gordon Hldrs on left,2nd.Suffolk Regt in support.

6. 1st.Northd.Fus.,9th.Inf.Brigade,is attacking on the right of 8th.K.O.R.L.
1st.Irish Guards,1st.Guards Bde,is attacking on left of 1st.Gordon Hldrs.

7. 76th.Inf.Brigade will move forward to its assembly positions on Y/Z night at times and by routes to be specified separately.

8. TASKS.

8th.K.O.R.L.Regt. 8th.K.O.R.L.on the right will capture and consolidate the line of STATION AVENUE from Railway to junction with SCORN TRENCH both inclusive (in touch on right with 1st.Northd.Fus and on left with 1st.Gordon ...

1st.Gordon Hldrs. 1st.Gordon Hldrs on the left will capture and consolidate the line of STATION AVENUE from its junction with SCORN TRENCH to junction with BEET TRENCH both exclusive (in touch on right with 8th.K.O.R.L.and on left with 1st.Irish Guards).

2nd.Suffolk Regt. 2nd.Suffolk Regt will:-

(I).(a) Cover left and rear of the advance of 1st.Gordon Hldrs and if required assist in the taking of FLESQUIERES from the North West.

(b) Complete the mopping up of any enemy holding out in FLESQUIERES after 1st.Gordon Hldrs have passed on.

(c) Assist left of 8th.K.O.R.L. advancing along front line of HINDENBURG SUPPORT SYSTEM.

(d) Protect right flank and rear of 8th.K.O.R.L. For this purpose 1 Coy will move in rear of the left of 1st.Gordon Hldrs; 1 Coy in rear of centre of 1st.Gordon Hldrs; 1 Coy in rear of left coy of 8th.K.O.R.L.; 1 Coy so placed as to protect right flank and rear of 8th.K.O.R.L.

8. TASKS. 2nd.Suffolk Regt (contd.)

(II) When the BROWN Line objective has been gained a protective barrage will be formed 300 yards in front. 2 Coys 2nd.Suffolk Regt will pass through BROWN Line to secure and mop up HINDENBURG SUPPORT SYSTEM and any enemy between STATION AVENUE and the barrage so as to ensure the advance of 185th.Inf.Brigade.

(III) After 185th.Inf.Brigade has passed through these 2 Coys will follow, advancing in a South Easterly direction, mopping up HINDENBURG SUPPORT SYSTEM and protecting right flank of 185th.Inf.Brigade. They will also be ready to assist by their fire the advance of 187th.Inf.Brigade moving round north of RIBECOURT.

(IV) The other 2 Coys 2nd.Suffolk Regt will remain in Brigade Reserve in RAVINE AVENUE.

76th.L.T.M.B.
O.C.76th.L.T.M.B. will place one half battery of 1 Stokes' Mortar and rifle bombers under the orders of 8th.K.O.R.L. and the other half battery under those of O.C.1st.Gordon Hldrs.

"C" Coy.3rd.M.G.Bn.
1 section will be at the disposal of each battalion to protect their consolidation. The remaining section will protect right flank of 76th.Inf.Brigade during the advance and, on the BROWN Line objective being reached, will take up a position to deal with any hostile counter-attack from the valley between RIBECOURT and MARCOING.

MARK V TANKS. These will pass through 76th.Inf.Brigade on 1st.objective and, keeping close behind the barrage, will co-operate in the attack on the HINDENBURG SUPPORT LINE and FLESQUIERES.

9. BARRAGE. (a) The advance of 76th.and 9th.Inf.Brigades will be made under a creeping barrage moving at the rate of 100 yards in 4 minutes.

(b) As soon as the 2nd.objective has been gained a protective barrage will be put down 300 yards beyond the objective dwelling for 60 minutes.

10. If during the advance the line is held up troops in rear will on no account remain stationary but will press on moving round the parts held up. It is absolutely vital that Battalions should be up under the barrage in front of RED line at ZERO plus 110 minutes.

11. Each Battalion Commander will arrange to get in touch with flank Battalions at definite points to be mutually agreed upon beforehand.

12. SIGNALS.

(a) SUCCESS SIGNAL. In order to indicate that 2nd. objective has been gained 3 WHITE Very lights will be fired. This signal will only be made on the order of a Company Commander.

(b) FLARES. The leading troops will light RED flares when called for by a contact areoplane sounding its Klaxon horn or dropping white Very lights.

Flares will be called for at the following hours:-

ZERO plus 90 mins (1½ hrs).
ZERO plus 210 mins (3½ hrs).

3/

(c) COUNTER ATTACK. A counter-attack machine will be in the air from ZERO onwards. The signal to denote the assembly of the enemy to counter-attack is the dropping of a RED smoke bomb over the place where the enemy is seen assembling.

(d) TANK SIGNALS. All ranks will be made acquainted with the signals to be used between Tanks and Infantry.

13. DUGOUTS.

Troops are to be warned against entering dugouts before they have been examined by special Tunnelling Section.

14. WATCHES. An officer from each unit will report at 76th. Inf. Brigade H.Q.at 4 p.m. Y.day to synchronize watches.

15. 76th.Inf.Bde.H.Q.will close at I.12b.7.2.at 9 p.m. Y/Z night and open at SLAG HEAP,K.20c.65.80.pn arrival.

16. HEADQUARTERS. Headquarters will be as follows:-

3rd.Division................ J.24a.5.4.
76th.Inf.Bde (after 11 p.m.Y day) .... K.20c.65.80.in STAMPE TR.
76th.Inf.Bde advanced report centre.......... K.21a.3.0.near junction KNIGHTSBRIDGE & LONDON SUPPORT.
8th.K.O.R.L. / 1st.Gordon Hldrs } at commencement -do-
2nd.Suffolk Regt at commencement........ K.20c.65.80.

All Battalion H.Q.will move forward along the line of GEORGE STREET and SCREW TRENCH.

17. ACKNOWLEDGE.

C. Clifford Captain,
Brigade Major,76th.Infantry Brigade.

Issued at 2 p.m.

Copies to:-
x1. 8th.K.O.R.L.
x2. 2nd.Suffolk Regt.
x3. 1st.Gordon Hldrs.
x4. 76th.T.M.B.
x5. "C" Coy.3rd.Bn.M.G.C.
6. Fd.Co.R.E.
7. 3rd.Div."G".
8. " "Q".
9. 8th.Inf.Bde.
10. 9th. "
11. 1st.Guards Bde.
12. 185th.Inf.Bde.
13. 187th.Inf.Bde.
14. 20th.K.R.R.C.
15. Bn.Tank Corps.
16. C.R.A.,3rd.Div.
17. A.D.M.S.
18. G.O.C.
19. S.C.
20. I.O.
21. Sig.Offr.
22. File.
23. War Diary.
24. "
25.-28. } Retained.

x Map with above & nos. only.

SECRET.
****

76TH. INFANTRY BRIGADE ADMINISTRATIVE INSTRUCTIONS. Copy No. 12
Issued with 76th. Infantry Brigade Order No.145.

1. GENERAL.
Forthcoming operations will lead the 3rd. Division into territory which necessitates change of Railheads and Roads - which will be partly in IV Corps Area.

2. RAILHEAD.
Supplies:- VELU probably on ZERO day.
Reinforcements:- ACHIET LE GRAND.

3. ROADS. The 3rd Division will have the running rights over the Roads through FREMICOURT, VELU, BERTINCOURT, RUYALCOURT, HAVRINCOURT WOOD, HAVRINCOURT VILLAGE for Supplies and Ammunition.

The Canal Bed will be available for double lorry traffic from the RAMP in K.31a. to the Lock in K.15a.

There is a good sleeper road running through HAVRINCOURT WOOD.

4. WATER.
Storage Tanks (10,000 galls.) will be installed at:-
K.15a. central.
K.27c. central.

The filling of these Tanks will probably not begin until the evening of "Z" day. Water Carts can then be filled from these two points.

A Water Point at J.15b.4.3. (DOIGNIES) is nearing completion. There will be Troughs at this point, and it will also be available for the filling of Water Lorries and Water Carts.

Water Point at P.4a.9.9. (SLAG HEAP) is available for filling Water Lorries. There are Water Troughs both sides of the Canal at J.36 central which can be taken into use on "Z" day.

At K.31a.0.3. there is a Water Point at bottom of Canal (approached by the RAMP) from which small lorries can fill up.

Water at FLESQUIERES and RIBECOURT should be plentiful and will be exploited immediately we occupy those places.

One Water Lorry will be allotted to the Brigade.

5. DUMPS.
There will be A Brigade Dump established at K.32a.7.6., YORKSHIRE BANK, which will contain:-

30 Boxes	S.A.A.	20 Boxes	Smoke Bombs No.24.
60 "	Rifle Grenades No. 36	15 "	L.G.Ammunition.
60 "	" " " 23	10 "	Rifle Grenades 24
20 "	Rods & Cartridges.	6 "	Long Rods.
7 "	Very Lights.	60	Stokes Mortars.

There will also be 100 Tins Water on this Dump available as an emergency supply.

Corps Light Ammunition Dump will be at Slag Heap, P.4a.

The S.A.A. Section of 3rd. D.A.C. will move to a site near HAVRINCOURT WOOD by noon on "Z" day. Exact location will be wired later.

(continued)

6. PROVOST ARRANGEMENTS.

The Corps Prisoner of War Cage will be at J.20a.3.2. (BEAUMETZ)
The 3rd.Div. " " " " " " " J.29c.8.7. (HERMIES).
Collecting Post will be at HAVRINCOURT.

Battalions are responsible for the safe custody of Prisoners until handed over to the A.P.M. at this Post, after which the infantry escorts will rejoin their units at once. Receipts will be obtained from the A.P.M. and copies of these receipts will be handed in to Brigade H.Q.

7. SUPPLIES.

A double refilling for Infantry Brigades will take place on 26th. instant. Those are rations for consumption on 27th. and 28th. instants, and for which a larger proportion of Preserved Meat will be issued to units.

8. TRANSPORT.

Two extra G.S. wagons have been allotted to the Brigade. These will be available for the carriage of surplus stores, etc.

Application for the use of these wagons will be made to 2/Lt. EASTWOOD who will be at Rear Brigade H.Q. at I.18d.2.3.

It is impressed on all concerned that there is no further spare transport, and units must be prepared to move "light".

Anything that has to be left behind must be collected and placed under a guard.

[signature] Major,
25th. September 1918. for Staff Captain, 76th. Infantry Brigade.

Copies to:-
1. 8th.K.O.R.L.Rgt.
2. 2nd.Suffolk Rgt.
3. 1st.Gordon Hrs.
4. 76th. T.M.Battery.
5. 3rd. Div. "Q".
6. G.O.C.
7. B.M.
8. S.C.
9. I.O.
10. Sig.Off.
11. War Diary.
12. Do.
13. File.
14. Do.

XVIII

SECRET.
****

Copy No. 24.

76th. INFANTRY BRIGADE ORDER NO. 146.

Ref. Map 57c.N.E. Sept. 25th. 1918.

1. The 76th. Inf. Brigade will march into assembly positions on Y/Z night as under:-

Unit.	Route.	Remarks.
8th. K.O.R.L. with ½ 76th. L.T.M.B.	BEAUMETZ-HERMIES STN-CEMETERY J.30c.8.3.- track to canal crossing about K.26c.7.0.-WIGAN COPSE.	Not to start before 7.30 p.m.
1st. Gordon Hldrs with ½ 76th. L.T.M.B.	BEAUMETZ-J.21c.- skirt HERMIES to the north through J.24a.& b.- K.20c.	Not to start before 7.30 p.m.
2nd. Suffolk Regt.	-do-	Not to start before 8.30 p.m.

2. Movement will be by platoons at 100 yards distance.

3. Assembly Trenches:-

8th. K.O.R.L. .... RAILWAY TRENCH, KNAT TRENCH & KNAT ALLEY north of railway.
1st. Gordon Hldrs. SLOANE STREET & CANAL TRENCH.
2nd. Suffolk Regt. O.B.L. AVENUE in K.19 and 20, moving to east bank of canal before ZERO.

4. The following trenches will be kept clear for purposes of communication:-
JERMYN STREET, BELL TRENCH, FAGAN AVENUE, GONG TRENCH, and SLAG AVENUE between FAGAN AVENUE and BELL TRENCH.

5. Arrival of each Battalion in its assembly position will be reported at once to Bde. H.Q. at SLAG HEAP, K.20c.65.80., by runner.

6. 76th. Bde. H.Q. will close at I.12b.7.2. at 9 p.m. Y. day and open at SLAG HEAP, K.20c.65.80. on arrival.

7. Area at present occupied by 76th. Inf. Bde will be taken over on departure by units of 99th. Inf. Bde as follows:-

8th. K.O.R.L. area down to grid line separating squares J.13, 14 and J.19, 20 by 1st. K.R.R.C.
2nd. Suffolk Regt H.Q. by H.Q. 99th. Inf. Brigade.
-do- area by 23rd. Royal Fusiliers.
1st. Gordon Hldrs area by 1st. Royal Berks.
-do- H.Q. by H.Q. 1st. Royal Berks and H.Q. 23rd. Royal Fus.
76th. L.T.M.B. area by 99th. L.T.M.B.

8. Advance parties will probably arrive today, 25th. Sept.

8. ACKNOWLEDGE.

C. Clifford Captain,
Brigade Major, 76th. Infantry Brigade.

Issued at 4 p.m.

DISTRIBUTION OVER.

Copies to:-
1. G.O.C.
2. 8th.K.O.R.L.
3. 2nd.Suffolk Regt.
4. 1st.Gordon Hldrs.
5. 76th.T.M.B.
6. "C" Coy.3rd.Bn.M.G.C.
7. 529th.Fd.Co.R.E.
8. 3rd.Div."G".
9. " "Q".
10. 8th.Inf.Bde.
11. 9th. "
12. 1st.Guards Bde.
13. 185th.Inf.Bde.
14. 187th. "
15. 20th.K.R.R.C.
16. Bn.Tank Corps.
17. C.R.A.,3rd.Div.
18. A.D.M.S.
19. B.M.
20. S.C.
21. Q.O.
22. Sig.Offr.
23. File.
24. War Diary.
25. "
26.)
27.) Retained.
28.)

XIX

76th Infantry [illegible] O.R/17

1. In the event of the Brigade being ordered to move forward at short notice, all men will carry fighting kit. In the event of Haversacks and Jerkins being issued before moving, they will be carried [illegible]. All Packs and Greatcoats will be [illegible] separately and dumped in BILHEM CHAPEL TRENCH close to the Railway [illegible] [illegible].

2. The 2nd Suffolk Regt. will dump theirs in the trench N. of the railway line and 8th K.O.R.L. Regt., 1st Gordon Hrs., Bde. H.Q. and T.M. Battery in the trench S. of the Railway.

3. Each Battalion will detail 1 N.C.O. & 4 Light Duty men to remain behind as a guard over these kits. Bde. H.Q. will detail [illegible] O.R. and 76th T.M. Bty. 2 O.R. to remain behind. They will be provided with 10 days' Iron Rations each.

4. All articles surplus to establishment which Battalions cannot carry on their transport must be dumped. No guarantee can be given that these can be collected again.

Packs and Greatcoats will remain in the Trench under the Guard detailed until it is possible to arrange for [illegible] to take them forward to [illegible] new areas.

5. O.C. 76th T.M. Battery will arrange to dump his guns [illegible] [illegible].

6. Each unit will provide the necessary [illegible] for [illegible] and [illegible] before leaving the area.

7. All Packs and Greatcoats must be plainly marked to facilitate redistribution.

[signature] Captain

Staff Captain 76th Infantry Bde.

2?th Sept. 1918.

Copies to: 8th K.O.R.L. Regt. | 2nd [illegible]
2nd Suffolk Regt. | B.M.
1st Gordon Hrs. | War Diary (2)
76th T.M. Bty. | File
Brigade Q.M. Sgt.

"A" Form.

Army Form C. 2121
(In pads of 100.)

MESSAGES AND SIGNALS.

No. of Message.........

Prefix ...... Code .... m.	Words.	Charge.	This message is on a/c of:	Recd. at .... m.
Office of Origin and Service Instructions.	Sent		.... Service.	Date ....
	At .... m.			From ....
	To			
	By		(Signature of "Franking Officer.")	By ....

TO: [illegible], KADI, FINI

Sender's Number.	Day of Month.	In reply to Number.	AAA
* G 495	30		

BAMA will move tonight 30th to area L26 L27 aaa KADI [illegible] L27 [illegible] [illegible] RIBACOURT 5 pm aaa [illegible] L27 a and c start 5 pm aaa FINI L26 b and d start 5.30 pm aaa ~~[illegible]~~ LTMB start 6 pm (and L26a) aaa C [illegible] MG start 6 pm area L26c aaa Route [illegible] [illegible] [illegible] ~~BAMA~~ [illegible]

BAMA [illegible] L27 a b6 on arrival [illegible] [illegible] at 7.00 [illegible]

From	BAMA		
Place			
Time			

The above may be forwarded as now corrected. (Z)

Censor. Signature of Addressor or person authorised to telegraph in his name.

* This line, except AAA, should be erased if not required.

Wt. W 3253/P511. 500,000 Pads. 1/18. B. & S. Ltd. (E2389.)

"A" Form.

Army Form C. 2121 (In pads of 100.)

MESSAGES AND SIGNALS.

No. of Message..........

Prefix .... Code .... m.	Words.	Charge.	This message is on a/c of:	Recd. at .... m.
Office of Origin and Service Instructions.	Sent At .... m. To .... By		.... Service. (Signature of "Franking Officer.")	Date .... From .... By ....

TO	GEJA	C Coy MG	
	KABI	LTMB	
	FINI		

Sender's Number.	Day of Month.	In reply to Number.	AAA
* G 495	30		

BAMA will move today 30th to area L26 L27 aaa KABI allotted L27 b and d clears RIBECOURT 5pm aaa GEJA L27a and c start 5pm aaa FINI L26 b and d start 5.30pm aaa ~~[illegible]~~ LTMB start 6pm area L26a aaa C Coy MG start 6pm area L26c aaa Route road south of railway aaa BAMA closes 6pm opens X L27a 6.6 on arrival aaa Move by companies at 200 yards

From BAMA

Place

Time 4pm.

The above may be forwarded as now corrected. (Z) .... Censor.

Signature of Addressor or person authorised to telegraph in his name. [signature] Capt

* This line, except AAA, should be erased if not required.

Wt. W 3253/P511. 500,000 Pads. 1/18. B. & S. Ltd. (E2389.)

X Wrong Ref

XXI

REPORT ON OPERATIONS Sept.26th.-28th.1918

76th.INFANTRY BRIGADE.

****

Ref.Map 1/20,000 57c.N.E.

On the night of Sept.26/27th., the Brigade moved from the BEAUMETZ-MORCHIES Area to assembly positions preparatory for the attack on FLESQUIERES. The assembly positions had been previously reconnoitred and routes marked out and picketed by Battalions. Thanks to these arrangements the approach march was carried out without a hitch in spite of rain and the darkness of the night. Units were disposed in assembly positions as follows:-

Right front Battalion, 8th.King's Own (R.L.) Regt. -
RAILWAY TRENCH & KNAT TRENCH.
Left front Battalion, 1st.Gordon Highlanders -
SLOANE STREET, CANAL TRENCH and KNIGHTSBRIDGE.
Support Battalion, 2nd.Suffolk Regt, -
O.B.L.AVENUE.

All battalions were in by 11.45 p.m.. At 3.45 a.m.the 2nd.Suffolk Regt moved across to the East bank of the canal south of KNIGHTSBRIDGE. The crossing was much hindered by heavy hostile shelling and machine gun fire which commenced shortly before 4.30 a.m., but all companies were in position on the East bank before ZERO.

76th.L.T.M.B. was organised in two half batteries of 15 men each with 1 Stokes' Mortar and 9 rifle bombers. One half battery was attached to 8th.K.O.R.L. and one to 1st.Gordon Hldrs.

"C" Coy 3rd.Bn.M.G.C.assembled in BOND STREET & CITY TRENCH. 1 section followed each Battalion in the advance while the rôle of the remaining section was to guard the right flank.

76th.Brigade headquarters were established at K.20c.65.80. in STAMPE TRENCH.

As the wire behind LONDON TRENCH & LONDON SUPPORT still presented a considerable obstacle to movement in the dark, the right front battalion moved two companies forward at 4.30 a.m.up KNIGHTSBRIDGE and CLARGES AVENUE into LONDON SUPPORT, while the 1st.Gordon Hldrs on the left cut a large gap through which to pass the whole battalion by platoons after ZERO.

The enemy barrage before ZERO caused a certain number of casualties.

At ZERO, 5.20 a.m., the 8th.Brigade advanced to the attack on the RED line and the battalions of the 76th.Brigade followed in their wake. LONDON TRENCH & SUPPORT were crossed with some difficulty, but direction and formation were rectified in No Man's Land.

All three battalions advancing in close support of the 8th.Brigade became involved in the fighting about the RED line. The 8th.K.O.R.L.on the right cleared up several enemy machine gun nests in CLARGES AVENUE and copse in K.22a., while the 1st.Gordon Hldrs on the left fought their way into SNAKE & SEAL TRENCHES. A number of casualties and some disorganisation was occasioned, but by thus pressing forward the brigade was able to advance from the RED line at ZERO plus 110 close under the barrage.

This advance to the BROWN LINE was attended by very hard fighting, The 8th.K.O.R.L.moved with their right flank on the railway, while their left two companies worked their way along the front line of the HINDENBURG SUPPORT SYSTEM. Enemy machine gunners everywhere kept up a stiff resistance until rushed by our riflemen under cover of Lewis Gun fire and rifle bombs. At 9.45 a.m.this battalion was in position along the whole of its objective on the BROWN LINE, and at ZERO plus 270 troops of the 62nd.Division passed through.

contd......

The two leading companies of the 1st.Gordon Hldrs captured the Sunken Road and LINCOLN TRENCH in K.17d.with a large number of prisoners and some machine guns. The support companies then continued the advance and entered FLESQUIERES. Here they became very much mixed in hand to hand fighting with the enemy but succeeded in XXXXXXXXXX reaching SHERWOOD SWITCH east of the village in touch with the Irish Guards on the left. Further advance was held up for some time by very heavy machine gun fire from the left flank and the BEETROOT FACTORY and by field guns firing over open sights from the east and north east. Other parties had meanwhile reached the sunken road in K.24a. Owing to very heavy losses in N.C.O's disorganisation was extreme and the advance was further held up by two or three enemy machine guns in action in SCORN TRENCH. Reorganisation was undertaken as quickly as possible and the machine guns in SCORN TRENCH silenced. At this juncture troops of the 62nd.Division passed through and occupied STATION AVENUE on the front of this battalion without much opposition.

The company of the 2nd.Suffolk Regt in immediate support of the 1st.Gordon Hldrs fought their way through FLESQUIERES and across RAVINE AVENUE to the trench running from L.19a.55.30.to L.19a.7.7. They were then held up by enemy in STATION AVENUE,which they were about to clear when the 62nd.Division troops passed through.

The commander of the right front company of the 2nd.Suffolk Regt noticed a large gap on the right of the brigade. He therefore on his own initiative moved his company south of the railway to fill it and fought forward under the barrage to the western outskirts of RIBECOURT. He advanced conjointly with a company of 4th.Royal Fusiliers which had lost all its officers and was very ably commanded by its C.S.M. These two companies overcame heavy resistance on the way taking many prisoners and established themselves on the BROWN LINE south of the railway. When the 62nd.Division advanced from the BROWN LINE and passed round RIBECOURT these two companies went forward with them and right through the village taking 200 prisoners. After which they reorganised and fell back on to the BROWN LINE.

Another Suffolk company,seeing the leading company move off to the right took on their rôle in support of the 8th.K.O.R.L.,and had heavy fighting up to the objective taking many prisoners. They then reorganised in RAVINE AVENUE and dug in in front of it together with the reserve company of the battalion.

"C" Coy 3rd.Bn.M.G.C.rendered very valuable assistance in the attack and subsequent consolidation. The section commanders were allowed considerable freedom on manœuvre in their co-operation with battalions and showed great initiative in selection of positions. In one instance a hostile machine gun in L.14c.was effectually silenced by fire from a section in liaison with a company of 1st.Gordon Hldrs.

Orders were issued from Brigade as regards reorganising and consolidation in depth,and this was carried out after dark,the front system being held by 2nd.Suffolk Regt and 1st.Gordon Hldrs,with 8th. K.O.R.L.in reserve.

Another machine gun company was allotted by Division and both companies took up positions in depth for the defence of the line.

Signed C.L. Porter

Brigadier-General,
Commanding 76th.Infantry Brigade.

5/10/18.

POINTS BROUGHT OUT BY THE OPERATIONS.

1. The relief model on the ground constructed near MORCHIES by an R.E.officer kindly lent by the 529th.Field Company was invaluable in enabling all ranks of the brigade and machine gun company to get an idea of the ground beforehand.

2. The reconnaissance and picketing of assembly positions and the cross country routes thereto enabled the approach march to be carried out without a hitch,in spite of the darkness of the night. No guides were required from other formations. Battalion scouts proved extremely useful.

3. Instructions were given not to delay if troops in front became held up,but to push through or round,and on no account to lose the barrage. It is thought that the success of the attack largely depended on the dashing and determined way this was carried out.

4. The extreme value of leadership and initiative in fire unit commanders was once more proved,as also the pressing need for a plentiful supply of well trained N.C.O's to replace casualties.

5. The success in the attacking of machine gun nests under cover of fire from rifles or Lewis Guns showed that men had been well trained previously in "fire and movement".

6. Visual communication was established early but the difficulty came to light of maintaining touch between the forward station which had to take up its position according to the ground and the battalion headquarters which must move with the fighting.

Brigadier-General,
Commanding 76th.Infantry Brigade.

5/10/18.

AND SIGNALS

Prefix.........Code .... | Words. | Charge.

Office of Origin and Service Instructions.

Sent
At ....m.
To.............
By.............

This message is on a/c of:
.... *Service.*
(Signature of "Franking Officer.")

Recd. at ...... m.
Date..........
From..........
By...........

TO

Sender's Number.	Day of Month.	In reply to Number.	AAA
* T. 266			

Casualties September 1918
76th Inf. Bde

	Killed	Wounded	Missing
Officers	6	13	·
Other Ranks	98	498	18

From

Place

Time

The above may be forwarded as now corrected. (Z)

Censor. Signature of Addressor or person authorised to telegraph in his name.

* This line, except **AAA**, should be erased if not required.

Wt. W 3253/P511. 500,000 Pads. 1/18. B. & S. Ltd. **(E2389.)**

3rd Division

WAR DIARY & APPENDICES

B. H. Q.

76th INFANTRY BRIGADE

OCTOBER 1918

76th Brigade

3rd Division.

WAR DIARY

B. H. Q.

76th INFANTRY BRIGADE.

OCTOBER 1918.

Appendices under separate cover

October 1918. 13

WAR DIARY

~~or INTELLIGENCE SUMMARY~~

(Erase heading not required.)

Page I

76th Infantry Brigade

Vol 37

Army Form C. 2118.

Instructions regarding War Diaries and Intelligence Summaries are contained in F. S. Regs., Part II. and the Staff Manual respectively. Title Pages will be prepared in manuscript.

Place	Date	Hour	Summary of Events and Information	Remarks and references to Appendices
MARCOING L 22.a.6.6.	Oct. 1	6am	Barrage opened. Battns. did not reach assembly positions until zero hour, & No trace of M.G. Coy. attached to Bgde.	App. I 9.499.
		7.45am	100 prisoners collected at Bgde H.Q. & more coming in. Reported that 2nd Suffolk Regt. had penetrated the village of RUMILLY	App 2 9.501.
		8am	Observers report troops seen advancing East in G.17.c.	
		9am	A further lot of 200 prisoners reach Bgde H.Q.	
		4pm	Dispositions from all Battns received	App 3
		4.20pm	Lt. Col. Fraser ordered to attack RUMILLY with 2 Coys. assisted by all available men of the 2nd Suffolk Regt.	9 502
		4.50pm	1 Coy. of the Royal Scots attached to assist in mopping up RUMILLY.	App IV 9505
		7pm	8th Bgde take over part of front line relieving the 8th KORL.	App V 9507
		10.30pm	RUMILLY reported to be entirely in our hands.	App VI 9.509.
—"—	Oct. 2.	3.40am	Small groups of Germans come to life in RUMILLY. Left flank reported to be in the air.	App. VII 9.512.
		5am	Small bombing parties organised & the village again cleared with a few more prisoners.	

2449 Wt. W14957/M90 750,000 1/16 J.B.C. & A. Forms/C.2118/12.

October 1918. **WAR DIARY** or ~~INTELLIGENCE SUMMARY~~ Page 2

(Erase heading not required.)

76th Infantry Brigade

Army Form C. 2118.

Instructions regarding War Diaries and Intelligence Summaries are contained in F. S. Regs., Part II. and the Staff Manual respectively. Title Pages will be prepared in manuscript.

Place	Date	Hour	Summary of Events and Information	Remarks and references to Appendices
MARCOING 4.22.a.66.	Oct 2nd		The remainder of the day was moderately quiet	
		7.30pm	8th Brigade take over the front line, failing to push further forward	
		10pm	Battns reorganise in the RUMILLY SUPPORT, with the K.O.R.L's E of the village Gordons on the S side, 2nd Suffolk Regt in Support.	
	3rd		Very quiet day counter attack expected (prisoners statement)	
		8pm	2nd Suffolk Regt. take over from the K.O.R.L's E. of the village	
	4th		Support area very heavily shelled during the morning.	
		5pm	General C.C. Metcalf CMG. DSO. arrives, to take over command of the Bgde.	
		8pm	1st Gordon Highlanders take over from the 2nd Suffolk Regt.	
	5th		General Porter left for England today.	
			All troops resting in the support area, excellent weather moderately quiet	
	6th		Operation orders received for a further advance the 76th Bgde. being in reserve	App VIII

2449 Wt. W14957/M90 750,000 1/16 J.B.C. & A. Forms/C.2118/12.

Instructions regarding War Diaries and Intelligence Summaries are contained in F. S. Regs., Part II. and the Staff Manual respectively. Title Pages will be prepared in manuscript.

OCTOBER 1918 **WAR DIARY** *or* ~~INTELLIGENCE SUMMARY~~ *(Erase heading not required.)*

Page 111

76th Infantry Brigade

Army Form C. 2118.

Place	Date	Hour	Summary of Events and Information	Remarks and references to Appendices
MARCOING L.22.a.66	Oct 7th	10.00	Advance party proceeds to MASNIERS (Masnières)	
MASNIERS G.20.d.4.2		16.00	Brigade H.Q. opened in the Catacombs.	
			2nd Suffolk Regt. come under orders of the G.O.C. 9th Bgde	
		18.00	K.O.R.L. move to RUMILLY SUPPORT East of CAMBRAI ROAD	App IX G.A. 294. " 301
— " —	8th	04.30	Barrage opens.	
		04.07	2nd Suffolk Regt. reported to be on their objective	App X
		08.00	Further report from 2nd Suffolk	" XI
			Liaison was kept up at intervals with the 9th Bgde, whose Headquarters were also in the CATACOMBS.	
		10.00	K.O.R.L.'s placed under orders of the 9th Bgde.	" XII
		12.55	Remainder of Bgde placed under orders of 9th Bgde. & H.Q. withdrawn to MARCOING.	XIII
L.22.a.66		15.00	B.H.Q. again opened in MARCOING	
		18.00	Battns. under orders of the G.O.C. 9th Bgde. attack & capture the whole of the 2nd Objective.	XIV
	9th		1st Guards Brigade pass through & all Battns. are withdrawn in the early hours of the morning & march to HAVRINCOURT area still under orders of the G.O.C. 9th Bgde.	XV. XVI & Report on C...

2449 Wt. W14957/M90 750,000 1/16 J.B.C. & A. Forms/C.2118/12.

Army Form C. 2118.

Instructions regarding War Diaries and Intelligence Summaries are contained in F. S. Regs., Part II. and the Staff Manual respectively. Title Pages will be prepared in manuscript.

OCTOBER 1918 WAR DIARY or ~~INTELLIGENCE SUMMARY~~

(Erase heading not required.)

Page IV

1/6th Infantry Brigade

Place	Date	Hour	Summary of Events and Information	Remarks and references to Appendices
BOGGART HOLE. K.33.b.2.6.	9th	12.00	Brigade H.Q. opened in BOGGARTS HOLE. Battns. assemble in the HAVRINGCOURT area	
—"—	10th – 12th		Resting reorganising & baths.	
	13th	10.00	Brigade march to MARCOING, great congestion of traffic on the roads, arrived in billets at 01.00 hours.	App. XVII. B.O. 148.
MARCOING 10 Rue de la Gare L.23.a.7.9.	14th		All Battns. employed on salvage work, with very good results. Captain Chipper on leave replaced by Captn Russell, 2nd Suffolk Regt.	
—"—	15th & 16th		One Coy per Battn still employed in salvage work, remainder platoon training. Captain Russell called to 9th Bgde to act as Brigade Major, his work carried on by the Intelligence Officer (Capt Black)	
—"—	17th		Companies training in "fire & movement". 1/4 employed in salvage. General attends distribution of medals to 8th Bgde by Major General.	
—"—	18th		All Battns employed in salvage, very good results.	App. XVIII
—"—	19th		March to CATTENIERES, arriving there about 17.00 hours to find very good furnished billets.	B.O. 149.
CATTENIERES	20th		10.30 hours leave CATTENIERES, very wet day, & heavy marching. arrive in QUIEVY, very good billets at 13.30 hours	App. XIX B.O. XIX

2449 Wt. W14957/M90 750,000 1/16 J.B.C. & A. Forms/C.2118/12.

Instructions regarding War Diaries and Intelligence Summaries are contained in F. S. Regs., Part II. and the Staff Manual respectively. Title Pages will be prepared in manuscript.

OCTOBER 1918 WAR DIARY or ~~INTELLIGENCE SUMMARY~~

(Erase heading not required.)

Page V

76th Infantry Brigade

Army Form C. 2118.

Place	Date	Hour	Summary of Events and Information	Remarks and references to Appendices
QUIEVY	21st Oct		Brigade resting, & standing by at two hours notice ~~in Div~~	
			Warning order received that we were to attack on the 23rd Oct.	
—do—	22nd	04.15	Operation orders for the attack received.	
		09.30	Conference, all Battn Commanders. O.C.'s. 76th L.T.M.B., 529th Field Coy R.E. & C. Coy. 3rd Battn M.G.C.	
SOLESMES		17.00	Headquarters close at Quiévy, & open at SOLESMES at 19.00 hours all Battns reported in billets by 22.00 hours.	App. XX (March table)
			Very good billets here fully furnished houses in tact.	
		20.00	Watches synchronized with Div. H.Q. & all Battns.	
	23rd	01.00	S.O.S. put up in front line by the 20th Londons, causing our artillery to open out & heavy retaliation from the enemy.	
		02.15	Slight gas shelling of SOLESMES., Brigade Staff retire to the cellar	
		02.40	Signalling Officer going up to establish a forward Brigade report centre in ROMERIES.	
		03.20	Zero Barrage opens, drawing slight retaliation on the forward area.	App. XXI B00 150.

2449 Wt. W14957/M90 750,000 1/16 J.B.C. & A. Forms/C.2118/12.

OCTOBER 1918

WAR DIARY
or
INTELLIGENCE SUMMARY

Page VI

76th Infantry Brigade

Army Form C. 2118.

Instructions regarding War Diaries and Intelligence Summaries are contained in F. S. Regs., Part II. and the Staff Manual respectively. Title Pages will be prepared in manuscript.

(Erase heading not required.)

Place	Date Oct.	Hour	Summary of Events and Information	Remarks and references to Appendices
SOLESMES.	23	04.45.	12 Prisoners arrive at B.H.Q. from the 1st Gordon Hldrs.	App. XXII Report on opps.
		04.55	Report centre opened & line complete.	
		05.40	Reports received through the R.C. that the 1st Gordon Hldrs. have gained their objectives.	
		06.35.	Detailed reports arrive from Companies giving their exact dispositions	
		07.30	Prisoners collected at the H.Q. now total 15 Officers & 542 ORs.	
		08.15	Several low flying aeroplanes (enemy) over ROMERIES.	
		09.12	Div. report that progress on the right will be slow as the line taken over by the N.Z. Divisions, hangs back on the right.	
		09.45	O.C. Trench Mortar Battry reports heavy casualties in the Battery, only one section left to go on to the second objective.	
		10.25.	O.C. 1st Gordon Hldrs. reports by phone that several prisoners appear coming from W.16.d. attack appears to be going well. N.Z. Div. in touch on the right & 8th K.O.R.L. on the left. Walking wounded report the attack going well.	

2449 Wt. W14957/M90 750,000 1/16 J.B.C. & A. Forms/C.2118/12.

OCTOBER 1918.

WAR DIARY or INTELLIGENCE SUMMARY

(Erase heading not required.)

Army Form C. 2118.

Instructions regarding War Diaries and Intelligence Summaries are contained in F. S. Regs., Part II. and the Staff Manual respectively. Title Pages will be prepared in manuscript.

Page VII

76th Infantry Brigade.

Place	Date	Hour	Summary of Events and Information	Remarks and references to Appendices
SOLESMES.	23	11.00.	Support Coy. Cmdr. of the 8th K.O.R.L. Regt. reports 10.30 hours front Coys. consolidating on the GREEN LINE, support Coys. 100x in rear of sunken Road W.11.C. Casualties light.	
		11.10.	Telephone communication received from the Major General to reorganize in depth on the GREEN LINE. & that the Corps Cavalry, backed up by the 9th Brigade would pass through.	
		11.30.	These orders issued through the O.C. in ROMERIES.	
		12.15.	Brigade H.Q. close at SOLESMES, arrived at ROMERIES. 13.20.	
ROMERIES		13.25.	O.C. 8th K.O.R.L. reports DOTTED GREEN line reached with no opposition.	
		14.50.	Confirmation arrives of the capture of the DOTTED GREEN line giving Battn. dispositions.	
		15.40.	Div. Commander on the telephone, says our men seen approaching the BROWN Line (probably the 9th Bgde.)	
		16.35.	9th Bgde. now reported on the BROWN Line.	
		16.40.	Orders transmitted to O.C's. Battns. to reorganise in depth on the Green Line 9th Bgde. take over responsibility of the front line.	

2449 Wt. W14957/M90 750,000 1/16 J.B.C. & A. Forms/C.2118/12.

OCTOBER 1918.

WAR DIARY
or
INTELLIGENCE SUMMARY
(Erase heading not required.)

Page VIII.

76th Infantry Bgde.

Army Form C. 2118.

Instructions regarding War Diaries and Intelligence Summaries are contained in F. S. Regs., Part II. and the Staff Manual respectively. Title Pages will be prepared in manuscript.

Place	Date	Hour	Summary of Events and Information	Remarks and references to Appendices
ROMERIES	23	21.00	Battns assembled in the LA TROUSSE MINON. area	
	24th	10.00	All troops withdrawn into billets in ROMERIES.	
	25th		Day spent in resting the troops salvage parties collecting the Booty, & conversing with the civilians in the village.	
	26th	07.30	BHQ close at ROMERIES & opened at ESCARMAIN at 09.00 hours, 2nd Suffolk Regt. remain in ROMERIES.	App. XXIII B.O.O. 151.
	27th		All officers reconnoitre the forward area.	
			Brigade take over the left Corps front from 99th Brigade. 8th K.O.R.L. in the outpost line, 1st Gordon Hldrs. in support 2nd Suffolk Regt. in Reserve in CAPELLE.	App. XXIV B.O.O. 152.
			Brigade H.Q. open in CAPELLE at 19.00 hours.	
	28th		Situation very quiet on the whole front, slight gas shelling reported in RUESNES.	
	29th		Relieved by the 5th Inf. Bgde. commencing at 17.00 hours Relief complete at 19.00 hours. Brigade H.Q. move back to VERTAIN & open at 22.00 hours.	App. XXV B.O.O. 153

OCTOBER 1918.

Instructions regarding War Diaries and Intelligence Summaries are contained in F. S. Regs., Part II. and the Staff Manual respectively. Title Pages will be prepared in manuscript.

WAR DIARY
or
~~INTELLIGENCE SUMMARY~~
(Erase heading not required.)

Page IX.

76th Infantry Brigade

Army Form C. 2118.

Place	Date	Hour	Summary of Events and Information	Remarks and references to Appendices
VERTAIN	30th		Brigade resting in billets, 1st Gordon Hldrs. & 2nd ~~K.O.R.L.~~ Suffolk in ST PYTHON, 8th K.O.R.L. in VERTAIN.	
	31st		Brigade march back to CARNIERES to rest billets, long march but men march very well, arrive at CARNIERES at 14.30 hours, where Brigade Major rejoins from leave	

2nd Lt. [illegible] Clark,
for Brigadier General Comndg,
76th Infantry Brigade

2449 Wt. W14957/M90 750,000 1/16 J.B.C. & A. Forms/C.2118/12.

3rd Division

APPENDICES

76th INFANTRY BRIGADE

OCTOBER 1918.

"A" Form. Army Form C. 2121 (In pads of 100.)

MESSAGES AND SIGNALS.

No. of Message............

Prefix ...... Code .... m.	Words.	Charge.	This message is on a/c of:	Recd. at .... m.
Office of Origin and Service Instructions.	Sent		.... Service.	Date ....
	At .... m.			From ....
	To			
	By		(Signature of "Franking Officer.")	By ....

TO REFE MIHU

Sender's Number.	Day of Month.	In reply to Number.	AAA
*			

[illegible] midnight [illegible] RIBECOURT [illegible] RERO [illegible] not [illegible] found [illegible] REFE [illegible] MIHU

From RAMA

Place

Time

The above may be forwarded as now corrected. (Z)

.... *Censor.* Signature of Addressor or person authorised to telegraph in his name.

* This line, except **A A A,** should be erased if not required.

Wt. W 3253/P511. 500,000 Pads. 1/18. B. & S. Ltd. **(E2389.)**

"A" Form.

Army Form C. 2121.
(In pads of 100.)

MESSAGES AND SIGNALS.

No. of Message..........

Prefix .... Code .... m.	Words.	Charge.	This message is on a/c of:	Recd. at .... m.
Office of Origin and Service Instructions.	Sent		.... Service.	Date ....
	At .... m.			From ....
	To			By ....
	By		(Signature of "Franking Officer.")	

TO 3rd DIV G.

Sender's Number.	Day of Month.	In reply to Number.	AAA
* G.501.	1st		

Situation at 7.45AM AAA 2nd SUFFOLK penetrated into village on their right but held up on left by M.G. Fire on their left AAA 2 Coys 1st GORDON HIGHLS reported attempting to work round on SUFFOLK left AAA. No news from 8th KORL AAA Orders sent through O.C. SUFFOLK and by Brigade Major to O.C 8th KORL to push up on east side of RUMILLY, if they have not already done so AAA O.C 1st GORDON HIGHLS to send one Coy to work through RUMILLY from Southern end and round up enemy M.Gs in G.14.D and B AAA Stokes ~~[illegible]~~ being sent forward to assist SUFFOLK left AAA Report

From

Place

Time

The above may be forwarded as now corrected. (Z)

Censor. Signature of Addressor or person authorised to telegraph in his name

*This line, except **AAA**, should be erased if not required.

Wt. W 3253/P511. 500,000 Pads. 1/18. B. & S. Ltd. (E2389.)

"A" Form.

Army Form C. 2121.
(In pads of 100.)

MESSAGES AND SIGNALS.

No. of Message............

Prefix......... Code .... m.	Words.	Charge.		Recd. at .... m.
Office of Origin and Service Instructions.	Sent At .... m. To .... By		This message is on a/c of: .... Service. .... (Signature of "Franking Officer.")	Date .... From .... By ....

TO

Sender's Number.	Day of Month.	In reply to Number.	AAA
*			

post received our Infantry seen in B.22 A + B. Prisoners already passed through 100 more are coming in. Later report from F.O.O. states our Infantry seen advancing E in G.17.c presumably The KINGS OWN. Later Suffolk report one Coy battalion passed through village Eastwards Left still held up by M.G. fire from about junction of Road & Railway G.9.c also towards G.14 G.8.7 AAA Have no news of 2nd [illegible] AAA

From 76th INF Bde

Place

Time 9-40 AM

The above may be forwarded as now corrected. (Z)

.... Censor.

[illegible] Signature of Addressor or person authorised to telegraph in his name.

*This line, except AAA, should be erased if not required.

Wt. W 3253/P511. 500,000 Pads. 1/18. B. & S. Ltd. (E2389.)

"A" Form.
Army Form C. 2121
(In pads of 100.)

MESSAGES AND SIGNALS. No. of Message........

Prefix...... Code........ m. Office of Origin and Service Instructions.	Words.	Charge.	This message is on a/c of:	Recd. at........ m.
	Sent At........ m. To By		.... Service. SECRET (Signature of "Franking Officer.")	Date .... From .... By........

TO: 8th RWRL; 2nd Suffolk Regt; 1st Gordon Hdrs

Sender's Number.	Day of Month.	In reply to Number.	AAA
* G 502	1		

1. Our line appears to run G 23 d 2.3 in touch with New Zealand Div. along sunken road to G 23 b 1.6 thence to G 16 d 0.6 thence echeloned back into G 21 b with some men in G 16 a also RUMILLY SUPPORT in G 14 and men in G 14 a
2. 8th Inf Bde will advance in artillery formation at 6.20 pm from trenches [illegible] going North East past RUMILLY to line G 17 central G 10 central to join 2nd Division attacking from North.
3. 76 Inf Bde will mop up RUMILLY following a creeping barrage starting 6.30 pm. on southern outskirts of RUMILLY dwelling ten minutes and then advancing 100 yards in 6 mins
4. RUMILLY is being bombarded all afternoon special attention being paid to known

From machine gun nests in village and vicinity
Place The railway siding in G central is also being
Time bombarded From [illegible] to 6.20 pm [illegible] is being bombarded by 3 brigades of heavy arty

The above may be forwarded as now corrected. (Z)

Censor. Signature of Addressor or person authorised to telegraph in his name.

* This line, except AAA, should be erased if not required.

Wt. W 3253/P511. 500,000 Pads. 1/18. B. & S. Ltd. (E2380.)

"A" Form.

Army Form C. 2121.
(In pads of 100.)

MESSAGES AND SIGNALS.

No. of Message............

Prefix.......... Code ....m. | Words. | Charge. | This message is on a/c of: ....Service. (Signature of "Franking Officer.") | Recd. at ......m. Date...... From By.........

Office of Origin and Service Instructions.

Sent At..........m. To.......... By..........

TO

Sender's Number.	Day of Month.	In reply to Number.	AAA
* G 502 (contd)	1		

5. Lt Col FRASER, DSO MC, will be in command of 76 Bde attack on RUMILLY and will use what men he has of his two Coys 1st Gordon Hdrs together with all available men of 2nd Suffolk Regt and rifle bombers of LTMB attached plus 12 more rifle bombers of LTMB now being sent up.

6. The attack on RUMILLY will be supported by 3 bdes RFA including 3 batteries 4.5 hows. Also by 3 bdes heavy artillery firing on north of RUMILLY until necessary to lift for safety.

7. 2nd Suffolk Regt will push forward in cooperation and engage hostile MGs with every available LG and rifle.

8. Acknowledge by wire.

From 76th Inf Bde
Place
Time 4.20pm

The above may be forwarded as now corrected. (Z) .... Censor.

C. Chetham [illegible]
Signature of Addressor or person authorised to telegraph in his name.

*This line, except AAA, should be erased if not required.

Wt. W 3253/P511. 500,000 Pads. 1/18. B. & S. Ltd. (E2389.)

"A" Form.

Army Form C. 2121.
(In pads of 100.)

MESSAGES AND SIGNALS.

No. of Message..........

Prefix.......... Code.......... m. | Words. | Charge.

Office of Origin and Service Instructions.

Sent
At.......... m.
To..........
By..........

IV

This message is on a/c of:
.... Service.

SECRET

(Signature of "Franking Officer.")

Recd. at .... m.
Date..........
From..........
By..........

TO { [illegible]
2nd Suff [illegible]
[illegible] }

Sender's Number.	Day of Month.	In reply to Number.	AAA
* G 505	1		

1. [illegible] my G 502

2. 2nd Suffolk Regt will [illegible] forward [illegible]

3. [illegible]

4. [illegible]

5. [illegible] IV and V [illegible]

From 76 [illegible] Bde
Place
Time 9 50 pm

The above may be forwarded as now corrected. (Z) [illegible]

.... Censor. Signature of Addressor or person authorised to telegraph in his name.

* This line, except **AAA**, should be erased if not required.

Wt. W 3253/P511. 500,000 Pads. 1/18. B. & S. Ltd. (E2389.)

"A" Form.

MESSAGES AND SIGNALS.

Army Form C. 2121
(In pads of 100.)

No. of Message..........

Prefix .... Code .... m.	Words.	Charge.	This message is on a/c of:	Recd. at .... m.
Office of Origin and Service Instructions.	Sent		.... Service.	Date ....
	At .... m.		SECRET	From ....
	To		(Signature of "Franking Officer.")	By ....
	By			

TO: [illegible] 2nd Suffolk Regt, 1st Gordon Hdrs

Sender's Number.	Day of Month.	In reply to Number.	AAA
* G 502	1		

1\. Our line [illegible] G 23 d 2.3 in touch with New Zealand Div along sunken road to G 23 b 1 6 thence to G 16 d 0 6 thence [illegible] back to G 21 b with some [illegible] in G 16 a also RUMILLY SUPPORT in G 14 and [illegible] in G 9 a

2\. 8th Bde will advance in artillery formation at 6.30 pm from [illegible] G 21 d and 28 a [illegible] North East of RUMILLY to line G 17 central G 10 central [illegible] from North

3\. 76 Bde will [illegible] of RUMILLY following [illegible] [illegible] RUMILLY [illegible] 100 yards in 6 minutes

4\. RUMILLY is being [illegible] [illegible] The [illegible] in G 9 central is also being bombarded. From 6 to 6.20 pm the [illegible] is being bombarded by 3 Brigades heavy artillery

From

Place

Time

The above may be forwarded as now corrected. .... Censor.

(Z) .... Signature of Addressor or person authorised to telegraph in his name.

* This line, except AAA, should be erased if not required.

Wt. W 3253/P511. 500,000 Pads. 1/18. B. & S. Ltd. (E2389.)

"A" Form.
Army Form C. 2121.
(In pads of 100.)

MESSAGES AND SIGNALS.

No. of Message.........

Prefix........ Code........ m.	Words.	Charge.	This message is on a/c of:	Recd. at ...... m.
Office of Origin and Service Instructions.	Sent		.... Service.	Date ....
	At .... m.			From ....
	To			
	By		(Signature of "Franking Officer.")	By ....

TO

Sender's Number.	Day of Month.	In reply to Number.	
* G 502 (contd)	1		AAA

5. Lt Col FRASER. DSO. MC. will be in command of 76 Bde attack on RUMILLY and will use what men he has of his two Coys 1st Gordon Hdrs together with all available men of 2nd Suffolk Regt and rifle bombers of TMB attached plus 12 more rifle bombers of TMB now being sent up
6. The attack on RUMILLY will be supported by 3 bdes RFA including 3 batteries 4.5 hows. Also by 3 bdes heavy artillery firing on north of RUMILLY until necessary to lift for safety.
7. 2nd Suffolk Regt will push forward in cooperation and engage hostile MGs with every available LGs and rifles
8. Acknowledge by wire

From 76th Inf Bde
Place
Time 4.20pm.

The above may be forwarded as now corrected. (Z) C. Clifton Capt
Censor. Signature of Addressor or person authorised to telegraph in his name.

*This line, except **AAA**, should be erased if not required.

Wt. W 3253/P511. 500,000 Pads. 1/18. B. & S. Ltd. (E2389.)

"A" Form.

Army Form C. 2121.
(In pads of 100.)

MESSAGES AND SIGNALS.

No. of Message............

Prefix.......... Code.......... m. | Words. | Charge.

Office of Origin and Service Instructions.

Sent At..........m. To.......... By..........

This message is on a/c of: .... Service.

(Signature of "Franking Officer.")

Recd. at ......m. Date...... From By......

TO GESA KABI FINI

Sender's Number.	Day of Month.	In reply to Number.	AAA
* G 505	1		

Further to G502 GESA will push forward in cooperation and engage hostile MGs with ~~every~~ available LG and rifle aaa One coy ROYAL SCOTS QALI will be under orders Col FRASER and will report his HQ aaa They will follow remainder if late. aaa ~~Gen~~ Germans are retiring in front of fourth and fifth corps aaa Acknowledge

From BAMA

Place

Time 5.10pm

The above may be forwarded as now corrected. (Z) C. Chipps Capt.

Censor. Signature of Addressor or person authorised to telegraph in his name.

*This line, except A A A, should be erased if not required.

Wt. W 3253/P511. 500,000 Pads. 1/18. B. & S. Ltd. (E2389.)

"A" Form.

Army Form C. 2121.
(In pads of 100.)

MESSAGES AND SIGNALS.

No. of Message............

Prefix..........Code..........m.	Words.	Charge		Recd. at ....m.
Office of Origin and Service Instructions.	Sent		This message is on a/c of:	Date......
	At..........m.		..........Service.	From
	To..........			
	By..........		(Signature of "Franking Officer.")	By..........

TO: GEJA
KABI
FINI

Sender's Number.	Day of Month.	In reply to Number.	AAA
* G 507	1		

Tonight on completion of operations [illegible] will hold front line from Q23d15 to Q10 central disposed in depth aaa BAMA will hold RUMILLY with battalions disposed in depth GEJA in Q21 KABI in Q14 FINI posts round RUMILLY aaa MG Coy as ordered direct aaa acknowledge

From BAMA

Place

Time

The above may be forwarded as now corrected. (Z) C. Clifford Capt

Censor. Signature of Addressor or person authorised to telegraph in his name.

*This line, except AAA, should be erased if not required.

Wt. W 3253/P511. 500,000 Pads. 1/18. B. & S. Ltd. (E2389.)

"A" Form.

Army Form C. 2121.
(In pads of 100.)

MESSAGES AND SIGNALS.

No. of Message............

Prefix......... Code.......... m.	Words.	Charge.	This message is on a/c of:	Recd. at ...... m.
Office of Origin and Service Instructions.	Sent At......m. To...... By......		..........Service. (Signature of "Franking Officer.")	Date...... From...... By......

TO MIHU
QALI

Sender's Number.	Day of Month.	In reply to Number.	AAA
* G 509	1		

RUMILLY now entirely in our hands mopping up practically completed aaa Eighty prisoners including battalion commander claimed aaa FINI ordered to return aaa DVJU now finishing mopping up aaa Added MIHU repd QALI

From BKMA
Place
Time 10.35pm

The above may be forwarded as now corrected. (Z) C Clifford Capt

Censor. Signature of Addressor or person authorised to telegraph in his name.

*This line, except **A A A**, should be erased if not required.

Wt. W 3253/P511. 500,000 Pads. 1/18. B. & S. Ltd. **(E2389.)**

"A" Form. Army Form C. 2121. (In pads of 100.)

MESSAGES AND SIGNALS. No. of Message

Prefix Code m. | Words. | Charge. | This message is on a/c of: | Recd. at m.

Office of Origin and Service Instructions. | Sent At m. To By | Service. (Signature of "Franking Officer.") | Date From By

TO MIHU QALI

Sender's Number.	Day of Month.	In reply to Number.	
* G 512	2		AAA

as neither QALI nor BAMA have been able to get touch with Division on left we are forming defensive flank along sunken road in G10 c and d and ~~round~~ north west of RUMILLY ~~onto~~ CAMBRAI road aaa Large clearing up party is being organised to scour RUMILLY completely as small ~~parties~~ groups of Germans have come to life aaa added MIHU rptd QALI

From BAMA

Place

Time 3.40 am

The above may be forwarded as now corrected. (Z) C. Clapper Capt

Censor. Signature of Addressor or person authorized to telegraph in his name.

*This line, except AAA, should be erased if not required.

Wt. W 3253/P511. 500,000 Pads. 1/18. B. & S. Ltd. (E2389.)

7th Oct 1918

VIII

76th Infantry Brigade Order No 147

SECRET

Ref Map 57C N.W.

Copy No 13

1. In conjunction with operations elsewhere the VI Corps is to continue its advance. The attack of the VI Corps will be carried out by the 3rd Division on the right and 2nd Division on the left. The New Zealand Division will be attacking on the right of the 3rd Division.

2 Boundaries and objectives are shewn on the map already issued.

3. The advance on the 3rd Division front will be carried out by the 9th Inf. Bde which will pass through the 8th Inf. Bde at zero hour.

4. 2nd SUFFOLK REGT. and the two Machine Gun Coys. in Divisional reserve will come under the orders of G.O.C. 9th Inf. Bde.

5. 76th Inf. Bde (less 2nd Suffolk Regt) and attached Machine Gun Company will be in Divisional reserve and will be prepared:-

(a) either to support the 9th Inf. Bde in their attack on the 2nd Objective for which purpose they will come under the orders of the G.O.C. 9th Inf Bde, or:-

(b) on receipt of orders from Divisional H.Q. to pass through the 9th Inf. Bde. on the 2nd objective under the orders of G.O.C. 76th Inf. Bde and capture the 3rd objective

6. The Guards Division will be prepared to pass through 3rd Division according as the situation developes, and will in any case take over from or pass through the 3rd Division on night Z/Z+1. When the Guards Division has passed through and taken over responsibility for the front the Division will be withdrawn to the HAVRINCOURT-HERMIES area and become Right Reserve Division.

7. On night Y/Z —

2nd SUFFOLK REGT will move under orders of G.O.C. 9th Inf. Bde.

8th K.O.R.L.Rgt will move to assembly positions about the MASNIERES-CAMBRAI road north of present headquarters G.20.d.25.30.

1st GORDON HDRS will move to assembly positions about the MASNIERES-CAMBRAI road south of 8th K.O.R.L.

RUMILLY to be cleared by 20.00 hours Y day. Accommodation at present occupied by 2nd Suffolk Regt will not be available till 01.30 hours Z day. No movement in areas open to enemy observation will take place before 19.00 Y day. Positions will be previously reconnoitred and occupied as speedily as possible on account of moves of other formations.

8th Inf. Bde. will be thinning out their line and withdrawing their reserve battalion to vicinity of 8th Bde HQ in L.2.a.c.

9th Inf. Bde and two M.G. Coys. will be moving up clearing their present area east of RIBECOURT by 19.00 hours.

8. The attack by the 9th Inf. Bde will be made with 1st Northumberland Fusiliers, right front battn
4th Royal Fusiliers, left front battn
2nd Suffolk Regt, right support battn
13th King's, left support battn

9. Barrage. The attack will be supported by 5 brigades field artillery and 1 brigade heavy artillery.

The creeping barrage will come down at zero hour about 100 yards west of road running through G24a and c where it will rest for 10 minutes. It will subsequently advance at the rate of 100 yards in 4 minutes. The fire of the four M.G. Coys will be used to assist in covering the advance of the 9th Inf. Bde.

There will be a pause of 30 minutes on the 1st objective. Troops advancing to the 2nd objective will pass the 1st objective at zero + 130

10 Tanks. 6 Mark IV Tanks of 12th Tank battalion will cooperate in the attack and will follow in rear of the 9th Infa Bde. 4 Tanks will operate against SERANVILLERS and 2 Tanks on the high ground west of the village.

11 Success Signal. In order to indicate that the 1st and 2nd objectives have been gained the "success signal" (rifle grenade, white over white over white) will be fired. This signal will only be made on the order of a company commander.

12. Flares. The leading troops will light RED flares when called for by contact aeroplane sounding its Klaxon horn or dropping white Very lights. Flares will be called for at Zero + 1 hour 55 minutes and Zero + 3 hours 20 minutes.

13. Counter attack. A counter attack machine will be in the air from Zero onwards. The signal to denote the assembly of the enemy to counter attack is the dropping of a RED smoke bomb over the place where the enemy is seen assembling.

14. Tank Signals. All ranks will be made acquainted with the signals in use between tanks and infantry.

15. Synchronization. An officer from each unit will be sent to Brigade H.Q. at 16.00 to synchronize watches.

16 Headquarters. 76th Inf. Bde and 9th Inf. Bde G20d7.2
Right battn 9th Inf. Bde G27b1.7,
Left battn 9th Inf. Bde G22c8.5, Battns 76th Inf. Bde G20d25.30

17 Z day will be Oct. 8th. Zero hour will be notified later.

18. Acknowledge.

C. Clipper Capt
Bde Major
76th Inf. Bde.

Issued at 07.00

Copies					
1	8th KORL	9	3rd New Zealand Bde	17	File
2	2nd Suffolk Rgt	10	99th Inf. Bde	18	New Divns
3	1st Gordon Hdrs	11	3rd Div G	19	
4	76th LTMB	12	9th Fd. Ambce.	20	Retained
5	C Coy 3rd M.G. Bn.	13	S.O.	21	
6	Group R.F.A	14	Staff Capt	22	
7	8th Inf. Bde	15	Sig. Offr	23	
8	9th Inf. Bde	16	Int. Offr	24	

K00/18.

Administrative Instructions. Ref 76th Bde Order No 147

Medical Arrangements.

O.C. No 142 Field Ambulance will be responsible for the evacuation of wounded from 9th Infantry Brigade. O.C. No 7 Field Ambulance from 76th Infantry Brigade.

Evacuation of wounded will be carried out in the first part of the operation along the present line, viz, either to the Advanced Dressing Station at G.19d.9.7, or to the Advanced Dressing Station at G.26c.6.5, whichever route is the more suitable.

Walking Wounded will be directed to the Advanced Dressing Stations, where collecting stations will be formed. O's C. No.7 and No.142 Field Ambulances will have the routes flagged as far as possible on "Y/Z" night.

Supply of Ammunition & Grenades

The Brigade Ammunition Dump at present Brigade H.Q. in L.22.a.6.7 will remain under our charge.

Capt MATTHEWS is being left behind in charge when Brigade H.Q. moves forward. All indents will continue to be sent to the Staff Captain, who will arrange direct with Capt MATTHEWS for issue of Ammunition and Grenades required.

Rations

All ranks will carry Rations for consumption 8th inst on the man, in addition to the Iron Rations.

Tools &c

Each man will carry 2 Sandbags. All available Picks & Shovels will be distributed and carried.

T.J. [illegible]
Captain
Staff Captain 76th Infantry Brigade.

7/10/18

Copies to: – 3 Battalions
76th T.M. Bty
Battalion Details
Brigade
B.M.
S.C.

"C" Form
MESSAGES AND SIGNALS.

Army Form C. 2123.
(In books of 100.)

No. of Message

Prefix SM Code Words 30

£ s. d.

Charges to collect

Service Instructions.

Received From Tck By

Sent, or sent out At m. To By

Office Stamp.

Handed in at MIHU Office 1802 m. Received 1857 m.

TO BAMA

*Sender's Number	Day of Month	In reply to Number	AAA
GA297	7		

RUMILLY SUPPORT and RUMILLY FRENCH are required for accommodation of other troops these trenches will not therefore be occupied by Troops of this Division

FROM
PLACE & TIME MIHU 18.50

* This line should be erased if not required.

(B 8070) Wt. w. 7496—M857 250,000 Pads. 10/16 H&S (E436.) Forms/C.2123/3.

"C" Form

MESSAGES AND SIGNALS.

Army Form C. 2123.
(In books of 100.)

No. of Message

Prefix AR Code 23.005 Words

Received From GEN By

Sent, or sent out At m. To By

Office Stamp.

Charges to collect

Service Instructions. Priority

Handed in at M.H.Q. Office 22.00 m. Received 23.05 m.

TO Same (76th Bde)

*Sender's Number	Day of Month	In reply to Number	AAA
GA 301	7		

Reference GA 297 aaa this refers
only to RUMILLY SUPPORT
and RUMILLY TRENCH
West of MASNIERES CAMBRAI
road aaa Trenches East of
the road are available for
troops of this Division

FROM M.H.Q.

PLACE & TIME 22:50

* This line should be erased if not required.

(B 8070) Wt. w. 7496—M857 250,000 Pads. 10/16 H & S (E436.) Forms/C.2123/3.

"C" Form

MESSAGES AND SIGNALS.

Army Form C. 2123.
(In books of 100.)

No. of Message

Prefix ...... Code ...... Words	Received.	Sent, or sent out.	Office Stamp.
£ s. d.	From	At m.	
Charges to Collect	By	To	
Service Instructions		By	

Handed in at Raby Office 0845 m. Received 0910 m.

TO Bama

*Sender's Number	Day of Month.	In reply to Number	AAA
	8		

am on first objective can only raise ten suffolk men am going to kings liverpools to try and get help

FROM Lt Mann

PLACE & TIME 07 07

* This line should be erased if not required.

9/M1970 50m 4/17 W. & Co. Ltd. E1213

"C" Form
Army Form C. 2123.
(In books of 100.)

MESSAGES AND SIGNALS.

No. of Message..............

Prefix.......... Code........Words..........	Received.	Sent, or sent out.	Office Stamp.
£ s. d.	From..............	At .... m.	
Charges to Collect	By	To..............	
Service Instructions		By..............	

Handed in at Kabi Office 0840 m. Received 0907 m.

TO Bama

*Sender's Number	Day of Month.	In reply to Number	AAA
	8		

report KABI and GEBI holding line west of SERRINVILLERS.

FROM
PLACE & TIME 2nd Bt Coote 8.40

* This line should be erased if not required.

W528/M1970 50m 4/17 W. & Co. Ltd. E1213

"C" Form — Army Form C. 2123. (In books of 100.)

MESSAGES AND SIGNALS.

No. of Message ....

Prefix SO Code .... Words ....

£ s. d.

Charges to collect

Service Instructions.

Received From .... By ....

Sent, or sent out At ....m. To .... By ....

Office Stamp.

Handed in at .... Office ....m. Received ....m.

TO (BAMH) 76 Bde.

*Sender's Number	Day of Month	In reply to Number	AAA
GL 809	8		

BAMH will place one Battn in addition to 2 [illegible] at disposal of GOC 9 Bde for gaining the objective added GAEA and BAMH

FROM PLACE & TIME (HIHU) 3 Divn

* This line should be erased if not required.

(B 8070) Wt. w. 7496—M857 250,000 Pads. 10/16 H & S (E436.) Forms/C.2123/3.

"C" Form

Army Form C. 2123.
(In books of 100.)

MESSAGES AND SIGNALS. No. of Message

Prefix SM Code 1405 Words 32

Received From YC By

Sent, or sent out At m. To By

Office Stamp.

£ s. d.

Charges to collect

Service Instructions.

Handed in at YC Office 1205 m. Received 1210 m.

TO CAMA

*Sender's Number	Day of Month	In reply to Number	AAA
GC 313	8/10		

~~[illegible]~~ The Remaining Bty of Cama is Placed under Orders of GOC QAFA aaa Cama Hqrs will move for Hqrs at L22A6.6 on Receipt of this order

FROM MIHV

PLACE & TIME 12:55

* This line should be erased if not required.

Wt. w. 7496—M857 250,000 Pads. 10/16 H&S (E436.) Forms/C.2123/3.

"C" Form
MESSAGES AND SIGNALS.

Army Form C. 2123.
(In books of 100.)

No. of Message

Prefix SM Code 2340 Words 38

Received. From YC By WHV

Sent, or sent out. At m. To By

Office Stamp.

Charges to Collect

Service Instructions

Handed in at YC Office 2340 m. Received 0010 m.

TO 76th Bde

*Sender's Number	Day of Month.	In reply to Number	AAA
Ga 331	8		

attack	carried	out	at
18.00	hours	completely	
successful	aaa	Whole	of
2nd	objective	now	occupied
units	in	touch	with
one	another	and	with
NZ	divn	on	right

FROM 3rd Div

PLACE & TIME 2305

* This line should be erased if not required.

528/M1970 50m 4/17 W. & Co. Ltd. E1213

"C" Form
MESSAGES AND SIGNALS.

Army Form C. 2123.
(In books of 100.)
No. of Message

Prefix SM Code 2236 Words 124

Received. From YC By ...

Sent, or sent out. At m. To By

Office Stamp.

£ s. d.

Charges to Collect

Service Instructions

1 of 3 adds

Handed in at YC Office 2236 m. Received 2359 m.

TO 76th Infy Bde

*Sender's Number	Day of Month	In reply to Number	AAA
GB325	8		

In	continuation	of	GA 324
of	this	date	aaa
Bns	of	9th	and
76th	Infy	Bdes	on
withdrawal	will	march	to
areas	as	stated	in
GB300	dated	oct	7th
under	the	orders	of
GOC	9th	Infy	Bde
who	will	allot	routes
in	consultation with		GOC's
of	two	leading	bdes
Guards	div	aaa	Two mg
coys	attached	9th	Infy
Bde	will	march	to
area	L25c and d		under orders
of	GOC	9th Inf	Bde aaa

FROM

PLACE & TIME

* This line should be erased if not required.

W528/M1970 50m 4/17 W. & Co. Ltd. E1213

"C" Form

MESSAGES AND SIGNALS.

Army Form C. 2123.
(In books of 100.)

No. of Message..............

Prefix.......... Code........Words........ £ s. d. Charges to Collect	Received. From.............. By..............	Sent, or sent out. At ....m. To.............. By..............	Office Stamp.
Service Instructions			

Handed in at .... Office ....m. Received ....m.

TO

*Sender's Number	Day of Month.	In reply to Number	AAA
2	remaining	mg	coys
will	march	to	the
area	on	road	between
BEAUMETZ	and	VELU	tomorrow
on	time	to	clear
area	at	present	occupied
before	arrival	of	2
coys	attached	9th	Infy
Bde	aaa	acknowledge	aaa
added	9th Infy	Bde	DMGC
repeated	76th	Infy	Bde
Q	signals		

FROM 3rd Div

PLACE & TIME 22.20

* This line should be erased if not required.

[18958] W528/M1970 50m 4/17 W. & Co. Ltd. E1213

XVI

SECRET.

REPORT ON OPERATIONS OCTOBER 1st.1918.

76th. INFANTRY BRIGADE.

On the afternoon of September 30th the Brigade received orders to move into the area L.26 and 27 East of RIBECOURT and be prepared to pass through 62nd. Division next day and continue the advance.

Battalions and attached Machine Gun Company commenced moving off about 17 hours; G.O.C.76th.Inf.Bde reported at headquarters 62nd. Division near FLESQUIERES at 18.00 hours to attend a conference. Here verbal orders were received that 76th.Inf.Bde was to capture RUMILLY and line of road running N.and S.through G.17b.and d,G.23b.and d.

After the conference,G.O's.C.186th and 187th Inf.Bdes were interviewed at 187th.Inf.Bde H.Q.as regards provision of guides,and arrangements were made after conferring at H.Q.4th.York & Lancaster (62nd.Div.). 8th.K.O.R.L.were to attack on the right and 2nd.Suff on the left with 2 Coys 1st.Gordon Hldrs in close support of each Battalion.

Battalions moved off between 01.00 and 01.45 Oct.1st assembly positions behind RUMILLY TRENCH East and West of the MASNI CAMBRAI road. The guides for the left sector were excellent and assembly was carried out without a hitch in spite of extreme darkness heavy rain showers. On the right,however,owing to heavy going and gui losing their way,the troops only arrived just before ZERO hour.

At ZERO,06.00,the barrage came down on the line of RUMILLY SUPPORT where it rested for 6 minutes before advancing at the rate of 100 yards in 6 minutes. The barrage was rather ragged and caused several casualties. Troops on the right got forward without much opposition and by about 08.00 were reported to be consolidating on their objective in G.23 in touch with the New Zealand Division.

2nd.Suffolk Regt on the left met opposition immediately in RUMILLY TRENCH and found RUMILLY SUPPORT strongly held and full of machine guns. Over 300 prisoners were taken out of the latter and many Germans killed. By the time these two trenches had been dealt with our troops had lost the barrage and the left companies came under intense machine gun fire from the flanks and front which inflicted severe casualties and made further advance impossible. The right company, however,was shielded by the ground from flanking fire and,pushing through RUMILLY,reached the trench line in G.16a.killing and capturing many of the enemy. Here they were held up by further machine guns East of the village. The two supporting companies of 1st.Gordon Hldrs working forward on the left had got into a position facing N.E.in G.14b.,where they were stopped by very heavy machine gun fire from a quarry in front and from the railway sidings in G.9c. 2nd.Division had been unable to advance owing to machine gun fire from MONT SUR L'OEUVRE.

After the barrage had passed the enemy started trickling back into RUMILLY eventually compelling troops on the East to refuse their left flank to face the village. About 11.00,the enemy commenced to advance from the direction of SERANVILLERS apparently intending to counter-attack. He was engaged at long range with rifle and artillery fire and retired back to the village. About the same time heavy shell fire was directed on our right flank,which was rather crowded. This flank was therefore thinned out and reorganised to gain depth and save casualties.

As RUMILLY appeared to be again in the hands of the enemy, our posts and patrols were withdrawn from the outskirts,and the village and machine gun nests were re-bombarded during the afternoon. Orders were received to re-capture RUMILLY under a creeping barrage at 18.30 with any available men,in conjunction with the advance of the 8th.Inf.Bde and troops of 2nd.Division on the flanks.

Two (weak) companies of 1st.Gordon Hldrs with about 100 men of the 2nd.Suffolk Regt and the 76th.L.T.M.B.(without mortars) were collected and organised for the attack by O.C.1st.Gordon Hldrs. The attack was completely successful and about 80 prisoners were taken

contd...... /

including a battalion Commander. Elements of the enemy which came to life again during the night were finally dispoéed of at dawn. Our casualties were light and were mostly caused by irregularities in the barrage.

A company of 2nd.Royal Scots lent by the 8th.Inf.Bde were not able to arrive in time for the commencement of the operation, but rendered valuable assistance in "mopping up".

After dark the Brigade was reorganised and the position consolidated in depth.

(signed) F.E. Metcalfe

Brigadier-General.

10/10/18. Commanding 76th.Infantry Brigade.

R C/16

SECRET

Administration Instructions Ref 76th Inf Bde Order No. 147

Medical Arrangements

O.C. No. 142 Field Ambulance will be responsible for the evacuation of wounded from 9th Infantry Brigade. O.C. No. 7 Field Ambulance from the 76th Infantry Brigade.

Evacuation of wounded will be carried out in the first part of the operation along the present lines, by either to the Advanced Dressing Station at G 19 d 9 7, or to the Advanced Dressing Station at G 26 c 1 5, whichever road is the more suitable.

Walking Wounded will be directed to the Advanced Dressing Stations, where Collecting Stations will be formed. O.C. No. 7 and No. 142 Field Ambulances will have the routes flagged as far as possible on 7/8 night.

Supply of Ammunition & Grenades.

The Brigade Ammunition Dump at present Brigade H.Q. in L 22 a 6 7 will remain under our charge.

Capt MATTHEWS is being left behind in charge when Brigade H.Q. move forward. All indents will continue to be sent to the Staff Captain who will arrange direct with Capt MATTHEWS for issue of Ammunition & Grenades required.

Rations

All ranks will carry Rations for consumption 8th inst. on the move in addition to the Iron Rations.

Tools etc

Each man will carry 2 Sandbags. All available Picks and Shovels will be distributed and carried.

Captain

7/10/16

Staff Captain 76th Infantry Bde.

Copies to 3 Battalions
Battalion Details
Brigade
T.M.
S.C.

XVII

SECRET.

76th. INFANTRY BRIGADE ORDER NO.148. Copy No.....

Ref, 57c.N.E.

1. 76th.Inf.Brigade with 56th.Field Coy., R.E. will march to MARCOING area as below:-

Starting point:- Cross Roads in HAVRINCOURT, K.27 484

Route via RIBECOURT.

2nd.Suffolk Regt	-	pass starting point	10.15 hours.	Oct 13th
8th.K.O.R.L.	-	do.	10.30 "	"
1st.Gordon Hldrs	-	do.	10.45 "	"
Bde H.Q.& 76th. L.T.M.B.	-	do.	11.00 "	"
56th.Field Co.R.E.	-	do.	11.05 "	"

To be clear of RIBECOURT by 12.30 hours.

2. Each Battalion will be followed by its transport.

3. The following distances will be maintained on the march:-

Between Companies.................................. 100 yards.
Between Battalion and its transport............. 100 yards.
Between Battalions................................. 100 yards.

4. Administrative Instructions will be issued separately.

5. ACKNOWLEDGE.

6. 76th Bde HQ will close at BOGGARTS HOLE at 10.30 hours and open at L 23a7.9 on arrival (near station MARCOING)

C. Clipper Captain,

Issued at 21.30hours. Oct 12th/18.

Brigade Major, 76th. Infantry Brigade.

Copies to:-
1. G.O.C.
2. 8th.K.O.R.L.
3. 2nd.Suffolk Rgt.
4. 1st.Gordon Hldrs.
5. 76th.T.M.B.
6. Bde Sig.Offr.
7. Bde Int.Offr.
8. No.2 Co.Train.
9. 3rd.Div."G".
10. " "Q".
11. 56th.Fld.Co.R.E.
12. 7th.Field Amb.
13. 8th.Inf.Bde.
14. 9th. "
15. Bde.Transport Offr.
16. SMC.
17. War Diary.
18. "
19. File.

SECRET.
****

Copy No..8.....

76TH. INFANTRY BRIGADE ADMINISTRATIVE INSTRUCTIONS.

1. The Brigade will move from present area to MARCOING Area to-morrow, 13th. instant. Time of move will probably be after midday.

2. Billeting parties of 1 Officer and 5 O.R. per Battalion, 1 Officer and 2 O.R. of 56th.Field Coy.,R.E., 2 O.R. of 76th.T.M.Bty., and 2 O.R. of Brigade H.Q. will meet 2/Lt.J.CLARK, M.C., Brigade Intelligence Officer, at the Cross Roads, L.22a.9.3. at 08.30. 2/Lt. CLARK will allot billeting areas.

3. The majority of the Brigade will be billeted in houses and cellars in the village which require a good deal of cleaning up before they can be occupied. In order to cope with this, Battalions will arrange to send an advance party of 1 Platoon per Company forward to report to their billeting Officers at the Cross Roads, MARCOING, L.22a.9.3. at 10.30.

56th.Field Coy., R.E. should send a party of 20 O.R.
76th.T.M.Battery " " " " " 10 "
76th.Inf.Bde.H.Q. will " " " " 20 "

to report as above.

4. Billeting parties will arrange to meet their Units on arrival at the same Cross Roads. Probable times of arrival will be notified later.

T.F. Fennell
Captain,
Staff Captain, 76th.Infantry Brigade.

12th.Oct.1918.

Copies to:-
1. G.O.C.
2. 8th.K.O.R.L.Rgt.
3. 2nd.Suffolk Rgt.
4. 1st.Gordon Hrs.
5. 76th.T.M.Bty.
6. 56th.Fld.Coy.,R.E.
7. B.M.
8. Bde.Int.Off.
9. War Diary
10. Do.
11. File.
12. Do.

SECRET.

**AMENDMENT NO. 1 TO
76TH. INFANTRY BRIGADE ADMINISTRATIVE INSTRUCTIONS
DATED 12th. OCTOBER 1918.**

Reference para.2, line 4.

For 08.30 read 07.30.

Reference para.3, line 6.

For 10.30 read 09.30.

Reference para.4.

Billeting parties will meet their units as under:-

2nd.Suffolk Rgt.	FORK ROAD L.22a.0.1. at 11.45.			
8th.K.O.R.L.Rgt.	Cross Roads,	L.22a.9.3.	at	12.00.
1st.Gordon Hrs.	"	"	"	12.00.
Brigade H.Q. & T.M.Bty.	"	"	"	12.15.
56th.Fld.Coy.,R.E.	"	"	"	12.30.

The advance party should take a percentage of shovels with them.

The Spare Kit and Stores Dump at HAVRINCOURT will remain until further notice.

Dress:- Full Marching Order.

Transport will follow their units.

T. J. [signature]
Captain,
Staff Captain, 76th.Infantry Brigade.

12th.October 1918.

Copies to all recipients of Administrative Instructions and No. 7 Field Ambulance.

XVIII

SECRET.
****

Copy No. 16

76th. INFANTRY BRIGADE ORDER NO.149.

Ref. ~~sheets~~ 57c.N.E.)
57b.N.W.) 1/20,000.

18th.October 1918.

1. The Brigade Group will move to CATTENIERES tomorrow, Oct.19th.

2. Route:- MASNIERES - GREVECOURT - SERANVILLERS - LA TARGETTE - WAMBAIX.

3. Starting point and order of march as per march table over.

4. Steel helmets will be worn.

5. L.G.limbers will move with their companies. Remainder of "A" Echelon (1st. line transport) i.e., S.A.A., Bomb, Signal and tool limbers will march with units. "B" Echelon (2nd.line transport) will march with Brigade Group under orders of O.C., No.2 Coy 3rd.Div.Train and in rear of that unit.

6. Watches will be synchronized at 12.00 hours at Brigade H.Q.

7. Units will halt independently at 10 minutes to the clock hour.

8. Administrative Instructions will be issued separately.

9. Brigade H.Q. will close at MARCOING at 13.30 hours and re-open at Billet No.19, CATTENIERES on arrival.

10. Reports during march to head of column.

11. ACKNOWLEDGE.

J. Clark 3/4t/15
Captain,
Brigade Major, 76th. Infantry Brigade.

Issued at 20.00 hours.

Copies to:-

1. G.O.C.
2. 8th.K.O.R.L.
3. 2nd.Suffolk Rgt.
4. 1st.Gordon Hldrs.
5. 76th.T.M.B.
6. Bde.Transport Offr.
7. 7th.Field Amb.
8. No.2 Coy Train.
9. 529th.(E.R.)Fd.Co.
10. 187th.Inf.Bde.
11. 8th.Inf.Bde.
12. 9th. "
13. 3rd.Div."G".
14. " "Q".
15. T.M.CATENIERES.
16. Area Comdt.MARCOING.
17. A.P.M., 3rd.Div.
18. War Diary
19. "
20. Bde.Sig.Offr.
21. S.C.
22. File.

MARCH TABLE TO ACCOMPANY 76th.INF.BRIGADE ORDER No.149.

Shedule No.	Unit.	To pass starting point (Road junction L.24c.5.7.) at:-	Remarks.
1.	Brigade H.Q.) 76th.T.M.B.)	14.00 hours	
2.	8th.K.O.R.L.	14.04 hours	100 yards interval from No.1
3.	1st.Gordon Hldrs	14.24 hours	
4.	2nd.Suffolk Regt	14.44 hours	
5.	No.7 Field Amb.	15.10 hours	
6.	"C" Coy.3rd.Bn.M.G.C.	15.19 hours	
7.	529th.Field Co.R.E.	15.26 hours	
8.	No.2 Coy Train & Bde.Group Echelon "B".	15.36 hours	To give way to Nos.6 & 7 west of starting point.

Intervals as laid down in S.S.724 to be strictly observed;i.e.,100 yards between Coys.,100 yards between Battns.and their transport,500 yards between units,as well as additional road space of 50 yards between each section of 12 vehicles. Attention is directed to this office B/3128 of 13/10/18.

SECRET.
****
Copy No. 16

76TH. INFANTRY BRIGADE ADMINISTRATIVE INSTRUCTIONS
to accompany 76th. Infantry bde. Order No.

BILLETING PARTIES.

Billeting Parties of 1 Officer and 5 O.R. from each Battalion, 1 Officer and 3 O.R. from each of the following units :-
529th. (E.R.) Field Coy., R.E., No. 7 Field Ambulance.
"C" Coy., 3rd. Bn. M.G.C. No. 2 Coy. 3rd. Div. Train.
will report to Town Major at Billet No. 52, CATTENIERES, at 12.30 hours to-morrow, 19th. inst., for billets.

Units will, as far as possible, take over from the corresponding units of 187th. Inf. Bde., who will be vacating the billets at 17 hours.

Billeting party for Brigade H.Q. will proceed direct to H.Q. of No. 187 Inf. Bde., billet No. 19.

GUIDES.

All units will arrange for their billeting parties to meet them at the Fork Roads, Eastern entrance to CATTENIERES, H.11d.7.9. at 17 hours.

As the 2nd. line Transport of units will be brigaded and march at rear of Brigade, it is essential that one guide per unit is detailed to meet its transport.

CONVEYANCE OF BLANKETS.

Separate Instructions have been issued to units concerned.

BAGGAGE WAGONS.

Will be returned to Battalion at 08.00 hours to-morrow.

T. F. [signature] Captain,
18th. October 1918. Staff Captain, 76th. Infantry Brigade.

Copies to:-
1. G.O.C.
2. 8th. K.O.R.L. Rgt.
3. 2nd. Suffolk Rgt.
4. 1st. Gordon Hrs.
5. 76th. T.M. battery.
6. 529th. Fld. Coy. R.E.
7. No. 7 Field Ambulance.
8. "C" Coy., 3rd. Bn. M.G.C.
9. No. 2 Coy., 3rd. Div. Train.
10. Town Major, CATTENIERES.
11. B.M.
12. S.C.
13. Bde. Sig. Off.
14. Bde. Sig Off.
15. War Diary
16. Do.
17. File.

SECRET.
****

MARCH TABLE TO ACCOMPANY ORDER
19/10/18.

Ref.sheets 51a.& 57b. 1/40,000.

Shedule.	Unit.	To pass starting point Road junction C.28c.5.2. at:-	Route	Remarks.
1.	Bde.H.Q.) 76th.T.M.B.)	ZERO 11.00 hrs.	BEAUVOIS. BEVILLERS.	
2.	2nd.Suffolk Rgt	11.04 "		
3.	8th.K.O.R.L.	11.22 "		
4.	1st.Gordon Hdrs	11.40 "		
5.	No.7 Fld.Amb.	12.04 "		
6.	"C" Co.M.G.C.	12.13 "		
7.	529th.Fld.Co.R.E.	12.20 "		
8.	No.2 Coy Train & Bde Group Echelon "B"	)12.30 "		

Intervals as ordered in yesterday's march table to be strictly observed. As no lorries are available blankets will be carried.

Billeting parties will meet their units at the CALVAIRE, C.24b.central.

20/10/18.

J Clark 2/Lt.for Captain,
Brigade Major,76th.Infantry Brigade.

SECRET.
****

76TH. INFANTRY BRIGADE WARNING ORDER.

Copy No......

1. The Brigade Group will be prepared to move at two hours' notice after 07.00 hours, October 20th., from present area to QUIEVY.

2. Further details as to routes and times will be issued later.

3. Each Unit will detail an Officer to be prepared to report at Brigade H.Q. at 15 minutes notice to go forward with Staff Captain to billet.

At the same time a Billeting Party of 5 N.C.O.'s per Battalion and 2 from each of Brigade H.Q., 76th.T.M.Bty., "C"Coy.3rd.Bn.M.G.C., 529th.(E.R.)Field Coy. R.E., No.7 Field Ambulance, and No.2 Coy.,3rd. Div.Train will be held in readiness to proceed to QUIEVY on bicycles immediately after the departure of Billeting Officers to Brigade H.Q.

These Billeting Parties will meet Billeting Officers on arrival at QUIEVY.

4. If possible, Blankets will be conveyed by lorry. Failing this, they will be folded and carried on top of the Pack.

5. Dress as for march to-day.

6. Transport arrangements as for to-day. Water Carts will not travel with Battalions, but will march with 2nd. Line Transport in rear of Brigade.

7. O.C., No.2 Coy.,3rd.Div. Train will be in charge of 2nd.Line Transport.

T.F. [signature]
Captain,
Staff Captain, 76th.Infantry Brigade.

19th.October 1918.

Copies to:-
1. 8th.K.O.R.L.Rgt.
2. 2nd.Suffolk Rgt.
3. 1st.Gordon Hldrs.
4. 76th.T.M.Battery.
5. 529th.(E.R.) Fld.Coy.
6. "C" Coy.,3rd.Bn.M.G.C.
7. No.2 Coy., 3rd.Div.Train.
8. No.7 Field Ambce.
9. Brigade Sig.Off.
10. Brigade Q.M.Sgt.

76th. INFANTRY BRIGADE

MARCH TABLE FOR MOVE 22nd. OCTOBER 1918.
****

Shedule No.	Unit.	Time to pass starting point, Railway Bridge D.14c.9.3.	Route.	Remarks.
1.	1st. Gordon Hldrs	16.00 hours	FONTAINE AU TERTRE FME along the road through D.11 central.	100 yards between Platoons. 150 yards between Companies.
2.	8th. K.O.R.L.	17.00 hours.		
3.	2nd. Suffolk Regt	18.00 hours		
4.	Brigade H.Q. and) 76th. T.M.B.)	19.00 hours		
5.	"C" Coy 3rd. Bn. M.G.C.	20.00 hours.		

Transport will return via SOLESMES church E.1c.6.3. Road running S. to E.7c.8.8. - D.12d.9.9. - D.12c.25.10. - D.17c.4.3.- FONTAINE AU TERTRE FME. This road must be taken on return journey.

J Clarke Lt for Captain,
Brigade Major, 76th. Infantry Brigade.

22/10/18.

XXI

SECRET.
****

Copy No.....

76th.INFANTRY BRIGADE ORDER NO.150.
****

Ref.sheets 51a.S.E.)
57b.N.E.) 1/20,000.

22nd.October 1918.

1. The Third Army is to resume the advance on the 23rd.Oct.

2. (a) The attack on the VI Corps front will be carried out by the 3rd.Division on the right and the 2nd.Division on the left,which will pass through the 62nd.Div.and Guards Div.respectively.

(b) The 125th.Inf.Bde,42nd.Div.,will be on the immediate right of the 3rd.Division during the advance to the 1st.objective,and the 2nd.Inf.Bde,N.Z.Division during the advance from 1st.objective.

(c) The 5th.Inf.Bde,2nd.Div.,will be advancing on the immediate left of the 3rd.Division.

3. The attack on the 3rd.Div.front will be carried out at an hour ZERO to be notified later by the 76th.Inf.Bde on the right and the 8th.Inf.Bde on the left. The 9th.Inf.Bde and one M.G.Coy will be in Divisional Reserve.

4. The objectives,Inter-Brigade and Inter-Battalion boundaries are shown on the map issued to all concerned.

1st.Objective..............	RED.
2nd. "	GREEN.
3rd. "	DOTTED GREEN.
Final "	BROWN.

5. Instructions regarding the move to staging area are being issued separately.

6. ASSEMBLY.

The Brigade will assemble as follows:-

1st.Gordon Hldrs to be in position along Black Dotted line by ZERO minus 120 mins.

2nd Suffolk Regt }
8th.K.O.R.L. }to be assembled in artillery formation about the area W.26c.by ZERO minus 30 mins.
/and

76th.L.T.M.B. as for 1st.Gordon Hldrs.

"A" & "C" Coys 3rd.Bn.M.G.C. to be in position by ZERO minus 60 mins.

In leaving SOLESMES the 8th.K.O.R.L.will give way to 2nd.Suffolk Regt.

7. TASKS.

1st.Gordon Hldrs.

(a) Will advance at ZERO and (a) capture and consolidate the RED line inclusive. They will be responsible for "mopping up" ROMERIES and picquetting the town vide instructions issued in this office A/125/10.

(b) They will be supported in the attack by 2 half batteries of 76th.L.T.M.B.

At ZERO plus 370 they will move two Coys forward to the BLUE line in support to the leading battalions on the 2nd.Objective.

6-10 hours later

7. ...... TASKS contd.

8th.K.O.R.L.& 2nd.Suffolk Regt

Will pass through the RED line at ZERO plus 260 mins (2nd.Suffolk Regt on the right) and will capture and consolidate the GREEN line, pushing patrols forward to clear up RAVIN DU SOURD.

At ZERO plus 472 mins they will continue the advance from the GREEN line and will capture and consolidate the 3rd.Objective (DOTTED GREEN LINE).

They will be prepared to continue the advance from 3rd. to Final Objective if ordered to do so from Brigade H.Q.

76th.L.T.M.B.

Will be divided into two half batteries and will (a) support the attack of 1st.Gordon Hldrs on ROMERIES and RED line under the orders of the C.O. of that unit.

(b) Pass through the RED line and continue the advance in support of the attacks on 2nd.and 3rd.Objectives, left half battery under command of C.O., 8th.K.O.R.L. and right half battery under command of C.O. 2nd.Suffolk Regt.

"C" Coy.3rd.Bn.M.G.C.

In conjunction with "A" Coy 3rd.Bn.M.G.C. will support the attack on 1st.Objective with barrage fire.

"A" Coy will subsequently move into Divisional Reserve and "C" Coy will move forward by bounds in support of the attack on 2nd.and 3rd.Objectives, being finally disposed in depth about the area W.10c., W.16a.& b.

In every case strong patrols will be pushed forward of each objective by Battns to clear up the situation and to maintain touch with the enemy.

8. Should the enemy have retired or the opposition be very slight, immediate information will be sent to Brigade Headquarters, and the 76th.and 8th.Inf.Bdes will push on to the BROWN line with the 9th.Inf. Brigade in Reserve.

The time table now laid down will be observed and the advance made by the bounds indicated by the coloured lines on map issued, until orders to the contrary are issued from Brigade Headquarters.

9. Counter-attack aeroplanes will be in the air from daylight onwards.

Contact aeroplanes will call for flares at 07.00 hours, 10.00 hours and 14.00 hours.

10. The leading troops will light flares when called for by contact aeroplanes and will fire "success signals" when the objectives have been gained. They will only be fired on the order of a Company Commander.

11. Battalions will maintain liaison with similar units on the flanks at definite and pre-arranged points on their boundaries.

12. Watches will be synchronized at 76th.Inf.Brigade H.Q.at 20.00 hours on the 22nd.October.

13. Artillery Table will be issued separately.

14. ACKNOWLEDGE.

J Clarke Lt Captain,

Issued at 12.00 hours. Brigade Major, 76th.Infantry Brigade.

distribution over........ /

Copies to:- 1. G.O.C.
2. 8th.K.O.R.L.
3. 2nd.Suffolk Regt.
4. 1st.Gordon Hldrs.
5. 76th.T.M.B.
6. 529th.(E.R.)Fd.Co.R.E.
7. 7th.Field Amb.
8. No.2 Coy Train.
9. 8th.Inf.Brigade.
10 9th. "
11. 125th. "
12. 2nd.(N.Z.) "
13. 5th.Inf.Bde.
14. "A" Coy.3rd.Bn.M.G.C.
15. "C" Coy "
16. 3rd.Bn.M.G.C.
17. 3rd.Div."G".
18. " "Q".
19. C.R.A.,3rd.Div.
20. A.D.M.S.,3rd.Div.
21. 20th.K.R.R.C.
22. S.C.
23. Bde.Sig.Offr.
24. War Diary.
25. "
26. File.

** ** ** **

ADDENDA TO 76th. INF BRIGADE ORDER NO..150. SECRET.

1. Should the IV Corps not be in a position to advance from the 2nd. Objective (GREEN) at 12.12 hours, VI Corps will not advance beyond this objective until IV Corps is ready. Unless an order to the contrary is issued it is understood that the advance is to continue.

If the advance is delayed and it is not possible to convey the order to the Infantry, the artillery creeping barrage will be ordered to remain stationary and will not quicken up in any way, but the Infantry must be prepared to resume the advance as soon as the artillery opens fire at intense rates.

2. Two sections of Field Artillery per group will advance in close support to the Infantry.

3. Approximate moves of Brigade H.Q. and Forward Report Centres.

(a) ZERO minus 60 mins. Forward report centre and telephone about W.26b.central.

(b) ZERO plus 190 mins. Forward Brigade H.Q. opens in ROMERIES about the CHATEAU.

As soon as (b) is open, Brigade H.Q. will close at SOLESMES and re-open at same hour at ROMERIES.

4. ZERO hour is 03.20 hours, not 04.20 hours as previously stated.

5. Ref. para. 7. of Order No. 150. Patrols will not enter the RAVIN DU SOURD, as protective barrage will be on that line.

In the event of leading Bn. continuing the advance to final objective i.e. (BROWN LINE) they will leave 3. Objective at 14.30 hours

T. J. Funnell
Captain,
for Brigade Major, 76th. Infantry Brigade.

22/10/18.

Copies to all recipients of Order No. 150.

XXII

SECRET.

****

REPORT ON OPERATIONS OCTOBER 22nd.- 24th.1918.

76th. INFANTRY BRIGADE.

On the night of Oct.22nd., the Brigade was located in Staging Billets in SOLESMES preparatory to moving to forward assembly areas before ZERO pn Oct.23rd.

PLAN OF ATTACK.

Owing to the pause of about 4 hours which was to elapse between the capture of the RED line and the advance therefrom to the subsequent objectives, it was decided to commit the capture of the RED line to one Battalion (1st.Gordon Hldrs.) unsupported, the other two units being retained in assembly positions when it was probable that they would escape casualties from the enemy barrage and be able to advance later with comparatively little inconvenience.

The 2nd.Suffolk Regt and the 8th.K.O.R.L. were to pass through the troops on the RED line (the latter Battn. on the left) at 08.40 hours and advance to the 2nd.Objective where they were to pause for 02.42 hours and continue the advance to the 3rd.Objective at 12.12 hrs. In case the Division on the right should be held up at any period of the attack, the 1st.Gordon Hldrs were ordered to be prepared to refuse their right flank approximately along the line of the light railway running into W.28b. from the arrêt in W.22c. Definite liaison points were also laid down to be made good at LE TROUSSE MINON and on the GREEN DOTTED line with troops of the N.Z.Division operating on our right. No special orders were given regarding liaison points with the 8th.Inf.Brigade on our left as the time table for the advance of both Brigades to the various objectives was identical.

THE ASSEMBLY.

The 1st.Gordon Hldrs were ordered to be in position on a line taped by troops of the 62nd.Division by ZERO minus 120 minutes, subsequently altered owing to the simplicity of the approach march to ZERO minus 60 minutes.

The 8th.K.O.R.L. and 2nd.Suffolk Regt were to occupy preliminary assembly positions in W.26c.& d by ZERO minus 30 minutes to avoid enemy shelling of the exits of SOLESMES after the attack commenced.

The approach march of the 1st.Gordon Hldrs presented no difficulties so far as the ground was concerned, and would have been accomplished without trouble had it not been for an unfortunate S.O.S. signal sent up from the front line about W.26b. at 24.30 hours which brought down a fairly heavy enemy barrage together with heavy shelling of the outskirts and exits of SOLESMES and a considerable amount of gas throughout the area. The 1st.Gordon Hldrs suffered some casualties from shell fire on their way forward, but as they had not left SOLESMES when the S.O.S. went up they were able to pick their way to some extent and thereby avoid the worst parts of the area.

The 8th.K.O.R.L. and 2nd.Suffolk Regt were able to choose their times for emerging from SOLESMES and escaped casualties in consequence.

The forward positions and all exits from SOLESMES were reconnoitred by officers of all units immediately upon the arrival of the Brigade in SOLESMES, and guides from the troops in the line were not required. I consider that the carrying out of the approach and assembly under the conditions obtaining when the troops actually moved forward, and the avoidance of casualties through careful leadership and forethought reflects great credit on the junior officers concerned.

THE ATTACK.

The barrage for the attack on the RED line was placed at 100 yards per 6 minutes and worked very well. The barrage was good.

The plan of mopping up the village by the establishment

contd..... /

of posts in previously allotted positions by Platoons detailed for the purpose answered well.

The 1st.Gordon Hldrs attacked on a two company front on the leap frog system, the leading coys making good the line of the River HARPIES. The right Coys met with a little opposition from M.G. nest on the railway and in the outskirts of the village, but the RED line was reached on the right under the barrage.

On the left the leading Coys were not so fortunate. Strong opposition was encountered from the Cemetery which was very strongly held by M.G's as was also the orchard behind it and the barrage had gone on before the first line of these posts was captured. The advance on this flank was subsequently carried on by rushes and by enveloping attacks on nests as they appeared. On the whole however, the resistance was not such as might have been expected considering the strength of the garrison and the number of T.M's and M.G's opposed to us.

The co-operation of the left half of 76th.L.T.M.Battery was good, and the value of a Stokes' gun fired from between the knees for dealing with isolated enemy posts was fully demonstrated.

In the village itself some determined opposition was encountered from groups of the enemy here and there, one house opposite the Chateau being very stoutly defended, but on the whole the enemy surrendered easily and 22 officers and 636 O.R. were captured including a Battalion Commander and his H.Q.staff.

The enemy made no attempt to counter-attack nor was retaliation by shell fire very heavy except in the village of ROMERIES itself which was heavily shelled and gassed from about 06.00 hours till after 11.00 hours. The 8th.K.O.R.L.and 2nd.Suffolk Regt had to make considerable detours in order to pass through the RED line at 08.40 hours.

2nd.OBJECTIVE.

The advance to the 2nd.Objective was not attended with much fighting, the enemy putting up no resistance except in isolated posts which surrendered quickly when attacked by platoons or sections from a flank. Several well placed M.G's were abandoned by their crews without firing a shot and it quickly became apparent that the enemy was hopelessly disorganised and that serious opposition was at an end. LA TROUSSE MINON was garrisoned by 3 officers and 50 O.R. who only offered a moderate resistance to an attack from a flank pushed with great dash by the 2nd.Suffolk Regt.

The casualties to both Battalions in the advance are reported to have been slight and caused almost entirely by some very short shells in our own barrage.

3rd.OBJECTIVE.

At 12.12 hours the advance of the 8th.K.O.R.L.and 2nd. Suffolk Regt to the GREEN DOTTED line commenced.

A certain amount of wild M.G.fire was met with from posts about the objective and from artillery at LA SABLONNIERE & LE MARI, but as a general rule the resistance was slight, and when attacked from a flank the enemy usually either bolted or surrendered, only very isolated cases of stout resistance being met with. Our own barrage again reported to have caused most of the casualties and some of the shells appear to have been very short indeed.

BROWN LINE.

The advance on the BROWN line was begun at 14.30 hours, closely supported by troops of the 9th.Inf.Brigade and was occupied without resistance.

The Brigade was subsequently withdrawn into support and disposed on the GREEN line and about W.16 central for the night Oct.23rd./24th., being finally withdrawn into billets at ROMERIES by 10.00 hours on Oct.24th.

Brigadier-General,
Commanding 76th.Infantry Brigade.

1/11/18.

P.T.O.

POINTS BROUGHT TO NOTICE.

1. S.O.S. during assembly hours. - I suggest that it should either be forbidden or that the artillery should be warned not to answer it. The infantry in the line must be prepared to defend their positions with the arms at their disposal. If active patrolling is resorted to a false alarm is much less likely.

2. Barrage maps issued to Battalions were very useful. When time permits they should be issued to company commanders.

3. Communications worked well and Battalions were always in touch with Brigade. A forward report centre right up behind the jumping-off line moving forward by bounds as the attack progresses is imperative when attacking to depth. Mounted D.R's will be used whenever possible in future. In the present case artillery horsed orderlies brought back reports on several occasions much quicker than any cyclists.

4. The system of establishing posts for mopping up villages is sound. The enemy has practically no chance of "bobbing up" after leading troops move forward.

5. The question of barrages when attacking in depth is a difficult one. From personal experience I have always been opposed to an H.E. barrage where a stout enemy has to be dealt with, and I am of opinion that even now it would be risky to depend on an H.E. barrage for a first objective. On the other hand, complaints of short bursts in a first objective are rare. In barrages on subsequent objectives however, complaints of shorts have been common during the past year and it seems that this is due to lack of proper supervision in manufacture and not to careless fuze setting on the part of the artillery.

If the use of H.E. will do away with short bursts I am of opinion that it is a question whether the barrage should not be regarded from a purely moral point of view and H.E. substituted in toto for shrapnel after the 1st. objective.

6. The forward sections of field artillery were not seen by the infantry. Where the supply of artillery officers allows, I have always found an F.O.O. with the Battalion commander very valuable. In the present case it is obviously unfair to condemn the roving gun as counter-attacks were not attempted and no enemy tanks appeared, but the closest possible liaison with Battalions is, I am sure, essential to success.

Brigadier-General,

1/11/18. Commanding 76th. Infantry Brigade.

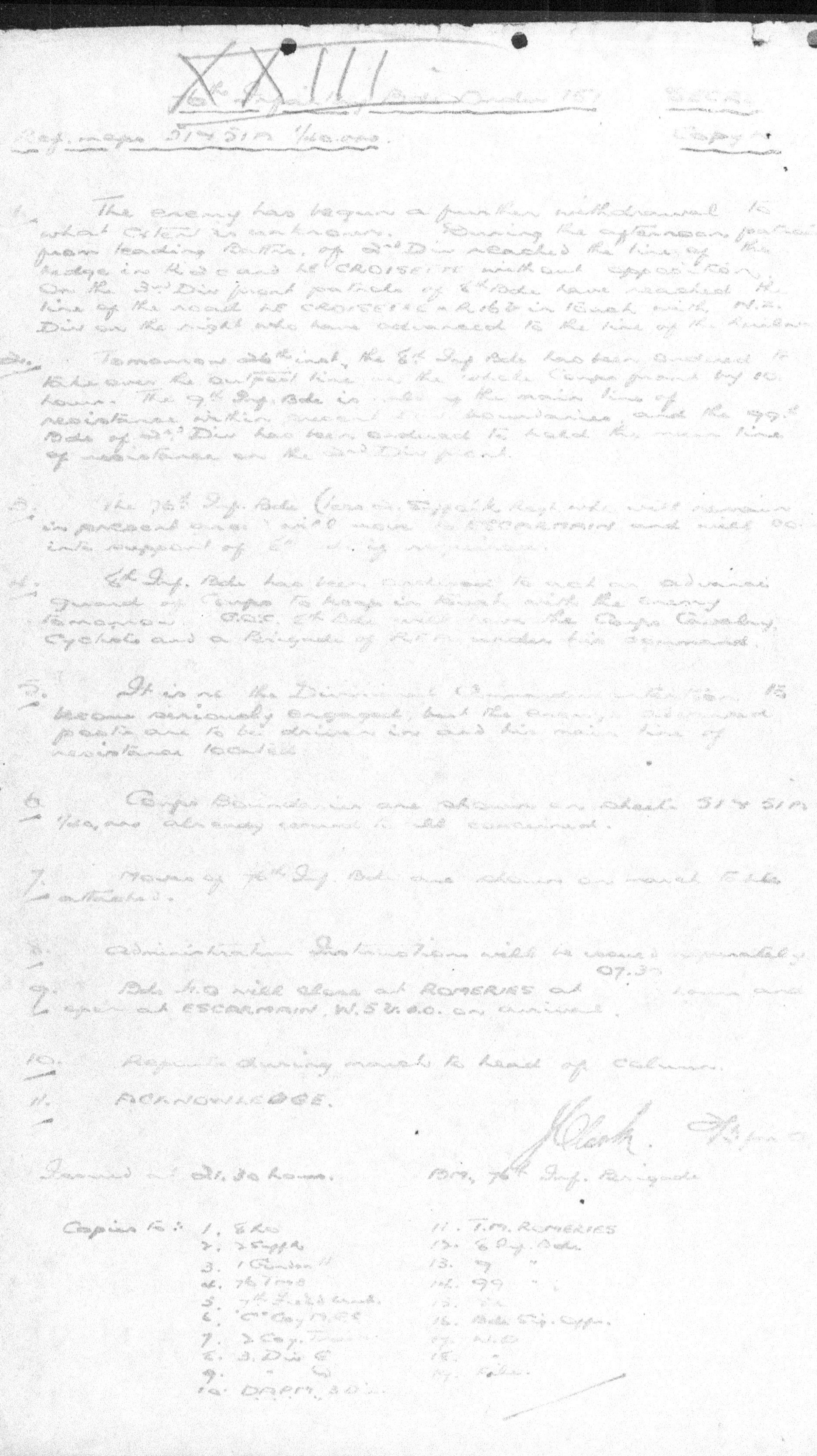

XXIII

76th Infantry Bde. Order 151. SECRET

Ref. maps 51 & 51A 1/40,000. Copy No.

1. The enemy has begun a further withdrawal to what extent is unknown. During the afternoon patrols from leading Battns. of 2nd Div reached the line of the ridge in [illegible] and [illegible] CROISETTE without opposition. On the 3rd Div front patrols of 8th Bde have reached the line of the road [illegible] CROISETTE & [illegible] in touch with N.Z. Div on the right who have advanced to the line of the [illegible].

2. Tomorrow 26th inst, the 8th Inf Bde has been ordered to take over the outpost line on the whole Corps front by [illegible] hours. The 9th Inf. Bde is [illegible] the main line of resistance within present [illegible] boundaries, and the 99th Bde of 2nd Div has been ordered to hold the main line of resistance on the 2nd Div front.

3. The 76th Inf. Bde (less [illegible] Suffolk Regt who will remain in present area) will move to ESCARMAIN and will be into support of 8th [illegible].

4. 8th Inf. Bde has been ordered to act as advance guard of Corps to keep in touch with the enemy tomorrow. G.O.C. 8th Bde will have the Corps Cavalry, Cyclists and a Brigade of R.F.A. under his command.

5. It is not the Divisional Commander's intention to become seriously engaged, but the enemy's advanced posts are to be driven in and his main line of resistance located.

6. Corps Boundaries are shown on sheets 51 & 51A 1/40,000 already issued to all concerned.

7. Moves of 76th Inf. Bde are shown on march table attached.

8. Administrative Instructions will be issued separately.

9. Bde H.Q will close at ROMERIES at 07.30 hours and open at ESCARMAIN, W.5 [illegible] on arrival.

10. Reports during march to head of column.

11. ACKNOWLEDGE.

J. Clark. [illegible]

Issued at 21.30 hours. B.M., 76th Inf. Brigade

Copies to:
1. 8 K.O.
2. 2 Suffk.
3. 1 Gordon H.
4. 76 T.M.B.
5. 7th Field Amb.
6. "C" Coy M.G.C.
7. 2 Coy. Train
8. 3. Div G
9. " Q
10. D.A.P.M. 3 Div
11. T.M. ROMERIES
12. 8 Inf. Bde.
13. 9 "
14. 99 "
15. [illegible]
16. Bde Sig. Offr.
17. W.D.
18. "
19. File.

XXIV

SECRET.
****

Copy No.....

76th. INFANTRY BRIGADE ORDER NO.152.
****

Ref.sheets 51 & 51a.,1/40,000.
51a.S.E.1/20,000. 27th.October 1918.

1. The 76th.Infantry Brigade will relieve the 99th.Inf.Bde and a portion of the 8th.Inf.Bde in the area lying between the boundaries shown on the attached Tracing "A" (issued to Battns and M.G.C.Coys only), on the night 27th./28th.October 1918.

2. All details will be arranged between C.O's concerned.

3. Moves are shown on Table attached.

4. All stores, dumps etc., within the area will be taken over and copies of receipts forwarded to Brigade H.Q.by 10.0.a., 28th.inst.

5. Brigade H.Q.will close at ESCARMAIN at 19.00 hours and re-open at CAPELLE, Q.35c.5.7. at the same hour.

6. ACKNOWLEDGE.

J Clark Capt.
Captain,
Issued at 16.30 hours. Brigade Major, 76th. Infantry Brigade.

Copies to:- 1. G.O.C.
2. 8th.K.O.R.L.
3. 2nd.Suffolk Regt.
4. 1st.Gordon Hldrs.
5. 76th.T.M.B.
6. "A" Coy M.G.C.
7. "C" " "
8. 7th.Field Amb.
9. 8th.Inf.Bde.
10. 9th. "
12. 99th. "
13. 3rd.Div."G".
14. " "Q".
15. D.A.P.M., 3rd.Div.
16. T.M., ESCARMAIN.
17. S.C.
18. Bde.Sig.Offr.
19. War Diary.
20. "
21. File.

TABLE OF RELIEFS TO ACCOMPANY 76th.BRIGADE ORDER NO.152.

Shedule No.	Unit.	In relief of:-	Area	Route	Remarks.
1.	8th.K.O.R.L.	7th.K.S.L.I.at H.Q. at R.13d.9.3.	Outpost system.	PONT DU BUAT.	Relief to be complete by 02.00 hours 28th.Oct. To give way to No.2 S.W. of Railway in R,8.
2.	1st.Gordon Hldrs. less 2 Coys	1st.K.R.R.C. H.Q.R.13d.8.3.	Main line of resistance.	PONT DU BUAT.	Relief to be complete by 20.00 hours. Oct. 27th
3.	2 Coys 1st.Gordon Hldrs.	1st.Royal Berks. H.Q.Q.28b.2.9.	Support of No.2.	PONT DU BUAT.	Reloef to be complete by 20.00 hours. Oct 27th
4.	2nd.Suffolk Regt.	23rd.Royal Fus. H.Q. Q.35c.5.7	Brigade Reserve	ESCARMAIN - CAPELLE.	Relief to be complete by 18.00 hours Oct.27th.
5.	"C" Coy M.G.C.	M.G.C.Group H.Q. Q.35c.5.9.	Covering outposts and main line.	Any.	Relief to be complete by 02.00 hours 28th.Oct.
6.	76th.Bde.H.Q.	99th.Bde H.Q.	CAPELLE Q.35c.5.7.	ESCARMAIN-CAPELLE.	
7.	76th.T.M.B.	99th.L.T.M.B.	CAPELLE.	ESCARMAIN-CAPELLE.	Relief to be complete by 18.00 hours Oct.27th.

XXV

SECRET.
****

Copy No....

76th.INFANTRY BRIGADE ORDER NO.153.

Ref.sheets 51a.S.E.,1/20,000.
51 & 51a.1/40,000.

29th.October 1918.

1. The 76th.Infantry Brigade will be relieved by the 5th.Inf. Brigade (2nd.Div.) on night 29th./30th.October.

2. 24th.Roy.Fus.will relieve 8th.K.O.R.L.
52nd.Light Inf." " 1st.Gordon Hldrs.
2nd.H.L.I. " " 2nd.Suffolk Rogt.
5th.T.M.B. " " 76th.T.M.B.

3. The head of 5th.Brigade column (in above order) is not expected to arrive at CAPELLE before 16.30 hours.

4. O.C.M.G.Group will arrange all details regarding relief with his opposite number and will move after relief under orders of 3rd.Bn.M.G.C.

5. On relief,Battalions will move to staging areas as follows:-

8th.K.O.R.L............ VERTAIN.
1st.Gordon Hldrs....... ST.PYTHON.
2nd.Suffolk Rogt....... ST.PYTHON.

The PONT DU BUAT crossing is not to be used. A new bridge has been constructed at Q.29b.5.1. and several foot-bridges have been made on both sides of the PONT DU BUAT crossing.

6. Administrative Instructions will be issued separately.

7. Brigade H.Q.will close at CAPELLE on completion of relief and re-open at VERTAIN,W.15a.9.1.at same hour.

8. ACKNOWLEDGE.

J. Clark, ?/ Captain,
Brigade Major,76th.Infantry Brigade.

Issued at 12.30 hours.

Copies to:- 1. G.O.C.
2. 8th.K.O.R.L.
3. 2nd.Suffolk Regt.
4. 1st.Gordon Hldrs.
5. 76th.T.M.B.
6. "A" Coy M.G.C.
7. "B" " "
8. 7th.Field Amb.
9. 8th.Inf.Bde.
10. 9th. "
11. 5th.Inf.Bde.
12. 3rd.Div."G".
13. " "Q".
14. D.A.P.M.
15. T.M.,VERTAIN.
16. S.C.
17. Bde.Sig.Offr.
18. War Diary.
19. "
20. File.

3rd Division

WAR DIARY & APPENDICES

76th INFANTRY BRIGADE

NOVEMBER 1918

76th Brigade.

3rd Division.

B. H. Q.

76th INFANTRY BRIGADE.

NOVEMBER 1918.

Appendices under separatecover

Instructions regarding War Diaries and Intelligence Summaries are contained in F. S. Regs., Part II. and the Staff Manual respectively. Title Pages will be prepared in manuscript.

NOVEMBER 1918.

WAR DIARY or INTELLIGENCE SUMMARY

(Erase heading not required.)

76th Infantry Brigade

Army Form C. 2118.

Page I

V.8 38

Place	Date Nov.	Hour	Summary of Events and Information	Remarks and references to Appendices
CARNIERES	1 2		Four hours training in the morning. Sports in the afternoon.	
QUIEVY.	3.		Brigade march to QUIEVY, leaving CARNIERES at 16.00 hours. HQ opened at QUIEVY at 19.00 hours.	App. I. B.O.O. 155.
ROMERIES	4.		Brigade ordered to march to ESCARMAIN. Advance parties find the village full up with 62nd & 2nd Division troops. Brigade billeted in ROMERIES. Standing by at an hours notice to follow up the 62nd Div.	App. II. B.O.O. 156.
"	5.		Still at an hours notice, orders issued for a march to ORSINVAL but no time stated. Staff Captain & 1 Officer per Battn go forward & reconnoitre billets in ORSINVAL.	
"	6.		Visited by the Major General, who says we are not likely to move for some little time yet. The advance is continuing with very little opposition so that we may not be called upon to go up. Very wet day impossible to do any training.	
"	7.		Orders received that we are to march through the Guards	

2449 Wt. W14957/M90 750,000 1/16 J.B.C. & A. Forms/C.2118/12.

Instructions regarding War Diaries and Intelligence Summaries are contained in F. S. Regs., Part II. and the Staff Manual respectively. Title Pages will be prepared in manuscript.

NOVEMBER. 1918.

WAR DIARY
or
~~INTELLIGENCE SUMMARY~~
(Erase heading not required.)

16th Infantry Brigade

Army Form C. 2118.

Page. II.

Place	Date Nov.	Hour	Summary of Events and Information	Remarks and references to Appendices
			& 62nd Division as advance guard to the 3rd Army.	
ROMERIES.	8th		Brigade march to FRASNOY. Very poor accomodation, 1st Gordon Hldrs. have to go on to billets in GOMMEGNIES.	App. III B.O.O. 158.
FRASNOY.	9		All available men working on the roads. Great rumours about armistice.	
	10.		Brigade march to LA LONGUEVILLE. Railway bridge at BAVAI blown up, causing considerable trouble with the heavy transport, which did not reach the village until 08.00 hours.	App. IV B.O.O. 159.
LA LONGUEVILLE			Delegates reported to have crossed the frontier armistice expected	
	11.		All preparations completed for the Brigade to move forward as an advance guard. Units were paraded ready to move off when the G.S.O. III from Corps H.Q. arrived to say that the armistice had been signed & that all hostilities were to cease at 11. o'clock, & we were to remain in our present areas.	
	12.		Working on the roads again today, they are blown in many places.	

2449 Wt. W14957/M90 750,000 1/16 J.B.C. & A. Forms/C.2118/12.

NOVEMBER 1918.

WAR DIARY
or
~~INTELLIGENCE SUMMARY~~

(Erase heading not required.)

76th Infantry Brigade. III

Page III.

Army Form C. 2118.

Instructions regarding War Diaries and Intelligence Summaries are contained in F. S. Regs., Part II. and the Staff Manual respectively. Title Pages will be prepared in manuscript.

Place	Date	Hour	Summary of Events and Information	Remarks and references to Appendices
LALONGUEVILLE	12.		Great rejoicing among the civilians, all regimental bands playing in the GRAND PLACE.	
"	13.		Lecture to all Officers N.C.O's. & men, on demobilisation & education by the Div. educational officer, the Major General in the chair. 50% of the men working on the roads.	
"	14.		All men employed on the roads. 1st Gordon Hldrs. have baths in the afternoon	
	15.		Brigade move to NEUF MESNIL, very short march, & men turn out very well.	App. V. G 406.
NEUF MESNIL	16. } 17 }		Brigade supposed to start the advance towards the frontier. but great delay, owing to transport difficulties, Bgde. resting.	
"	18.		Brigade march to LOUVROIL. Very short march, considerable transport difficulties, necessitating a different route.	App VI. BOO. 162.
"	19.		The advance again delayed, troops spend the day in cleaning up.	
"	20.		Brigade Group ~~again~~ march to the COUSOLRE area. men march very well & all arrive in billets before 13.00 hours.	App VII. BOO. 163.

2449 Wt. W14957/M90 750,000 1/16 J.B.C. & A. Forms/C.2118/12.

Instructions regarding War Diaries and Intelligence Summaries are contained in F. S. Regs., Part II. and the Staff Manual respectively. Title Pages will be prepared in manuscript.

NOVEMBER 1918

WAR DIARY or ~~INTELLIGENCE SUMMARY~~

(Erase heading not required.)

Page IV

Army Form C. 2118.

76th Infantry Brigade

Place	Date NOV.	Hour	Summary of Events and Information	Remarks and references to Appendices
COUSOLRE	21.		All men employed clearing the roads. Working parties greatly handicapped by a most severe frost.	
— " —	22.		Again working on the roads. Lorries run to MONS & CHARLEROI, to convey Officers for the day. Brigadier goes to BRUSSELS to see the triumphal entry of the King & Queen.	
— " —	23.		Unable to move again today, the supply question still obscure. Three Battalions have the use of the baths	
— " —	24.		Brigade march to THUIN - LOBBES area, arriving in billets by 13.00 hours. Troops taking full advantage of their first opportunity of visiting the Belgian estaminets	App VIII. B.O.O. 164
THUIN.	25.		Group march to NALINNES ~~area~~. Rations arrive very late, men have to start off without any breakfast.	App IX. B.O.O. 165.
NALINNES.	26.		Group march to METTET, arriving in billets 12.30 hours. The first appearance of German guns, handed over as part of the armistice conditions	App X. B.O.O. 166.
METTET.	27		Waiting today to collect a group of artillery, which is joining the Brigade group, but orders afterwards cancell[ed]	

2449 Wt. W14957/M90 750,000 1/16 J.B.C. & A. Forms/C.2118/12.

NOVEMBER 1918.

WAR DIARY
or
~~INTELLIGENCE SUMMARY~~
(Erase heading not required.)

Army Form C. 2118.

Page V.

76th Infantry Brigade

Instructions regarding War Diaries and Intelligence Summaries are contained in F. S. Regs., Part II. and the Staff Manual respectively. Title Pages will be prepared in manuscript.

Place	Date Nov.	Hour	Summary of Events and Information	Remarks and references to Appendices
METTET.	27th	contgd	Officers of the Brigade Group give a very successful Ball to the local inhabitants. who were greatly impressed.	
— " —	28.		Group march to ANNEVOIE ROUILLON area. Very heavy rain came on at 11.00 hours. Brigade headquarters opened at CHATEAU ROUILLON, where the staff were made guests of the Countess Henri De La Meuse.	App XI. B.O.O. 167.
ROUILLON.	29.		Group march to the NATOYE-BRAIBANT area. Billeting area very scattered, limited accommodation, & very poor rations.	App XII. B.O.O. 168.
BRAIBANT.	30.		Brigade group march to PESSOUX-CINEY area.	
JANNÉE.			Headquarters open at JANNÉE CHATEAUX at 12.30 hours Billeting area very scattered.	App XIII. B.O.O. 169.

2449 Wt. W14957/M90 750,000 1/16 J.B.C. & A. Forms/C.2118/12.

3rd Division.

76th Infantry Brigade.

A P P E N D I C E S

76th INFANTRY BRIGADE

NOVEMBER 1918.

SECRET.
****

Copy No.....

76th.INFANTRY BRIGADE ORDER NO.155.

Ref.Sheet 57b.,1/40,000. November 1st.1918.

1. The 76th.Inf.Brigade Group (less Field Co.R.E.and 7th.Field Amb.) will march to the QUIEVY area on November 3rd as follows:-

Route:- BOUSSIERES - BEVILLERS.

Starting Point:- Cross Roads in BOUSSIERES C.21a.5.4.

1.Bde.H.Q.& 76th.T.M.B. pass starting point	17.01 hours.	
2.8th.K.O.R.L.	do.	17.04 "
3.2nd.Suffolk Regt	do.	17.13 "
4.1st.Gordon Hldrs.	do.	17.22 "
5.No.2 Coy Train & Bde Group Transport.	do.	17.33 "

2. 3rd.Bn.Machine Gun Corps will march to BEVILLERS ~~area~~ ~~passing~~ the cross roads in BOUSSIERES C.21a.5.4. at 18.01 hours.

3. The only distances to be maintained on the march will be 300 yards between Battalions and 100 yards between Battalions and their transport.

4. L.G.limbers will move with their companies; remainder of 1st. line transport in rear of units: 2nd.line transport under orders of O.C.,No.2 Coy Train.

5. Brigade H.Q.will close at CARNIERES at 16.00 hours and open at QUIEVY on arrival.

Reports during march to head of column.

6. Administrative Instructions will be issued later.

7. ACKNOWLEDGE.

C. Chitty Captain,
Brigade Major,76th.Infantry Brigade.

Issued at 19.30 hours.

Copies to:-
1. G.O.C.
2. 8th.K.O.R.L.
3. 2nd.Suffolk Regt.
4. 1st.Gordon Hldrs.
5. 76th.T.M.B.
6. 7th.Field Amb.
7. No.2 Coy Train.
8. 3rd.Bn.M.G.C.
9. 3rd.Div."G".
10. " D.A.P.M.
11. Town Major CARNIERES.
12. " QUIEVY.
13. Bde Supply Offr.
14. Bde Transport Offr.
15. Bde Int.Offr.
16. S.C.
17. War Diary.
18. "
19. Bde Signal Offr.
20. File.

SECRET.

76TH. INFANTRY BRIGADE ADMINISTRATIVE INSTRUCTIONS
(To accompany 76th.Inf.Bde.Order No. 155) Copy.No. 15

1. BILLETS. The following Billets and Billeting areas have been allotted:-

8th.K.O.R.L.Rgt. Eastern end of PETITE RUE.
RUE DE BOIS.
PETITE RUE DE BOIS.
Battalion H.Q.:- No. 19 PETITE RUE DE BOIS.

2nd.Suffolk Rgt. RUE DES JUIFS. Western end of PETITE RUE.
PLACE D'ARMES. Unoccupied houses in RUE CAMBRAI.
Battalion H.Q.:- No.37, GRANDE RUE, taking over from Devon Rgt.

1st.Gordon Hrs. GRANDE RUE. RUE DE SOLE.
Battalion H.Q.:- No.6,8 & 9, GRANDE PLACE, taking over from London Rgt.

76th.T.M.Battery. 1st.Bn.Gordon Hldrs will allot accommodation for 2 Officers and 40 O.R. of 76th.T.M.Bty. in their area.

No.2 Coy.,3rd.Div.Train. Billets now occupied by 62nd.Div.Train Coy. on ST HILAIRE Road.

76th.Inf.Bde.H.Q. Billets No.54, GRANDE RUE and Signal Offices attached, taking over from 185th. Inf.Bde.

2. BILLETING PARTIES. Billeting Parties of :-
1 Off. and 6 O.R. per Battalion.
1 Off. and 2 O.R. No.2 Coy.,3rd.Div.Train.
2 O.R. 76th.T.M.Battery, and 2 O.R. Bde. H.Q.
will report to Town Major, QUIEVY, at his Office, GRANDE RUE, at 10-00 hours, Nov.3rd.

3. DRESS. Full Marching Order (including Packs). Steel helmets will be worn, and 1 Blanket rolled and carried on top of Pack.

4. GUIDES. Guides from Billeting Parties will meet their units at the Crucifix, C.24b.4.6. (entrance to QUIEVY) at the following times:-
Bde.H.Q. and 76th.T.M.Bty.)
8th.K.O.R.L.Rgt.) 18-15 hours.
2nd.Suffolk Rgt.)

1st.Gordon Hrs.)
No.2 Coy.,3rd.Div.Train & 2nd.Line Transport.) 18-30 hours.
Billeting Officers will ensure that a guide from each unit is detailed to meet its 2nd.Line Transport.

5. 1st.Line Transport. Will march with Coys. and Battalions as detailed for march to CARNIERES on Oct.31st.
2nd.Line Transport. Will march in rear of Brigade Group under orders O.C.No.2 Coy.,3rd.Div.Train. They will rendezvous between CARNIERES Church and CARNIERES-BOUSSIERES Road with head of column at Road Junction, C.19b.8.8., at 16.45 hours.

6. CLEANLINESS OF BILLETS. All billets must be left as they were taken over from Guards Brigade - scrupulously clean.

7. BRIGADE DUMP, QUIEVY. All units will arrange to clear the houses now occupied by them for Kit and Pack Dumps, as these will be occupied by 9th.Inf.Bde. from 12-00 hours, 3rd. instant.

8. MEDICAL ARRANGEMENTS. No.7 Field Ambulance will continue to administer the VIth.Corps Rest Station at CARNIERES.
O.C. No.142 Field Ambulance will be responsible for the collection of the sick from both the 9th. and 76th.Infantry Brigades.

T.F. [signature] Captain,
Staff Captain, 76th.Infantry Brigade.

2nd.Nov.1918.

Copies to all recipients of Order No. 155.

II

SECRET.
****

Copy No.....

76th.INFANTRY BRIGADE ORDER NO.156.

Ref.sheets 57b.,51a.,51. 1/40,000. 3rd.November 1918.

1. The 76th.Inf.Brigade Group (less Field Coy R.E.and 7th.Field Amb.) together with "C" Coy 3rd.Bn.M.G.C. will march to ESCARMAIN and ROMERIES tomorrow Nov.4th.,as follows:-

Route:- Railway crossing D.12a.,SOLESMES,Cross roads E.1b.0.9.,ROMERIES.

Starting point:- Cross roads D.16c.4.4.

1.	Bde H.Q.& 76th.T.M.B.pass starting point		07.45
2.	1st.Gordon Hldrs	do.	07.48
3.	8th.K.O.R.L.	do.	08.10
4.	2nd.Suffolk Regt	do.	08.19
5.	"C" Coy M.G.Bn.	do.	08.28
6.	No.2 Coy Train & Brigade Group Transport	do.	08.35

2. Distances to be maintained on the march 300 yards between battalions and 100 yards between battalions and their transport.

3. L.G.limbers will move with their companies; remainder of 1st.line transport in rear of units: 2nd.line transport under orders of O.C.,No.2 Coy 3rd.Div.Train.

4. Brigade H.Q.will close at Billot No.54,GRANDE RUE,QUIEVY at 06.30 and re-open on arrival at a place to be notified later.

Reports during march to head of column.

5. Administrative instructions will be issued separately.

6. ACKNOWLEDGE.

C. Clifford Captain,
Brigade Major,76th.Infantry Brigade.

Issued at 15.00 hours.

Copies to;-
1. 8th.K.O.R.L.
2. 2nd.Suffolk Regt.
3. 1st.Gordon Hldrs.
4. 76th.T.M.B.
5. 7th.Field Amb.
6. No.2 Coy Train.
7. "C" Coy M.G.C.
8. 3rd.Bn.M.G.C.
9. 3rd.Div."G".
10. D.A.P.M.
11. Brigade Supply Offr,
12. " Transport Offr.
13. " Signal Offr.
14. " Int.Offr.
15. G.O.C.
16. S.C.
17. War Diary,
18. "
19. } File.
20. }

SECRET.
****

Copy No. 16

76TH. INFANTRY BRIGADE ADMINISTRATIVE INSTRUCTIONS
(To accompany 76th.Inf.Bde. Order No.156).

1. DUMPING OF PACKS AND BLANKETS.
All Packs and Blankets will be dumped in the School in GRANDE RUE to-night. 1 O.R. from each unit will be left behind as guard. Each man will be provided with 10 days' rations.

2. BILLETS.
Brigade H.Q.,76th.T.M.Bty., 8th.K.O.R.L.Rgt.,2nd.Suffolk Rgt. and 1st.Gordon Hrs. with first line Transport, Cookers and Water Carts will be accommodated in ESCARMAIN.
"C"Coy.,3rd.Bn.M.G.C., No.2 Coy.,3rd.Div.Train and Brigade Group Transport, including all Battalion Q.M.Stores, will find accommodation in ROMERIES.
Accommodation in these villages is very scarce and close billoting will be the rule. It is not expected that the Brigade will remain in that area for a night.

3. BILLETING PARTIES.
1 Off. and 5 O.R. from each Battalion and 1 Off. and 2 O.R. from Bde H.Q. will report to the Town Major, ESCARMAIN, for accommodation at 08-00 hours to-morrow, 4th. instant.
1 Off. and 2 O.R. from each of No.2 Coy. Train and "C" Coy. 3rd.Bn.M.G.C., and 1 N.C.O. from each of the Battalions will report to the Town Major, ROMERIES, at 08-00 hours for accommodation.

4. GUIDES.
Guides from billeting parties for units moving to ESCARMAIN will meet their units at Fork Road, W.5c.2.1., at 10-00 hours.
Guides for units moving to ROMERIES will meet their units at Road Junction, W.26b.9.6., at 09-35 hours.

5. AMMUNITION AND GRENADES.
The 2 Grenades per man which will be carried by all men (less Lewis Gunners) will be issued at ESCARMAIN,and not at QUIEVY as previously arranged.

6. BATTLE SURPLUS.
Will move with Battalions until further notice.

7. Battalions will arrange to serve dinner to their men immediately on arrival at their destinations.

T.J. Finnell
Captain,
Staff Captain, 76th.Infantry Brigade.

3rd.Nov.1918.

Copies to:-
1. 8th.K.O.R.L.Rgt.
2. 2nd.Bn.Suffolk Rgt.
3. 1st.Gordon Hrs.
4. 76th.T.M.Bty.
5. 7th.Field Ambce.
6. No.2 Coy.,3rd.Div.Train.
7. "C"Coy.3rd.Bn.M.G.C.
8. D.A.P.M.
9. Bde. Supply Off.
10. Bde. Signal Off.
11. Bde.Q.M.Sgt.
12. Bde.Int.Off.
13. Town Major, ESCARMAIN.
14. Town Major, ROMERIES.
15. G.O.C.
16. B.M.
17. War Diary (2)
18. File.

W.D
III

SECRET.
****

76th. INFANTRY BRIGADE ORDER NO.158.
****

Ref.sheets 51a.,51.,1/40,000.

7th.November 1918.

1. 76th.Inf.Bde Order No.157 is cancelled.

2. 76th.Brigade Group will march to FRASNOY area tomorrow November 8th.,as follows:-

Route:- BEAUDIGNIES - LE QUESNOY.
Starting point:- Cross Roads in W.17c.North east of ROMERIES.

1. Brigade H.Q.& 76th.T.M.B.pass starting point .... 09.00 hours
2. 8th.K.O.R.L. do. 09.05
3. 2nd.Suffolk Regt do. 09.30
4. 1st.Gordon Hldrs do. 10.05
5. "C" Coy 3rd.Bn.M.G.C. do. 10.30
6. No.2 Coy 3rd.Div.Train and Brigade 2nd.line transport. do. 10.40
7. Bearer Section 7th.Field Amb do. 11.05

3. Distances to be maintained on the march:-

100 yards between companies.
300 yards between Battalion and its transport.
1,000 yards between Battalions.

4. Brigade H.Q.will close at ROMERIES at 08.00 at open at FRASNOY on arrival.

Reports during march to head of column.

5. L.G.limbers will move with their companies; remainder of 1st.line transport and cookers in rear of units: 2nd.line transport including water carts under orders of O.C.,No.2 Coy 3rd.Div.Train.

6. ACKNOWLEDGE.

C. Chipper
Captain,
Brigade Major,76th.Infantry Brigade.

Issued at 23.00 hours.

Copies to:-
1. 8th.K.O.R.L.
2. 2nd.Suffolk Regt.
3. 1st.Gordon Hldrs.
4. 76th.T.M.B.
5. "C" Coy M.G.C.
6. Section 7th.Field Amb
7. No.2 Coy Train.
8. Bde Supply Offr.
9. " Transport Offr.
10. " Signal Offr.
11. " Int.Offr.
12. G.O.C.
13. S.C.
14. 3rd.Div."G".
15. " "Q".
16. D.A.P.M.
17. 9th.Inf.Bde.
18. Town Major ROMERIES.
19. " FRASNOY.
20. War Diary.
21. "
22.)
23.) File.
24.)

SECRET.
****

76TH. INFANTRY BRIGADE ADMINISTRATIVE INSTRUCTIONS Copy No. 18.
(To accompany 76th. Inf. Bde. Order No. 158).

BILLETING PARTIES.

1 Off. from each Battalion and 1 from each of the following units - "C" Coy., 3rd. Bn. M.G.C., No.2 Coy. 3rd. Div. Train and No. 7 Field Ambulance - will report at Brigade H.Q. at 06-00 hours to-morrow, 8th. inst., They will go forward in a car with the Staff Captain.

Billeting Parties of 6 N.C.O.'s per Battalion, 2 for "C" Coy., 3rd. Bn. M.G.C., 2 for No.2 Coy., 3rd. Div. Train, 1 for 76th. T.M. Battery and 2 for Brigade H.Q. will meet their Billeting Officers at 09-45 hours at the Area Commandant's Office in the Main Street, FRASNOY.

2. TRANSPORT.

1st. Line Transport will march with Coy.'s and Battalions as usual.

2nd. Line Transport will be brigaded and will march in the rear of the column under the orders of O.C. No.2 Coy., 3rd. Div. Train. They will rendezvous at Road Junction, W.22c.0.7., at 10-10 hours.

3. DRESS.

Fighting Order with one Blanket carried on the man.

4. GUIDES.

Guides from Billeting Parties will meet their units at Road Junction. M.11c.0.0.

5. BILLETING CERTIFICATES.

Will be rendered to the Maire at Brigade H.Q. before leaving the village.

6. CLEANLINESS OF BILLETS.

All billets will be left in a clean and sanitary condition.

7. BATTLE SURPLUS.

Will march with their Battalions to the new area.

T. J. Funnell
~~Captain,~~ Captain,
7th. Nov. 1918. Staff Captain, 76th. Infantry Brigade.

Copies to:-
1. 8th. K.O.R.L. Rgt.
2. 2nd. Suffolk Rgt.
3. 1st. Gordon Hrs.
4. 76th. T.M. Bty.
5. "C" Coy., 3rd. Bn. M.G.C.
6. 7th. Field Ambce.
7. No.2 Coy., 3rd. Div. Train.
8. Bde. Supply Off.
9. " Transport Off.
10. " Signal Off.
11. " Int. Off.
12. G.O.C.
13. B.M.
14. 3rd. Div. "Q".
15. D.A.P.M.
16. Town Major, ROMERIES.
17. " " FRASNOY.
18. War Diary.
19. Do.
20. File.

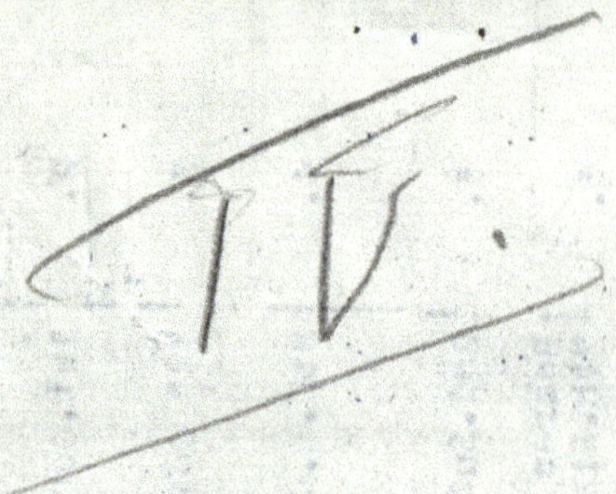

SECRET.
****

Copy No.....

76th.INFANTRY BRIGADE ORDER NO.159.

Ref.sheet 51 1/40,000. November 9th.1918.

1. 76th.Inf.Bde.Group will march to LA LONGUEVILLE area tomorrow Nov.10th.,in accordance with march table overleaf.

2. 529th.Field Coy R.E.and 7th.Field Ambce will move under orders of 3rd.Division to LA LONGUEVILLE where they will come under orders of G.O.C.,76th.Inf.Brigade.

3. Distances to be maintained on the march:-

100 yards between companies.
300 yards between Battalion and its transport.
1,000 yards between Battalions.

4. On portions of road where traffic is heavy units will march in file.

5. L.G.limbers will move with their companies; remainder of 1st.line transport and cookers in rear of units: 2nd.line transport including water-carts under orders of O.C.,No.2 Coy 3rd.Div.Train.

6. Brigade H.Q.will close at FRASNOY at 08[illegible]00 and open at LA LONGUEVILLE on arrival.

Reports during march to head of column.

7. ACKNOWLEDGE.

C. Clifford Captain,
Brigade Major,76th.Infantry Brigade.

Issued at 2[illegible].30 hours.

Copies to:-
1. 8th.K.O.R.L.
2. 2nd.Suffolk Regt.
3. 1st.Gordon Hldrs.
4. 76th.T.M.B.
5. "C" Coy M.G.C.
6. Section 7th.Field Amb.
7. No.2 Coy Train.
8. Bde Supply Officer.
9. " Transport "
10. " Signal "
11. " Int. "
12. G.O.C.
13. S.C.
14. 3rd.Div."G".
15. " "Q".
16. D.A.P.M.
17. C.R.E.
18. A.D.M.S.
19. 9th.Inf.Bde.
20. War Diary.
21. "
22. File.

MARCH TABLE TO ACCOMPANY 76th.BRIGADE ORDER NO.159.

Shedule No.	Unit.	From	Starting Point.	Time.	Route.	Remarks.
1.	76th.Bde H.Q. & 76th.T.M.B.	FRASNOY.	Road junction H.32d.7.0. near AMFROIPRET.	10.01	AMFROIPRET - BERLAIMONT - BAVAY.	Route to starting point road junct.M.12a.8.8.- road through N.1a
2.	1st.Gordon Hldrs	LE GRAND SART	do.	10.06	do.	Route to starting point road through N.18a.& c.
3.	"C" Coy M.G.Bn.	GOMMEGNIES Stn.	do.	10.31	do.	Route to starting point GOMMEGNIES - PETIT GOMMEGNIES.
4.	8th.K.O.R.L.	FRASNOY.	do.	10.41	do.	Route to starting point Rd.junct.M.12a.8.8. - road through N.1a
5.	2nd.Suffolk Regt	do.	do.	11.16	do.	do.
6.	Bearer Section 7th.Field Amb.	do.	do.	11.41	do.	do.
7.	No.2 Coy Train & Bde 2nd.line transport	do.	do.	11.44	do.	do.

SECRET.

Copy No....

76TH. INFANTRY BRIGADE ADMINISTRATIVE INSTRUCTIONS
(To accompany 76th.Inf.Bde. Order No.159).

1. BILLETING PARTIES.

1 Officer from each of the following units will report at Brigade H.Q. at 07-30 hours to-morrow, 10th.inst., to go forward with the Staff Captain :-
8th.K.O.R.L.Rgt.,2nd.Suffolk Rgt., 2 Coy.3rd.Div. Train, 529th.(E.R.) Field Coy., R.E.

1 Officer from each of the following units will meet the above party at Cross Roads, M.12a.7.7.,, at 07-40 hours:-
1st.Bn.Gordon Hldrs., "C" Coy.,3rd.Bn.M.G.C.

6 N.C.O.'s from each Battalion and 2 N.C.O.'s from each of the following - No.2 Coy.,3rd.Div.Train, 529th.Field Coy.,R.E., "C" Coy. 3rd.Bn.M.G.C., 76th.T.M.Battery and Bde.H.Q. - will be sent forward in time to meet their Billeting Officers at the Church,La LONGUEVILLE, at 09-00 hours.

2. TRANSPORT.

1st.Line Transport will move with Coy.'s and Battalions as usual. Water Carts must march with 2nd. Line Transport.

2nd.Line Transport will march in the rear of the Brigade under orders of O.C. No.2 Coy. 3rd. Div. Train.

2nd. Line from units at FRASNOY will rendezvous at H.Q. of No.2 Coy. Train, M.10b.2.0., at 10-30 hours.

2nd. Line Transport of 1st.Gordon Hldrs. will meet the remainder of 2nd line transport at H.32d.7.0. at 11-44 hours and will march in the rear of the column.

Units must be particularly careful not to obstruct the roads in FRASNOY before moving off. Until they move to their rendezvous they must be kept off the roads as much as possible.

3. DRESS.

Fighting Order. Each man will carry one Blanket rolled in the Waterproof Sheet.

4. GUIDES.

Guides from Billeting Parties will meet their units at road junction, I.29b.3.0.

5. BILLETS.

Billets at present occupied will be taken over by 9th. Inf.Bde. to-morrow. They must be left in a clean and sanitary condition.

Captain,
Staff Captain, 76th. Infantry Brigade.

9th.Nov.1918.

Copies to all recipients of Order No. 159.

SECRET.

Copy No. 15.

76TH. INFANTRY BRIGADE ADMINISTRATIVE INSTRUCTIONS
(To accompany 76th. Inf.Bde. Order No. G.706).

1. BILLETING PARTIES.

Billeting Parties of 1 Off. and 6 O.R. from each Battalion, 1 Off. and 2 O.R. from each of 529th.(E.R.) Field Coy., R.E., 7th. Field Ambulance, No.2 Coy.,3rd.Div.Train, 76th. T.M.Battery, and 2 O.R. of Brigade H.Q. will meet the Staff Captain at Road Junction, GRAVAUX, P.17a.4.9., at 08-30 hours, 16th. instant.

2. GUIDES.

Guides from Billeting Parties will meet their units at Road Junction, GRAVAUX, P.17a.4.9., at the following times:-

Brigade H.Q. & 76th T.M.Bty.) 8th.K.O.R.L.Rgt.)	12-00 hours.
1st.Gordon Hrs.	12-15 "
2nd.Suffolk Rgt.	12-30 "
529th.Field Coy.,R.E.	12-45 "
7th.Field Ambulance.	12-50 "
No. 2 Coy.,3rd.Div.Train &) Guides for 2nd.Line Transport)	13-00 "

3. DRESS.

Full Marching Order with Box Respirators. Caps will be worn and Steel Helmets will be carried on the man.

4. BLANKETS.

One lorry per Battalion has been asked for for convoyance of Blankets. Lorries will do 2 trips. They will be used for Blankets only, and on no account will Stores or Furniture of any sort be convoyed on them.

5. RETURN OF ORDNANCE STORES.

Battalions will send back to D.A.D.O.S., on their lorry after it has finished carrying the Blankets, any Ordnance Stores not required.

6. PRESENT BILLETS.

Billets at present occupied will be taken over by 9th.Inf.Bde. Group. They must be left in a clean and sanitary condition.

Billeting Certificates will be rendered to the MAIRE for all billets in this village occupied, before leaving.

[signature]

Captain,
Staff Captain, 76th.Infantry Brigade.

15th. Nov.1918.

Copies to :-
1. G.O.C.
2. 8th.K.O.R.L.Rgt.
3. 2nd.Suffolk Rgt.
4. 1st.Gordon Hrs.
5. 529th.(E.R.) Field Coy., R.E.
6. 7th.Field Ambulance.
7. No.2 Coy.,3rd.Div.Train.
8. 76th.T.M.Battery.
9. B.M.
10. Bde.Signal Off.
11. Bde.Q.M.Sgt.
12. War Diary.
13. Do.
14. File.

"A" Form.

Army Form C. 2121.
(In pads of 100.)

MESSAGES AND SIGNALS.

No. of Message.........

Prefix .... Code .... m. | Words. | Charge.

Office of Origin and Service Instructions.

Sent
At .... m.
To
By

This message is on a/c of:

.... *Service.*

(Signature of "Franking Officer.")

Recd. at .... m.
Date
From
By

TO 8 Koch. 529 Fd. Co. R.E. 76 T.M.B.
2 Suff. Regt. 7th Fd. Amb.
1 Gdn. Hdrs. 2 Coy. Train

Sender's Number.	Day of Month.	In reply to Number.	
* G. 706	15		AAA

1\. 76th Bde. Group will move to NEUF MESNIL – MONPLAISIR area tomorrow 16th as follows:–

Route: – LES PETITES MOTTES – NEUF MESNIL P156

Starting Point: – Road junction I 31 c. 0. 5

Bde. H.Q. & 76 T.M.B. pass starting point		11.01
8 Koch.	"	11.04
1 Gordon Hdrs.	"	11.16
2 Suffolk Regt.	"	11.29
529 (E.A.) Fd. Co. R.E.	"	11.41
7th Field Amb.	"	11.48
No. 2 Coy. Train & 2nd Line Transport	"	12.04

2\. 1st Line transport in rear of Battns. Baggage & supply wagons under orders O.C. 2 Coy. Train. 50 yds distance between companies, 200 yds between Battns.

3\. Administrative instructions will be issued later.

From

Place Acknowledge.

Time

The above may be forwarded as now corrected.

(Z)

Censor.

Signature of Addressor or person authorised to telegraph in his name

[illegible] Capt.
Bde. Maj.
76th Inf. Bde.

* This line, except AAA, should be erased if not required.

Wt. W 3253/P511. 500,000 Pads. 1/18. B. & S. Ltd. (E2389.)

SECRET.
****

Copy No....

76th. INFANTRY BRIGADE ORDER NO.162.

Ref.VAL.1000,000. 17th.November 1918.

1. 76th.Inf.Bde Order No.161 is cancelled.

2. 76th.Inf.Bde Group will move to LOUVROIL area tomorrow 18th, as follows:-

(a) PERSONNEL ONLY.

ROUTE:- Road along south edge of railway; pontoon bridge 200 yards north of last L in LOUVROIL.

STARTING POINT:- Level crossing just north of U in LOUVROIL.

PERSONNEL.

Brigade H.Q.& 76th.T.M.B.	pass starting point (a)	12.08 hours.
1st.Gordon Hldrs	"	.09
8th.K.O.R.L.	"	.15
2nd.Suffolk Regt	"	.20
20th.K.R.R.C.	"	.25
529th.Field Coy R.E.	"	.30
7th.Field Amb.	"	.32

(b) ALL TRANSPORT.

ROUTE. HAUTMONT Bridge - red road just north of 160 contour.

STARTING POINT:- Crossing of LONGUEVILLE-HAUTMONT road and BACHANT-MAUBEUGE railway in HAUTMONT.

All 1st.linetransport of Brigade Group under Lt.Mc.GUFFIE, 8th.K.O.R.L., pass starting point (b) 12.30 hours.

No.2 Coy Train and all 2nd.line transport of Brigade Group and ambulances pass starting point (b) 12.45 hours.

3. Distances to be maintained on the march:-

In rear of an Infantry Company.......... 10 yards.
In rear of an Infantry Battalion........ 50 yards.
In rear of other units.................. 25 yards.

4. ACKNOWLEDGE.

Captain,
Brigade Major, 76th.Infantry Brigade.

Copies to:-
1. 8th.K.O.R.L.
2. 2nd.Suffolk Regt.
3. 1st.Gordon Hldrs.
4. 76th.T.M.B.
5. 7th.Field Amb.
6. 529th.Field Coy R.E.
7. No.2 Coy Train.
8. 20th.K.R.R.C.
9. Bde Transport Officer.

SECRET.

Copy No......

76th. INFANTRY BRIGADE ORDER NO.163.

Ref. VALENCIENNES) 1/100,000.
NAMUR)

19th. November 1918.

1. The 3rd. Division will commence the advance towards the frontier.

2. 76th. Infantry Brigade Group will march tomorrow Nov. 20th., to the area COUSOLRE - BERSILLIES L'ABBAYE - BOUSIGNIES as follows:-

ROUTE:- CERFONTAINE - COLLERET.

STARTING POINT:- Level crossing ½ mile N.W. of F in FERRIERE LA GDE. (NAMUR Sheet).

No.1. 76th. Bde. H.Q., 76th. T.M.B.
& 1 Sect. 529th. Field Co. R.E., pass starting point....... 08.30 hours.
2, 2nd. Suffolk Regt........................"........................32
3. 1st. Gordon Hldrs........................"........................39
4. 8th. K.O.R.L.............................."........................47
5. 20th. K.R.R.C. (Pioneers)...................".....................09.04
6. 529th. (E.R.) Fd. Co. R.E. (less 1 Sectn.) "........................12
7. 7th. Field Amb.............................."........................18½
8. 1st. line transport of Group.............."........................20
9. No.2 Coy Train, G.S. Tool Wagons of
20th. K.R.R.C. & all 2nd. line transport......... under orders of O.C., 3rd. Div. Train.

3. All orders laid down in 76th. Inf. Brigade Instructions for the Advance, Nos. 1, 2 & 3, are to be strictly complied with.

4. Brigade H.Q. will close at LOUVROIL at 07.30 hours and open at COUSOLRE on arrival. Reports during march to head of column.

5. ACKNOWLEDGE.

C. Clifford Captain,
Brigade Major, 76th. Infantry Brigade.

Issued at 18.30 hours.

Copies to:- 1. 8th. K.O.R.L.
2. 2nd. Suffolk Regt.
3. 1st. Gordon Hldrs.
4. 76th. T.M.B.
5. 7th. Field Amb.
6. 529th. (E.R.) Field Co. R.E.
7. No.2 Coy Train.
8. 20th. K.R.R.C.
9. Brigade Transport Offr.
10. " Signal Offr.
11. " Int. Offr.
12. S.C.
13. 3rd. Div. "G".
14. War Diary.
15. "
16. File.

War Diary

SECRET.

Copy No....16

76th. INFANTRY BRIGADE ORDER NO.....164

Ref. Map 1/100,000 ....Nov 23rd.......... 1918.

1. The Brigade Group will move tomorrow Nov 24th in accordance with march table overleaf to THUIN-LOBBES area

2. Brigade H.Q. will close at present location at 09.00 and open at THUIN on arrival.

3. ACKNOWLEDGE.

C. Clifford Captain,
Issued at 12.00 hours. Brigade Major, 76th. Infantry Brigade.

Distribution:-
1. 8th. K.O.R.L.
2. 2nd. Suffolk Regt.
3. 1st. Gordon Hldrs.
4. 76th. [illegible]
5. [illegible]
6. [illegible] Field Co. R.E.
7. 7th. Field Amb.
8. No. [illegible] Coy Train.
9. Bde Transport Offr.
10. " Signal "
11. " Int. "
12. S.C.
13. 3rd. Div. "G".
14. File.
15.)
16.) War Diary.

IX

SECRET.

Copy No.....

76th. INFANTRY BRIGADE ORDER NO. 165

Ref. map 1/100,000. NOV. 24th 1918.

1. The Brigade Group will move tomorrow NOV. 25th in accordance with march table overleaf to NANINNES - SOMZEE - THY LE CHATEAU area

2. Brigade H.Q. will close at present location at 10.00 and open at NANINNES on arrival.

3. ACKNOWLEDGE.

[signature]
Captain,
for Brigade Major, 76th. Infantry Brigade.

Issued at hours.

Distribution:-
1. 8th. K.O.R.L.
2. 2nd. Suffolk Regt.
3. 1st. Gordon Hldrs.
4. 76th. T.M.B.
5. 20th. K.R.R.C.
6. 529th. Field Coy R.E.
7. 7th. Field Amb.
8. No.2 Coy Train.
9. Bde. Transport Offr.
10. " Signal "
11. " Int. "
12. S.C.
13. 3rd. Div. "G".
14. File.
15.)
16.) War Diary.

SECRET.
Copy No. 15

76TH. INFANTRY BRIGADE ADMINISTRATIVE INSTRUCTIONS.
(To accompany 76th. Inf. Bde. Order No.165).

1. **BILLETS.** Units will be accommodated to-morrow as under:-

20th.K.R.R.C.,2nd.Suffolk Rgt., Brigade H.Q.	NALINNES.
529th.Field Coy.R.E., No.7 Field Ambce.	SOMZEE.
No.2 Coy.Train, 76th.T.M.Bty.	GOURDINNE.
1st.Gordon Hrs.,8th.K.O.R.L.Rgt.	THY-LE-CHATEAU.

2. **BILLETING PARTIES.** 1 Officer from each of 1st.Gordon Hrs. and 2nd. Suffolk Rgt., and the Interpreter of 2nd.Suffolk Rgt., will meet a car at LOBBES Church at 07-15 hours. This car will then proceed to Brigade H.Q. to meet the Staff Captain.'

1 Officer from each of 8th.K.O.R.L.Rgt.,20th.K.R.R.C.,529th.Field Coy.,R.E.,No.7 Field Ambulance, No.2 Coy.3rd.Div.Train,76th.T.M.Bty.,and the Interpreter of 8th.K.O.R.L.Rgt. will meet the Staff Captain at Brigade H.Q. at 07-30 hours.

6 N.C.O.'s from each of 20th.K.R.R.C. and 2nd.Suffolk Rgt., and 2 N.C.O.'s of Brigade H.Q. will go forward on bicycles and will meet their Billeting Officers at the Bandstand in the Square at NALINNES at 08-30 hours.

2 N.C.O.'s from each of 529th.Field Coy.,R.E. and No.7 Field Ambulance will meet their Billeting Officers at SOMZEE Cross Roads at 09-00 hours.

2 N.C.O.'s from each of No.2 Coy.Train and 76th.T.M.Bty. will meet their Officers at the Mairie, GOURDINNE, at 08-45 hours.

6 N.C.O.'s from each of 1st.Gordon Hrs. and 8th.K.O.R.L. will meet their Officers at the Mairie, THY-LE-CHATEAU at 08-30 hours.

3. **GUIDES.** Guides will meet their units as under:-

Brigade H.Q.,20th.K.R.R.C.,2nd.Suffolk Rgt. At Cross Roads 100 yds. S.E. of T in CLAQUEDENT at 12-15 hours.
529th.Field Coy.) at Bridge across River on GOURDINNE-SOMZEE
No.7 Field Ambulance) Road at 14-00 hours.
76th.T.M.Bty. At western entrance to GOURDINNE at 13-00 hours.
No.2 Coy.3rd.Div.Train Do. Do. on arrival.
8th.K.O.R.L.Rgt. At Road Junction by BERZEE Station at 12-35 hours.
1st.Gordon Hrs. Do. Do. 13-00 "

Guides for First Line Transport will meet their units at the eastern outskirts of their villages

Guides for Secon Line Transport will meet their units at HAM-SUR-HEURE at 14-00 hours.

4. **TRANSPORT.** First Line Transport will rendezvous at Road Junction due N. of X in LES TRIEUX at 10-45 hours.

Second Line Transport will report to O.C.No.2 Coy.Train at his H.Q., Places de Chant des Oiseaux, THUIN,(at top of GRAND RUE) at 10-45 hours.

5. **PRESENT BILLETS.** Billets at present occupied will be left in a clean and sanitary condition. Billeting certificates will be rendered to the Maire of the respective Communes before departure.

All units (less 529th.Field Coy,) billeted in THUIN will leave a rear party behind until 12-40 hours to hand over billets to 8th.Inf. Bde.

T. F. [signature]
Captain,
Staff Captain, 76th. Infantry Brigade.

24/11/18.

(Copies to all recipients of Order No.165)

SECRET.

Copy No..11.

76th.INFANTRY BRIGADE ORDER NO..166.

Ref.Map 1/100,000 Nov. 20th 1918.

1. The Brigade Group will move tomorrow Nov. 26th in accordance with march table overleaf to METTET - PONTAURY - BIESME area

2. Brigade H.Q.will close at present location at 08.30 and open at METTET on arrival.

3. ACKNOWLEDGE.

C. Clifton Captain,

Issued at hours. Brigade Major,76th.Infantry Brigade.

Distribution:-
1. 8th.K.O.R.L.
2. 2nd.Suffolk Regt.
3. 1st.Gordon Hldrs.
4. 76th.T.M.B.
5. 20th.K.R.R.C.
6. 529th.Field Coy R.E.
7. 7th.Field Amb.
8. No.2 Coy Train.
9. Bde.Transport Offr.
10. " Signal "
11. " Int. "
12. S.C.
13. 3rd.Div."G".
14. File.
15.) War Diary.
16.)

MARCH TABLE.

ROUTE:- GERPINNES - FROMIEE - BIESME.

STARTING POINT:- Cross roads 30.00.75.(300 yards South West of T in TARCIENNE.)

Schedule No.	Unit.	Time to pass starting point.	Instructions.
1.	529th.Field Coy R.E. & 76th.T.M.B.	10.00 hours.	BCRY } METTET
2.	Brigade H.Q.	10.03	
3.	20th.K.R.R.C.	.04	BIESNES
4.	2nd.Suffolk Regt.	.09	} METTET
5.	1st.Gordon Hldrs.	.14	
6.	8th.K.O.R.L.	.19	DONTAURY
7.	7th.Field Amb.	.24	ESTROY
8.	1st.line transport of Group.	.28	→ BCRY
9.	No.2 Coy Train, R.E. Tool Wagons of 20th.K.R.R.C. and all 2nd.line transport.	.40	

** ** ** **

SECRET.

76TH. INFANTRY BRIGADE ADMINISTRATIVE INSTRUCTIONS.
(To accompany 76th. Inf.Bde. Order No. 166)

Copy No. 15

1. BILLETS. Accommodation has been allotted to units in the new area as under:-

Brigade H.Q., 76th.T.M.Bty. 2nd.Suffolk Rgt., 1st.Gordon Hldrs.	METTET.
No. 7 Field Ambce.	ESTROY.
8th.K.O.R.L.Rgt.	PONTAURY.
529th.Field Coy., No.2 Coy.3rd.Div.Train.	SCRY.
20th.K.R.R.C.	BIESME.

2. BILLETING PARTIES. 1 Officer from each of 20th.K.R.R.C., 7th.Field Ambce., 529th.Field Coy., R.E. and 2nd.Suffolk Rgt., and the Interpreter of 2nd.Suffolk Rgt. will report to Brigade H.Q. at 07-45 hours.

1 Officer from each of 1st.Gordon Hrs., 8th.K.O.R.L.Rgt., No.2 Coy.Train, 76th.T.M.Bty., and the Interpreter of 8th.K.O.R.L. will be met by a car at GOURDINNE Church at 07-30 hours. This car will then proceed to Brigade H.Q. in the Square, NALINNES.

6 N.C.O.'s of each of 2nd.Suffolk Rgt., 1st.Gordons, 8th.K.O.R.L., and 2 N.C.O.'s of each of Brigade H.Q., 76th.T.M.Bty., No.7 Field Ambce., 529th.Field Coy. and No.2 Coy.3rd.Div.Train will report at the Church in the Square, METTET, at 09-00 hours.

6 N.C.O.'s of 20th.K.R.R.C. will report at the Mairie, BIESME at 09-30 hours.

3. GUIDES. Guides from Billeting Party of 20th.K.R.R.C. will meet their Battalion at Road Junction on BIESME - GERPINNES Road at figure 0 of 1740 at 12-00 hours.

Guides from remainder of units in Brigade Group will meet their units at bend of BIESME-METTET Road, 200 yards S. of the C in SCRY at the following times:-

529th.Field Coy., 76th.T.M.Bty., Bde.H.Q.	12-30 hours.
2nd.Suffolk Rgt.	12-35 "
1st.Gordon Hrs.	12-40 "
8th.K.O.R.L.Rgt.	12-45 "
7th.Field Ambce.	12-50 "
1st. Line Transport.	12-55 "
No.2 Coy.Train & 2nd.Line Transport.	13-05 "

4. TRANSPORT. (a). First Line Transport of Bde.H.Q., 20th.K.R.R.C., and 2nd.Suffolk Rgt. will rendezvous at starting point - Road Junction 300 yds. S.W. of the T in TARCIENNE at 10-26 hours.

(b). First Line Transport of 529th.Field Coy., 1st.Gordons, 8th.K.O.R.L. and 7th.Field Ambce. will rendezvous at SOMZEE in schedule order, with head at Cross Roads, and will follow No.7 Field Ambce. to Starting Point, where they will arrive at 10-26 hours.

Second Line Transport of (a) will join No.2 Coy.3rd.Div.Train at Starting Point at 10-40 hours.

Second Line Transport of (b) will rendezvous in schedule order at SOMZEE Cross Roads at 10-00 hours unders orders of O.C. No.2 Coy. Train.

5. PRESENT BILLETS. Billets at present occupied will be left in a clean and sanitary condition. 8th.Inf.Bde. will take over all billets occupied by this Brigade in NALINNES and SOMZEE 20th.K.R.R.C., 2nd.Suffolk Rgt., Bde.H.Q., 529th.Field Coy. and 7th.Field Ambce. will each leave a rear party to hand over billets to units of 8th. Brigade. Rear parties will leave area at 12 noon and will proceed to join units in new area. Billeting certificates will be rendered by all units to the Maire of their respective villages before leaving.

25/11/18.

T. F. Kinnell
Captain,
Staff Captain, 76th. Infantry Brigade.

(Copies to all recipients of Order No.166).

XI

SECRET.

Copy No......

76th. INFANTRY BRIGADE ORDER NO...167.

Ref. map 1/100,000. Nov. 27th 1918.

1. The Brigade Group will move tomorrow Nov. 28th in accordance with march table overleaf to ANNEVOIE ROUILLON – WIRANANT – ANHEE area.

2. Brigade H.Q. will close at present location at 09.00 and open at ANNEVOIE ROUILLON on arrival.

3. ACKNOWLEDGE.

C. Clifton Captain.

Issued at 16.00 hours. Brigade Major, 76th. Infantry Brigade.

Distribution:-
1
2. 8th. K.O.R.L.
3. 2nd. Suffolk Regt.
4. 1st. Gordon Hldrs.
5. 76th. T.M.B.
6. 20th. K.R.R.C.
7. 526th. Field Coy R.E.
8. 7th. Field Amb.
9. No.2 Coy Train.
10. Bde. Transport Offr.
11. " Signal Offr.
12. " Int. "
13. S.C.
14. 3rd. Div. "G".
15. File.
16.) War Diary

MARCH TABLE.

ROUTE:- RIGUL; dividing at road junction 2J.87.02., East of RIGUL.

STARTING POINT:- Cross roads 21.38.75.(1,000 yards North West of FURNAUX).

Schedule No.	Unit.	Time to pass starting point:-	Instructions.
1.	Bde.H.Q.& 76th.T.M.B. + 1 Sectn.229th.Field Coy.	10.00	
2.	2nd.Suffolk Regt.	.01	
3.	1st.Gordon Hldrs.	.05	
4.	8th.K.O.R.L.	.10	
5.	20th.K.R.R.C.(Pioneers).	.14	
6.	229th.Field Co R.E.(less 1 Sectn.)	.19	
7.	7th.Field Amb.	.22	
8.	1st.line transport of Group.	.24	
9.	No.2 Coy Train, Tool wagons of 20th.K.R.R.C., and all 2nd.line transport.	.40	

\- \- \- \- \-

"A" Form.

Army Form C. 2121.
(In pads of 100.)

MESSAGES AND SIGNALS.

No. of Message..........

Prefix........ Code:........ m. Office of Origin and Service Instructions.	Words. / Charge. Sent At........ m. To........ By........	This message is on a/c of: .... Service. (Signature of "Franking Officer.")	Recd. at........ m. Date........ From........ By........

TO

8th KORL	76th LTMB	No 2 Coy Train
2nd Suffolk Rgt	529 Fd Coy RE	20th KRRC
1st Gordon Hdrs	7th Fd Amb	

Sender's Number.	Day of Month.	In reply to Number.	AAA
* G 755	27		

Ref Bde Order No 167

Route to starting point for all units & transport except 7th Fd Ambce:- road from METTET Church by the Station and through second E in METTET

From 76th Inf Bde

Place

Time

The above may be forwarded as now corrected.

Censor.

(Z) C Chiffer Capt

Signature of Addressor or person authorised to telegraph in his name.

Bde Major

* This line, except AAA, should be erased if not required.

Wt. W 3253/P511. 500,000 Pads. 1/18. B. & S. Ltd. (E2389.)

SECRET.
============

ADMINISTRATIVE INSTRUCTIONS TO ACCOMPANY
76th.INF.BRIGADE ORDER NO.187.

Copy No.....

BILLETS.

Units will be accomodated tomorrow as under:-

1st.Gordon Hldrs 8th.K.O.R.L. No.2 Coy Train	ANHEE.
529th.Field Coy R.E. No.7th.Field Amb 76th.T.M.B.	WARNANT.
Brigade H.Q. 2nd.Suffolk Regt. 20th.K.R.R.C.	ANNEVOIE ROUILLON and HUN.

BILLETING PARTIES.

1 Officer and 2 O.R.each of 1st.Gordon Hldrs,~~xxx~~ 8th.K.O.R.L. 2nd.Suffolk Regt and 20th.K.R.R.C.,and 1 Officer and 1 O.R. of No.2 Coy Train,7th.Field Amb.,76th.T.M.B. and Brigade Headquarters will report at Brigade Headquarters at 07.45 hours.

4 N.C.O's from each of 1st.Gordon Hldrs and 8th.K.O.R.L.,and 2 N.C.O's from No.2 Coy Train will proceed on bicycles to ANHEE Church,where they will meet their billeting officer at 08.00 hours.

4 N.C.O's from each of 2nd.Suffolk Regt and 20th.K.R.R.C. will proceed on bicycles and will meet their billeting officers at cross roads ANNEVOIE ROUILLON at 09.15 hours.

2 N.C.O's from each of 529th.Field Coy R.E.and 7th.Field Amb., will meet their billeting officers at WARNANT Church at 09.30 hours.

GUIDES.

Guides from billeting parties will meet their units as follows:-

1st.Gordon Hldrs 8th.K.O.R.L.	At HALTE on ANHEE - WARNANT Road at 12.00 hours.
No.2 Coy Train	-do- at 12.30 hours.
76th.T.M.B. -	At eastern entrance to WARNANT on BIOUL-WARNANT Road at 12.15 hours.
529th.Field Coy -	-do- at 12.30 hours.
7th.Field Amb. -	-do- at 12.30 hours.
Brigade H.Q. 2nd.Suffolk Regt	At eastern entrance to ANNEVOIE ROUILLON on main road at 12.15 hours.
20th.K.R.R.C. -	-do- at 12.30 hours.

Billeting officers will ensure that one guide is detailed to meet unit's 2nd.line transport.

TRANSPORT.

1st.line will rendezvous at starting point at 10.30 hours under Brigade Transport Officer.

2nd.line will rendezvous at starting point at 10.40 hours under O.C.,No.2 Coy Train.

PRESENT BILLETS. Will be left in a clean and sanitary condition. No rear parties need be left behind. Billeting certificates will be rendered by all units to the MAIRE of their respective villages before leaving.

LIGHTS & SMOKING. C's.O.Units will ensure that all men are warned against smoking in barns.All lights must be enclosed in tins to prevent fires.

Captain,
Staff Captain,76th.Infantry Brigade.

27/11/18.
Dist.as for O.O.187

Int. Offr XII

SECRET.

Copy No......

76th. INFANTRY BRIGADE ORDER NO. 162

Ref. map 1/100,000   Nov. 28th 1918.

1. The Brigade Group will move tomorrow Nov. 29th in accordance with march table overleaf to NATOYE - BRAIBANT SOVET area

2. Brigade H.Q. will close at present location at 07.30 and open at BRAIBANT on arrival.

3. ACKNOWLEDGE.

C. Chipper Captain,
Brigade Major, 76th. Infantry Brigade.

Issued at 16.30 hours.

Distribution:

1. 8th. K.O.R.L.
2. 2nd. Suffolk Regt.
3. 1st. Gordon Hldrs.
4. 76th. T.M.B.
5. 20th. M.G.C.
6. 529th. Field Coy R.E.
7. 7th. Field Amb.
8. No.2 Coy Train.
9. Bde. Transport Offr.
10. " Signal "
11. " Int. "
12. S.C.
13. 3rd. Div. "G".
14. File.
15.) War Diary.
16.)

MARCH TABLE.

ROUTE:- VER HAILLES - CORIBEE.

STARTING POINT:- Bridge BR.S9.8#. (Iron bridge at YVOIR).

Schedule No.	Unit.	Time to pass starting point.	Instructions.
1.	Bde.H.Q., 76th.I.N.B. & 1 Sectn.529th.Fd.Coy R.E.	09.00.	
2.	1st.Gordon Hldrs.	.01	
3.	8th.K.O.R.L.	.06	
4.	20th.K.R.R.C.	.10	
5.	2nd.Suffolk Regt.	.15	
6.	529th.Field Coy (less 1 Section)..	.19	
7.	7th.Field Amb.	.23	
8.	1st.line transport of Group		.... Under orders of O.C., 3rd.Divl.Train.
9.	No.2 Coy Train, Tool wagons of 20th.K.R.R.C., all 2nd.line transport		

-- -- -- --

ADDENDUM TO 76th.INF.BRIGADE ORDER NO.188.

****

Special Instructions for March Nov.29th.1918.

1. 1st.LINE TRANSPORT.

Vehicles laid down in B/8811/4 will accompany units as usual. Remainder of 1st.line transport in order of Groups will move in rear of "C" Group under orders of O.C.,3rd.Divl.Train,who will issue orders direct to Brigade Transport Officer as regards starting point and hour of start. .

2. TRAIN TRANSPORT.

As soon as the 1st.Line Transport of Groups have crossed the bridge at YVOIR,the whole of the Train (less No.1 Coy with D.A.) will close up with its head on the bridge and will cross the bridge in rear of the 1st.Line Transport in order of Groups.

3. PARTY TO ASSIST TRANSPORT.

1st.Gordon Hldrs will leave a party of 2 Officers and 50 other ranks in YVOIR to report to O.C.,3rd.Div.Train at East end of YVOIR bridge.

As soon as party is no longer required,O.C.,Divl. Train will order it to rejoin unit.

4. SPARE HORSES.

All spare horses will be handed over to O.C.,No.2 Coy 3rd.Div.Train before commencing the march on Nov.29th.

5. OVERLOADED WAGONS.

A Divisional Staff Officer will be on the hill just East of YVOIR with orders to dump excess baggage on overloaded wagons.

6. ACKNOWLEDGE.

[illegible signature]
Captain,
28/11/18. Brigade Major,76th.Infantry Brigade.

Copies to all recipients of Order No.188.

XII

SECRET.

76TH. INFANTRY BRIGADE ADMINISTRATIVE INSTRUCTIONS
(To accompany 76th.Inf.Bde.Order No.188)

Copy No. 16

1. BILLETS. Units will be accommodated as under:-

8th.K.O.R.L.Rgt.,20th.K.R.R.C., 7th.Field Ambce.	NATOYE.
1st.Gordon Hrs.,76th.T.M.Bty.,Bde.H.Q., No.2 Coy. Train.	BRAIBANT & HALLOY.
2nd.Suffolk Regt.	SOVET.
529th.Field Coy.,R.E.	MIANNOYE.

2. BILLETING PARTIES. 1 Off. and 2 O.R. from each of 20th.K.R.R.C. and 2nd.Suffolk Regt. will report at Brigade H.Q. at 07-15 hours.

1 Off. and 2 O.R. from each of 1st.Gordon Hrs, 8th.K.O.R.L.Rgt., No.2 Coy. Train, 529th. Field Coy., 7th.Field Ambce and 76th. T.M.Bty. will meet the Staff Captain on W. side of Iron Bridge across the MEUSE at YVOIR N.E.20.33 at 07-45.

Billeting Parties of 4 N.C.O.'s from each of 8th.K.O.R.L.,20th. K.R.R.C., and 2 N.C.O.'s of No.7 Field Ambce. will proceed on bicycles and will meet their Billeting Officers at NATOYE Station at 09-00 hours.

4 N.C.O.'s of 1st. Gordon Hrs., and 2 from each of Brigade H.Q., No.2 Coy.Train and 76th.T.M.Bty. will proceed on bicycles and will meet their Billeting Officers at BRAIBANT Church at 09-00 hours.

4 N.C.O.'s of 2nd.Bn.Suffolk Regt. will meet their Billeting Officer at the Mairie, SOVET, at 09-00 hours.

2 N.C.O.'s of 529th.Field Coy.,R.E. will meet their Billeting Officer at MIANNOYE Church at 09-00 hours.

3. GUIDES. Guides from Billeting Parties will meet their units as under:

1st.Gordon Hrs., 76th.T.M.Bty. and Brigade H.Q.	Western entrance to BRAIBANT	at 12-00 hours.
No.2 Coy. Train	Do.	at 14-00 hours.
8th.K.O.R.L.Rgt.	Railway Crossing near E in NATOYE	" 12-00 "
20th.K.R.R.C.	Railway Crossing near E in NATOYE	" 12-05 "
7th.Field Ambce.	Railway Crossing near E in NATOYE	" 12-20 "
529th.Field Coy.,R.E.	Eastern entrance to MIANNOYE	" 12-00 "
2nd.Suffolk Rgt.	Western entrance to SPONTIN	" 11-30 "

4. PRESENT BILLETS. Will be left scrupulously clean. Billeting Certificates will be rendered to the BOURGMESTRE of villages before departure of units.

5. YVOIR HILL. In view of the steepness of this hill, units should, if possible, take some ropes on their Cookers in case it is necessary to manhandle them up the hill.

[signature] Captain,
Staff Captain, 76th. Infantry Brigade.

23/11/18.

XIII

SECRET.
****

Copy No....

76th.INFANTRY BRIGADE ORDER NO.169.

Ref.map 1/100,000. Nov.29th.1918.

1. The Brigade Group will move tomorrow Nov.30th.,in accordance with march table overleaf to PESSOUX - CINEY - MOHIVILLE area.

2. 1st.line transport and baggage wagons will move in rear of Groups (a),(b),(c) in march table.

3. Brigade H.Q.will close at present location at 09.00 hours and open at JANNEE CHAU.on arrival.

4. ACKNOWLEDGE.

C. Chipper Capaain,
Brigade Major,76th.Infantry Brigade.

Issued at 2230 hours.

Distibution:-
1. 8th.K.O.R.L.
2. 2nd.Suffolk Regt.
3. 1st.Gordon Hldrs.
4. 76th.T.M.B.
5. 20th.K.R.R.C.
6. 529th.Field Coy R.E.
7. 7th.Field Amb.
8. No.2 Coy Train.
9. Bde.Transport Offr.
10. " Signal "
11. " Int. "
12. S.C.
13. 3rd.Div."G".
14. File.
15. War Diary.
16. " "

MARCH TABLE.
****

	Unit.	Starting point.	Hour of passing starting point.	Route.	Destination.	Instns.
Grp. (a)	(8th.K.O.R.L.	Rd.junct.at first E.in EMBLINNE.	09.00	EMPTINNE - Road junct.3B.85.72.	MOHIVILLE.	
	(20th.K.R.R.C.		09.05		PESSOUX,	
	(7th.Field Amb.		09.10		RY.	
	(529th.Fd.Coy.		09.12		SCY.	
Grp. (b)	(Bde.H.Q.& (76th.T.M.B.	Bridge over Rly.just East of HALLOY.	09.20	CINEY STA.- CINEY.	JANNEE CHAU.	
	(1st.Gordon H.		09.21	CINEY STA.	CINEY CHAU	
	(No.2 Coy Train.		09.26	CINEY STA.- CINEY.	TRISOGNE.	
Grp. (C)	(2nd.Suffolk Regt	———		CINEY	TRISOGNE.	To be clear of CINEY by 10.00 hrs.

MESSAGES AND SIGNALS. No. of Message..........

Prefix.......... Code.......... m | Words. | Charge. | This message is on a/c of: | Recd. at........ m.

Office of Origin and Service Instructions.

Sent At............ m. To .... By ....

.... *Service.*

(Signature of "Franking Officer.")

Date .... From .... By ....

TO

Sender's Number. | Day of Month. | In reply to Number. | AAA

Casualties for month of November 1918

Nil

From

Place

Time

The above may be forwarded as now corrected. (Z)

Censor. Signature of Addressor or person authorised to telegraph in his name.

* This line, except **AAA**, should be erased if not required.

Wt. W 3253/P511. 500,000 Pads. 1/18. B. & S. Ltd. (E2389.)

SECRET.

76TH. INFANTRY BRIGADE ADMINISTRATIVE INSTRUCTIONS. Copy No. 15
(To accompany 76th. Inf.Bde. Order No. 169)

1. BILLETS. Units will be accommodated to-morrow as under :-

Brigade H.Q.	JANNEE Chateau.
Do. and 76th.T.M.Bty.	JANNEE.
20th.K.R.R.C.	PESSOUX.
2nd.Suffolk Rgt. and No.2 Coy.Train.	TRISOGNE.
8th.K.O.R.L.Rgt.	MONIVILLE and SCOVILLE.
529th. Field Coy.,R.E.	SCY.
No.7 Field Ambce.	HY.
1st.Gordon Hldrs.	CINEY.

2. BILLETING PARTIES. Billeting Party of 1st.Gordon Hldrs. will proceed to CINEY and will report to Town Major for Billets at 08-30 hours Location of Town Major:- Billet No.17, 1st. turning on left past the Town Hall.

Billeting Parties of 1 Officer and 1 N.C.O. each of No.2 Coy. Train and 76th. T.M.Bty., and 1 Off. and 2 O.R. of 2nd.Suffolk Rgt. will meet the Staff Captain at Brigade H.Q. at 07-30 hours.

1 Officer and 2 O.R. from each of 8th.K.O.R.L.Rgt., 20th. K.R.R.C., 529th.Field Coy.R.E. and No.7 Field Ambce. will meet Staff Captain at 08-00 hours at NATOYE Church.

4 N.C.O.'s from 20th.K.R.R.C. will meet their Billeting Officer at PESSOUX Church at 09-00.

4 N.C.O.'s from 2nd.Suffolk Rgt. and 2 from No.2 Coy. Train will meet their Billeting Officers at Cross Roads, TRISOGNE at 09-15 hrs.

4 N.C.O.'s from 8th.K.O.R.L.Rgt. will meet their Billeting Officer at MONIVILLE Church at 09-00 hours.

3. GUIDES. Guides from Billeting Parties will meet their units as under :-

Brigade H.Q. and T.M.Bty. at PESSOUX Cross Roads at 1120 hours.

20th. K.R.R.C. Road Junction 200 yds.N.of X in PESSOUX at 1100 "
8th.K.O.R.L. " " 200 " N. of V in MONIVILLE at 1100 hours.
2nd.Suffolk Rgt. " " 200 " S. of N in TRISOGNE CONVENT at 1100 hours.
No.2 Coy. Train " " " " at 1040 "
529th.Field Coy. Western entrance to SCY at 1110 "
No.7 Field Ambce. N.W. " " HY at 1100 "

4. PRESENT BILLETS. The whole of the billets occupied by the Brigade wi[ll] be taken over by 9th. Inf.Bde. to-morrow. All Billets will be left scrupulously clean.

Each unit will leave a small rear party behind to hand over billets to units of 9th.Bde. After handing over, they will proceed to join their units. Billeting Certificates will be rendered to the Maire of respective villages before departure of units.

[illegible signature]
Captain,
29/11/18. Staff Captain, 76th. Infantry Brigade.

3rd Division.

B. H. Q.

76th INFANTRY BRIGADE

DECEMBER 1918.

Appendices under separate cover

Sent

At .... m. To .... By ....

.... *Service.* (Signature of "Franking Officer.")

Date .... From .... By ....

TO

Sender's Number.	Day of Month.	In reply to Number.	AAA
*			

Casualties for Month of December 1918

1 officer 1st Gordon Hdrs ~~Attd~~ died of pneumonia

~~Nil.~~

From

Place

Time

The above may be forwarded as now corrected. (Z) C. Chipper Capt

Censor. Signature of Addressor or person authorised to telegraph in his name.

* This line, except **AAA**, should be erased if not required.

Wt. W 3253/P511. 500,000 Pads. 1/18. B. & S. Ltd. **(E2389.)**

Instructions regarding War Diaries and Intelligence Summaries are contained in F. S. Regs., Part II. and the Staff Manual respectively. Title Pages will be prepared in manuscript.

DECEMBER. 1918.

WAR DIARY or ~~INTELLIGENCE SUMMARY~~

(Erase heading not required.)

HQ 76th Infantry Brigade Page I.

Army Form C. 2118.

WR 39

Place	Date Dec.	Hour	Summary of Events and Information	Remarks and references to Appendices
JANNEE.	1 2 3		Resting in the JANNEE area.	
	4.		Brigade march to BAILLONVILLE area, arriving at 13.00 hours very wet.	App. I. BOO. 170.
BAILLONVILLE SOY.	5.		Move to the SOY-HOTTON area. Long march & very bad roads did not arrive till 14.00 hours.	App. II BOO 171.
MANHAY.	6.		Move to ODEIGNE - GRANDMENIL area, BHQ. opened at MANHAY. at 13.00 hours.	App. III 172.
HEBRONVAL	7.		Move to OTTRE-MALEMPRE area. BHQ. opened in estaminet at HEBRONVAL. at 14.00 hours	App. IV BOO. 173.
CERREUX (HALTE)	8.		Move off at 9.30 am. Advanced billeting parties find the allotted area still occupied by the Canadian troops. 1st Gordon Hldrs. & 8th K.O.R.L. Regts. halt at SALMCHATEAUX until accomodation is found. 8th K.O.R.L. go to VIELSALM. 1st Gordon Hldrs. to COURTIL, arriving in soon after dark.	App. V. BOO. 174.

2449 Wt. W14957/M90 750,000 1/1[illegible] J.B.C. & A. Forms/C.2118/12.

DECEMBER. 1918.

Army Form C. 2118.

WAR DIARY ~~or INTELLIGENCE SUMMARY~~

(Erase heading not required.)

Page 11.

76th Infantry Brigade.

Instructions regarding War Diaries and Intelligence Summaries are contained in F. S. Regs., Part II. and the Staff Manual respectively. Title Pages will be prepared in manuscript.

Place	Date Dec.	Hour	Summary of Events and Information	Remarks and references to Appendices
CIERREUX CHATEAUX	9.		Closing in the Brigade area. Headquarters remain in CIERREUX	App. VI. G.491.
— " —	10.		No move today, troops cleaning up, preparatory to crossing the frontier.	
— " — GRUFFLINGEN	11.		March accross the frontier, past the Corps Commander, with the Major General & his staff at the head of the column. B.H.Q. open at GRUFFLINGEN.	App VII. BOO. 175.
MANDERFIELD	12.		March to MANDERFIELD area. Very long march for all units and very heavy rain. Arriving in area at 14.00 hours.	App VIII. BOO 176.
BAASEM	13.		BHQ. opened in BAASEM at 14.00 hours. Slight improvement in the weather, roads still very bad	App IX. BOO. 177.
BLANKENHEIM	14.		Move to BLANKENHEIM area, weather fine, roads still bad. H.Q. opened in the KÖLNER HOF hotel at 13.00 hours.	App X. BOO 178.
EICHERSCHEID.	15.		Move to EICHERSCHEID – TONDORF area, great improvement in the roads & weather. H.Q. opened at 13.00 hours.	App XI. BOO 179.

2449 Wt. W14957/M90 750,000 1/16 J.B.C. & A. Forms/C.2118/12.

DECEMBER. 1918. **WAR DIARY** *or* ~~INTELLIGENCE SUMMARY~~ *(Erase heading not required.)* Page III. 76th Infantry Brigade. Army Form C. 2118.

Instructions regarding War Diaries and Intelligence Summaries are contained in F. S. Regs., Part II. and the Staff Manual respectively. Title Pages will be prepared in manuscript.

Place	Date Dec.	Hour	Summary of Events and Information	Remarks and references to Appendices
MUNSTEREIFEL	16th.		Short march to MUNSTEREIFEL. H.Q. opened in the HOTEL HILLEBRAND. at 11.00 hours.	App. XII. B.O.O. 180.
EUSKIRCHEN	17th		Arrive at EUSKIRCHEN at 12.00 hours, very good roads for the march, & everyone very comfortably billeted.	App. XIII. B.O.O. 181.
AHREM.	18th		March to AHREM - ERP. area. 529 Field Coy. R.E.s & 20 K.R.R.C. (Pioneers), return to Division, no longer under orders of the G.O.C. 76th Infy. Bgde.	App. XIV. B.O.O. 182.
GYMNICH. CHATEAUX.	19th		Brigade march to the final area. Brigade H.Q. open at the Schloss at GYMNICH. Slight snow shower in the afternoon.	App. XV. B.O.O. 183.
— " —	20th.		G.O.C. interviews all the village Headmen of the Brigade area.	
— " —	21st		Brigadier visits the Battn. areas. All units busy arranging dining halls for the men & messes for the sergeants.	
— " —	22nd		First instalment of the demobilisation forms arrive. Brigade concert party collect & have their first rehearsal.	

2449 Wt. W14957/M90 750,000 1/16 J.B.C. & A. Forms/C.2118/12.

Instructions regarding War Diaries and Intelligence Summaries are contained in F. S. Regs., Part II. and the Staff Manual respectively. Title Pages will be prepared in manuscript.

DECEMBER. 1918.

WAR DIARY
or
INTELLIGENCE SUMMARY
(Erase heading not required.)

Page IV

76th Infantry Brigade.

Army Form C. 2118.

Place	Date Dec	Hour	Summary of Events and Information	Remarks and references to Appendices
GYMNICH.	23rd		Conference of Football representatives from each unit to arrange fixtures for the Bgde. Football League	App. XVI
— " —	24th		Major General visits all Battns. accompanied by the Staff Captn. Brigadier indisposed	
— " —	25th		Staff Captain visits all Battns. at their dinners, which had to be purchased locally & were none too good. The Div. canteen supplies fail to arrive, in spite of a previous plentiful promise.	
— " —	26th		Brigadier still indisposed	
— " —	27th		Very wet today, all football matches postponed. 2nd Suffolk Regt. have a very successful boxing tournament. Brigade concert party give a performance to No 2. Coy Train	
— " —	28th		Again very wet today no football. Splendid performance by the Bgde. concert party in the Brigade Hall at GYMNICH.	

2449 Wt. W14957/M90 750,000 1/16 J.B.C. & A. Forms/C.2118/12.

Instructions regarding War Diaries and Intelligence Summaries are contained in F. S. Regs., Part II. and the Staff Manual respectively. Title pages will be prepared in manuscript.

DECEMBER 1918.

~~WAR~~ DIARY ~~or INTELLIGENCE SUMMARY.~~

(*Erase heading not required.*)

Page V

Army Form C. 2118.

76th Infantry Brigade -

Place	Date Dec.	Hour	Summary of Events and Information	Remarks and references to Appendices
GYMNICH	29.		Men demobilized December.	
	30			
	31			

~~28th~~	Coalminers	Demobilizers & Pivotals	Any Service	Watford Detail	
28th	57	2	3.	0	62
29th	65	0	4	0	69
30th	30	0	4	0	34
31st	0	0	0	13	13.
					178

Training started. 2 hours a day military training. Drill, guards and ceremonial chiefly. Cross-country running, football and boxing in afternoon and evening. Education held up for lack of books and stationery.

Intelligence Officer went on leave 29th.

Much work in connection with civil administration.

Weather very mild.

C. Cliffe Capt
for GOC 76th Inf Bde
Dec 31/18

A5834 Wt. W4973/M687 750,000 8/16 D. D. & L. Ltd. Forms/C.2118/13.

3rd Division.

APPENDICES

76th INFANTRY BRIGADE

DECEMBER 1918.

XVI

76th. INFANTRY BRIGADE FOOTBALL LEAGUE.

F I X T U R E S.

Jan.4th.	8th.K.O.R.L.	V.	2nd.Suffolk Regt.
	1st.Gordon Hldrs	V.	No.7 Field Amb.
Jan.8th.	Bde.H.Q.& T.M.B.	V.	8th.K.O.R.L.
	2nd.Suffolk Regt	V.	1st.Gordon Hldrs.
Jan.11th.	7th.Field Amb.	V.	Bde.H.Q.& T.M.B.
	8th.K.O.R.L.	V.	1st.Gordon Hldrs.
Jan.15th.	Bde.H.Q.& T.M.B.	V.	2nd.Suffolk Regt.
	8th.K.O.R.L.	V.	7th.Field Amb.
Jan.18th.	1st.Gordon Hldrs	V.	Bde.H.Q.& T.M.B.
	2nd.Suffolk Regt	V.	7th.Field Amb.
Jan.22nd.	2nd.Suffolk Regt	V.	8th.K.O.R.L.
	7th.Field Amb	V.	1st.Gordon Hldrs.
Jan.25th.	8th.K.O.R.L.	V.	Bde.H.Q.& T.M.B.
	1st.Gordon Hldrs	V.	2nd.Suffolk Regt.
Jan.29th.	Bde.H.Q.& T.M.B.	V.	7th.Field Amb.
	1st.Gordon Hldrs	V.	8th.K.O.R.L.
Feb.1st.	2nd.Suffolk Regt	V.	Bde.H.Q.& T.M.B.
	7th.Field Amb	V.	8th.K.O.R.L.
Feb.5th.	Bde.H.Q.& T.M.B.	V.	1st.Gordon Hldrs.
	7th.Field Amb.	V.	2nd.Suffolk Regt.

** ** ** **

The usual association rules will apply.

All games will start at 14.30 hours prompt and play 35 minutes each way.

The "Home" team, i.e. the first mentioned in each case above, will provide the referee, who will notify Bde.H.Q. the result of the game as soon after as possible.

Games which cannot be played owing to bad weather etc., will be arranged for on a future date.

** ** **

I

SECRET.
****

Copy No....

76th.INFANTRY BRIGADE ORDER NO...178

Ref.1/100,000 map. Dec 3rd 1918.

1. The Brigade Group will move tomorrow Dec. 4th in accordance with March table overleaf to BAILLONVILLE - HETTINNE - SINSIN Area

2. Brigade H.Q.will close at present location at 08.30 and open at BAILLONVILLE CHAU. on arrival.

3. ACKNOWLEDGE.

4. Billets at present occupied will be taken over by 9th.Inf.Bde.Group. Units will leave small parties to hand over.

Issued at 11.30 hours.

C Cliffe Captain,
Brigade Major,76th.Infantry Brigade.

Distribution:-
1. 8th.K.O.R.L.
2. 2nd.Suffolk Regt.
3. 1st.Gordon Hldrs.
4. 76th.T.M.B.
5. 20th.K.R.R.C.
6. 529th.Field Coy R.E.
7. 7th.Field Amb.
8. No.2 Coy Train.
9. Bde.Transport Offr.
10. " Signal "
11. " Int. "
12. S.C.
13. 3rd.Div."G".
14. File.
15. War Diary.
16. "

MARCH TABLE.

ROUTE:- JAMBES - HEURE.

STARTING POINT:- Cross roads 800 yards South West of JAMBES CHAU.

SCHEDULE NO.	UNIT.	TIME TO PASS STARTING POINT.		INSTRUCTIONS.
			Destination:-	
1.	Bde.H.Q.,76th.T.M.B. 1 Sectn.229th.Fd.Coy R.E.......	10.00	BAILLONVILLE Area.	
2.	8th.K.O.R.L......................	10.02	SINSIN.	
3.	20th.K.R.R.C.(Pioneers)........	10.07	BAILLONVILLE Area.	
4.	2nd.Suffolk Regt................	.12	NETTINNE	
5.	229th.Fd.Coy (less 1 Sectn)...	.17	KARESSEN.	
6.	7th.Field Amb...................	.20	HEURE.	
7.	1st.line transport of Group (less 1st.Gordon Hldrs)....	.22	....	Rendezvous at starting point.
8.	No.2 Coy Train,Tool wagons of 20th.K.R.R.C.,all Train Transport (less baggage wagons of 1st.Gordon Hldrs)...	.30	HEURE..................	Rendezvous at starting point.
9.	1st.Gordon Hldrs with 1st.line transport & baggage wagons....	11.00	SINSIN.	

** ** ** ** **

II

SECRET.
****

Copy No.....

76th. INFANTRY BRIGADE ORDER NO..171
****

Ref: Map 1/100,000. ....Dec. 4th........ 1918.

1. The Brigade Group will move tomorrow Dec. 5th in accordance with march table overleaf to SOY - HOTTON - MONVILLE area

2. Brigade H.Q. will close at present location at 09.00 and open at SOY on arrival.

3. ACKNOWLEDGE.

S Eashwood 2Lt for
Captain,

Issued at hours. Brigade Major, 76th. Infantry Brigade.

Distribution:-

1. 8th. K.O.R.L.
2. 2nd. Suffolk Regt.
3. 1st. Gordon Hldrs.
4. 76th. T.M.B.
5. 20th. K.R.R.C.
6. 529th. Field Coy R.E.
7. 7th. Field Amb.
8. No.2 Coy Train.
9. Bde. Transport Offr.
10. " Signal "
11. " Int. "
12. S.C.
13. 3rd. Div. "G".
14. File.
15. War Diary.
16. "

MARCH TABLE.
****

ROUTE:- NOISEUX - FRONVILLE. Personnel for SOY via NY, but all transport via HOTTON.

STARTING POINT:- Main cross roads 1,000 yards East of BAILLONVILLE.

Schedule No.	Unit.	Time to pass starting point.	Instructions.
			Destination:-
1.	Bde.H.Q.,76th.T.M.B.) & 1 Sectn.529th.Fd.Coy)	10.00	~~SOY.~~ FISENNE ~~NY.~~ SOY
2.	20th.K.R.R.C.(Pioneers)	10.02	MELREUX.
3.	2nd.Suffolk Regt.	10.07	SOY. To drop one company at starting point to follow No.9.
4.	1st.Gordon Hldrs.	10.11	HOTTON.
5.	8th.K.O.R.L.	10.16	HOTTON.
6.	529th.Fd.Coy.R.E.(less 1 Sectn)	10.21	~~NY.~~ SOY
7.	7th.Field Amb.	10.24	~~[illegible]~~. HOTTON
8.	1st.Line Transport of Group	10.26	Rendezvous at Starting Point.
9.	No.2 Coy Train, Tool Wagons of 20th.K.R.R.C., all Train Transport of Group	10.40	HOTTON. Rendezvous at starting point.

** ** ** ** **

1 G.H. Tr
1 Coy Tr
7 F.A.
25th

SECRET.
****

Copy No......

76TH. INFANTRY BRIGADE ADMINISTRATIVE INSTRUCTIONS.
(To accompany 76th. Inf.Bde.Order No.171).

1. BILLETS. Units will be accommodated in the new area to-morrow as follows:-

Bde. H.Q., 76th.T.M.Bty., 2nd.Suffolk Rgt.	SOY. FISENNE
529th.Field Coy.R.E.	~~ST.~~ SOY
1st.Gordon Hrs., 8th.K.O.R.L., No.2 Coy.Train.	HOTTON.
20th.K.R.R.C.	MELREUX.
No.7 Field Ambce.	HOTTON ~~[illegible]~~.

2. BILLETING PARTIES. The billeting lorry will collect billeting parties as under :-

1 Officer, 1 Interpreter and 2 N.C.O.'s of each of 8th.K.O.R.L., 1st.Gordon Hrs., and 2nd.Suffolk Rgt. will meet the lorry at NETINNE at 07-15 hours.

1 Officer and 1 N.C.O. of each of 529th. Field Coy. and No.2 Coy.Train will meet the lorry in the Main Street, HEURE, at 07-35 hours.

The lorry will then proceed to Brigade H.Q. to pick up 1 Off. and 1 O.R. of T.M.Bty., 1 Off. and 2 N.C.O.'s of 20th.K.R.R.C., and Staff Captain at 08-00 hours.

Billeting Parties of 4 N.C.O.'s from each Battalion and 2 from each of 529th.Field Coy., 7th.Field Ambce and 76th.T.M.Bty. will proceed on bicycles to their various villages.

3. GUIDES. Guides will meet their units at the entrance to their villages at times to be arranged by Billeting Officers.

4. PRESENT BILLETS. Will be left scrupulously clean. Billeting Certificates will be rendered to the BURGERMEISTER of respective villages before departure of units.

The 9th.Inf.Bde. will take over billets of 20th.K.R.R.C. at BAILLONVILLE.

The 8th.Inf.Bde. will take over billets of all units (less 20th.K.R.R.C.).

Rear Parties will be left behind to hand over to Billeting Officers of these Brigades. They will proceed to join their units after handing over.

S Eastwood 2Lt for
Captain,
Staff Captain, 76th. Infantry Brigade.

4/12/18.

S.C.

III

SECRET.
****

Copy No.....

76th. INFANTRY BRIGADE ORDER NO..172..
****

Ref. Map 1/100,000. ....Dec 5th.......... 1918.

1. The Brigade Group will move tomorrow Dec. 6th in accordance with march table overleaf to ODEIGNE - GRANDMENIL area

2. Brigade H.Q. will close at present location at 09.30 and open at MANHAY on arrival.

3. ACKNOWLEDGE.

C. Clifford Captain,
Brigade Major, 76th. Infantry Brigade.

Issued at 16.30 hours.

Distribution:-
1. 8th. K.O.R.L.
2. 2nd. Suffolk Regt.
3. 1st. Gordon Hldrs.
4. 76th. T.M.B.
5. 20th. K.R.R.C.
6. 529th. Field Coy R.E.
7. 7th. Field Amb.
8. No.2 Coy Train.
9. Bde. Transport Offr.
10. " Signal "
11. " Int. "
12. S.C..
13. 3rd. Div. "G".
14. File.
15. War Diary.
16. "

MARCH TABLE.

ROUTE:- EREZEE - GRANDMENIL.

STARTING POINT:- Cross roads [illegible]. (800 yards North East of O in SOY).

Schedule No.	Unit.	Time to pass starting point.	Instructions.
			Destination:-
1.	Bde.H.Q.,[illegible]th.I.B.& 1 Sectn.[illegible]th.Fd.Co.R.E.	10.00	MANHAY.
2.	2nd.Suffolk Regt.	.02	ODEIGNE.
[illegible]	1st.Gordon Hldrs.	.06	LA FOSSE and OSTER.
4.	8th.K.O.R.L.	.11	VAUX CHAVANNE.
[illegible]	20th.K.R.R.C.(Pioneers).	.16	GRANDMENIL. 1 Coy to report to No.2 Coy Train at HOTTON to follow No.8.
6.	[illegible]th.Fd.Co.R.E.(less 1 Sectn.).	.21	MALEMPRE.
7.	[illegible]th.Field Amb.	.24	MALEMPRE.
8.	1st.Line Transport of Group.	.26	.... Rendezvous HOTTON. Pick up vehicles of Nos.1,2 & 6 at SOY.
[illegible]	No.4 Coy Train,Pool Wagons of 20th.K.R.R.C.,all Train Transport of Group.	.40	MANHAY. Rendezvous HOTTON. Pick up vehicles of Nos.1,2 & 6 at SOY.

\-\- \-\- \-\- \-\- \-\-

III

SECRET.

Copy No. 12......

1.. BILLETS. Accommodation in the new area will be allotted as under:-

2nd.Suffolk Rgt. and 76th.T.M.Bty.	ODEIGNE.
1st.Gordon Hrs.	LA FOSSE A OSTER.
20th.K.R.R.C.	GRANDMENIL.
8th.K.O.R.L.Rgt.	VAUX CHAVANNE.
No.7 Field Ambce. & 529th.Field Coy.	MALEMPRE.
Brigade H.Q. & No.2 Coy. Train.	MANHAY.

2. BILLETING PARTIES. The billeting lorry will pick up 1 Officer and 2 N.C.O.'s from each of 1st.Gordon Hrs., 20th.K.R.R.C. and 8th.K.O.R.L., and 1 Officer and 1 O.R. from each of No.2 Coy. Train and 7th. Field Ambce. at the Bridge across the river at HOTTON at 07-30 hours to-morrow, 9th.Instant.

The lorry will then proceed to Brigade H.Q., FISENNE, where it will pick up 1 Officer and 2 N.C.O.'s of 2nd.Suffolk Rgt., 1 Officer and 1 N.C.O. each of 529th.Field Coy. and 76th.T.M.Bty., and the Staff Captain at 08-00 hours.

4 N.C.O.'s from each Battalion and 2 N.C.O.'s from each of 7th.Field Ambce., 529th.Field Coy. will proceed on bicycles to their respective areas, meeting their Officers on arrival.

3. GUIDES. Will meet their units under arrangements to be made by Billeting Officers.

4. PRESENT BILLETS. Will be left scrupulously clean. Billeting certificates will be rendered to the BURGERMEISTER of respective villages before departure of units.

All billets at SOY and HOTTON will be taken over by 8th.Inf. Bde. A rear party will be left behind to hand over billets to advance parties of 8th. Inf.Bde.

Billets in new area are poor, both for Officers and men. Billeting Officers must be prepared to billet close to ensure that all men are under cover.

G. Eastwood 2Lt for
Captain,
Staff Captain, 76th. Infantry Brigade.

8/12/18.

SECRET.

Copy No.12.....

76TH. INFANTRY BRIGADE ADMINISTRATIVE INSTRUCTIONS.
(To accompany 76th. Inf.Bde. Order No. 178)

1. BILLETS. Accommodation in the new area is allotted as under :-

2nd. Suffolk Rgt.	ODEIGNE.
1st.Gordon Hrs.	MALEMPRE.
20th.K.R.R.C., No. 2 Coy. Train.	GRANDMENIL.
8th.K.O.R.L.Rgt.	VAUX CHAVANNE.
No.7 Field Ambce.	LA FOSSE.
529th.Field Coy.R.E.	OSTER LE BATTE.
Brigade H.Q. & T.M.Bty.	MANHAY.

2. BILLETING PARTIES. The billeting lorry will pick up 1 Officer and 2 N.C.O.'s from each of 1st.Gordon Hrs., 20th.K.R.R.C. and 8th.K.O.R.L., and 1 Officer and 1 O.R. from each of No.2 Coy. Train and 7th. Field Ambce. at the Bridge across the river at HOTTON at 07-30 hours to-morrow, 9th.instant.

The lorry will then proceed to Brigade H.Q., FISENNE, where it will pick up 1 Officer and 2 N.C.O.'s of 2nd.Suffolk Rgt., 1 Officer and 1 N.C.O. each of 529th.Field Coy. and 76th.T.M.Bty., and the Staff Captain at 08-00 hours.

4 N.C.O.'s from each Battalion and 2 N.C.O.'s from each of 7th.Field Ambce., 529th.Field Coy. will proceed on bicycles to their respective areas, meeting their Officers on arrival.

3. GUIDES. Will meet their units under arrangements to be made by Billeting Officers.

4. PRESENT BILLETS. Will be left scrupulously clean. Billeting certificates will be rendered to the BURGERMEISTER of respective villages before departure of units.

All billets at SOY and HOTTON will be taken over by 8th.Inf. Bde. A rear party will be left behind to hand over billets to advance parties of 8th. Inf.Bde.

Billets in new area are poor, both for Officers and men. Billeting Officers must be prepared to billet close to ensure that all men are under cover.

G Eastwood 2Lt for.
Captain,
Staff Captain, 76th. Infantry Brigade.

8/12/18.

IV

War Diary

SECRET.
****

Copy No.....

76th.INFANTRY BRIGADE ORDER NO..173
****

Ref.Map 1/100,000. ....Dec 6th.... 1918.

1. The Brigade Group will move tomorrow Dec. 7th in accordance with march table overleaf to OTTRE - MALEMPRE area

2. Brigade H.Q.will close at present location at 09.00 and open at HEBRONVAL on arrival.

3. ACKNOWLEDGE.

Captain,
Issued at hours. Brigade Major, 76th. Infantry Brigade.

Distribution:-

1. 8th.K.O.R.L.
2. 2nd.Suffolk Regt.
3. 1st.Gordon Hldrs.
4. 76th.T.M.B.
5. 20th.K.R.R.C.
6. 529th.Field Coy R.E.
7. 7th.Field Amb.
8. No.2 Coy Train.
9. Bde.Transport Offr.
10. " Signal "
11. " Int. "
12. S.C..
13. 3rd.Div."G".
14. File.
15. War Diary.
16. "

MARCH TABLE.

ROUTE:- BELLE HAIE - REGNE.

STARTING POINT:- Road junction 51.Y7.42. (1000 yards South East of Y in MANNAY).

Schedule No.	Unit.	Time to pass starting point:-	Instructions. Destination:-
1.	Bde.H.Q.	10.00	[illegible]CONVAL.
2.	2nd.Suffolk Regt.	10.01	O[illegible]IGNE.
3.	1st.Gordon Hldrs.	10.05	O[illegible].
4.	8th.K.O.R.L.	10.10	R[illegible]NE.
5.	1st.Line Transport of Nos.1,2, 3 and 4.	10.15	Rendezvous MANNAY.
6.	[illegible] Train and S.S.wagons of Nos.1 to 4.	10.20	REGNE. Rendezvous MANNAY.
7.	20th.K.R.R.C.(Pioneers).	10.30	[illegible]. via cross roads 71.35.39.
8.	[illegible].W.Co.R.E.& 76th.T.M.B.	10.35	[illegible]RAITURE. via LES ANNAIS.
9.	7th.Field Amb.	10.38	[illegible]IGNE. via LES ANNAIS.
10.	1st.Line transport and baggage wagons of Nos.7,8 and 9.	10.40	

SECRET.

Copy No. 12...

76TH. INFANTRY BRIGADE ADMINISTRATIVE INSTRUCTIONS
(To accompany 76th.Inf.Bde. Order No. 17[illegible]).

1 BILLETS. Units will be accommodated in the new area to-morrow as under :-

Brigade H.Q.	~~[illegible]~~ HEBRONVAL.
1st.Gordon Hrs.	OTTRE.
8th.K.O.R.L.Rgt.	REGNE.
2nd.Suffolk Rgt.& 7th.Field Ambce.	ODEIGNE.
20th.K.R.R.C.	MALEMPRE.
529th. Field Coy. & 76th. T.M.Bty.	FRAITURE.
No. 2 Coy.Train.	Main Road, REGNE.

2. BILLETING PARTIES. Billeting Parties of 2nd.Suffolk Rgt., 20th. K.R.R.C. and No.7 Field Ambce. will proceed to new areas under their own arrangements.

Billeting Parties of 529th.Field Coy. and 76th. T.M.Bty. will meet ~~[illegible]~~ the billeting lorry at FANZEL Church at 07-30 hours.

The lorry will then proceed to Brigade H.Q., where it will pick up billeting parties of 1 Officer, 1 Interpreter and 2 N.C.O.'s from each of 8th.K.O.R.L.Rgt. and 1st.Gordon Hrs., 2 N.C.O.'s of Bde H.Q., and 1 Officer and 1 N.C.O. of No.2 Coy. Train at 08-00 hours.

4 N.C.O.'s from each of 8th.K.O.R.L., and 1st.Gordon Hrs., and 2 N.C.O.'s of 529th.Field Coy. and No.2 Coy. Train will proceed on bicycles to their various villages to meet Billeting Officers.

3. GUIDES. Guides will meet their units at times and points to be arranged by their Billeting Officers.

4. PRESENT BILLETS. Will be taken over by 9th. Inf.Bde. They must be left scrupulously clean. Each units will leave a rear party to hand over billets to advance parties of 9th.Inf.Bde.

Billeting Certificates will be rendered to the BURGERMEISTER of the Commune in which villages are situated before departure of units.

[signature]
Captain,
6/12/18. Staff Captain, 76th. Infantry Brigade.

VI

War Diary

SECRET.
****

Copy No.....

76th. INFANTRY BRIGADE ORDER NO. 174.
****

Ref. Map 1/100,000. ....Dec 7th........ 1918.

1. The Brigade Group will move tomorrow Dec 8th in accordance with march table overleaf to BOVIGNY - JOUBIEVAL area

2. Brigade H.Q. will close at present location at 09.30 and open at CIERREUX HALTE on arrival.

3. ACKNOWLEDGE.

C. Clutter
Captain,
Brigade Major, 76th. Infantry Brigade.

Issued at 15.30 hours.

Distribution:-

1. 8th. K.O.R.L.
2. 2nd. Suffolk Regt.
3. 1st. Gordon Hldrs.
4. 76th. T.M.B.
5. 20th. K.R.R.C.
6. 529th. Field Coy R.E.
7. 7th. Field Amb.
8. No.2 Coy Train.
9. Bde. Transport Offr.
10. " Signal "
11. " Int. "
12. S.C..
13. 3rd. Div. "G".
14. File.
15. War Diary.
16. "

MARCH TABLE.

ROUTE:- SALMCHATEAU.

STARTING POINT:- Crossing of JOUBIEVAL - SART Road with main HEBRONVAL - SALMCHATEAU Road.

Schedule No.	Unit.	Time to pass starting point.	Instructions. Destination:-
1.	Bde.H.Q., 76th.T.M.B. & 1 Sectn. [illegible] Fd.Co.	10.30	CIERREUX HALTE.
2.	1st.Gordon Hldrs	10.32	COUSTIL.
3.	8th.K.O.R.L.	10.37	BOVIGNY.
4.	1st.Line transport of Nos.1, 2 and 3	10.42	
5.	Head.Coy Train and [illegible] wagons of Nos.1, 2 and 3	10.47	LONGCHAMPS.
6.	[illegible]	11.07	CIERREUX.
7.	9th.Field Amb.	11.10	HONVELEZ.
8.	2nd.Suffolk Regt.	11.12	GRAND SART.
9.	20th.K.R.R.C.(Pioneers)	11.16	PETIT SART & JOUBIEVAL.
10.	1st.Line transport and baggage wagons of Nos.6,7,8,9.	11.21	

-- -- -- -- --

SECRET.

Copy No...16...

76TH. INFANTRY BRIGADE ADMINISTRATIVE INSTRUCTIONS.
(To accompany 76th.Inf.Bde Order No. 174).

1. BILLETS. Units will be accommodated in the new area as follows:-

1st. Gordon Hrs.	COURTIL.
8th.K.O.R.L.Rgt.	BOVIGNY.
529th.Field Coy.,R.E.	CIERREUX.
Brigade H.Q. and 76th.T.M.Battery.	CIERREUX Chateau.
No.2 Coy.,3rd.Div.Train.	LONGCHAMPS.
2nd.Suffolk Rgt.	GRAND SART.
20th.K.R.R.C.	PETIT SART. + JOUBIEVAL
No.7 Field Ambce.	HONVELEZ.

2. BILLETING PARTIES. 1 Officer and 2 N.C.O.'s from each of 2nd. Suffolk Rgt. and 20th.K.R.R.C. will meet the Billeting Lorry at the Cross Roads from MALEMPRE to ODEIGNE on the Main Road by the 99 Kilo.Post at 07-15 hours. The lorry will then proceed to Brigade H.Q., where it will pick up 1 Officer and 2 N.C.O.'s from each of 8th.K.O.R.L.Rgt., and 1st.Gordon Hrs., and 1 Officer and 1 N.C.O. of each of 529th.Field Coy., 76th.T.M.Battery and No.2 Coy. Train at 08-00 hours.

4 N.C.O.'s from each of 8th.K.O.R.L., 2nd.Suffolk Rgt.,1st. Gordon Hrs. and 20th.K.R.R.C., and 2 N.C.O.'s each of 529th. Field Coy., 76th.T.M.Bty. and No.2 Coy. Train will proceed on bicycles to meet their Billeting Officers at their respective villages.

3. GUIDES. Will meet their units at times and points to be arranged by their Billeting Officers.

4. PRESENT BILLETS. Will be taken over by 9th.Inf.Bde. They must be left perfectly clean. Each unit will leave a rear party to hand over billets to advance parties of 9th.Inf.Bde.

Billeting Certificates will be rendered to the BURGOMEISTER of respective villages before departure of units.

T.J. [signature]
Captain,
Staff Captain, 76th. Infantry Brigade.

7/12/18.

"A" Form. Army Form C. 2121. (In pads of 100.)

MESSAGES AND SIGNALS.

No. of Message............

Prefix........ Code.......... m. | Words. | Charge.

Office of Origin and Service Instructions.

Sent At........m. To........ By........

This message is on a/c of: .... *Service.* (Signature of "Franking Officer.")

Recd. at .... m. Date........ From........ By........

TO { 8th KORL 76th IMB 7th Yd Ambce. 2nd Suffolk Regt 20th KRRC No 2 [illegible] Train 1st Gordon Hdrs 529 Fd Coy RE 3rd D.A.C.

Sender's Number.	Day of Month.	In reply to Number.	AAA
* 9791	8		

1 Following moves will take place tomorrow Dec 9th :-

Unit	From	To	Start
1st Gordon Hdrs	COURTIL	BEHO	10.00
8th KORL	VIELSALM	COURTIL	09.00
20th KRRC	COMTÉ	BOVIGNY	09.45
2nd Suffolk Regt	SART	ROGERY	09.45
7th Yd Ambce	CIERREUX	HONVELEZ	09.00
No 2 Coy Train	CIERREUX	LONGCHAMPS	09.20
529 Fd Coy RE	no move		
Bde HQ 76 IMB	no move		

2 Acknowledge

From 76 Inf Bde

Place

Time 22.00

The above may be forwarded as now corrected. (Z) C. Clutterbuck Capt

Censor. Signature of Addressor or person authorised to telegraph in his name.

*This line, except AAA, should be erased if not required.

Wt. W 3253/P511. 500,000 Pads. 1/18. B. & S. Ltd. (E2389.)

VII

War Diary

SECRET.
****

Copy No.....

76th. INFANTRY BRIGADE ORDER NO. 175.
****

Ref. Map 1/100,000. (Paper) ....Dec. 10th.......... 1918.

1. The Brigade Group will move tomorrow Dec. 11th in accordance with march table overleaf to NEUNDORF - NEIDINGEN - THOMMEN area.

2. Brigade H.Q. will close at present location at 07.30 and open at 1000 yds north west of first G in GRUFFLINGEN on arrival.

3. ACKNOWLEDGE.

4. All troops will march past the Corps Commander with fixed bayonets. Officers will not wear cloaks.

C. Chippin, Captain,
Brigade Major, 76th. Infantry Brigade.

Issued at 20.15 hours.

Distribution:-

1. 8th. K.O.R.L.
2. 2nd. Suffolk Regt.
3. 1st. Gordon Hldrs.
4. 76th. T.M.B.
5. 20th. K.R.R.C.
6. 529th. Field Coy R.E.
7. 7th. Field Amb.
8. No.2 Coy Train.
9. Bde. Transport Offr.
10. " Signal "
11. " Int. "
12. S.C..
13. 3rd. Div. "G".
14. File.
15. War Diary.
16. "

MARCH TABLE.

ROUTE:- MALDINGEN.

STARTING POINT:- Road junction 500 yards North of R in BEHO.

Schedule No.	Unit.	Time to pass starting point.	Instructions.
			Instructions:-
1.	Bde.H.Q.& 76th.T.M.B.	10.00	1000 yds.[illegible] of first G in GRUFFLINGEN.
2.	229th.Field Coy.R.E.	10.01	[illegible]
3.	1st.Gordon Hldrs.	10.05	[illegible] via ST.VITH.
4.	8th.K.O.R.L.	10.10	KRONBACH via [illegible]
5.	20th.K.R.R.C.	10.15	THOMMEN.
6.	2nd.Suffolk Regt.	10.20	BRAUNLAUF & [illegible].
7.	7th.Field Amb.	10.24	GRUFFLINGEN.
8.	1st.Line Transport of Group....	10.26	
9.	No.2 Coy Train, G.S.Tool Wagons of 20th.K.R.R.C., all Train Transport............	10.36	GRUFFLINGEN.

-- -- -- -- -- --

War Diary

VII

SECRET.
****

Copy No.....

76th. INFANTRY BRIGADE ORDER NO. 175.
****

Ref. Map 1/100,000. (Paper) ......Dec. 10th....... 1918.

1. The Brigade Group will move tomorrow Dec. 11th in accordance with march table overleaf to NEUNDORF – NEIDINGEN – THOMMEN Area.

2. Brigade H.Q. will close at present location at 07.30 and open at 1000 yds north west of first G in GRUFFLINGEN on arrival.

3. ACKNOWLEDGE.

4. All troops will march past the Corps Commander with fixed bayonets. Officers will not wear cloaks.

C. Chiffin. Captain.
Brigade Major, 76th. Infantry Brigade.

Issued at 20.45 hours.

Distribution:-

1. 8th. K.O.R.L.
2. 2nd. Suffolk Regt.
3. 1st. Gordon Hldrs.
4. 76th. T.M.B.
5. 20th. K.R.R.C.
6. 529th. Field Coy R.E.
7. 7th. Field Amb.
8. No.2 Coy Train.
9. Bde. Transport Offr.
10. " Signal "
11. " Int. "
12. S.C.
13. 3rd. Div. "G".
14. File.
15. War Diary.
16. "

G.O.C.

SPECIAL ORDER OF THE DAY
by Brigadier-General F.E. METCALFE, C.M.G., D.S.O.,
Commanding 76th. Infantry Brigade.

TO ALL TROOPS OF 76TH. INFANTRY BRIGADE GROUP.

In a few days' time you will have crossed the frontier and will be part of the Allied Army in occupation of German Territory. Do not allow your natural kindness of heart to blind you to the fact that you are in an enemy country and that the residents are still our enemies, in spite of any protestations they may make to the contrary.

They are the same people whose national boast for 40 years was the coming of "THE DAY" when they would destroy the British Empire and set their foot upon the neck of Europe;

who have consistently and brazenly broken and derided all international Laws of War;

who boasted that treaties are "scraps of paper" to be cast aside with impunity along with their pledged word and their national honour ;

who introduced into a struggle of unparalleled bitterness horrors and abuses never previously conceived in the history of the world, adding to the sum of their despicable crimes the use of gas and the explosive bullet ;

Who rejoiced in the bombing of open cities and the murder of innocent women and children ;

Who, as a mark of national triumph, rang joybells throughout the country and struck and distributed special medals to commemorate the sinking of the "LUSITANIA" and the murder of her civilian passengers, whilst the Commander of the submarine responsible for the atrocity was decorated with the highest award that the Emperor could bestow ;

whose women, at COLOGNE in 1914, spat at wounded and starving British Prisoners, and threw soup in their faces rather than alleviate their agony ;

who, in the same year, foully tortured, and finally cut to pieces, the Mayor and Curé of SPONTIN because they endeavoured to protect civilians from murder and rape.

They hated us then. Do they love us now that we have been so largely instrumental in bringing their evil plans to nought ?

You have endured over 4 years of horrors such as have never been known before. There can be but few among you who have not lost relatives or dear friends in defence of Honour, Justice and Right.

DO NOT FORGET IT.

Your wounded have been bayonetted, your prisoners have been starved, tortured, driven mad and murdered by the people amongst whom you will presently be living. They will endeavour to make you believe that they know nothing of these things, that they are animated with the warmest feelings towards you, and that the sins of the minority must not be visited on the majority.

Do not be blinded to facts. The proofs that the atrocities repeatedly committed by the German Armies were fully supported by the German Nation are overwhelming. " Leave the conquered nothing but their eyes to weep with " has been the National Motto. At the bottom of their hearts they hate us all. Friendliness on our part will be regarded as national weakness.

Let your demeanour be consistently courteous, as it has always been, but have no friendly dealings with any of them.

Respect scrupulously the property and houses which you may occupy.

Let the German nation learn that an Army of Occupation can conduct itself honourably, and, seeing your conduct and your contempt of their advances, let them thereby measure the more accurately the depth to which they have fallen in the eyes of Europe and of all just and right-thinking people.

:-:-:-:-:-:-:-:

In the Field.

9th.December 1918.

SECRET.

Copy No....15....

76TH. INFANTRY BRIGADE ADMINISTRATIVE INSTRUCTIONS.
(To accompany 76th.Inf.Bde.Order No.178)

1. BILLETS. Accommodation in new area is allotted as under :-

		Accommodation demanded from village headmen.	
		Officers.	Other Ranks.
1st.Gordon Hrs.	BREITFELD.	15	400
	NEIDINGEN.	20	500
8th.K.O.R.L. Rgt.	KROMBACH.	35	800
2nd.Suffolk Rgt.	WEISTEN.	10	200
	BRAUNLAUF.	20	500
	Battalion H.Q.:- BRAUNLAUF.		
20th.K.R.R.C.	THOMMEN.	30	800
529th.Field Coy.	NEUNDORF.	9	250
Brigade H.Q.) No.7 Field Ambce.,No.2 Coy. Train.)	GRUFFLINGEN.	20 Off.	800
76th.T.M.Battery.	NEUBRÜCK.		

2. BILLETING PARTIES. No Billeting Lorry is available. Billeting Parties will proceed under own arrangements to their various villages. Village Headmen have been ordered to meet Billeting Parties as follows:-

1st.Gordon Hrs.	BREITFELD	at Post House	at 09-00 hours.
	NEIDINGEN	" Church	" 09-00 "
8th.K.O.R.L.Rgt.	KROMBACH	" Church	" 09-00 "
2nd.Suffolk Rgt.	BRAUNLAUF	" Church	" 08-30 "
20th.K.R.R.C.	THOMMEN	" Church	" 09-00 "
529th.Field Coy.	NEUNDORF.	" Church	" 09-00 "
Bde.H.Q., 7th.F.A.) No.2 Coy.Train.)	GRUFFLINGEN N.W. of 1st.G in GRUFFLINGEN	" Cross Roads ½ mile	" 09-00 "

All Billeting Parties should, if possible, include an Officer or N.C.O. who can speak German.

3. PRESENT BILLETS. Will be left in a clean and sanitary condition. The billets of 1st.Gordon Hldrs. will be taken over by 9th.Inf.Bde. A rear party will be left behind by this Battalion to hand over billets to advance party of 9th.Inf.Bde. Billeting Certificates will be rendered to the BURGERMEISTER of various Communes before departure of units.

10/12/18.

Captain,
Staff Captain, 76th. Infantry Brigade.

War Diary

VIII

SECRET.
****

Copy No.....

76th. INFANTRY BRIGADE ORDER NO. 176
****

Ref. Map 1/100,000. (Belgium) Dec 11th 1918.

1. The Brigade Group will move tomorrow Dec. 12th in accordance with march table overleaf to MANDERFELD - SCHÖNBERG Area

2. Brigade H.Q. will close at present location at 07.30 and open at MANDERFELD on arrival.

3. ACKNOWLEDGE. (100 yards S.W. of church)

C. Chaplin Captain.

Issued at hours. Brigade Major, 76th. Infantry Brigade.

Distribution:-

1. 8th. K.O.R.L.
2. 2nd. Suffolk Regt.
3. 1st. Gordon Hldrs.
4. 76th. T.M.B.
5. 20th. K.R.R.C.
6. 529th. Field Coy R.E.
7. 7th. Field Amb.
8. No.2 Coy Train.
9. Bde. Transport Offr.
10. " Signal "
11. " Int. "
12. S.C.
13. 3rd. Div. "G".
14. File.
15. War Diary.
16. "

MARCH TABLE.

ROUTE:- AITZRATH.

STARTING POINT:- Railway crossing 400 yards South of 2 in ST.VITH.

Schedule No.	Unit.	Time to pass starting point.	Instructions.
			Destination:
1.	Bde.H.Q.& 78th.[illegible]	10.00	WANDERFELD.(100 yds [illegible]
2.	89th.Field Coy R.E.	10.01	ANDLER.Not to [illegible] Road.
3.	1st.Gordon Hldrs.	10.08	EMETINKEL & WANDERFELD.Not to pass starting point beforehand.
4.	8th.K.O.R.L.(less 1 Coy)	10.10	WANDERFELD [illegible] RHEDORF [illegible] ST.VITH [illegible]
5.	20th.K.R.R.C.(Pioneers)	10.15	BRUGH,AITZRATH [illegible]
6.	2nd.Suffolk Regt.	10.20	SCHONBERG.[illegible] ST.VITH Rd.
7.	7th.Field Amb.	10.24	SCHONBERG.
8.	1st.Line Transport of Group	10.26	
9.	No.2 Coy Train,R.E.Tool Wagons of 20th.K.R.R.C.,all Train Transport	10.30	SCHONBERG.
10.	1 Coy 8th.K.O.R.L.,to follow No.9 from starting point.		

\-\- \-\- \-\- \-\- \-\- \-\-

IX

SECRET.
****

Copy No.....

76th.INFANTRY BRIGADE ORDER NO. 177

Ref: Map 1/100,000. (paper) Dec 13th 1918.

1. The Brigade Group will move tomorrow Dec 13th in accordance with march table overleaf to BAASEM - HALLSCHLAG area

2. Brigade H.Q. will close at present location at 10.00 and open at Post House BAASEM on arrival.

3. ACKNOWLEDGE.

C. Clutter Captain,
Issued at hours. Brigade Major, 76th: Infantry Brigade.

Distribution:-

1. 8th.K.O.R.L.
2. 2nd.Suffolk Regt.
3. 1st.Gordon Hldrs.
4. 76th.T.M.B.
5. 20th.K.R.R.C.
6. 529th.Field Coy R.E.
7. 7th.Field Amb.
8. No.2 Coy Train.
9. Bde.Transport Offr.
10. " Signal "
11. " Int. "
12. S.C..
13. 3rd.Div."G".
14. File.
15. War Diary.
16. "

MARCH TABLE.

****

ROUTE:- HALLSCHLAG.

STARTING POINT:- Road junction 700 yards East of MANDERFELD.

Schedule No.	Unit.	Time to pass starting point.	Instructions. Destination:-
1.	Bde.H.Q.& 76th.T.M.B.	11.00	BAASEM. Via road junct.1500 yards South of M in BAASEM.
2. *	529th.Field Coy R.E.	11.01	FRAUENKRON. Leave transport at road junct. 1100 yards North of S in HALLSCHLAG.
3.	8th.K.O.R.L.	11.05	BAASEM. Via road junct.1500 yards South of M in BAASEM.
4. *	20th.K.R.R.C.	11.10	HALLSCHLAG.
5. *	2nd.Suffolk Regt.	11.15	KRONENBURG.
6. *	7th.Field Amb.	11.19	BERK. Leave transport at road junct.1100 yards North of S in HALLSCHLAG.
7. *	1st.Line Transport of above	11.21	Rendezvous MANDERFELD.
8. *	No.2 Coy Train,G.S.Tool Wagons of 20th.K.R.R.C.,all Train Transport of above	11.26	KRONENBURG. Rendezvous MANDERFELD.
9.	1st.Gordon Hldrs with 1st.Line Transport and Baggage Wagons		FACTORY 1 mile S.W.of HALLSCHLAG.(Not on map).Any Route. Not to leave MANDERFELD till No.8 is clear. To be clear of area by 12.00.

* Note hill with bad surface East of ANDLER.

** ** ** ** **

SECRET.

Copy No....15...

76TH. INFANTRY BRIGADE ADMINISTRATIVE INSTRUCTIONS.
(To accompany 76th.Inf.Bde.Order No.176).

1. BILLETS. Accommodation is allotted in the new area as under :-

		Accommodation demanded from Burgermeister or Village Headman.	
		Officers.	O.R.
1st.Gordon Hldrs.	KREWINKEL.	20	400
	MANDERFELD.	12	350
	(Battalion H.Q.:- MANDERFELD).		
8th.K.O.R.L.Rgt.	MANDERFELD.	20	600
	HASENVENN.	6	200
	(Battalion H.Q.:- MANDERVELD).		
2nd.Suffolk Rgt.	SCHONBERG.	25	800
20th.K.R.R.C.	HEUEM.	15	400
	ATZERATH.	12	300
	SETZ.	8	200
	(Battalion H.Q.:- HEUEM).		
529th.Field Coy.R.E.	ANDLER.	9	160
76th.T.M.Battery.	ANDLER.	5	40
No.7 Field Ambce.	SCHONBERG.	4	100
Brigade H.Q.	MANDERFELD.	8	150
	(Brigade H.Q.:- Billet No.88).		

2. BILLETING PARTIES. No billeting lorry is available. Billeting Parties will proceed under own arrangements to their various villages.

Burgermeister and Village Headmen have been ordered to meet billeting parties as follows:-

1st.Gordon Hrs.	KREWINKEL	at Billet No.1	at	09-00 hours.
	MANDERFELD.	Burgermeister's Office (Billet No.82)	at	09-00 "
Brigade H.Q.	Do.	Do.		Do.
8th.K.O.R.L.	MANDERFELD) HASENVENN)	Do.		Do.
2nd.Suffolk Rgt.	SCHONBERG.	Burgermeister's Office (Billet No.32) (Turn left by bridge over river).		08-30 hours.
No.7 Field Ambce.	Do.	Do.		Do.
No.2 Coy.3rd.Div.Train.	Do.	Do.		Do.
529th.Field Coy.) 76th.T.M.Bty.)	ANDLER	Billet No.11	at	09-00 hours.
20th.K.R.R.C.	SETZ	Billet No.7(Post House)		08-15 "
	ATZERATH	Bridge across stream		08-15 "
	HEUEM.	Billet No.16		08-30 "

Close billeting will be necessary in all cases to avoid long marches on bad roads.

3. PRESENT BILLETS. 9th.Inf.Bde. will take over all billets unit for unit. Each unit will leave a rear party to hand over billets to advance party of 9th.Inf.Bde.

All billets must be left scrupulously clean.

/12/18.

Captain,
Staff Captain, 76th. Infantry Brigade.

SECRET.

Copy No. 16.

76th. INFANTRY BRIGADE ORDER NO. 178.

Ref: Map 1/100,000. (paper) 13th Dec 1918.

1. The Brigade Group will move tomorrow 14th Dec. in accordance with march table overleaf to BLANKENHEIM-DAHLEM Area

2. Brigade H.Q. will close at present location at 10.00 hours and open at KÖLNER HOF, BLANKENHEIM on arrival.

3. ACKNOWLEDGE.

C. Chipps
Captain,
Issued at hours. Brigade Major, 76th. Infantry Brigade.

Distribution:-

1. 8th. K.O.R.L.
2. 2nd. Suffolk Regt.
3. 1st. Gordon Hldrs.
4. 76th. T.M.B.
5. 20th. K.R.R.C.
6. 529th. Field Coy R.E.
7. 7th. Field Amb.
8. No.2. Coy Train.
9. Bde. Transport Offr.
10. " Signal "
11. " Int. "
12. S.C.
13. 3rd. Div. "G".
14. File.
15. War Diary.
16. "

MARCH TABLE.

****

ROUTE:-

DAHLEM.

STARTING POINT:-

Road Junction 1000 yards North-West of S in STADTKYLL.

Schedule No.	Unit.	Time to pass starting point.	Instructions.
1.	Bde.H.Q. and T.M.Bty.	11-00 hours.	BLANKENHEIM (KÖLNER HOF)
2.	529th.Field Coy.	11-01 "	BLANKENHEIM.
3.	8th.K.O.R.L.Rgt.	11-05 "	SCHMIDTHEIM.
4.	20th.K.R.R.C.(less 1 Coy.)	11-10 "	SCHMIDTHEIM.
5.	2nd.Suffolk Rgt.	11-14 "	DAHLEM.
6.	1st.Gordon Hrs.	11-18 "	DAHLEM.
7.	7th.Field Ambce.	11-23 "	BLANKENHEIM.
8.	1st.Line Transport of Group	11-25 "	
9.	No.2 Coy.Train, G.S.Tool Wagons of 20th.K.R.R.C.; all Train Transport	11-35 "	BLANKENHEIM.
10.	1 Coy.20th.K.R.R.C.	to follow No. 9.	

NOTE:- There are two long, steep hills on the march, one between starting point and DAHLEM, and the other between DAHLEM and SCHMIDTHEIM.

SECRET.

Copy No. 16......

76TH. INFANTRY BRIGADE ADMINISTRATIVE INSTRUCTIONS.
(To accompany 76th.Inf.Bde.Order No.178).

1. BILLETS. Accommodation in the new area is allotted as follows:-

		Officers.	O.R.
Brigade H.Q. and 76th.T.M.Bty.	BLANKENHEIM.	11	190
229th.Field Coy.,R.E.	Do.	9	200
No.7 Field Ambce.	Do.	9	200
	(Brigade H.Q.:- Hotel KÖLNERHOF).		
8th.K.O.R.L.Rgt.	SCHMIDTHEIM (Schloss and N.end)	27	700
20th.K.R.R.C.	SCHMIDTHEIM	30	800
1st.Gordon Hrs.	DAHLEM.	32	750
2nd.Suffolk Rgt.	DAHLEM.	25	650

2. BILLETING PARTIES. No billeting lorry is available. Billeting Parties will proceed under own arrangements to their various villages.
Billeting Officers should report to Bürgermeister as follows and hand in attached Billet Demands:-

BLANKENHEIM. Bürgermeister's House in Main St. at 09-00 hours.

SCHMIDTHEIM. Town Hall (under railway bridge & turn left) at 09-00 "

DAHLEM. Billet No.110 (Western entrance to village) at 08-30 "

3. PRESENT BILLETS. Will be taken over unit for unit by 9th.Inf.Bde. Each ~~[illegible]~~ unit will leave a rear party to hand over billets to advance parties of 9th.Inf.Bde. All billets must be left ~~[illegible]~~ scrupulously clean.
Divisional H.Q. will take over Factory now being occupied by 1st.Gordon Hldrs.

H Eastwood Lt for
Captain,
Staff Captain,76th. Infantry Brigade.

13/12/18.

XI

SECRET.
****

Copy No..15...

76th.INFANTRY BRIGADE ORDER NO...179

Ref. Map 1/100,000. ....Dec 14th........ 1918.

1. The Brigade Group will move tomorrow Dec 15th in accordance with march table overleaf to EICHERSCHEID - TONDORF Area

2. Brigade H.Q. will close at present location at 09.00 and open at EICHERSCHEID on arrival.

3. ACKNOWLEDGE.

C. Chiffer
Captain,
Brigade Major, 76th. Infantry Brigade.

Issued at hours.

Distribution:-

1. 8th.K.O.R.L.
2. 2nd.Suffolk Regt.
3. 1st.Gordon Hldrs.
4. 76th.T.M.B.
5. 20th.K.R.R.C.
6. 529th.Field Coy R.E.
7. 7th.Field Amb.
8. No.2 Coy Train.
9. Bde.Transport Offr.
10. " Signal "
11. " Int. "
12. S.C..
13. 3rd.Div."G".
14. File.
15. War Diary.
16. "

MARCH TABLE.

****

ROUTE:- TONDORF.

STARTING POINT:- Bend in road 1000 yards North of [illegible] in BLANKENHEIM.

Schedule No.	Unit.	Time to pass starting point.	Instructions. Destination:-
1.	Bde.H.Q.,76th.T.M.B. & 1 Sectn.529th.Fd.Co.	10.30	EICHERSCHEID via HOLZMÜLHEIM - SCHÖNAU.
2.	8th.K.O.R.L.	10.32	BOUDERATH & ENGELGAU via ENGELGAU.
3.	20th.K.R.R.C.	10.37	SCHÖNAU via HOLZMÜLHEIM.
4.	2nd.Suffolk Regt.	10.42	FROHNGAU & BUIR.
5.	1st.Gordon Hldrs.	10.46	TONDORF.
6.	529th.Field Co.(less 1 sectn)	11.01	HOLZMÜLHEIM.
7.	7th.Field Amb.	11.04	EICHERSCHEID via HOLZMÜLHEIM.- SCHÖNAU.
8.	1st.Line Transport of Group	11.06.	
9.	No.2 Coy Train,G.S.Tool Wagons of 20th.K.R.R.C.,all Train Transport	11.16	EICHERSCHEID via HOLZMÜLHEIM - SCHÖNAU.

** ** ** ** ** ** **

SECRET.

Copy No. 15

76TH. INFANTRY BRIGADE ADMINISTRATIVE INSTRUCTIONS.
(To accompany 76th.Inf.Bde.Order No.179)

1. BILLETS. Accommodation in new area is allotted as follows:-

		Officers.	Other Ranks.
Brigade H.Q. & T.M.Bty.	EICHERSCHEID.	11	200
No.7 Field Ambce.	Do.	9	200
No. 2 Coy.Train.	Do.	5	180
	(Brigade H.Q. Billet No.14)		
20th.K.R.R.C.	SCHÖNAU	35	900
8th.K.O.R.L.Rgt.	BOUDERATH.	12	200
	RODERATH.	10	200
	ENGELGAU.	25	500
2nd.Suffolk Rgt.	FROHNGAU.	20	650
	BUIR	10	200
1st.Gordon Hrs.	TONDORF.	35	900
529th.Field Coy.R.E.	HOLZMÜLHEIM	9	200

2. BILLETING PARTIES. Will proceed to new areas under own arrangements. Billeting Parties should report to village headmen as follows and hand in attached Billet Demands.

Bde.H.Q., T.M.Bty. 7th.Field Ambce.,2 Coy.Train.	Billet 25, EICHERSCHEID	at 09-00 hrs
20th.K.R.R.C.	Billet 51, SCHÖNAU	" 09-00 "
2nd.Suffolk Rgt.	Billet 42, FROHNGAU.	" 09-00 "
1st.Gordon Hrs.	Billet 7, TONDORF.	" 09-00 "
8th.K.O.R.L.Rgt.	Billet 18, BOUDERATH. Billet 5, RODERATH. Billet 25, ENGELGAU	" 09-00 "
529th.Field Coy.	Billet 15, HOLZMULHEIM.	" 09-00 "

3. PRESENT BILLETS. Present billets will be taken over unit for unit by 9th.Inf.Bde. Each unit will leave a rear party to hand over billets to advance parties of 9th.Inf.Bde. All billets must be left scrupulously clean.

T. H. [signature]

Captain,

Staff Captain, 76th. Infantry Brigade.

14/12/18.

XII

SECRET.
****

Copy No....

76th.INFANTRY BRIGADE ORDER NO. 180
****

Ref.map 1/100,000. Dec 15th 1918.

1. The Brigade Group will move tomorrow Dec 16th in accordance with march table overleaf to WEINGARTEN – MÜNSTEREIFEL Area

2. Brigade H.Q.will close at present location at 09.00 and open at MÜNSTEREIFEL (HOTEL HILLEBRAND) on arrival.

3. ACKNOWLEDGE.

C. Clifford
Captain,
Brigade Major,76th.Infantry Brigade.

Issued at hours.

Distribution:-
1. 8th.K.O.R.L.
2. 2nd.Suffolk Regt.
3. 1st.Gordon Hldrs.
4. 76th.T.M.B.
5. 20th.K.R.R.C.
6. 529th.Fd.Co.R.E.
7. 7th.Field Amb.
8. No.2 Coy Train.
9. Bde.Trans.Offr.
10. " Signal "
11. " Int. "
11. S.C.
13. 3rd.Div."G".
14. File.
15. War Diary.
16. "

MARCH TABLE.

ROUTE:-

STARTING POINT:- Road junction 300 yards West of first E in EICHERSCHEID.

Schedule No.	Unit.	Time to pass starting point:-	Instructions. Destination:-
1.	Bde.H.Q.,76th.T.M.B. & 1 Sectn.209th.Fd.Co.R.E.	10.00	MÜNSTEREIFEL (HOTEL HILLEBRAND).
2.	20th.K.R.R.C.	10.05	KIRSPENICH & ARLOFF.
3.	2nd.Suffolk Regt.	10.09	IVERSHEIM. Via ROTHEN? or SCHÖNAU.
4.	1st.Gordon Hldrs.	10.14	MÜNSTEREIFEL. Via [illegible]-SCHÖNAU.
5.	8th.K.O.R.L.	10.18	MÜNSTEREIFEL.
6.	209th.Fd.Co.(less 1 sectn.)	10.21	MÜNSTEREIFEL. Via SCHÖNAU.
7.	7th.Field Amb.	10.24	MÜNSTEREIFEL.
8.	1st.Line Transport of Group	10.28	Rendezvous EICHERSCHEID.
9.	No.2 Coy Train,R.E.Tool Wagons of 209th.F.[illegible].R.E.,all Train Transport	10.38	WEINGARTEN. Rendezvous EICHERSCHEID.

-- -- -- -- -- --

SECRET.

Copy No.....16.....

76TH. INFANTRY BRIGADE ADMINISTRATIVE INSTRUCTIONS.
(To accompany 76th.Inf.Bde. Order 180).

1. BILLETS. Accommodation in new area is allotted as under :-

		Offs.	O.R.
Brigade H.Q. & T.M.Battery.	MÜNSTEREIFEL.	11	200
1st.Gordon Hrs.	Do.	35	850.
8th.K.O.R.L.Rgt.	Do.	30	800.
529th.Field Coy.,R.E.	Do.	9	200.
No. 7 Field Ambce.	Do.	10	200.
(Brigade H.Q.:- Hotel Hillebrand).			
2nd.Suffolk Rgt.	IVERSHEIM.	30	800
20th.K.R.R.C.	KIRSPENICH & ARLAFF.	35	900
No.2 Coy.,3rd.Div.Train.	WEINGARTEN.	5	120

2. BILLETING PARTIES. Will proceed under own arrangements to new areas, reporting to BURGERMEISTER and Village Headmen as follows and handing in attached Billet Demands :-

MÜNSTEREIFEL	Town Hall in Square	at 09-00 hours.
IVERSHEIM.	Billet No.79 (N.end of village)	09-00 "
KIRSPENICH & ARLAFF.	at large Farm with towers on river, S. end of ARLAFF.	09-00 "
WEINGARTEN.	Billet No.46	09-00 "

3. PRESENT BILLETS. Will be taken over unit for unit by 9th.Inf.Bde. Each unit will leave a rear party to hand over billets to advance parties of 9th.Inf.Bde. All billets must be left scrupulously clean.

15/12/18.

for C. Chiffer Captain,
Staff Captain, 76th.Infentry Brigade.

XIII

SECRET.
****

Copy No....

76th.INFANTRY BRIGADE ORDER NO....161

Ref.map 1/100,000. Dec 16th 1918.

1. The Brigade Group will move tomorrow Dec 17th in accordance with march table overleaf to EUSKIRCHEN

2. Brigade H.Q.will close at present location at 07.30 and open at EUSKIRCHEN on arrival.

3. ACKNOWLEDGE.

C. Clifford
Captain,
Issued at hours. Brigade Major,76th.Infantry Brigade.

Distribution:-

1. 8th.K.O.R.L.
2. 2nd.Suffolk Regt.
3. 1st.Gordon Hldrs.
4. 76th.T.M.B.
5. 20th.K.R.R.C.
6. 529th.Field Coy R.E.
7. 7th.Field Amb.
8. No.2 Coy Train.
9. Bde.Trans.Offr.
10. " Signal "
11. " Int. "
12. S.C.
13. 3rd.Div."G".
14. File.
15. War Diary.
16. "

MARCH TABLE.

ROUTE:-

STARTING POINT:- Road junction 300 yards East of last N in WEINGARTEN.

Schedule No.	Unit.	Time to pass starting point.	Instructions.
1.	Bde.H.Q.,76th.T.M.B. & 1 Sectn.529th.Fd.Co.R.E.	10.00	
2.	20th.K.R.R.C.	10.02	
3.	2nd.Suffolk Regt.	10.07	
4.	1st.Gordon Hldrs.	10.11	
5.	8th.K.O.R.L.	10.16	
6.	529th.Fd.Co.R.E.(less 1 Sectn.)	10.21	
7.	7th.Field Amb.	10.24	
8.	1st.Line Transport of Group	10.26	
9.	No.2 Coy Train,G.S.Tool Wagons of 20th.K.R.R.C.,all Train Transport	10.36	

** ** ** **

SECRET.

Copy No.....16....

76TH. INFANTRY BRIGADE ADMINISTRATIVE INSTRUCTIONS.
(To accompany 76th.Inf.Bde.Order No.181).

1. BILLETS. The whole Brigade Group will be quartered in EUSKIRCHEN.

2. BILLETING PARTIES. The billeting lorry will leave Brigade H.Q. at 08-00 hours and will convey 1 Officer and 1 Interpreter from each of 8th.K.O.R.L 1st.Gordon Hrs., 529th.Field Coy., 7th.Field Ambce. and Bde.H.Q. These Officers and Interpreters will report at Bde.H.Q. at 08-00 hours. The lorry will pick up Officers and Interpreters of 2nd.Suffolk Rgt., 20th. K.R.R.C. and No.2 Coy. Train as under:-

2nd.Suffolk Rgt. IVERSHEIM. at 08-20 hours.
20th.K.R.R.C. at Main Road where WACHENDORF-KIRSPENICH Road crosses Main Road at 08-30 hours.
No.2 Coy., 3rd.Div.Train. WEINGARTEN. at 08-35 "

Billeting N.C.O.'s will proceed on bicycles.

All billeting parties will report ~~as~~ at Main Billeting Office, Town Hall, EUSKIRCHEN, at 09-00 hours.

3. PRESENT BILLETS. Present billets must be left in a clean and sanitary condition. Unless further orders are received, no rear parties will be left behind to-morrow, as it is not expected that 9th.Inf.Bde. will take over the area now occupied by us.

T.J. Kerr
Captain,
Staff Captain, 76th. Infantry Brigade.

16/12/18

XIV

SECRET.

Copy No....

76th. INFANTRY BRIGADE ORDER NO....182

Ref. map 1/100,000. .....Dec. 17th..... 1918.

1. The Brigade Group less 20th K.R.R.C. & 529 Fd. Coy R.E. will move tomorrow Dec 18th in accordance with march table overleaf to AHREM – ERP – WEILER area

2. Brigade H.Q. will close at present location at 07.30 and open at AHREM on arrival.

3. ACKNOWLEDGE.

C. Clifford
Captain,
Brigade Major, 76th. Infantry Brigade.

Issued at hours.

Distribution:-
1. 8th. K.O.R.L.
2. 2nd. Suffolk Regt.
3. 1st. Gordon Hldrs.
4. 76th. T.M.B.
5. 20th. K.R.R.C.
6. 529th. Field Coy R.E.
7. 7th. Field Amb.
8. No.2 Coy Train.
9. Bde. Trans. Offr.
10. " Signal "
11. " Int. "
12. S.C.
13. 3rd. Div. "G".
14. File.
15. War Diary.
16. "

MARCH TABLE.

ROUTE:- LOMMERSUM - NIEDERBERG.

STARTING POINT:- Road junction 300 yards North East of E in KESSENICH.

Schedule No.	Unit.	Time to pass starting point.	Instructions.
1.	Bde.H.Q.& 76th.T.M.B.	10.00 hours.	
2.	2nd.Suffolk Regt.	10.03	
3.	1st.Gordon Hldrs.	10.08	
4.	8th.K.O.R.L.	10.10	
5.	7th.Field Amb.	10.1[illegible]	
6.	1st.Line Transport of Group	10.17	
7.	No.2 Coy Train,all Train Transport	10.22.	

-- -- -- -- --

SECRET.

Copy No. 16

76TH. INFANTRY BRIGADE ADMINISTRATIVE INSTRUCTIONS.
(To accompany 76th.Inf.Bde.Order No.182).

1. BILLETS. Accommodation in the new area is allotted as under:-

Bde.H.Q., 76th.T.M.Bty. & No.2 Coy. Train. AHREM.
(Brigade H.Q.:- Billet No. 34).

1st.Gordon Hrs. will take over billets of 2nd. Scots Guards at ERP.

2nd.Suffolk Rgt. " " " " " 4th.Gds.M.G.Battn. at ERP.

No.7 Field Ambce. " " " " " Guards F.A. at ERP.

8th.K.O.R.L.Rgt. " " " " " 4th.Gren.Gds. at FRIESHEIM.

2. BILLETING PARTIES. Billeting Parties will proceed under own arrangements, and will report for Billeting Lists to Village Headmen or BÜRGERMEISTER as follows:-

ERP. At Town Hall, close to Church at 09-00 hours.
FRIESHEIM. At BÜRGERMEISTER's Office, Billet No. 71 at 09-00 hours.
AHREM. At Billet No. 41 at 09-00 hours.

3. PRESENT BILLETS. Present Billets will be taken over unit for unit by 9th.Inf.Bde. All units will leave a rear party behind to hand over billets to advance parties of 9th.Inf.Bde. All billets must be left scrupulously clean.

T.F. Innes
Captain,
17/12/18. Staff Captain, 76th. Infantry Brigade.

War Diary

XV

SECRET.

Copy No.....

76th. INFANTRY BRIGADE ORDER NO. 183

Ref.map 1/100,000. Dec 18th 1918.

1. The Brigade Group will move tomorrow Dec 19th in accordance with march table overleaf to final area

2. Brigade H.Q. will close at present location at 08.30 and open at GYMNICH BURG on arrival.

3. ACKNOWLEDGE.

C. Clifford Captain,
Issued at hours. Brigade Major, 76th. Infantry Brigade.

Distribution:-
1. 8th. K.O.R.L.
2. 2nd. Suffolk Regt.
3. 1st. Gordon Hldrs.
4. 76th. L.T.M.B.
5. 7th. Field Amb.
6. No.2 Coy Train.
7. Bde. Transport Offr.
8. " Signal "
9. " Int. "
10. S.C.
11. 3rd. Div. "G".
12. File.
13. War Diary.
14. "

MARCH TABLE.

ROUTE:- DIRMERZHEIM.

STARTING POINT:- Main cross roads in LECHENICH.

Schedule No.	Unit.	Time to pass starting point.	Instructions.
			Destination:-
1.	Bde.H.Q.& 76th.T.M.B.	10.00	GYMNICH BURG.
2.	2nd.Suffolk Regt.	10.01	GYMNICH.
3.	1st.Gordon Hldrs.	10.05	KIERDORF and BRÜGGEN.
4.	8th.K.O.R.L.	10.10	TÜRNICH and BALKHAUSEN.
5.	7th.Field Amb.	10.15	DIRMERZHEIM.
6.	1st.Line Transport of Group	10.17	
7.	No.2 Coy Train and all Train Transport	10.22	GYMNICH.

** ** ** ** ** **

JANUARY. 1919

Instructions regarding War Diaries and Intelligence Summaries are contained in F. S. Regs., Part II. and the Staff Manual respectively. Title pages will be prepared in manuscript.

WAR DIARY ~~or~~ INTELLIGENCE SUMMARY.

(*Erase heading not required.*)

Page I

Army Form C. 2118.

76th Infantry Brigade.

VR 40

Place	Date JAN.	Hour	Summary of Events and Information	Remarks and references to Appendices
GYMNICH	1.			
– " –	2.		3 hours training in the morning, recreation in the afternoon	
– " –	3.			
– " –	4.		22 men left today to proceed to their various dispersal stations, 12 of which were coal miners, the remainder were special classes	
– " –	5			
– " –	6		Usual training programme. Excellent weather.	
– " –	7.			
– " –	8.		22 men demobilized today, 6 were coal miners, & 12 were men with over 2 years colour service. Results of Bgde. football league. 8th K.O.R.L. 7. Bgde. H.Q. & T.M.B. 0. 1st Gordon Hldrs 3. 2nd Suffolk Regt. 0.	
– " –	9.			
– " –	10.		Inter Company football competitions.	
– " –	11.		50 men demobilized today, 22 were men of 2 years colour service 8 were coal miners, 7 demobilizers & pivotal, 5 guarantee letter men & 2 teachers. Bgde. football results. No 4 F.A. 6. Bgde. H.Q. & T.M.B. 1. 1st Gordon Hldrs. 4 8th K.O.R.L. 1.	
– " –	12.			
– " –	13		Usual training programme.	
– " –	14.			

A5834 Wt. W4973/M687 750,000 8/16 D. D. & L. Ltd. Forms/C.2118/13.

Instructions regarding War Diaries and Intelligence Summaries are contained in F. S. Regs., Part II. and the Staff Manual respectively. Title pages will be prepared in manuscript.

JANUARY 1919

WAR DIARY or ~~INTELLIGENCE SUMMARY~~. (Erase heading not required.)

Page 11

Army Form C. 2118.

76th Infantry Brigade.

Place	Date	Hour	Summary of Events and Information	Remarks and references to Appendices
GYMNICH	15.		40 men proceeded to their various dispersal stations today. 12 were men with over 2 years colour service, 7 were guarantee letter men, 8 coalminers, & 2 were teachers. Staff Captain went on leave today, replaced by Major Burman 2nd Suffolk Regt.	
— " —	16. 17.		2nd Lieut CHAMBERLAIN. H.A.C. takes up the duties of Bgde. Provost Officer.	
— " —	18.		32 men demobilized today. 8 guarantee letter men, 8 demobilizers & pivotal men, 6 coal miners, 3 teachers.	
— " —	19.		Div. cinema gave a splendid preformance today.	
— " —	20.		Classification of boxers for the Brigade tournament. Cinema performed at TURNICH.	
— " —	21.		2nd Cross Country run was won by ~~Captn~~ Major Burman today	
	22		28 men were demobilized today, 21 of which were demobilizers & pivotal men. 1st round of Bgde boxing competition. App. Div. competition A 23rd Bgde. R.F.A 3. 8th K.O.R.L. 2. Brigade Gymkhana postponed owing to the severe frost. Concert party gave an excellent show tonight at Gymnich.	App. I

A5834 Wt. W4973/M687 750,000 8/16 D. D. & L. Ltd. Forms/C.2118/13.

Instructions regarding War Diaries and Intelligence Summaries are contained in F. S. Regs., Part II. and the Staff Manual respectively. Title pages will be prepared in manuscript.

JANUARY 1919.

WAR DIARY or ~~INTELLIGENCE SUMMARY~~.

(Erase heading not required.)

Page III

76th Infantry Brigade

Army Form C. 2118.

Place	Date JAN	Hour	Summary of Events and Information	Remarks and references to Appendices
GYMNICH	24.		The G.O.C. addresses the 2nd Suffolk Regt. on "Demobilization"	
			Div. football competition A. 1st K.S.L.I. 5 2nd Suffolk Regt. I.	
— " —	25.		Brigade matches postponed, 1st Gordon Hldrs. beat the 7th K.S.L.I. 4–1.	
			G.O.C. addresses the 8th K.O.R.L. on "Demobilization".	
— " —	26.		20 Men demobilized today, 9 pivotal, 4 guarantee letters, & the remainder demobilizers.	
			2nd Suffolk Officers team beat the 1st Battn Gordon Hldrs. 3–0. in a very exciting game today.	
			Major Fox of the Scots Guards gave a splendid lecture on his experiences & escape from Germany.	
— " —	27.		Fall of snow during the night about 3 inches all over.	
			Lecture by Captn. Bless. R.W.F. on "How we won the war"	
			Major General & Captn Goulding lunch with the Brigade Staff	
— " —	28.		All Brigade horses classified today. Sports stopped owing to the snow. Skating on the lake at Gymnich	
— " —	29.		59 men demobilized ~~…~~ mostly agriculturalists. skating on the lake.	

A5834 Wt. W4973/M687 750,000 8/16 D. D. & L. Ltd. Forms/C.2118/13.

Instructions regarding War Diaries and Intelligence Summaries are contained in F. S. Regs., Part II. and the Staff Manual respectively. Title pages will be prepared in manuscript.

JANUARY. 1919

WAR DIARY

~~or~~

~~INTELLIGENCE SUMMARY.~~

(Erase heading not required.)

Page IV.

76th Infantry Brigade

Army Form C. 2118.

Place	Date JAN.	Hour	Summary of Events and Information	Remarks and references to Appendices
GYMNICH	30.		Ground still unsuitable for football, very severe frost.	
	31.		All cross country running & bicycle races postponed.	
			Skating on the lake in the afternoon.	
			Total number of men demobilized for the month.	
			– 273. – Groups 1 & 43, special classes, 10% longservice men.	

J. Clark Lieut.
for G.O.C. 76th Infantry Brigade
31st January 1919.

A5834 Wt. W4973/M687 750,000 8/16 D. D. & L. Ltd. Forms/C.2118/13.

FEBRUARY. 1919.

Instructions regarding War Diaries and Intelligence Summaries are contained in F. S. Regs., Part II. and the Staff Manual respectively. Title pages will be prepared in manuscript.

WAR DIARY
or
~~INTELLIGENCE SUMMARY~~.
(Erase heading not required.)

HQ 76th Infantry Brigade.

Page 1.

Army Form C. 2118.

V.8 41

Place	Date FEB	Hour	Summary of Events and Information	Remarks and references to Appendices
GYMNICH	1.	11.00.	Brigade lecture in TURNICH hall by Lord Denbigh.	
			2nd round of the Boxing tournament had to be postponed at the last minute, owing to the failure of the electric light.	
— " —	2.		Staff Captain returns from leave.	
— " —	3.		Second round of the boxing tournament at GYMNICH tonight.	
— " —	4.		Major General inspects the TURNICH – KIERDORF area today	
— " —	5.		" " " GYMNICH – KONRADSHEIM " "	
— " —	6.		Brigade concert party at GYMNICH.	
			Brigadier went on leave today. Colonel The Hon W. Fraser D.S.O. M.C. 1st Battn Gordon Highlanders, in command.	
— " —	7.		1st Gordon Hldrs. beat Bgde. H.Q. & T.M.B. today 6–0.	
— " —	8.		Lecture on "Alsace Lorraine" by Mr Masterman-Smith at BRUGGEN.	
			Finals of the Bgde. Boxing Tournament at BRUGGEN.	

A5834 Wt. W4973/M687 750,000 8/16 D. D. & L. Ltd. Forms/C.2118/13.

Instructions regarding War Diaries and Intelligence Summaries are contained in F. S. Regs., Part II. and the Staff Manual respectively. Title pages will be prepared in manuscript.

FEBRUARY 1919.

WAR DIARY ~~or INTELLIGENCE SUMMARY.~~

(Erase heading not required.)

Page. II.

Army Form C. 2118.

76th Infantry Brigade.

Place	Date FEB.	Hour	Summary of Events and Information	Remarks and references to Appendices
GYMNICH	9.	}		
— " —	10	}	2nd rounds of the inter company Knock out Competitions.	
— " —	11	}		
— " —	12	}		
— " —	13.		4th Cross country run, won by Sgt Richardson 2nd Suffolk Regt.	
			3rd Bicycle race, only one team enters.	
— " —	14.		Semi-finals Brigade inter coy. football.	
			Lecture by 2nd Lt. Pettigrew-Young "France & the French" at BRUGGEN.	
			" " Dr Lambert K.O.R.L. "Venereal Disease" at GYMNICH.	
— " —	15.		1st Battn Gordon Hldrs draw in the semi-final with the H.T. Column.	
— " —	16.		Thaw precautions adopted today no lorries allowed on the road.	
			Visited by General Stubbs, late C.O. of the 2nd Suffolk Regt	
— " —	17.	}	No football today, ground unsuitable.	
		}	Div. cinema at GYMNICH.	
— " —	18.	}		
— " —	19.		Committee meeting (sports) at Brigade H.Q.	

A5834 Wt. W4973/M687 750,000 8/16 D. D. & L. Ltd. Forms/C.2118/13.

FEBRUARY. 1919.

WAR DIARY or ~~INTELLIGENCE SUMMARY.~~

(Erase heading not required.)

Page 111.

76th Infantry Brigade

Army Form C. 2118.

Instructions regarding War Diaries and Intelligence Summaries are contained in F. S. Regs., Part II. and the Staff Manual respectively. Title pages will be prepared in manuscript.

Place	Date FEB.	Hour	Summary of Events and Information	Remarks and references to Appendices
GYMNICH	20.		Several cases of measles reported at BALKHAUSEN.	
			Semi-final of Div. football competition. 1st Gordon Hldrs.	
			beat the Div. M.T. Company 4-0.	
—"—	21.		Brigade Major visits Cologne to arrange relief of guards.	
—"—	22.		Bgde league game cancelled owing to the 8th K.O.R.L. Regt. being	
			placed out of bounds.	
—"—	23.		Advance officers proceed to Cologne to look over new area.	
—"—	24.		1st Gordon Hldrs. beat the R.A.M.C. in semi-final Div. football competition	
			Summary Court at Gymnich today.	
—"—	25.		Div. Cinema at GYMNICH	
—"—	26.		2nd Suffolk Regt. move into RIEHL Barracks today	
			& relieve the Coldstream Guards.	
—"—	27.		Rehersal of presentation of colours for the 8th K.O.R.L. Regt.	
			Ceremonial parade 1st Gordon Hldrs. Major General's farewell.	
			20th Durham L.I. arrive at COLOGNE to take the place	
			of the 8th K.O.R.L. who are to be disbanded.	
			20th D.L.I. take over from the Gren. Guards in RIEHL Barracks.	

A5834 Wt. W4973/M687 750,000 8/16 D. D. & L. Ltd. Forms/C.2118/13.

FEBRUARY 1919

Instructions regarding War Diaries and Intelligence Summaries are contained in F. S. Regs., Part II. and the Staff Manual respectively. Title pages will be prepared in manuscript.

WAR DIARY
or
~~INTELLIGENCE SUMMARY~~.
(Erase heading not required.)

Page IV

Army Form C. 2118.

76th Infantry Brigade

Place	Date FEB.	Hour	Summary of Events and Information	Remarks and references to Appendices
GYMNICH	28.		Presentation of colours to the 8th K.O.R.L. Regt. at TURNICH by the 2nd Army Commander. The 1/4 York & Lancaster Regt. arrived today at HORREM, to take the place of the 1st Gordon Hldrs. who are to be disbanded. They march to KERPEN & billet there for the night. Total number demobilized for the month 5 Officers & 326 OR's. Groups 1843. 10% longservice. J. Clark Lieut. for G.O.C. 76th Infy. Brigade. 28th Feb. 1919.	

A5834 Wt. W4973/M687 750,000 8/16 D. D. & L. Ltd. Forms/C.2118/13.

Instructions regarding War Diaries and Intelligence Summaries are contained in F. S. Regs., Part II. and the Staff Manual respectively. Title pages will be prepared in manuscript.

MARCH 1919

WAR DIARY ~~or~~ ~~INTELLIGENCE SUMMARY.~~

(Erase heading not required.)

Page I.

16th Infantry Brigade.

Army Form C. 2118.

Vol 42

Place	Date MARCH	Hour	Summary of Events and Information	Remarks and references to Appendices
GYMNICH.	1.		Brigade Headquarters move into COLOGNE, (59. HOHENSTAUFEN RING.). Transport & details accomodated in PIONEER BARRACKS, RHIEL.	
COLOGNE.	2.		1/4th York & Lancaster Regt. move into RHIEL BARRACKS. (No 2.). 20th Durham Light Infantry take over the Guard duites from the 2nd Suffolk Regt.	
—„—	3.		The Army Commander inspects the Barracks.	
—„—	4	}	Units training in guard duties.	
—„—	5.	}		
—„—	6		52nd Durham Light Infy arrived from England today. Farewell parade for 2nd Suffolk Regt	
—„—	7		1st Inspection by the Major General of 20th D.L.I.	
—„—	8th		51st D.L.I. arrived today.	
—„—	9th		Div. boxing competition in Y.M.C.A. central.	
—„—	10th		Inspection by the Army Commander of the 51st & 52nd Battn. D.L.I. All retainable men of the 8th KOYL Regt left today to join the 16th Lancashire Fusiliers.	

A5834 Wt. W4973/M687 750,000 8/16 D. D. & L. Ltd. Forms/C.2118/13.

Instructions regarding War Diaries and Intelligence Summaries are contained in F. S. Regs., Part II. and the Staff Manual respectively. Title pages will be prepared in manuscript.

MARCH 1919

WAR DIARY
or
~~INTELLIGENCE SUMMARY.~~
(Erase heading not required.)

Page 11

76th Infantry Brigade.

Army Form C. 2118.

Place	Date MARCH	Hour	Summary of Events and Information	Remarks and references to Appendices
COLOGNE	11		Final of the intercompany football competition at BLUCHER PARK No 1 Section D.A.C v. ~~Z~~ Company 1st N.Fs.	
—"—	12		3rd Division R.A.M.C beat the Corps Troops 2 – 0 at BLUCHER PARK	
—"—	13		Demonstration of Guard mounting by 3rd Div. M.G.C. at RHIEL BARRACKS.	
—"—	14		All training areas near RHEIL BARRACKS reconnoitred also ranges. Guard mounting demonstration by the 20th D.L.S. Performers congratulated by the G.O.C.	
—"—	15		The 20th D.L.S were beaten by the Argyle & Sutherlands in the IV Corps final competition. Reception at Brigade HQ. to which all officers of the Bgde, the G.O.C. & Div. Staff are invited. The 2nd Bttn Suffolk Regt provide their orchestra.	
—"—	16		The Nth Div. R.A.M.C. draw with 35th Bgde R.G.A. in the Corps final	
—"—	17th		R.A.M.C. win the Corps final.	

A5834 Wt. W4973/M687 750,000 8/16 D. D. & L. Ltd. Forms/C.2118/13.

MARCH.

Instructions regarding War Diaries and Intelligence Summaries are contained in F. S. Regs., Part II. and the Staff Manual respectively. Title pages will be prepared in manuscript.

WAR DIARY
~~or~~
~~INTELLIGENCE~~ SUMMARY.
(Erase heading not required.)

1919.

Page 111

76th Infantry Brigade

Army Form C. 2118.

Place	Date MARCH	Hour	Summary of Events and Information	Remarks and references to Appendices
COLOGNE. 59 HOHENSTOFEN RING	18	}	Battns. practicing guard duties	
	19	}	First firing on the range near REIHL BARRACKS.	
	20			
"	21.		All Battn. Cadres come under the orders of General Potter C.M.G. D.S.O.	
	22.		2nd Battn. Royal Scots accommodated in the BARRACKS today.	
"	23		All Demobilization & leave cancelled today owing to strike in England. 20th Durham L.I. take over guards today.	
"	24.		Demobilization reopened.	
"	25		Lecture on the French Army by Marechal des Logis Salverton.	
"	26		All troops confined to Barracks for the afternoon. Guards doubled. Trouble expected from the Spartacists	
"	27.		52nd Durham L.I. take over the guard duties.	
"	28.		20th D.L.I. supply Guard of honour to receive the C in C at Cologne Main Station. Lecture by Major Ratcliffe Dugmore "Big game hunting with the camera in Africa"	

A5834 Wt. W4973/M687 750,000 8/16 D. D. & L. Ltd. Forms/C.2118/13.

Army Form C. 2118.

MARCH 1919.

WAR DIARY

~~or~~

~~INTELLIGENCE SUMMARY~~

(Erase heading not required.)

Page IV

7/6th Infantry Brigade.

Instructions regarding War Diaries and Intelligence Summaries are contained in F. S. Regs., Part II. and the Staff Manual respectively. Title Pages will be prepared in manuscript.

Place	Date March	Hour	Summary of Events and Information	Remarks and references to Appendices
COLOGNE. 59 HOHENSTAUFEN RING.	29		Major Lumley G.S.O. II. expected to arrive as Brigade Major.	
	30.		Reinforcements arrive for the "West Yorks" Battns. & are accomodated in RHEIL. BARRACKS.	
— " —	31		Usual training programme. Total number demobilized for the month. 330.	

J Clark Lieut.
for G.O.C. 7/6th Infy Bgde.
30/3/19.

2449 Wt. W14957/M90 750,000 1/16 J.B.C. & A. Forms/C.2118/12.

www.ingramcontent.com/pod-product-compliance
Lightning Source LLC
Chambersburg PA
CBHW081424300426
44108CB00016BA/2295
9781474504690